Spectacles of Realism

CULTURAL ✌ POLITICS

A series from the Social Text Collective

Aimed at a broad interdisciplinary audience, these volumes seek to intervene in debates about the political direction of current theory and practice by combining contemporary analysis with a more traditional sense of historical and socioeconomic evaluation.

Spectacles of Realism: Body, Gender, Genre

Margaret Cohen and
Christopher Prendergast, editors
(for the Social Text Collective)

Cultural Politics, Volume 10

 University of Minnesota Press
Minneapolis
London

"The Morgue and the Musée Grévin: Understanding the Public Taste for Reality in Fin-de-Siècle Paris," by Vanessa R. Schwartz, was previously published in *The Yale Journal of Criticism* 6, no. 2. Reprinted with permission of Blackwell Publishers.

"A Question of Reference: Male Sexuality in Phallic Theory," by Charles Bernheimer, was previously published in somewhat different form as "Penile Reference in Phallic Theory," *differences: A Journal of Feminist Cultural Studies* 4, no. 1 (Spring 1992): 116-32. Reprinted with permission.

"Courbet's *L'Origine du monde*: The Origin without an Original," by Linda Nochlin, was previously published in *October* 37 (Summer 1986). Copyright MIT Press, Cambridge, Massachusetts, reprinted with permission.

Published by the University of Minnesota Press
111 Third Avenue South, Suite 290, Minneapolis, MN 55401-2520
Printed in the United States of America on acid-free paper
Second Printing, 1996

Library of Congress Cataloging-in-Publication Data
Spectacles of realism : body, gender, genre / Margaret Cohen and Christopher Prendergast,
    editors (for the Social Text Collective).
        p.   cm. — (Cultural Politics ; v. 10)
    Includes bibliographical references and index.
    ISBN 0-8166-2520-4 (hard : alk. paper). — ISBN 0-8166-2521-2 (pbk. : alk. paper)
    1. Feminist theory. 2. Realism. 3. Feminism and literature. I. Cohen, Margaret. II. Prendergast, Christopher. III. Series: Cultural politics (Minneapolis, Minn.); v. 10.
HQ1190.R435   1995
305.42'01—dc20   94-37016

Contents

Preface:
Reconfiguring Realism

Margaret Cohen

> *Realism is an issue not only for literature; it is a major political,*
> *philosophical and practical issue and must be handled and ex-*
> *plained as such—as a matter of general human interest.*
>
> —Bertolt Brecht, "On the Formalistic Character of the
> Theory of Realism," 1938

Realism has been enjoying unprecedented prestige in one vital
arena of recent critical debate. Slippery and problematic as the
term has become, the texts, images, and critical writings once
unified under the rubric "realism" constitute *the* single set of artifacts most widely cited by gender studies as this interdisciplinary
discipline has consolidated itself during the past fifteen years.
Inquiry into the occulted gender experience and sexual politics
embedded in dominant discourses on truth, knowledge, pleasure,
power, and art; investigations of how representations participate in
the social ordering of sexuality; considerations of how gender and
sexuality are implicated in the construction of ideology and identity—all have had an uncanny way of passing through cultural artifacts once called realist. Even the resistance/subversion wing of
feminist theory concerned with the micropolitical potential of non-
hegemonic practices has evinced a fascination with realism, albeit
couched in highly negative terms. As the celebrated notion of *écri-
ture féminine* exemplifies, realism there received validation as the
enemy, equated with the existing phallocentric domination feminism sets out to critique.

The centrality of realism as a reference point for feminisms is, however, at odds with the fact that realism has recently been out of fashion as a literary-cultural problematic. Heatedly elaborated, defended, and demystified in the mid-century by Marxist theoreticians concerned with its relation to a self-proclaimed epistemologically and aesthetically superior "modernism," realism was then a major focus of structuralist classification and poststructuralist dismantling in the 1960s and 1970s. But the concept has faded from the crucial postmodern debates around reference, construction, representation, aesthetics, and ideology, although it continues to serve some function in the realm of pedagogic practice.

In large part as a result of this fading, gender studies too has an odd relation to the realism of the artifacts it has found so useful. Realism constitutes a dense field of representational practices where much of gender studies' hard labor of the concept has been situated but whose importance as such the discipline has been reluctant to address in detail. The reasons for this reluctance are complex, extending beyond the postmodern distaste for realism as a critical problematic to the urgent agendas of identity politics informing the consolidation of gender studies in the late 1970s and the 1980s. In the struggle to demonstrate gender as a constitutive practice of social differentiation, realism was the least of the problems, particularly given the extent to which realism had been laid to rest by both the Marxist and structuralist/poststructuralist lineages so important to the theoretical foundations of gender studies itself. But as Walter Benjamin knew so well, theory receives its full significance only with an understanding of its relation to the historical artifacts upon which it is articulated. The consolidation of gender studies, whatever threat of ossification it poses, has at least the advantage of constituting a stable institutional and epistemological frame in which to carry through on Benjamin's imperative.

The critical wager of this volume is to elucidate the elective affinity between realist artifacts and gender studies by resuscitating realism in all its historical unevenness, as cultural practice traversing media and as critical problematic. What, to put the question in its most general form, is the relation between the concerns of gender studies and the realist artifacts it seems to prefer? More precisely, how is realism complicit with the historically specific ideologies challenged by gender studies? To what extent is realism a piece of

the prehistory of gender studies? To what extent does realism constitute itself around precisely those issues of reference, construction, relation, and representation central to gender studies as well?
Which is to say that the methodology unifying the essays in this volume is that of a gender-sensitive cultural studies. Although it has
been claimed that "cultural studies in fact has no distinct methodology," cultural studies is unified by a fundamental methodological
commitment at issue here.[1] This commitment is the Benjaminian
imperative to clarify the dialectical relation between theory and history, with history understood as including the historical artifacts
upon which a theory is articulated, the historical conditions in
which a theory is produced, and the historical processes of its reception and dissemination.

This volume's effort to elucidate the nexus of realism, sexuality,
and gender, it should be stressed, in no way breaks with gender
studies' foundational texts. Rather, we seek to build on these texts'
brilliant but uncompleted insights. Thus, in a way, the contributions
to this book can be considered elaborations of powerful formulations like Naomi Schor's statement that "realism is that paradoxical
moment in Western literature when representation can neither accommodate the Otherness of Woman nor exist without it."[2] But
there is an important distance covered between such theoretical insights and the historically specific and extensive archaeology of realism we are undertaking here. To take the example of Schor's statement, we build on it with the following sorts of questions: What
cultural practice of realism—textual, visual, as critical problematic? Realism in which specific historical and geocultural situation?
According to what constructions of Woman? What constructions of
Man? Other in what way? From our discussion, it should become apparent that gender studies is in the process of doing for realism concerning the problematic of gender and sexuality what mid-century
Marxism did for realism concerning the problematic of class and
what structuralism/poststructuralism did for realism concerning the
problematic of reference—and what these critical moments interro-
gating realism did not do as well. Gender and sexuality in the domains of both social relations and aesthetic representation remain
undertheorized in these prior moments of realism's critical prestige.

The chapters in this collection focus on the cultural practices—
textual, visual, and critical—collected under the rubric of realism in

nineteenth-century France. This focus derives in part from our quarrel with the ahistoricity of the previous two important moments of theoretical debate on realism. Theoretical inquiry has had a tendency to lump together all realist practices, as if geocultural and historical variations were immaterial in this form of representation, participating, as has been argued by the Marxist lineage positioning realism, above all others in the consolidation of the bourgeois nation-state.

At the same time, the vicissitudes of realism in the French context lend it a particular exemplarity, making it a privileged site from which to view the social and cultural factors at issue in realism across geopolitical divisions. In no other consolidation of a national literary-cultural realism with what used to be called "world historical importance" have these social and cultural factors intersected with the same temporal simultaneity and density as in nineteenth-century France. The heyday of realism in France is the moment that has been termed, in short, the invention of modernity. To put it more elaborately, realism in France was a state-of-the-art visual and textual practice and the site of polemical debate during the half century that saw the explosion of industrial production and the industrial metropolis; the institutionalization of the bourgeois nation-state; the displacement of aristocratic class power and the creation of the proletariat; the invention of technologies of the spectacle, mechanical reproduction, notably photography, and mass media, notably the mass press; the height of France's imperial project; the consolidation of modern experimental science; the creation of the first modern socialisms as well as the first modern feminist movements; and a period characterized by the preeminence of gender as a system of differentiation central to hegemonic political and social organization and hence to this organization's contestation as well.

The essays collected in this volume are attentive to the diversity of social and cultural practices at issue in realism as well as to the unevenness of the realist artifact itself (I lean heavily on the term *unevenness* because it is located at precisely the nexus of history and theory under examination in this collection; Marx, after all, proposed the notion of "unequal development" in a series of notes also raising the problem of the "relation between the previous idealistic methods of writing history and the realistic method" in the same year that Flaubert published *Madame Bovary*).[3] Under the rubric of realism, this collection includes literary texts; fashion plates; paintings; caricatures; popular spectacles such as wax museums, the morgue, and the World's Fair; and ideologico-discursive constructs elaborated in critical polemic and legal dispute. Accompanying our interest in the diversity of artifacts that have been designated as "realist" is an understanding of interdisciplinarity as itself a practice of unevenness. If this collection brings together work by critics from literary studies, history, art history, and anthropology, such diversity should not imply that it lacks methodological precision. Rather, the authors of the essays collected here preserve the specificity of disciplinary method even as they question disciplinary boundaries. They are committed to the proposition that interdisciplinary inquiry worthy of its name can exist only as a dialogue *among* disciplines attentive to divergence, to the uneven textures of disciplinary conventions, to the differing foundations of disciplinary projects.[4]

In our attentiveness to the unevenness of the realist artifact, our excavation of realism contrasts markedly with previous moments of realism's critical prestige. Here, the disparities among realist practices are neither minimized nor employed as a way to dismantle the concept itself. As a result, this very unevenness emerges as a source of realism's power. The diverse accounts collected in the volume show realism as a relation. Realism consists precisely in a complicated slippage among a wide variety of discursive practices, a slippage where concerns of gender and sexuality play a crucial mediating role. Our attention from the outset to historical specificity should make clear that this claim is emphatically not an effort to bring realism back into fashion by turning it into a form of early postmodernism. At the same time, reconfiguring realism as a relation does suggest that the dialogue between realism and postmodernism is far more complex than postmodernist reductions of realism often admit, reductions that treat realism as an outmoded concept and/or as the old enemy of modernism. Several essays in this collection, moreover, pursue the complexity of this dialogue explicitly. They frame their archaeology of realism not only in relation to gender studies but also in relation to postmodern conceptualizations and constructions of the real.

Jean-Marie Schaeffer comments, "Genre theory . . . though thoroughly discredited by modern literary theory and practice, has in fact always entertained a privileged relationship with [a certain] historical materialism";[5] in the present volume, the problem of genre emerges as of paramount importance to a gender-sensitive cultural studies as well. Here, however, genre is understood not as limited to the aesthetic realm but more broadly, as Anne Higonnet's essay citing Fredric Jameson reminds us, as a social contract of representation functioning both interdiscursively and intersemiotically, across discourses and across signifying media as well. In this context, a word should be said about the organization of the essays in this collection. Because of the essays' common construction of realism as a relation among textual and visual practices both high and low, aesthetic, critical, scientific, ethnographic, legal, political, ideological, it proved difficult to maintain our initial project to categorize them according to the forms of realism that constituted their dominant fields of inquiry. So, too, the essays could not be categorized as investigating how one isolated aspect of modernity came to representation in realist practices. Rather, the essays "work through" a consistent set of factors informing realist practices that are synonymous with the salient features of modernity enumerated above. We have thus opted for a roughly chronological organization, as the essays follow practices of realism across the nineteenth-century invention of modernity.

One last methodological reason for our focus on nineteenth-century France deserves mention. The essays collected in this volume exemplify the critical terrain of French cultural studies, the importance of which has, for several important institutional reasons, unjustly been downplayed. Cultural studies has historically positioned itself as a phenomenon of the Anglophone world, both in its methodology (with some reference, however, to poststructuralism) and in its objects of study. At the same time, cultural studies has sometimes been ill received within French departments in the United States and Great Britain, which include it, above all in its feminist incarnation, as part of the theory that is the object of recent backlash. Given the conservatism now prevailing in certain French departments, it is particularly important that French cultural studies integrate itself into cultural studies more generally. With this collection, we hope to show that French cultural studies is of more than local significance. It constitutes a powerful tool for understanding the theoretico-historical pressures informing current critical debate.

NOTES

1. Cary Nelson, Paula A. Treichler, and Lawrence Grossberg, "Cultural Studies: An Introduction," in *Cultural Studies,* ed. Lawrence Grossberg, Cary Nelson, and Paula A. Treichler (New York: Routledge, 1992), 2.

2. Naomi Schor, *Reading in Detail: Aesthetics and the Feminine* (New York: Columbia University Press, 1985), xi.

3. Karl Marx, *The Grundrisse,* trans. David McLellan (New York: Harper & Row, 1971), 43.

4. I thank Vanessa Schwartz for help in articulating this point.

5. Jean-Marie Schaeffer, *Qu'est-ce qu'un genre littéraire?* (Paris: Seuil, 1989), 105 (my translation).

Introduction:
Realism, God's Secret, and the Body
Christopher Prendergast

Moments of Realism

Realism, as a literary-cultural concept, has had a strange history. Not the least interesting feature of that history is that it is not yet over; despite many modernist and postmodernist declarations of its death, the concept has an uncanny capacity for springing, Lazarus-like, back to life, returning again and again to the agenda of discussion. If it appeared to have been escorted definitively offstage by the high modernism of the early twentieth century, how then is it that the question of "realism" remains so actively central, though subject to varying evaluations, in the late twentieth century, in, say, the critical work of Roland Barthes or Raymond Williams? What exactly is at stake in these constantly renewed returns, including the return proposed by the following collection of essays? One line of interest is strictly scholarly, as part of the continuing endeavor to explore a historical field (as here in the many studies, broadly new-historicist style, of "cases" from the relevant archive of representations, on a spectrum from texts to museums). It is of course no accident if *relevant* here means essentially the nineteenth century and in particular nineteenth-century France: the exemplary place and moment of what we conventionally understand as the great tradition of realism, in both literature and painting (what Engels, in the well-known letter to Miss Harkness, called the "triumph of realism").

Yet the history is not simply an archival one. Viewed as a *cultural* history in the broadest sense, it displays the following, somewhat paradoxical, property: if the nineteenth century is the age of the flowering of realism as a set of literary and pictorial practices, it is not the age of its sophisticated conceptual articulation (famously, the nineteenth century, whether in terms of defense or attack, theorized the idea of realism in exceptionally naive terms). As developed concept, "realism" belongs rather to the twentieth century, in the form of the abiding, even obsessive, returns we have noted. Here we can distinguish three crucial moments of inquiry and evaluation. First, there is the moment of Marxism, notably the elaboration and defense of the idea of realism in the work of Georg Lukács, where realism is promoted as epistemologically and aesthetically superior to an allegedly antirealist modernism. This is a line of argument continued in the work of Raymond Williams, with the added twist, however, that much of the modernism rejected by Lukács (for example, Proust and Joyce) is incorporated by Williams as experimental extension of the realist canon itself.

Second, there was the moment of structuralism and poststructuralism, developed largely as critique of the idea of realism, most influentially in Barthes's seminal *S/Z*, arguably *the* critical-theoretical text of and for the post-1968 generation. Barthes's key move was to look at realism less in terms of substantive representational claims than as *forms* of representation, constructed and constructing practices, but where it was characteristically a feature of the practices (as well as of the acompanying panoply of legitimating theoretical ideas) to present the forms as if they were substances, or, in the well-known semiological formulation, to "convert culture into nature." Literary realism, in short, was the cultural brother of ideology, or more accurately was itself an ideological "operator," performing the primary task of ideology, the function of naturalizing socially and historically produced systems of meaning. (The distance of Barthes's approach from that of Lukács is conveniently measured by contrasting the latter's attachment to the category of the "type," as the very ground of representation, with the former's insistence on the "stereotype," as the mark of realism's incorrigible complicity in the conservatism and bad faith of ideology.)

Third, there was—and continues to be—the moment of feminism, often in harness with critical themes from poststructuralism, and notably in a particularly active deployment of issues and categories from psychoanalysis, the basic drift of which has been to align the representational strategies of realism with the production and reproduction of the ideological terms of patriarchy. This last moment is one that will especially preoccupy us here, above all by virtue of its strong focus on the body, on the tracing of representation from and across the body (a concern echoed in the title of this collection of essays). On the other hand, in distinguishing these three exemplary moments, we should also be wary of drawing too neatly differentiating a map or too simple a set of endorsements. The picture is more complex. It does not, for instance, form a simple chronology; there are many relations of overlap among all three. There are also intellectual convergences, as well as some knots and tangles. For example, if Barthes's literary semiology is to be read, at one level, as working *against* Lukács, it does so to some considerable extent from within the space of Marxism, especially, as a form of critical analysis (what in *Mythologies* Barthes calls a "semioclasm") concerned with ideology, in its use of notions from *The German Ideology*. Or again, if we think of psychoanalytic theory as a major "modernist" source for disrupting the field of representation (through the agency of unconscious desire), what do we make of Raymond Williams's curious suggestion that the best way to read the Freudian text is as realist novel? Is this merely a perverse antimodernism, anxious to hold on to the realist canon at all costs? Or does it direct attention toward a subtler and more tenacious life within the concept of realism, to which we must attend?

One shorthand for gaining some intial purchase on these different questions and problems is by way of a form of shorthand within many of the arguments and positions themselves. It is probably no accident that one proper name recurs throughout the history and variety of debate: "Balzac." For Lukács, Balzac is the quintessential representative of the great realist tradition. For Barthes—analyzing the story *Sarrasine* in *S/Z*—Balzac stands for the intimate relation between literary realism and the workings of ideology (the "cultural codes"). In certain feminist arguments, Balzac is the pure demonstration of the relation between the order of realism and the order of patriarchy (Balzac characteristically fantasizes the artist on analogies with the father, the king, the emperor, and God); indeed, in one version of the feminist case, even to *speak* of Balzac today, whatever the actual terms of the critical discourse in question, is to perpetuate a system of thought and values from which we need urgently to free ourselves (by speaking instead of, say, George Sand). This seems, however, a somewhat rigid polarization of the matter. Much is lost in simplifying Balzac as "Balzac," a metonym displaying exactly the same fetishizing and immobilizing force associated with the method of metonymic nomination that Jakobson advanced as the basic technique of realism itself.

God's Secret

It may in fact serve our purposes well, in presenting this collection of essays, to return once more to the example of Balzac, and in particular to that relatively unknown masterpiece, situated at the edges of the *Comédie humaine,* called *The Unknown Masterpiece.* The story involves a painter, Frenhofer, obsessed for ten years with painting the naked body of his dead mistress. When Frenhofer finally shows his canvas to his painter friends, Poussin and Porbus, they see only a chaos of lines and colors, with but a trace of the body of a woman (significantly, a foot). Frenhofer despairs and, in the concluding sentence of the story, the next day the two painters "learned that he had died during the night, after burning his pictures." Balzac's magnificent tale of passion, madness, and death around an issue of *representation,* and specifically, of course, the representation of a female body by a male painter, gives us a set of terms for thinking the problematics of realism. At its most euphoric, Frenhofer describes his project, in one of his many feverish speeches to his two colleagues, as nothing other than the attempt to "steal God's secret," thus at a stroke (a brush stroke, one is tempted to say) aligning representation, metaphysics, and sexuality. "God's secret" here is an alleged "essence" of Woman, and the project of pictorial representation the effort to master (thus touching one of the problematic senses of "masterpiece") a sexuality posed as radically other, as a mysterious essence and metaphysical ground of being.

There are several reasons why the story of Balzac's crazy painter may serve as a parable or allegory of realism. One concerns its use of the visual arts, not simply as contingent literary representation of the act of painting, but because the visual arts work importantly as an analogy for literary representation itself, as based on a tacit but founding invitation to visualization (realism invites us above all to *look* at the world). A second reason has to with the object of representation, the body—specifically, the female body. This again is a far from contingently chosen object, but reaches deep into the logic and structure of representation. It is, for example, also part of the lesson of Barthes's *S/Z,* where the bar between the two letters signifies the slash of gender and the barrier of sexual difference: Sarrasine and Zambinella, the former another male artist (a sculptor) obsessed with the body of Zambinella, but in the form of a category mistake (the male castrato taken for a woman). The question of sexual difference is thus at the very heart of the text, not only thematically but also formally, in its constitution as text, notably at that level of its organization commanded by the "symbolic code." The "symbolic" in Barthes's scheme of five basic codes governing the realist text is understood in a roughly Lévi-Straussian and Lacanian sense, the symbolic order based on very general binary oppositions and, crucially, the binary system of sexual difference (which, however, as "limit text," *Sarrasine* does as much to disrupt as to confirm).

In this view, questions of the body, of gender and sexuality, are not just "themes" of the realist corpus; they connect with basic presuppositions and furnish constitutive categories. They give flesh, so to speak, to what elsewhere (in the essay "Diderot, Brecht, Eisenstein") Barthes describes more abstractly as the "triangular" model of realist representation: a subject positioned as a viewer carves out a field shaped as a triangle, with the viewer's eyes as the apex. This of course recalls the classical model of perspective, and shows why analogies with vision and the visual are so important (in Barthes's scheme the visual reference covers the nonvisual arts as well). In this account, realism is best understood as an economy of positions and drives based on the relation of actual or imaginary looking, an economy where there is typically, or stereotypically, a male looker (painter, narrator, or the like) and one of the privileged objects of vision is the body of a woman. The latter attracts the gaze of the former as the figure of the "mystery" of sexual difference, as figure of the "origin," the ground of the symbolic order. In the case of painting, the two most notorious nineteenth-century images of the female body are Manet's *Olympia* and Courbet's aptly named *L'Origine du monde.* In the former, the woman's left hand lies flexed over the genitalia as a provocative game of hide-and-seek with the imperative to look, a "secret" withheld (or perhaps as a tongue-in-cheek statement to the effect that there is no secret other than in the head of the viewer); in the latter (the "original" of which disappeared immediately into the private collection of its—male—commissioner, never to be seen again other than in reproduction), the focus of the gaze is fully on the female genitalia, though as "dark continent," thus leaving endlessly open the question as to whether the term of its title, "origin," is intended ironically or is merely the symptom of a scopic, voyeuristic interest in the object that steers close to the idiom of pornography.

It is therefore of considerable significance that in very many of the essays in this collection the naked female body should figure so frequently as object of display or "spectacle." The nineteenth-century archive continuously discloses its own secret, or rather its abiding preoccupation with a "secret." It is a preoccupation also shadowed by an anxiety, the anxiety that "God's secret" might turn out to be unmanageable (in Balzac's story it generates rivalry, hatred, violence, madness, and death). The "secret," or rather the assumption of a secret, may prove to be dangerous. This is one reason the grounding analogy between the written and the visual in the theoretical articulation of realism is not simply a theoretical point, but also connects with a precise cultural and institutional politics; as Matlock's essay in this volume shows, the various nineteenth-century literary trials turned to a large extent on the prosecution's claim that the texts in question contained dangerous solicitations to *visualization,* "a rhetoric of seeing too much," notably around the questions of the body and sexuality.

If the body and sexuality hold out the promise of contact with an origin, thus anchoring the representation of reality in the ultimate "unveiling" of a truth (in Plato's terms, the moment of *aletheia;* in Aristotle's, the moment of "recognition," the *anagnorisis;* or in Barthes's, the moment of the fulfillment of the "hermeneutic code"), that truth (if such it is) threatens mayhem and panic. Plato famously fears mimesis because it menaces the body politic with noxious fakes. It is less commonly remarked that mimesis is also feared because of an association with the uterus (Plato's example in censuring mimesis is the practice of the womenfolk telling "emotional" stories to children) or, more accurately, with the uterus convulsed

(Maxime du Camp described the body in Courbet's picture as "convulsé"), with, that is, the condition of *hysteria*. For all the confidence of its presuppositions, models, and strategies, realism's engagement with the female body is permanently hedged about by the worry of something running out of control, at once fueling and exceeding the will to truth and knowledge. "Woman" (or, in Lacan's self-erasing phrase, "The Woman") is always a point of trouble for the classic tradition of realist writing. This is one reason so many of the relevant narratives are stories of female adultery and families falling apart, with a corresponding stress on the containing authority of the male sexual body (the "phallus"), the emphasis both in and on narrative—crucially the tradition of the European *Bildungsroman*—as the story of socialization into the order of property, filiation, and descent commanded by the Name of the Father. The *Bildungsroman* is, as it were, the other side of the coin to the anxiety represented by what Freud calls the *Familenroman,* the former part of the symbolic apparatus for covering over what is revealed in the fantasy structure of the latter, namely, the knowledge that there is no knowledge, that, in Freud's curious slippage into Latin, *pater semper incertus est.*

Body-Realism

Here then is the deep ambiguity of the project of realism, predicated on a desire for stable knowledge while encountering the conditions of its impossibility. The ambiguity is not, however, a contradiction, or, if so, it is a dialectical contradiction in the sense that the conflicting terms are the mutually constitutive terms of a general logic. Whether as drive to mastery or encounter with the unmasterable, realism is involved in the production of knowledge regimes across the body as an economy of the knowable and the unknowable, each reinforcing the other. This is Foucault's principal point regarding the historical culture that produced simultaneously the modern discourses of realism and "sexuality"; the common assumption is that the body, in particular the female body, houses a mystery, an enigma wrapped around an essence, that may or may not be known but that supplies the key to being.

Freeing ourselves from these metaphysical and ideological notions of hidden essence has been at the forefront of contemporary critical theory and literary practice. But the offered terms of opposition and rejection are themselves problematic and raise questions that bear directly on how we might continue to understand the idea of realism today. For example, the notion of "essence" attaches controversially to one of the principal spokeswomen for the antirealist critique in the name of, precisely, the "body," Hélène Cixous. As is well known (notably from the essay "Le Rire de la Méduse"), one of Cixous's principal concerns is to bring writing back to the reality of the body in ways that liberate both: the body and the text freed from the systems of control and the syndromes of paranoia into which they allegedly have been locked by the traditional practices of literary realism. But it is then immediately a question as to whether in this version the body reappears, in what is otherwise proposed as an antifoundationalist aesthetic of dispersal, as yet again a kind of foundation, guarantee of contact with the "real," and more precisely with an "origin." Does the place of the body in Cixous's argument in effect involve not so much a rejection of realism as its redefinition in late-twentieth-century conditions? Might we not be tempted to say that the argument that demands a return of writing to the pulses and rhythms of the body, and in particular the female body, is an argument in defense of a "feminist" realism (were it not that this might start to sound like a parody of Polonius's proliferating distinctions)?

In several of its aspects, Cixous's argument certainly looks like this. Indeed, in one vital respect it even comes across as *plus royaliste que le roi,* and that is in its very deployment of the category of the "body" itself. The text Cixous envisages is not merely "about" the body, it is itself a body ("Texte, mon corps"), the body of the text as material incarnation and end to the regime of the arbitrariness of the sign. This desired relation between body and text is one way of stating one of the wildest dreams of realism, the dream according to which representation becomes *embodiment,* in which the text no longer stands for something but is itself a presentation of that of which it speaks. As Cixous puts it in one of her essays, significantly titled "Le Dernier tableau ou le portrait de Dieu," it is the dream of a writing that would be a "présent absolu," where the "present" and the presentation in question would be the movements of bodily sensation and perception (the aesthetic act thus restoring something of the old sense of *aesthesis*). In the conception of such a project it is therefore perhaps no surprise that the terms of both God and painting should reappear, commanding not only the title of the essay but also its whole argument. The notion of God's portrait, in which we might *see* God ("voir Dieu," again the relation of looking and seeing), is a figure for an ideal of material incarnation and the ground of an analogy between writing and painting: "Je voudrais écrire comme un peintre. Je voudrais écrire comme peindre."

The idea here of a painterly writing is not at all that of a merely descriptive writing. It is rather the idea of a performatively embodying one, which will close the gap between words and things, signs and sensations, body and soul. This uncannily recalls, though in a very different register, the project of Balzac's Frenhofer to put onto canvas "God's secret." It also confirms the importance, and continuing life, of the painterly analogy in the deep structure of thinking and fantasizing about realism, not simply as imperative to look but also, and more radically, as desire for embodiment. Painting, or the visual arts generally, is the closest we get to (the illusion of) an art of embodiment, above all when the object is the body, human flesh itself. Cixous thinks of Cézanne as she meditates on the theme of "God's portrait"; Cézanne was obsessed with Frenhofer; Frenhofer in turn is obsessed with Titian; and it is Titian's way with flesh and blood that inspired the astonishing remark by one of his contemporaries: "It is to me as if Titian in painting this body has used flesh to make his colors." This both reverses and abolishes the normal view of signification and representation as based on a system of substitutions; it thinks not of paint substituting for blood, but of blood *being* paint; one could scarcely imagine a more dramatic statement of the idea of art as a making incarnate, as "body" pure and simple.

Does all this then serve to confirm the stubbornly enduring life of the idea of realism, along with its incurable complicities with metaphysical essentialism and foundationalism, or are there still further possibilities within the idea to be retrieved and explored? Raymond Williams, for example, also insists on a relation between the body, language, and knowledge, specifically knowledge of the social and its articulations as "experience." This web of relations enters decisively into his account of both the novel and the drama in the nineteenth and twentieth centuries, where the categories of the body and of knowledge converge in the complex existential and historical weave that Williams names the "structure of feeling." From within this structure, the plots of literary realism are identified as forms that actively make possible certain kinds of understanding of the social world. In this respect Williams is close to Bakhtin as well as to Lukács, and against Foucault (or rather a polemically simplified version of "Foucault"). Knowledge is not so much knowledge that incarcerates in the prevailing forms of the symbolic order as knowledge of *what* incarcerates in that order. It works by making "connections" that are otherwise hidden from view in the mystificatory moves of ideology (for example, the knowledge of the city made possible by the plots of Dickens's novels).

The connecting energies of realism may well be a value to hold on to in the ongoing debate, in counterpoint to the fashionable emphases on dispersal and fragmentation. It may also help us make sense of Williams's otherwise curious remark about reading Freud as realist novel. It is worth remembering, against the grain of those (often very persuasive) readings of Freud as protomodernist, all laterality, textual expansion, digression, and tangle, that the word *connection* is a very powerful one in the Freudian narrative and analytic lexicon (it appears literally dozens of time in the Dora story). Thus, if psychoanalysis is to be one of the paradigms of a questioning of the realist paradigm, then a veritable Pandora's box is opened, out of which tumble all sorts of intractable and intriguing paradoxes. In the meantime, the debate continues.

Female Sexuality and the Referent of Enlightenment Realisms

April Alliston

Twentieth-century historians of the novel generally distinguish the emerging genre from earlier (romance) narrative by its increased "realism," variously defined in terms of referentiality to the details of a quotidian experience shared by readers.[1] Judged by this standard, theorized as it is from the practice of nineteenth-century high realism, most eighteenth-century novels tend to appear underdeveloped, still uncomfortably close to the romance genre satirized in one of the first novels, *Don Quixote* (itself, of course, hardly "high realist"). Early novels may well be making a gesture of reference to something they identify as "the real," and in that sense it is appropriate to call them "realist." But it is not appropriate to assume that the logic of that gesture remains the same over the course of the novel's history, enabling critics to judge more and less successful expressions of the realist endeavor by a single, and often anachronistic, standard. The logics of referentiality at work in eighteenth-century fiction are multiple, and are based on conceptions of evidence that differ importantly from the one that came to dominate the later high realist tradition.

One effect of the normalized failure to recognize the multiplicity of realisms in eighteenth-century fiction is the marginalization of early women novelists. Accepted histories of the novel tend to associate women's work at the origins of the genre not with alternate concepts of how truth (or "reality") is evidenced, but with an underdeveloped execution of a singular model of realism. This critical judgment repeats the gesture of high realism itself in excluding alternate systems for representing reality from the literary canon, most often by adopting the very nineteenth-century metaphor of "natural" selection. After outlining a typology of the main varieties of eighteenth-century realism as I see them, I hope to open to debate the gender politics of various realist strategies, and then of twentieth-century criticism that describes the history of the novel in the rhetorical terms of biological evolution.

Three Types of Evidence, Three Types of Realism

The eighteenth-century novel differs starkly from later fiction in its frequent claims to factual truth, in the documentary forms of narration with which it evidences those truth claims, and in the wide acceptance of them by contemporary readers. The truth claimed was, generally speaking, a private truth (even when it concerned public figures, as in the "scandalous histories" of Delariviere Manley and Eliza Haywood). The documentary forms were therefore private documents or personal, eyewitness accounts: familiar letters, journals, memoirs, travelogues. Up to this point, I remain in agreement with Ian Watt's classic description of eighteenth-century realism. But where Watt constructs an ultimately unitary conception of "formal realism" as vacillating dialectically through the eighteenth century until it achieves synthesis in the novels of Austen, I would like to propose a nonhierarchical tripartite model of Enlightenment realisms.[2] I do not assert that three categories of realism exist by theoretical necessity, but that there were during the period at least three distinct types, representing three significantly different conventions for referring to reality, and that these intersected and competed with one another.

Watt refers to the "realism of representation" because these forms did not *represent* "reality" or events as much as, and except insofar as, they *presented* private testimony. But Watt conflates the technique of presentation with reliance upon a sense of plausibility for the construction of nontraditional plots. That is where I would like to draw an important distinction. More often than not, eighteenth-century novels presented reality as fantastic truth rather than plausible fiction.[3] Defoe's fictional *A Journal of the Plague Year* was initially read as a factual account, Diderot's reclusive friend actually made an effort to assist the fictive nun in distress, and Americans wept all the way through the nineteenth century at the grave of their first fictional heroine, Charlotte Temple (her tombstone still stands in New York's Trinity Churchyard).[4] These contemporary responses to eighteenth-century fiction do not by any means indicate that Defoe's remarkable episodes, the scenes of lesbian sex in a downright Gothic setting of incarceration and torture related by Diderot's nun, or the moral beatification of a young woman who "falls" and is abandoned as a result of her error corresponded to any Enlightenment sense of verisimilitude. What it does indicate is that the documents of private testimony, regardless of mechanical reproduction, were taken seriously as evidence of truth, and that such evidence was if anything supported by the implausibility of the events related.[5] Indeed, the idea of plausibility has always been accompanied by a certain awareness, more or less uneasy at different times, that its law is a law for narration, for the accounting for fact, and not for the facts themselves, which often seem to have no regard whatsoever for its dictates. What established the relationship of a text to the real for the eighteenth-century reader, then, was not the plausibility of a representation, but rather the presentation of documentary evidence of a firsthand or eyewitness account.[6] I shall refer to this form of realism as *evidentiary realism.*

If evidentiary realism prevailed during the first half of the eighteenth century, another type came to prominence with the works of Richardson and Rousseau, coexisting to the end of the century with "evidentiary" works like *Charlotte Temple,* but becoming increasingly important as the century proceeded. I shall distinguish this type from the first with the term *exemplary realism.* Whereas in evidentiary realism the (re)presentation of proof—documentation and eyewitness accounts—establishes the factuality of the account for the reading public, in exemplary realism the perceived exemplarity of the account begins to *create* factual truth according to its own model. In evidentiary realism, the text's status as presentation (of evidence) takes precedence over its status as representation (of what is proven by the evidence); in exemplary realism, the text's status as exemplum again takes precedence over its status as representation, so that it is read in terms of imitation rather than in terms of mimesis. That is, the text asks to be read as an example capable of generating real action through imitation, rather than as an imitation of real action. The church bells rang for Pamela's wedding and young men shot themselves in yellow vests that matched Werther's not because there was anything plausible about such representations (as Fielding so acidly observed), but because their perceived moral exemplarity generated its own imitative reality.[7]

Evidentiary and exemplary realism are in fact closely connected to one another in both conception and practice (especially Richardson's). Only a shift of emphasis differentiates them: the truth claim of exemplary realism no longer emphasizes as much the establishment of the exemplary person or event's individual and unique existence as fact; rather, it simultaneously asserts the exemplar's uniqueness and her existence, or at least her potential existence in multiple reproductions, by dint of imitation. Her "truth" as exemplar is supported by this double proof: she is unique (otherwise she would not be exemplary) and at the same time she is presented as worthy of imitation. This shift in emphasis also entails one from event to character. Not events, but characters, generally though not always female ones, are held up as examples. The emphasis on character remains in force for mimetic realism, and, like it, is very much alive to the present day.

The high realism of the nineteenth century takes the figure of example and turns it from the logic of imitation to that of mimesis. The characters of mimetic realism are presented as *examples*, like those of "exemplary" realism, but another shift of emphasis has occurred, this time in the meaning of the term *example*. The characters of mimetic realism are no longer examples in the sense that they are presented as models for imitation, but they are examples in the other, evidentiary sense: they are the particular instances that prove a maxim or precept—in this case an implicit statement of general truth about "reality"—by standing for it, representing it. What connects all three is the private nature of the truth in question, whether that truth be evidenced through documentation, presented as example, or mimetically represented. All the documentary forms mentioned above enact the public disclosure of private truth. When public truths are referred to (such as the actions of public figures in the early scandal chronicles or well-known historical events in mimetic realism), the gesture of the fiction is to involve those public truths within a private context that must remain a matter of public ignorance or doubt, unprovable by any but uncertain forms of evidence: that of private, unsubstantiated testimony; that of circumstantial evidence; or that of the authority of an omniscient narrator.

The Reality of Legitimacy

The truth-referent of realism, then, is historically a *private* truth. Eighteenth-century novels in England, France, and Germany come back obsessively to one private truth in particular: the truth about female sexuality and its conformity (or lack thereof) to patriline control. This preoccupation is so characteristic of fiction of the "longer eighteenth century" in Western Europe that it would almost be deceptive to describe it from a reading of specific instances.[8] The anxiety over woman's virtue and its corollary, man's legitimacy, is a preoccupation that the novel inherits from romance. Eighteenth-century realisms represent a search for new ways of either demonstrating or destabilizing the old romance truth about legitimacy of succession and transmission in terms of Enlightenment conceptions of evidence. In patriline terms, the question of female sexuality is identical with the question of legitimacy, and hence of legality; thus the logic of its demonstration historically follows changes in the dominant forms of legal evidence, culminating in the hegemony of mimetic realism's logic of verisimilitude.

The link between realism and patriline anxiety over legitimacy has its roots in classical aesthetics, where "recognition" as an essential aspect of mimetic representation is theorized by Aristotle from the praxis of tragic recognition. "Recognition" in Greek tragedy is generally recognition of a kinship relation; thus, I would trace it to the epic anxiety over recognition as evidence of patriline legitimacy.[9] "You must be, by your looks, Odysseus' boy?" says Athene (and Nestor, and Menelaos) to Telemachos, "Yes, how like him!" Telemachos replies, "thoughtfully": "My mother says I am his son; I know not/surely. Who has known his own engendering?"[10] A mother's word has never been, and by definition cannot be, adequate evidence to establish the legitimacy of a child in patriline terms. From this point of view, much of Western narrative since Homer has been an exercise in *not* simply taking women's words for it—a search for evidence that would establish the truth or false-hood of a mother's word on legitimacy without allowing her to remain the ultimate authority on the subject.

Michael McKeon describes the novel as a dialectical motion away from romance that negates it even while commemorating its ancient knowledge that "lineage existed to resolve questions of virtue and truth with a tacit simultaneity, making both a causal claim of genealogical descent attesting to an eminence of birth, hence worth, and a logical claim of testimonial precedent validating all present claims as true."[11] What is left out of this convincing account is that what most persists from that romance knowledge, and persists well through the period of mimetic realism's heyday, is the cultural value of patriline legitimacy, along with the anxious recognition, as represented by Telemachos's answer to the question of his lineage and his identity, of the very fragility of its own evidence.

Although anxiety about control over female sexuality and the evidence of legitimacy is as ancient as patriarchy, Enlightenment discourse moves the scene of recognition from the public theater of tragedy (or of Renaissance romance), itself originally modeled on the Athenian law court, to a domestic theater. *Clarissa* stages the "trial" of its heroine's virtue in the family sitting room, complete with pleading, testimony, material evidence (the letters), jury, judge, accuser, and incarceration of the defendant between sessions, in a kind of private theatricals taken seriously as courtroom drama (whereas playful private theatricals will become, for Jane Austen, a frivolous threat to the very feminine virtue these are staged to discover).[12] The real jury, of course, is not the Harlowe family, but the reading public. The members of the real jury are moved to sympathize with the defendant, not directly by her performance or by the pleadings of those who speak on her behalf, both of which fail to move the fictive jury, but rather by the evidence of their own senses, by the familiar letters, which they see as evidence of her sincerity. The letters are of course the very thing the Harlowe family, the jury in representation, views as evidence of her disobedience, regardless of their content.[13] What changes the perspective is an intersection of two things: the differing personal investments in the interpretation of the evidence for the jury of characters and the jury of readers, and the differing amounts and types of evidence presented to each. Only the readers see all the correspondence, with its several perspectives that tend further to verify the heroine's sincerity. To complement the presentation of evidence, a sympathetic response *outside* the situation of the courtroom drama is inscribed within the text in the mother-daughter relation.

Richardson takes advantage of the readers' lack of personal (i.e., *private*) investment in Clarissa's acting according to the will of her family—despite the fact that the same readers are likely to be so invested when it comes to real daughters in their own families—to present the more comprehensive evidence that proves Clarissa's virtue. Thus, he creates the illusion of having proved that Clarissa's word can be taken for her own virtue, and also demonstrates the narrowness and bias of the familial perspective. In placing the question, not only of a heroine's virtue, but moreover of her sincerity, of whether her own word can be taken for the truth of her virtue, within the play of difference between readers' and characters' evidence and interpretation of the evidence, Richardson is working (to his own different ends) with a feminine strategy of resistance to the norms of verisimilitude that points back to Marie de Lafayette's *La Princesse de Clèves*.[14]

Virtue and Verisimilitude

In *La Princesse de Clèves* as in *Clarissa,* a woman's statements about her own fidelity to patriarchal norms of female sexual conduct are judged by a fictive audience that possesses only the partial evidence of the senses (the Harlowes' of Clarissa's performance and her partial correspondence; the prince of Clèves's of his manservant's glimpse of Nemours going over the garden wall), as well as by readers of the novel, who are in possession of fuller evidence: a more complete correspondence in the case of *Clarissa,* and the omniscient narrator's presentation of the princess's private thoughts and actions in the other. Those private thoughts and actions include the princess's famous *aveu*. The *aveu* is a pledge of fidelity, of faithfulness to patriline law, but it is one whose evidence, for its fictive judge, consists in nothing other than its own status as a free, unforced confession.[15] It is thus paradoxical, because the confession of female desire inherently threatens the very law to which it pledges fidelity. Such an act of confession already constitutes a transgression, for both fictive and actual readers, of the law of verisimilitude, which prescribes that women maintain the *appearances* of female fidelity, as interpreted and judged by an authoritative male viewer or male-dominated community of viewers.[16] Writers throughout the eighteenth century, most of them women, imitated and transformed the "inimitable" strategy of the princess of Clèves for resistance to the normative hegemony of verisimilitude as an unstable category whose interpretation would always be manipulated in the service of the ruling hierarchy.[17] The princess's strategy for resistance to the demand for the evidence of plausibility, for the appearances that would prove, according to the evidentiary logic particular to the law of verisimilitude, the truth of the narrative of female virtue, is to attempt to keep the scene of that narration entirely within the realm of the private. The princess is unsuccessful in this project, and has to relinquish desire in order to become mistress of her own private state, estate, status, and story.

Rather than expose, like Richardson, the trials of woman's virtue to the reading public on its domestic bench, eighteenth-century women novelists often attempt to circumvent the trial scenario altogether, by turning the nonfictional private documentary forms and the perceived instability of history in relation to verisimilitude (the recognition, referred to above, that plausibility is a category of narrative and not of reality) into forms of evidence that would force *the reader's recognition,* and hence legitimation, of the authority of the woman as narrator to determine the truth value of her own narrative.[18] Even when they do stage the heroine's trial of virtue, thereby conforming to a law of verisimilitude for what women authors might publish, they quite often undercut the reader's ability to judge of that trial on any evidence but that of the heroine's own word. They do so by writing the trial in the form of a letter- or memoir-novel that includes no masculine or skeptical demand for corroborating evidence, except where the heroine's own testimony portrays that skepticism as mistaken and its demand as silencing.

As I have said, the ultimate private truth, the truth that would always lack authoritative testimony and have to be judged by the standards of plausibility, was identified by Mme de Lafayette in *La*

Princesse de Clèves as the truth about female sexual conduct and its conformity (or lack thereof) to the reproduction of patriline legitimacy. This indeed remains the ultimate truth for fiction in France and England, at least through the time of Dickens and Collins, for example, or of Balzac, whose work consistently explores questions of legitimacy and legitimate transmission. Lafayette and the writers who followed her (many of them women or "feminocentric" writers like Richardson) authorized private testimony in opposition both to traditional received authority and to the new logic of plausibility. Private testimony was identified with feminine narration through the linkage of the domestic sphere with femininity, and its truth value was evidenced not by plausibility, but by the very implausibility of the act of *free* "confession" of female desire, which constituted an inherently transgressive act in its potential threat to patriline legitimacy. Throughout the eighteenth century this strategy of free feminine narration—a hallmark of sentimentalism—competed in fiction with the authority of plausibility, which quickly came to dominate legal and historical proof (*Northanger Abbey* itself, a parodic commentary on the implausibility of Gothic romance, is a good example of this conflict). The logic of plausibility eventually won out in fiction, too, in the mimetic realism of the nineteenth century. This conflict and its resolution accounts for the shift from the immense popularity of epistolary fiction in the eighteenth century as a form of private documentary testimony to the use of letters in nineteenth-century fiction more exclusively as material evidence: conclusions drawn from the material evidence of the letter supersede the authority of its text as testimony.

The period between the publication of Richardson's novels and the triumph of mimetic realism saw the production of a strong body of fiction by women that presents the history of a heroine's virtue strictly through the private documentation of the heroine's own letters and their sympathetic reception by a female confidante. This form limits the evidence of virtue, and the force of its example, to the woman's own word for her history and conduct. Given the long history of literary anxiety over how the reality of a woman's sexual fidelity can be faithfully represented, it cannot be a matter of pure chance or pure aesthetic value that this pattern of evidence is *not* the one to be found in the canonical works of the same period that also present the exemplary history, in letters, of a virtuous heroine.[19] Neither Richardson, Rousseau, Burney, Laclos (whose skepticism about female virtue and its evidence is only more extreme than the others), nor Austen limits the evidence of the heroine's virtue to her own account, so that Austen, on the verge of high realism, at last drops the letters altogether in favor of a skeptical, omniscient narrator. In doing so, she demands of any heroine who is to prove her virtue the utmost fidelity to the principles of verisimilitude.

Conclusion: The Legitimacy of Reality

Although evidentiary and exemplary realisms, the realisms of Defoe and Richardson, may seem clunky and archaic when viewed, as they tend to be, as Cro-Magnons in the "evolution" of the novel as the genre of transcendent mimetic realism, contemporary women's fiction, whenever it has been subjected to the same standard of comparison, comes out looking like a horde of Neanderthals. Were they capable of speech? critics seem to be asking of early novels by women. Were their brains as big? Were these strange-looking texts the ancestors of the novel as well, did they contribute equally to the genesis of the genre of realism, or do they simply constitute a dead-end freak mutation?

The rhetoric of the "evolution" of *the* realist novel turns out to be identical with the discourse of mimetic realism itself; it is no accident that this metaphor is borrowed from the period of mimetic realism's heyday. One emphasizes the formal "perfection" of the representation, the other the "reality" that is to be perfectly represented, but both discourses locate the value of the representation or the represented in terms of a logic akin to that of patriline legitimacy. If the idea of plausibility is based upon the fiction of a consensus of likelihood, centered on and originating in a masculine, first aristocratic and then bourgeois consensus about the likelihood of female sexual conduct and of the truth of a woman's word about it, the idea of evolution similarly devalues the production that it labels as indeterminate (for plausibility, the reality of paternity and the truth of a woman's word; for evolution, mutation or the production of new forms) by judging it according to the criterion of "selection." The logic of natural selection, like that of patriline descent, ascribes a higher value to that which it designates as "fit" or "legit" by distinguishing it from and opposing it to a field of other possibilities defined as an indiscriminate chaos of production (or reproduction). In so doing, both allay potential anxieties about the reality of indeterminacy by creating a legible line of descent, whether of the "fit" or of the "legit," that cuts through what would otherwise be, it seems, not a history but a cacophony.

Some individual historians of the novel overtly emphasize or even insist on an evolutionary metaphor, but even when they overtly reject it, some version of it often pervades their language, an inevitable connotation of words such as *development* and *rise*. John J. Richetti's main objection to Watt's *The Rise of the Novel*, for example, is what he identifies as the latter's "teleological bias," which "imposes an untenable pattern of growth and development upon the history of prose fiction. This preconception reduces any study of the material in question to the rather thankless, and to my mind meaningless, task of pointing out small 'advances' in realistic technique in various otherwise hapless hacks." I could not agree more with this critique of the evolutionary conception of literary history. Yet Richetti, too, in his epilogue, significantly titled "The Relevance of the Unreadable," leaves his hacks, most of them female hacks, as haplessly unread and unredeemed as ever—and for the same reason. He, too, is trying to read them through the dark glasses of late realism: "Defoe's narratives are often garrulous and disjointed *by modern standards of narrative coherence;* his imitators are merely diffuse or incoherent without any of his *saving realism.*"[20] Richetti is willing to give Defoe the benefit of his historical difference on the score of "narrative coherence" because his "realism" is *at times* more akin than others' to the mimetic realism, with its logic of plausibility, that has since been codified as the transparent representation of a reality that can never be diffuse or incoherent.[21]

I have just argued that the metaphor of literary evolution so pervasive in writing about the history of the novel as a genre, like all metaphors of descent in a patriarchal culture, masks the indeterminacy inherent in relations of patriline descent, in much the same way that Athene, Nestor, Helen, and Menelaos reassure Telemachos about the undecidability of Penelope's honesty by telling him that he looks just like his father. Those who use the metaphor most self-consciously, however, do emphasize the role of indeterminacy in evolutionary processes. English Showalter writes: "The evolutionary analogy describes quite well how progress emerged from *such chaos*" (i.e., the diversity of fictional forms produced in eighteenth-century Europe). Chaos exists, the chaos of diverse possibility, as Telemachos would be the last to deny; indeed, it is only the acknowledgment of the indeterminate as *all too real* that creates the anxious necessity of social and symbolic systems to devalue it. What emerges from the reality of chaos through these processes of selection, we must reassure ourselves, is at once *natural* (as implied by the rhetorical force of the evolutionary analogy) and representative of "progress."

Showalter continues:

> Given the literary situation, ranging from the tastes of potential readers to the mechanics of publishing, certain elements had greater fitness for survival than others. Whenever such an element occurred, it *naturally* seemed outstandingly successful, and was therefore imitated by subsequent writers, most of whom added nothing to it, but a few of whom perhaps advanced the genre one more evolutionary step by some new idea or device. During these prehistoric days, many offshoots of the original genre were headed for extinction; the gigantic romances of the seventeenth century resemble dinosaurs in more ways than one. At the same time, the early ancestors of the modern novel were toiling away in obscurity, profiting from their insignificance to adapt better and faster to new conditions.[22]

I have included the above passage because it vividly describes, with the detail of a *National Geographic* artist's rendition, two recurrent aspects of the evolutionary analogy that might seem to clear it of the present critique: the fittest literary forms (and their authors) are originally "insignificant" and "obscure" (although, apparently, also outstandingly successful from the outset), laboring in the shadow of such "dinosaurs" as the *roman de longue haleine,* a strongly *feminine*-identified genre. When this strategy of representation is examined, the outlines of romance emerge: what we have in the evolutionary analogy taken at its word is a romance of the novel, in which the genre-hero begins in an orphaned obscurity of unidentifiable lineage, but, recognized in time by its own inherently superior merits, ends by becoming fully legitimated, its ancient lineage seen to stretch back, finally, to the heroic epic. The evolutionary discourse modifies this implicit romance narrative, to be sure, by shifting the evidence mark of superiority from "nobility" (in its full sense, in which the ideas of "best" and "purest" include and occlude that of class superiority) to "fitness," a term that implies a more relative sense of superiority, not necessarily absolute superiority, but one determined by environmental necessity.

One of the most recent, and certainly the most rigorous, of the proponents of the evolutionary analogy for the history of the novel repeats the twin moves just described in Showalter's work. Franco Moretti more strongly insists upon the role of indeterminacy in producing literary forms in the eighteenth century, and on that of "social necessity" in selecting from among them the fittest genre for survival into the nineteenth: the *Bildungsroman,* which he also identifies as the "most bastard" genre.[23] Thus he repeats and develops further perhaps not so much a romance as a *Bildungsroman* of the novel's development: in his Marxist adaptation of natural selection he is careful to de-emphasize strictly aesthetic values ("saving realism" or "pleasing readers") in favor of social norms as the determining factors, just as, he argues, the *Bildungsroman* abandons the romance interest in the inherently extraordinary or noble to mark the "normal" as worthy of interest.[24]

In any case, like the orphaned nobles of romance or the obscurely normal heroes of *Bildungsromane,* the "bastard genre" ends by becoming legitimated. As Moretti writes, "The most bastard of these forms [i.e., of the various novelistic forms competing for survival at the end of the eighteenth century] became—the dominant genre of Western narrative."[25] It became so, as always, at the expense of the other bastards who remain bastards, thereby maintaining the meaningfulness of the opposition between the bastard and the legitimate. If the *Bildungsroman* is a "bastard" genre because it is a *hybrid* (a term more in keeping with the evolutionary rhetoric, whereas *bastard* evokes romance), then the women's novels of the eighteenth century described in the preceding sections might fairly contest with it for the title of "most bastard," for they actually undo the opposition of "classification" to "transformation," which, according to Moretti, finds its compromise position in the *Bildungsroman,* thus giving it the flexibility to survive the conflict between the two.[26] They combine the marriage plot identified with "classification" with the open-ended form identified with "transformation," and they do it through an embedded repetition of similar narratives that combine differing, multiple versions of "classificatory" endings, resisting the prioritization of any one of them, and thus resisting classification itself by creating an undecidable, openended form. They, too, are bastard forms, but they have remained the bastards of literary history as well, instead of becoming "the dominant genre of Western narrative."

What is the reason for the difference in the histories of these two bastards? Moretti identifies the selective factor, in keeping with his adaptation of the evolutionary metaphor to a Marxist literary history, as "social necessity."[27] "Social" it indubitably is; "necessity"—there's the rub. What Moretti's most evolved species of the evolutionary analogy allows us to see is that it does indeed provide an accurate representation of the processes of modern literary history, though not an absolute standard for judging the value, the perfection, or the readability of literary works. Insofar as the former—the accurate representation of what happened in literary history—was the project of all of the critics I have just mentioned, as I believe it was, they are right. The problem is that to represent the social in terms of a discourse of natural necessity is to perform, if inadvertently, a rhetorical gesture parallel to that of mimetic realism: one of its effects is to mask the social contingency and the constructedness of reality—whether of an individual's or of a genre's history—as something *natural* (or real), and hence unquestionably necessary. Romance becomes biology—or perhaps biology is simply post-Enlightenment romance. We need (which, as usual, means *some of us* need; it has now become "socially necessary") to question the investment of such critical moves, for of course the representation of literary history retrospectively affects the readability of literary works. In order to reread early women's novels, we will have to rethink literary tradition.

A feminist reconsideration of fiction judged as archaic and unreadable by the standards of mimetic realism—which are the standards promoted and perpetuated by the discourse of literary evaluation—allows not only for a more informed appreciation of early women's novels through an understanding of the political differences in their epistemology and referentiality, but also for a greater awareness of the politics of epistemology and referentiality concealed in mainstream Enlightenment evidentiary and exemplary

realisms, in the mimetic realism that succeeded them in the nineteenth century, and in contemporary constructions of the history of
the novel.

NOTES

I would like to thank Paula Backscheider, Margaret Cohen, and Franco Moretti for
their generous help in reading and commenting on this essay. I am also grateful to
the American Council of Learned Societies for a Research Fellowship for Recent
Recipients of the Ph.D., which helped fund my research.

1. See, for example, Robert A. Day, *Told in Letters: Epistolary Fiction before
Richardson* (Ann Arbor: University of Michigan Press, 1966); J. Paul Hunter, *Before
Novels: The Cultural Contexts of Eighteenth-Century English Fiction* (New York: W.
W. Norton, 1990); John J. Richetti, *Popular Fiction before Richardson: Narrative
Patterns 1700–1739* (Oxford: Clarendon, 1992 [1969]); English Showalter, *The
Evolution of the French Novel, 1641–1782* (Princeton, N.J.: Princeton University
Press, 1972); Ian Watt, *The Rise of the Novel: Studies in Defoe, Richardson, and
Fielding* (Berkeley: University of California Press, 1957).

2. Watt, *The Rise of the Novel*, 295–97.

3. Delariviere Manley's preface to *The Secret History of Queen Zarah* (London,
1711) clarifies the latter distinction: "He that writes a True History ought to place the
Accidents as they Naturally happen, without endeavouring to sweeten them for to
procure a greater Credit, because he is not obliged to answer for their Probability;
but he that composes a History to his Fancy, . . . is obliged to Write nothing that is
improbable"; "To the Reader," n.p. See also Hunter, *Before Novels*, 193–96.

4. Cathy N. Davidson, "Introduction," in Susanna Rowson, *Charlotte Temple*
(New York: Oxford University Press, 1986), xiii; Robert Mauzi, "Preface," in Denis
Diderot, *La Religieuse* (Paris: Gallimard, 1972), 9–13. I am grateful to Paula R.
Backscheider for this information about Defoe's work.

5. As David Hume lamented in 1748, "When anything is affirmed utterly absurd
and miraculous, [the mind] rather the more readily admits of such a fact, upon account of that very circumstance, which ought to destroy all its authority." *Of
Miracles*, ed. Antony Flew (La Salle, Ill.: Open Court, 1985), 35.

6. This is in contrast to the later turn taken by both legal evidence and fictional
representation, as Alexander Welsh argues in *Strong Representations: Narrative and
Circumstantial Evidence in England* (Baltimore: Johns Hopkins University Press,
1992), 8: "By strong representations, I mean those of the later eighteenth and nineteenth centuries that openly distrust direct testimony, insist on submitting witnesses
to the test of corroborating circumstances, and claim to know many things without
anyone's having seen them at all."

7. See also Robert Darnton on *Julie*: "Reader and writer communed across the
printed page, each of them assuming the ideal form envisioned in the text."
"Readers Respond to Rousseau: The Fabrication of Romantic Sensitivity," in *The
Great Cat Massacre and Other Episodes in French Cultural History* (New York:
Vintage, 1985 [1984]), 248–49.

8. To illustrate from well-known examples, however, one might mention
Clarissa, Tom Jones, Corinne, La Nouvelle Héloïse, La Princesse de Clèves, The Castle

of *Otranto* (and indeed the Gothic in general, notably the works of Radcliffe and Lee), *Die Marquise von O; Geschichte des Fräuleins von Sternheim.*

9. See Sheila Murnaghan, *Disguise and Recognition in the Odyssey* (Princeton, N.J.: Princeton University Press, 1987); Marylin Katz, *Penelope's Renown: Meaning and Indeterminacy in the* Odyssey (Princeton, N.J.: Princeton University Press, 1991).

10. Homer, *The Odyssey,* trans. Robert Fitzgerald (Garden City, N.Y.: Anchor/ Doubleday, 1961), 20.

11. Michael McKeon, *The Origins of the English Novel, 1600–1750* (Baltimore: Johns Hopkins University Press, 1987), 420.

12. I refer to *Mansfield Park,* of course. The word *trial* appears on every other page of *Clarissa;* both the legal and religious senses of the word are played upon throughout the novel. See Watt, *The Rise of the Novel,* 34. See also Susan Pepper Robbins, "Jane Austen's Epistolary Fiction," in *Jane Austen's Beginnings: The Juvenilia and "Lady Susan,"* ed. J. David Grey (Ann Arbor: University of Michigan Research Press, 1989). Robbins notes that Jane Austen "knew that Clarissa's letters were documents in the case against Lovelace" (219).

13. Samuel Richardson, *Clarissa; or, The History of a Young Lady,* ed. Angus Ross (Harmondsworth, England: Penguin, 1985 [1747–48]). See, for example, 364–65.

14. Although Richardson, too, is resisting verisimilitude (as Fielding noticed), his "different ends" may be those identified by Paula Backscheider in " 'The Woman's Part': Richardson, Defoe, and the Horrors of Marriage," *Eighteenth-Century Studies* 26 (Spring 1994); or by Nancy Armstrong in *Desire and Domestic Fiction: A Political History of the Novel* (New York: Oxford University Press, 1987): *to place women at the center of domestic ideology* rather than to have them threaten patrilineage by controlling the meaning of their own words.

15. See Joan DeJean, "Lafayette's Ellipses: The Privileges of Anonymity," *PMLA* 99 (October 1984): 896–97.

16. See my *Virtue's Faults; or, Women's Correspondence in Eighteenth-Century Fiction* (Stanford, Calif.: Stanford University Press, forthcoming); on the relation between female "fidelity" and verisimilitude, see, again, DeJean, "Lafayette's Ellipses"; and Nancy Miller, *Subject to Change: Reading Feminist Writing* (New York: Columbia University Press, 1988), 25–46.

17. On the instability of plausibility in the history of legal argument, see Welsh, *Strong Representations:* "Thus circumstances typically told against the individual brought to trial as Johnson's definition of the word implies" (15). "[By the mid-Victorian period, when] defendants were fully represented, the weaknesses of circumstantial evidence could be advertised to the jury" (18).

18. This is the case in Eliza Haywood's *The British Recluse* (London, 1724 [1722]), Mme Riccoboni's *Histoire de Miss Jenny Revel* (Paris, 1764), Sophie von La Roche's *Geschichte des Fräuleins von Sternheim* (Stuttgart: Philipp Reclam jun., 1983 [Leipzig, 1771]), and Sophia Lee's *The Recess* (London, 1783–85), to name only a few. On the instability of the relations among history, fiction, and verisimilitude in seventeenth-century France, see Showalter, *The Evolution of the French Novel,* 15–16, 53–56.

19. See, for example, the works by Riccoboni and Lee mentioned in note 18. For a full account and bibliography of this fiction, see my *Virtue's Faults.*

20. Richetti, *Popular Fiction before Richardson,* 5–6, 262; emphasis added.

21. Though Crusoe may infer plausibility from circumstantial evidence, as Welsh argues (*Strong Representations*, 3–6), Defoe relies precisely on the force of the forms of eyewitness testimony to persuade his audience of Crusoe's truth.

22. Showalter, *The Evolution of the French Novel*, 5–6; emphasis added.

23. Franco Moretti, *Signs Taken for Wonders: Essays in the Sociology of Literary Forms* (London: Verso, 1988 [1983]), 264; Franco Moretti, *The Way of the World: The Bildungsroman in European Culture* (London: Verso, 1987), 10. Moretti emphasizes chance as that which distinguishes his Darwinian version of the metaphor from a Lamarckian one that would see formal variations as " 'oriented' and 'preferentially inclined towards variations' " (*Signs Taken for Wonders*, 262).

24. Richetti, *Popular Fiction before Richardson*, 262; Showalter, *The Evolution of the French Novel*, 349; Moretti, *The Way of the World*, 10–13.

25. Moretti, *The Way of the World*, 10.

26. Moretti borrows the terms *classification* and *transformation* from Yuri Lotman: the former "establishes a classification different from the original one but nevertheless perfectly clear and stable"; under the latter, "the opposite is true: what makes a story meaningful is its narrativity, its being an open-ended process" (*The Way of the World*, 7–9). On narrative structure in eighteenth-century women's epistolary fiction, see Alliston, *Virtue's Faults*.

27. Moretti, *Signs Taken for Wonders*, 263.

Censoring the Realist Gaze
Jann Matlock

"There is a very dangerous thing in literature," wrote Eugène Maron in 1847, "and that is the excess of truth. That excess leads to a method of observation without ideals or poetry, which recounts every fact and scrutinizes every feeling indiscriminately, randomly, and without a thought to whether they are by nature worthy of study." Like other critics of the July Monarchy and Second Empire, Maron insisted that he did not question either the "truth of manners" described by Balzac in *Les Parents pauvres* or the "exactitude of the observations." There were, however, things Maron just did not want to *see*: "Is it really necessary to paint such morals? Isn't there a corner of life that we should carefully hide and never unveil?" Like many of Balzac's critics over the previous decade, Maron saw these novels as examples of "incessant, merciless observation" that reduced the world to a "barren and practical reality."[1]

Railing against "that school that calls itself realist," ten years later, in 1857–58, critics found powerful metaphors to call for the censorship of what they saw as a new breed of novel owing its origins to that "father of physiology, Honoré de Balzac." The recently censored *Madame Bovary* was targeted for inheriting the methods of the nineteenth-century clinic, the subjects of hysteria and overwhelming passion, and an audience of pleased "great ladies and honorable *bourgeoises*." Critic Eugène Poitou protested this "realist literature" that would "expose our secret maladies" with the assurance that one might thus be cured, by likening it to the Musée Dupuytren, the pathological anatomy museum that harbored wax and other anatomical figures designed to share knowledge of the diseased body with medical students (Figure 3.1). "Anatomy, physiology . . . there is the muse of the new school," fumed Poitou, imagining that these novels, like the pathology museum, brought "together the terrifying images of the most hideous afflictions of humanity."[2]

The pathological anatomy museum known as the Musée Dupuytren (Figure 3.2) gained a special currency for the fantasmatic understanding of the body in the nineteenth century—despite the fact that the original museum, established in the École de Médecine in 1835 in honor of surgeon Guillaume Dupuytren (1777–1835), was almost never open to the general public. Unseen by those who could only imagine its horrors, its name conveyed an account of "monstrosities" and "maladies" that ought to have remained "secret" but that had, through the workings of science, nevertheless come to light.[3] Closed away in the buildings of the medical school, the Musée Dupuytren became an emblem of all that ought to remain hidden from view. Containing, in the words of a Second Empire commentator on Paris, "some pieces which are excessively curious, representing the ravages in the contexture of organs, and others, in wax, representing the most complete series of secret maladies," this collection was imagined so disturbing as to "drive all those who cannot tolerate this hideous image of the most disgusting of all maladies to flee as quickly as they can."[4]

The Musée Dupuytren, unseen by either literary critics or their readers, nevertheless became a compelling emblem through which to evoke the new novel's dangers and, ultimately, to call for its censure. If we are to "so expose our secret maladies," wrote Poitou, "why not make public the Musée Dupuytren?"[5] Let doctors describe "hideous lepers, awful cancers, and horrible wounds" in their books, wrote Louis-Gustave Vapereau: "Let a doctor model them in wax for his pathological museums, . . . but don't let him make from them either novels or paintings!"[6] The stories told about this "new" literature repeatedly relied, in this way, on its dangers, its corruptions, its depravities, and, ultimately, on how it *showed* more than one would want to see. The new novel had gone so far, critics declared from the 1830s forward, that one would have little choice but to ask the state to intervene to put an end to its dangers.

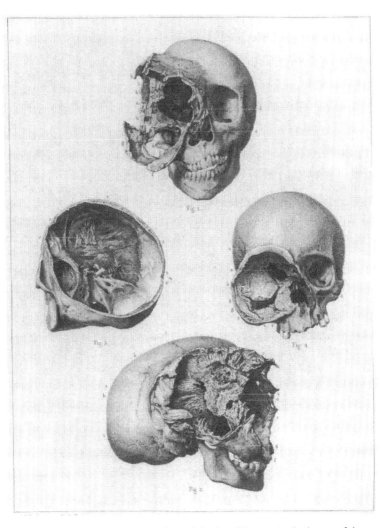

Figure 3.1. Emile Beau, *Altération des os de l'orbite* (Changes in the bones of the eye socket), lithograph from the "Atlas" of *Muséum d'Anatomie pathologique de la faculté de médecine de Paris ou Musée Dupuytren* (Paris: Béchet, 1842) (Bibliothèque Nationale, Paris). This catalog, published only seven years after the founding of the Musée Dupuytren, was to be one of several intended to itemize its collection of pathological anatomical pieces. It includes only descriptions and illustrations of bone ailments, and was the only such catalog published prior to the 1870s. Part of the museum's collection, like the bones illustrated here, consisted of actual human skeletons. Other parts, particularly those for which it became famous in the Second Empire, consisted of wax anatomical models resembling those in Figures 3.6 and 3.13.

Figure 3.2. *Façade du Musée Dupuytren,* anonymous engraving from Noé
Legrand, *Les Collections artistiques de la faculté de médecine de Paris* (Paris:
Masson, 1911), 31 (Bibliothèque Nationale, Paris).

These accounts of the novel's dangers belong to a distinct genre of contemptuous literary criticism of the July Monarchy and Second Empire, frequently published side by side in the press with the very newspaper novels it condemned. The novelists lambasted by the likes of Maron and Poitou were popular writers such as Balzac, Eugène Sue, Frédéric Soulié, George Sand, and Alexandre Dumas *fils,* whose texts took up the social world of their era, explicitly evoking the poverty and suffering of the working classes, women, and the marginalized. What unified these novelists was far less any aspect of their cumulative work than the accusations relayed by their critics. The rhetoric of seeing too much, of anatomical exposure, and of spectacles of depravity recurs in these critiques from the late 1830s through the 1860s, ever more explicitly cataloged under a rubric of "realism," and ever more insistently marginalized by critics for unveiling aspects of life one might have chosen not to see.[7]

Around the same time as Maron and others like him—Alfred Nettement, Charles-Augustin Sainte-Beuve, Armand de Pontmartin[8] —began codifying the disturbing and potentially dangerous "realism" of the novel, the state took up its arms in the battle against the novel. Beginning in 1847, with the trial of a *roman-feuilleton* in a small Fourierist weekly, a series of censorship battles ensued in the courts, complemented by a war on the newspaper novel that virtually obliterated it at the beginning of the Second Empire.[9] By 1856–57, with the censorship trials of Xavier de Montépin's *Filles de plâtre,* Sue's *Mystères du peuple,* and Flaubert's *Madame Bovary,* government intervention in the matters of the novel had become bound up in more than fantasmatic ways with the critical discourse of denigration. "Realism" had become a watchword for the state censors as well as for the conservative critics, who wanted texts like these wrenched from the grasp of endangered readers.[10]

I begin this chapter with two premises: that the "realism" imagined both by these critics and by the state censors of 1847 and 1857 can be associated with certain theories of looking, what I am here calling the "realist gaze," and that this gaze is forged out of a series of anxieties about looking. I will consider here how those anxieties fed into and gave rise to the categories we today associate with "realism" in literature and art.

"Lascivious" Views

In May 1847, nine months before the Revolution of 1848 rocked France, the Fourierist paper, *La Démocratie Pacifique,* began publishing a new *roman-feuilleton*. Fourteen chapters of Antony Méray's *La Part des femmes* had appeared when the state censors swept down, blocking the distribution of three issues of the newspaper including sequences in which a young bourgeois is set up with a woman and in which a "seduction" occurs. Despite an incomparable public outcry by newspapers as diverse as *Le Constitutionnel, La Gazette de France,* and *Le Charivari,* in September the jury found the newspaper's editors and Méray guilty as charged of "offenses against public morality and good morals." For their crimes, editor Cantagrel and Méray were each fined 100 francs and sentenced to one month in jail.

The trial of *La Part des femmes* was unprecedented in three ways. First, despite the rampant press, theater, and caricature censorship of the July Monarchy, novels were almost never subject to seizure in this period. Second, the state offered up an account of the novel that particularly emphasized the seductions that might be worked by the *paintings* of debauchery it depicted—an account of *visual* danger in a written text that, as we shall see, recurred in censorship trials of the mid-century, particularly those associated with "realism." Third, both the state and the defense arrived at a particularly odd conclusion: that certain kinds of texts were dangerous and that they could, indeed, seduce.

Like Maron, the state censor upheld an argument that some aspects of life ought to remain hidden. Like the critics of realism with whom we began, the prosecution embraced a rhetoric of visuality, a language of scenes, paintings, and pictures that pointedly fixes *viewpoints* imagined as potentially disruptive. This newspaper, argued prosecutor Bresson, had "overstepped all bounds in gathering together licentious pictures calculated to ruin the young." What the novel *showed* became the focus of the state—despite the fact that this novel bared almost nothing and showed far less than the prosecutor himself fantasized up. The representation he achieved, of what he calls "lascivious literary paintings," embedded a gaze that is not only voyeuristic, but promised far more than any blink through a keyhole. "Not only," declared the censor, "do [these

paintings] show you the young man succumbing to seduction, but
. . . they push the reader to the very foot of the bed; they make him
touch with a finger all his desires; they make palpable for him all
the charms that they describe with pleasure."[11]

Like all censorship trials, the trial of *La Part des femmes* put on
display the very sequences the newspaper's confiscation had rendered inaccessible. Reading extensively from the censored passages, the state prosecutor argued that the text should be censored
because the novel so closely resembled obscene engravings and
lithographs commonly circulating in the underground market of
the Palais-Royal. Like such images, argued the prosecutor, this text
should be banned because its *paintings* of "all the details of an
orgy" could easily risk the honor of the sons and daughters of the
bourgeoisie.[12]

Stunningly, the defense attorney entered the courtroom the following day carrying a roll of paper he declared to be a package of
obscene prints, which he had no intention of showing—"Je ne
veux pas me souiller de nouveau mes regards [I don't want to pol-
lute my vision again]"—but which, he insisted, bore no relation
whatsoever to the novel on trial. *La Part des femmes* used its potentially risqué scenes (a bit of shoulder, to be exact) to make
moral pleas for the improvement of the lot of the working classes.
Obscene imagery, he argued, had no such redeeming value.[13]
Astonishingly, both the prosecution and the defense agreed that
there was a kind of image that was dangerous, that there was a
kind of looking that could endanger, and that it could be figured in
terms of an undesirable unveiling. Like the critic Maron, with
whose 1847 speculations we began, both the prosecution and the
defense articulated positions through which one might be imagined to *see too much,* and from which one might wish to censor
such a gaze.

The imagery both the state censors and the defense summoned as
dangerous—part of a booming market of pornography whose increased availability was assured by, first, the introduction of lithographic processes in France in the early Restoration[14] and, eventually, the diffusion of photographic processes in the 1840s and
1850s[15]—was far more likely to have crossed the path of the male
jurors of 1847 than any of the anatomical models of the Musée
Dupuytren. These pictures, with such titles as *Comment l'esprit vient*

aux filles (How girls get spirit), *Plaisir sans crainte* (Pleasure without fear), and *Seule? Hélas-oui!* (Alone? Alas, yes!), had become such a subject of concern among July Monarchy moralists that they could be summoned as a point of reference for dangerous looking without ever being shown (see Figure 3.3).[16] The prosecutor of *La Part des femmes* managed in 1847 to convince the jury that the novel was guilty as charged of "outrage à la morale publique et aux bonnes moeurs [offending public morality and good morals]" without ever unfurling in the courtroom a single one of those "paintings fit to perturb the senses and excite . . . evil passions."[17]

The censored gaze put on display by the trial of *La Part des femmes* was not only that of the young bourgeois whose "improprieties" might lead to a marriage deemed inappropriate to his class and status. The state censors were equally concerned with the young *bourgeoise:* "Can an honorable and modest girl find in her hands descriptions like these?!" asked the prosecutor in a gesture that embedded the potential risks to the bourgeois girl in her simply *touching* such "paintings" of seduction.[18]

Not surprisingly, the focus of the censorious gaze of the state in 1857, Flaubert's *Madame Bovary,* was equally imagined seducing its women readers with "its brutal paintings, its coarse sensualism, its flattering pictures of libertinism, its poetry of vice and the ugly." The "great ladies and honorable *bourgeoises*" were imagined flocking to its "studies of depraved morals" in ways resembling men caught up by street prostitutes.[19] Just as in the trial of *La Part des femmes* in 1847, the text was imagined capable of seducing with its vivid "paintings." This rhetoric of visuality was accompanied, all the more powerfully, by a fantasy of gendered looking that all the more disturbingly seemed to require the censorship of critics and the state. And by 1857, all the censors seemed convinced that what threatened most belonged to a type of text they chose to call "realism."

"The offense against public morals" of Flaubert's *Madame Bovary,* according to the government prosecutor of 1857, lay precisely in the "lascivious pictures" such "realistic literature" deployed: "M. Flaubert knows how to embellish his paintings with all the resources of art, but without the circumspection of art. With him there is no gauze, no veils, it is nature in all its nudity, in all its crudity."[20] Despite its arguably "moral conclusion," Pinard com-

Figure 3.3. *Portes et fenêtres, No. 7,* lithograph (Bibliothèque Nationale, Paris). This anonymous lithograph, from the popular series *Portes et fenêtres,* is one of several dozen images that circulated in the July Monarchy that depicted voyeurs looking through keyholes, windows, and peepholes to spy on sexual activities within. Each lithograph had a moving door or window that enabled the human voyeur to peep inside as well, exposing with the flick of a wrist a much more scabrous scene.

plained, its dangers warranted the intervention of state censors precisely of the dangers of its "lascivious details" to an imagined female public:

> The frivolous pages [*les pages légères*] of Madame Bovary fall into hands still more frivolous [*des mains plus légères*], into the hands of young girls, sometimes of married women. Well, when the imagination has been seduced, when this seduction has fallen upon the heart, when the heart has spoken to the senses, do you believe that cold reason would have much power against this seduction of senses and feeling? . . . Lascivious paintings have generally more influence than cold reason. (F386, E33)

The "paintings of passion" Pinard imagines on display here are rendered "without bridle, without limits." "Art without rules," he explains, "is no longer art," but rather strangely like the character of the novel he would ban: "It is like a woman who would take off all her clothing" (F388, E36).

Fears about women's looking, here and elsewhere, have a strange way of slipping into accounts of women's exposure. In a century in which women's access to artistic training is prohibited in part because of debates over the life class, in which the nude body is turned into smut by ever-increasing concerns over women's access to the nude, and in which even the pornographic cashes in on women's gaze on display, the stories told about the female gaze repeatedly engage the woman's body in struggles over the positions from which she might be allowed to look. This is an era in which, rather than simply being "forbidden" in the terms of a recent essay by Tamar Garb, the woman's gaze is elicited, evoked, and problematized—in texts ranging from these trials to pornographic images to caricatures that explicitly poke fun at the limitations placed on women's vision.[21]

"Ladies were not under any circumstances admitted," reads the inscription next to the title page of Bertrand-Rival's revolutionary project for a wax anatomy museum in 1801. Anticipating museums like the Dupuytren, this museum used wax casts like those that would appear in the 1830s in medical schools. There, the medical sculptor sought to create a space where citizens might take their sons to learn of the human body, envisaged in its "normal state" as a nude male and a pregnant female, and where "moral instruction" might be achieved through the witnessing of bodies ravaged

Figure 3.4. Anonymous engraving depicting woman looking through "telescope" (Bibliothèque Nationale, Paris, Réserve du Cabinet des Estampes).

by disease—particularly by the malady of masturbation. Women were excluded from both museum and catalog with the same prurience that several decades later would mobilize the anxieties expressed about the Musée Dupuytren.[22] Poitou's 1858 question, "Why not make public the Musée Dupuytren?" thus comported not

Figure 3.5. Bourdet, *Béotismes parisiens,* lithograph from *Le Charivari,*
September 2, 1836. Reprinted with permission of Department of Printing and
Graphic Arts, The Houghton Library, Harvard University.

only a fear of the exposure of scientific knowledge—the hitherto
invisible made violently visible—but the exposure of women and
girls.

The politics of such exposures are reflected in contemporary
pornography in ways that suggest the dangers to girls who take
looking into their own hands (Figure 3.4) or in caricature in terms
suggestive of the erotics of vision, as in Bourdet's image (Figure
3.5) of a mother shown attributing a particularly disturbing female
malady to her daughter's visual intercourse: "Sir," pleads the
mother, "my daughter has a tumor [*grosseur*], we don't know what
it is and it worries us a great deal. Mightn't it be conjunctivitis [*une
opthalmie*]?" Women's entry into public spaces of the gaze seems,
repeatedly in such popular imagery, censorship trials, popular literary criticism, and, ultimately, even in the novel itself, to elicit fears
that some kinds of looking might expose simply too much. "The
overflowings of the powers of nature can be for the imagination a
spectacle," writes Vapereau of *Madame Bovary.* "Let us not forget

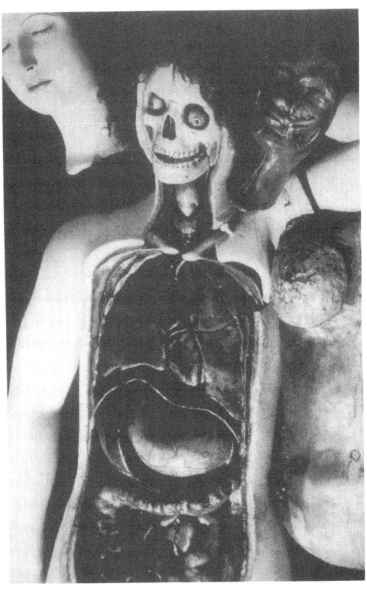

Figure 3.6. *La Vénus anatomique,* wax anatomical sculpture with forty movable pieces, including fetus, a centerpiece of Spitzner's "Grand Musée Anatomique et Ethnologique" (founded 1856). Illustration from *Cires anatomiques du XIXe siècle: collection du Dr. Spitzner* (exhibition catalog) (Paris: Centre Culturel de la Communauté française de Belgique, 1980), 14.

Figure 3.7. *Le Marchand de kaleidoscopes,* from engraving from Mme Alfred Heyman, *Les Lunettes et les lorgnettes de jadis* (Paris: Leroy, 1911), 37 (Bibliothèque Nationale, Paris). The caption reads: "Oui, j'en ai de toutes les formes, de grands, de petits, et d'énormes. Mesdames, entre nous, Comment les voulez-vous? [Yes, I have all shapes: large, small, and enormous. My ladies, between us, how do you want them?]."

that they are also for us plagues."[23] The association of spectacles with the ravages of disease relays with a kind of brutality the maladies imagined to evolve from a seduced gaze. This caricatured girl, pregnant with looking too much, is fixed in wax museums of her own era as naturally with child (Figure 3.6).[24]

And yet, in the first decades of the nineteenth century, women have a curious way of turning up whenever there is a question of looking in some new way. Depictions of new visual technology exploited female fascinations with the powers of looking. The kaleidoscope, invented in 1818, was quickly depicted—not without the innuendo regularly attached to all contraptions of vision—as drawing women in particular into intrigues (Figure 3.7). Pornographic imagery regularly positioned women in front of magic boxes and behind telescopes. Popular caricature reveled in the depiction of women's access to new optical instruments, as in the Daumier of 1845 (shown in Figure 3.8). "Mesdemoiselles, I forbid you to look at the moon," scolds the mother in the Bourdet of 1836 shown in Figure 3.9. "It seems that one sees men there . . . and horrors of men even!" Though the lorgnon began as the ornament of "tout homme bien né [every wellborn man]" (Figure 3.10), it was quickly "exiled" to the noses of "women of letters"[25] and taken up in a magic form as the subject of a novel by just such a woman, Delphine de Girardin.[26] Likewise, the lorgnette (Figure 3.11), depicted by a 1768 dictionary as a special mark of importance and honor for "les élégants," had become by the July Monarchy such a mark of bourgeois women's style that it was listed by the *Journal des Dames et des Modes* as one of the four objects that "a fashionable woman must have at the theatre."[27] During the July Monarchy, women's most favored fashion accessory, the fan, was adapted to current fads by the insertion of a small lorgnette in its center (Figure 3.12). Such eyeglasses gave a new twist to the stories told about curiosity, for they were particularly useful for women, whom they allowed to see close up from afar, all the while enabling them to maintain distances dictated by propriety. Yet the root of the word from which both lorgnette and lorgnon derive suggests a kind of looking repeatedly evoked by critics of realism as the source of textual danger: *lorgner*—to gaze with desire and covetousness, to cast a sidelong glance, to ogle, to leer, or, provocatively, to make eyes.

That Emma Bovary is shown early in Flaubert's novel wearing a special looking glass replicates a fascination with the objects that alter vision running from July Monarchy caricature through the Third Republic. What seems peculiar to the two or three decades mid-century during which fears of "realism" emerge is the emphasis on women's looking and the eroticism fantasmatically attached to that vision. "What was really beautiful about her was her eyes," writes Flaubert's narrator of Emma at the moment early in the novel when Charles first watches her pricking her fingers as she sews: "Her gaze came at you frankly, with a candid boldness" (F49). Significantly, however, Emma does not *look* through the special looking glass with which she might aggrandize her vision, but wears her "lorgnon d'écaille" (tortoiseshell eyeglass) dangled around her neck "like a man, thrust between two buttons of her blouse" (F50). Though her wearing of the eyeglass is depicted as

Figure 3.8. Daumier, *Subscribers Receiving Their Newspaper and Seeking the Way to Use It,* lithograph from the *Actualités* series, *Le Charivari,* January 31, 1845, 3. Reprinted with permission of Department of Printing and Graphic Arts, The Houghton Library, Harvard University.

Figure 3.9. Bourdet, *Béotismes parisiens,* lithograph from *Le Charivari,* April 6, 1836. Reprinted with permission of Department of Printing and Graphic Arts, The Houghton Library, Harvard University.

Figure 3.10. Horace Vernet, *Incroyable with lorgnon,* engraving from Roger-Armand Weigert, ed., *Incroyables et merveilleuses* (Paris: Rombaldi, 1956) (Bibliothèque Nationale, Paris).

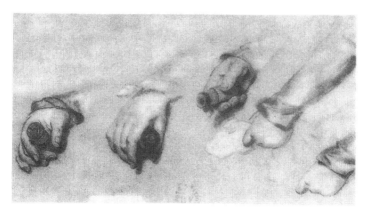

Figure 3.11. Boilly, *Etudes de mains tenant la lorgnette,* drawing from Mme Alfred Heyman, *Les Lunettes et les lorgnettes de jadis* (Paris: Leroy, 1911) (Bibliothèque Nationale, Paris).

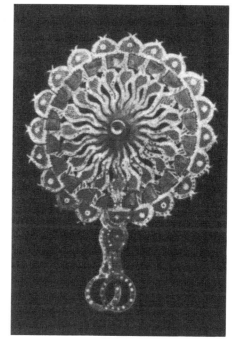

Figure 3.12. Fan with lorgnette in center, photograph from Mme Alfred Heyman, *Les Lunettes et les lorgnettes de jadis* (Paris: Leroy, 1911), facing p. 34 (Bibliothèque Nationale, Paris).

giving her a kind of male allure, it nevertheless seems to attract, from its provocative position at her bodice, quite another version of the male gaze.[28]

Yet it is precisely Emma's viewpoint that disturbs the critics and censors in 1857. "How the eyes of this woman enlarge!" exclaims the prosecutor Pinard, in his excoriation of the moments of the novel he believes glorify adultery and threaten to seduce the young women of France into thinking such pleasures desirable. She is, because of her eyes somehow, never more "dazzling as in the days after her fall," never more "ravishing" than after she has bared herself to adultery and illusions. What we see through Pinard's citations and commentary during the trial is a gaze upon this woman "without a veil" (F378, E19). Exposed to a gaze that is somehow not at all that of the women of France he believes endangered, Emma is imagined by the prosecutor in her physiognomic nakedness: "The poses are voluptuous, the beauty of Madame Bovary is a beauty of provocation" (F375, E14).

Emma's gaze at herself in the mirror, after her first encounter with Rodolphe, convinces Pinard that the "lascivious pictures" of this novel cannot be redeemed by some moral message in its ending. "From this first fault, from this first fall," fulminates the prosecutor, "she glorified adultery, she sang its song, its poetry, and its sensual pleasures. This, gentlemen, to me is much more dangerous and immoral than the fall itself!" (F377, E17). What Pinard says he wants here, "a sentiment of remorse that she feels, in the presence of this deceived husband who adores her," is replaced by Emma's own delighted vision of herself in her looking glass: "Never had she had eyes so large, so black, of so profound a depth," writes Flaubert of what she *saw* in the mirror (F191; trial citation, F377, E17). This greedy vision, these all-encompassing eyes, that covetous gaze of the adulteress, is precisely what the critics, the censors, and the Flaubertian narrator alike imagine as characterizing its protagonist. She is a woman imagined by the novel and censors alike as having both an expansive point of view and an indomitable moral vision of her own. The prosecutor claims, he confesses, to have "sought in this book a person who could rule this woman" and found "none there": "Only one person is right, rules, dominates, and that is Emma Bovary" (F387, E35).

That Emma Bovary's vision might "dominate" this text proves more than daunting to the novel's critics as well. Gustave Merlet treats the novel as a "realist" "exhibition of paintings," which might give the reader pleasure to "lorgner de près cette jeune fille [give a long hard look at this girl]" but ultimately might overwhelm.[29] Like those critics who summoned wax museums as reference points for the realism they believed endangered readers, Merlet compares Flaubert's novel to the closed rooms of the Museo Borbonico in Naples, otherwise known as the "secret museum," where sexually explicit material from Pompeii was hidden from the public until the 1860s. *Madame Bovary* is like, Merlet writes, a "cabinet reserved for a certain number of paintings that the crowd seems to seek out, but which we will not speak of, because, according to us, it would have been wise not to show them to the public. It would have rather been necessary to close them under lock and key."[30] Like the Musée Dupuytren, Merlet's imaginary censored "cabinet" serves as a touchstone for the contents of the "realist" novel. What Merlet will call its surgical dissections and cold-blooded anatomical work are likened to brutal paintings we would choose rather not to show publicly.[31] Abandoned to the "spectacle" Merlet believes ruled neither by heart nor by conscience, we are made to share the narrator's impassive "gaze"—an eye that is again compared explicitly to that of Emma Bovary. To the realism that "kills eloquence and poetry" and "pretends to please us with tastes for depraved things," Merlet gives the name of the one with whose vision he believes Flaubert too much colluded—"*le bovarisme*."[32]

Could we say, then, that "realism" names a way women look? Or a way women are imagined to look? Or is it, rather, a way men might look when they look *like* women (who ought not to be looking to begin with)? Or perhaps even the way men look who want to look like fallen women? No matter how we retell this story of imagined spectacles, we find that "realism" in these trials and in this criticism refers repeatedly back to a series of terrors about certain kinds of looking and certain kinds of viewers.

What these two trials and criticism ultimately put on display is a fantasmatic gaze—that of the potential readers who might be imagined *seduced* by these works or one like them. Like "paintings fit to perturb the senses and excite evil passions" or "lascivious details"

of imagined barings of bodies, these novels are imagined and spec-
ularized, given a kind of visual materiality through fantasized results. Even if contemporaries do not know what kind of paintings
might so perturb the senses, they have learned, by listening to
these diatribes, to imagine such visual exchanges. The "realism"
unveiled by the state turns out to be unfurled as a kind of fantasmatic dirty picture in the mind's eye of the readers of trial reports
and press criticism. And yet with those fantasies of wax monstrosities, anatomical dissections, and lurid imagery, each of these theo-
rizers of the realist gaze has fixed a woman's eye as a pinnacle of
disruptive vision. We should not, therefore, be surprised to discover that for the champions of realism as well as its critics, women
were privileged visionaries.

Women's Questions

Realism began with a woman's question, according to Champfleury
in his 1857 treatise, a forceful attempt to reclaim the language that
had for more than a decade surrounded certain kinds of literature
and art with deprecation: "A few years ago, a distinguished woman
asked me the following question: *Find* the causes and the means
which give the appearances of reality to works of art."[33] Without
giving too much significance to the gender or the class of the
woman who asked the critic and novelist to give meaning to mimesis, we might nevertheless wonder at her reappearance only a few
paragraphs later in the preface—this time, as the patient of one of
those doctors famed for their understandings of pathology— and,
perhaps even more remarkably, *pregnant*.

The "isms" to which "realism" belongs, explains Champfleury, do
nothing more than complicate the answers to questions like the one
posed by that "femme distinguée." If one wants such complications,
he suggests ironically, "I don't know why one would not admit to
the Academy . . . Professor Piorry, who calls pregnancies a hyper-
endometrotropia. A woman is no longer pregnant, she is 'hyperen-
dometrophic.' " If the word *réalisme* has been, as Champfleury argues, "invented by critics as a war-machine to incite hatred toward
a new generation,"[34] it nevertheless has a curious way of deriving

from the bodies of women. *Realism* thus has its beginnings—in this originary tract itself—as a synonym for *pregnant*.

Such analogies between pregnancy and looking, and reproduction and realism, suggest we might want to refocus one of the traditional ways of recounting the story of nineteenth-century realism. Although sexuality and the hierarchies it engenders have long been a central component in debates over realism, given prominence by such astute readers as Roland Barthes, Leo Bersani, Dorothy Kelly, and Naomi Schor, much of the important work in this domain has treated sexuality and sexual difference as a given, uninflected by historical transformations in production and reproduction. Thomas W. Laqueur has recently insisted on the the historically changing ways the body—and, with it, sexuality—serves as representational. We might argue, following the impressive recurrence of a pregnant realist gaze, that between the French Revolution of 1789 and the early Second Empire, anxieties about the gaze lodged in bodies specifically represented in relation to a particular inflection of sexual difference. Realism was a woman's question because the bodies of women were being exposed in radically new ways.[35]

The very anatomy museums that served Champfleury's enemies as a reference point for the impending dangers of realism had themselves depended upon fascinations with the physiology of the female body. One of the first individuals to practice wax modeling, Marie Catherine Bihéron (1719–96), earned her living from private showings of her "cabinet," whose "principal pieces" related to childbirth, though she did not, according to recent historians, "represent the 'delicate parts' of the female on her models."[36] The "masterpiece" of José de Flores, Guatemalan creator of "dissectible wax models," was a woman whose "accurately replaceable parts" would have shown various stages of pregnancy, various difficulties of delivery, and numerous pathological conditions of the reproductive organs.[37] Bertrand-Rival's pathology museum of the era just after the 1789 revolution depicted its "typical" female figure as pregnant, marked as normal by the very attributes of sexual difference.[38] The collection of Florentine Felice Fontana (1730–1805), known throughout Europe in the late eighteenth century for his anatomy cabinet and diffusion of techniques of wax modeling, equally centered on the wax model of a woman.[39] Though not intended for demonstrations of diseased bodies (such goals would have to await the Musée Dupuytren), Fontana's Specola museum had a peculiar way of pathologizing femininity—both in its wax figures and in its observers, as Elisabeth Vigée-Lebrun's memoirs attest:

> He had me see his cabinet which was full of anatomy pieces made in wax the color of flesh. What I saw first with admiration were the almost unseeable ligaments that surround our eye, and a bunch of other details especially useful to our preservation or our intelligence. . . . Until then I had seen nothing that would have made me feel anything painful, but, just as I saw a woman of natural size lying down [Figure 3.13], Fontana told me to approach her, then, raising a kind of cover, he offered to my gaze all the intestines, wound up like ours are. This view gave me such an impression that I felt close to turning away, to such an extent that I couldn't see a person without mentally removing the clothes or the skin, which put me in a deplorable nervous state. When I saw Mr. Fontana again, I asked his advice on how to deliver myself from the enormous susceptibility of my organs. I understand too much, I told him, I see too much, and I feel everything from the same source.[40]

Vigée-Lebrun's complaint to the wax modeler, which she qualifies as being about "cette vue excellente [that excellent sight]," suggests that the woman's gaze on realistic models of physiology is destabilized precisely at the instant that she sees her own internal anatomy. Observing the structures of the eye, Vigée-Lebrun is "persuaded of the existence of a divinity."[41] Observing what is hidden beneath the cover of a skin like her own, a woman asks what to do about organs that may or may not be the same ones, with the same fabled "susceptibility" to nervous disorders, she has seen exposed.[42] Realism again resonates as a woman's question.

Exposing the Realist Gaze

What are we to make of this curious conflation of women's exposure to dangerous visual stimulae and the exhibition of women's sexual difference? Even given private showings, these cabinets of disease and teratology attract the curious and elicit titillating commentary. Looking at women looking becomes a kind of show in itself, a visual or narrative intrigue that suspends the censor's condemnations just long enough to catch a glimpse of what women

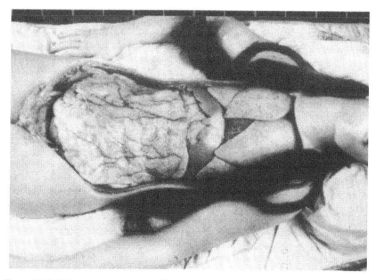

Figure 3.13. *Venus de Medici*, copied by Felice Fontana for his Speculo museum after a work by Bernini. This is most likely the wax model that Vigée-Lebrun saw. From Sander Gilman, *Sexuality: An Illustrated History* (New York: John Wiley, 1991), 184. Reprinted by permission of John Wiley & Sons, Inc.

expose in their regards. The criticism of realism cashes in on these intrigues in ways that suggest the discourse of the censor might serve as a further narrative of exposure.

If Flaubert's critics made him, like Balzac before him, into a demon with a scalpel,[43] they had not entirely misjudged the author's vision. Flaubert wrote to Louise Colet in 1852, as he composed *Madame Bovary*, of his interest in casting a "coup d'oeil médical [a medical glance]" at life.[44] Overdetermining the influence of biography on an artist's work, critic Sainte-Beuve had positioned Flaubert's interests in anatomy and physiology in the context of his relationship to that "distinguished doctor,"[45] Flaubert's father, who held a chair in anatomy at the Rouen Medical School, and who was himself trained by the founders of Rouen's first pathological anatomy museum. Yet Flaubert's own language suggests he was as consciously obsessed with his father's anatomical trade as critics would have liked to imagine: "I am only happy with . . . the subjects of analysis, of anatomy," he wrote in 1852.[46] In the later *Dictionnaire des idées reçues*, Flaubert joked about novels written "with the point of a scalpel. Ex.: *Madame Bovary*," making of

Figure 3.14. Poster from the popular Talrich "Dupuytren Museum" fair show of the early Third Republic (c. 1880). This show drew on the myths about the Paris Dupuytren museum but did not actually exhibit its collection (Musée de la Publicité, Paris).

Sainte-Beuve's criticism the source of Bouvard et Pécuchet's anatomy lessons in irony.[47] The "amphitheatre of dissection" that the Flaubertian novel was once criticized for resembling[48] itself became the topos in which that novel revels. But if visitors to such dissections may have been imagined as increasingly female, both metaphorically, as novel readers, and literally, as those who might be allowed to look on during medical practices, popular representations were far more likely to show those women lying exposed on dissection tables than gazing on.[49]

By the Third Republic, the very woman who was prohibited from entering private wax collections, who was warned away from the medical school museums and dissections, and who has been shown blanching before nudes in the Louvre,[50] will be invited into knock-offs of the Musée Dupuytren, assured that the wax figures there are "viewable for adults of both sexes"—presumably because all figures are covered by loinclothes (Figure 3.14).[51] Yet she will meet there the languorous nudity of the Olympialike "jeune fille tetramaze" extended on her divan, in the supposed interest of a science seeking to fight the "ignorance that leads to debauchery." Exposed to the "realistic" visions of the wax museum, the Third Republic woman can supposedly learn to control the urges that corrupted the body and the gaze of Emma Bovary. Though she is allowed to look, her gaze remains censored.[52] Though she is invited to peek into the mysteries of the body, it is her own body—and her very gaze on that body—that is put on display.

The gaze I have here called the "realist gaze" is an account of theories that accompanied looking over approximately three decades between the mid-1830s and the mid-1860s in France. Not just an account of observation and detail, as critics of the twentieth century have too frequently held, the realist gaze of which Balzac, Flaubert, and their contemporaries were constantly accused had a political content. Critics' aversions to physiology, dissection, and hysterical conversion masked a rage at the secularization of the medical profession. Accounts of readers led astray by the seductions of palpable textuality relayed fears about the newly literate readers of the July Monarchy and Second Empire—girls, women, and especially workers—moving out of the social roles critics believed appropriate. Such transgressions, whether of looking at the hitherto invisible, as in seeing the contents of wax museums, or of imagining the other desires, as evoked by lithographic erotica, could not be ignored by conservatives, moralists, or the state. The gaze summoned by these inventors of a discourse of realism was a politically expedient one—speculating on the ways that activities in the private sphere might spill into the public one, and focusing on imagined disruptions resulting from such improprieties. My goal is to return the political content to the theories of realism we have inherited from these censors. The fantasy of seeing too much has continued, in our own era, to be strangely coupled with fantasies about who might look. As in nineteenth-century discussions of the unseeable Musée Dupuytren and unseen pornography, the fantasy of a dangerous gaze has quite recently turned on a portfolio of images all but invisible in the press coverage of their exhibition and its NEA funding.[53] Only by seeing how the category of realism is invested in a rhetoric of denigration, I want to argue, can we begin to unravel the assumptions that continue to underlie censorious gazes.

Two recent shows, one in a suburb of Paris, the other in New York, suggest the stakes for reinterrogating what I have been calling the realist gaze. At the Cartier Foundation show at Jouy-en-Josas, *A Visage découverte* (June–October 1992), a striking installation was put in place to create a continuity between the eighteenth- and nineteenth-century wax museums and the expressive heads, masks, and sculptures of other cultures and eras. Using mirrors to multiply illusions and glass cubes to give a consistency to the framing of the objects on display, a darkened room re-created the atmosphere, as the catalog explained, of a pathological anatomy museum, complete, in this case, with the *Reclining Venus* and several other wax models from the Spitzner collection. Pulled out of their historical context and juxtaposed with skulls and African masks, the wax pathology sculptures of this nineteenth-century collection seemed garish, even exploitative. Almost exclusively female, the wax modeled bodies on display there told a familiar story of women's exposure to a gaze underwritten by medical interests. The absence of any commentary on how a collection such as Spitzner's was exhibited, circulated, and popularized in its own historical moment gave a kind of surreal quality to the Cartier Foundation's use of these wax models. How was one to read bodies on display so radically divorced from the identities and fantasies that had once invested them? Despite the installation's visual wizardry, viewers were inevitably positioned as prurient spectators to exposed body parts. What Poitou and Vapereau had most feared—the making public of wax pathology museums—had come to pass. But the gaze the show evoked cast no new light on what it may mean to remove such objects from censorship. In fact, the exhibit had a peculiar way of drawing on the thrill of that very exposure. Invited to look at what was staged as somehow illicit— evanescent body parts hidden behind mirrors and locked behind glass—the viewer had nothing to do but gawk.[54]

By contrast, Cindy Sherman's recent exhibition of photographs at Metro Pictures Gallery in New York (May 1992) took that censoring gaze and dislocated it. Like the Cartier Foundation show, Sherman appropriated a set of medical models, likewise wrenched from their ostensible functions. Purchased from medical supply companies, Sherman's anatomical models were marketed for uses in medical school training rooms.[55] By the time they emerged in photographs (Figure 3.15), they had become metaphors for quite another account of the destinies of anatomy. If realism in the nineteenth century named the way women looked, this show gave new meaning to those exposures.

Significantly, critics embraced both the language of realism and insisted on the dangers of looking these images evoked. "Beware," one review began, concluding nevertheless that Sherman made her "obviously fake" models "come to life" through her "skilled understanding of film as a medium and the 'art' of makeup."[56] "This time she's gone extreme," wrote Amei Wallach in the *Los Angeles Times,* comparing Sherman's work to "X-rated photos that even she might shrink from."[57] Like most reviewers, Wallach and others emphasized the potential shock value of Sherman's manipulation of dissected sexualized body parts and praised her for using them to confront the nightmares of censorship that have surrounded the sexually explicit imagery of other less well known artists.[58] Like their nineteenth-century forebears, however, Sherman's reviewers shared a fascination with the possible censorship written into images they repeatedly evoked in terms of *realism.* "We wander through this imagery wondering what is real and what is fabricated," wrote Elizabeth Hess.[59] Sherman's show "relentlessly demonstrates that pictures of the human anatomy bear no intrinsic rela-

Figure 3.15. Cindy Sherman, *Untitled (#264)*, 1992, color photograph from Metro Pictures show, May 1992 (Metro Pictures Gallery, New York). Sherman's allusion here to Manet's *Olympia* interrogates the censors implicated in the realist gaze of the nineteenth century even as it explicitly confronts the censorship of the 1990s. Copyright Cindy Sherman. Courtesy of Metro Pictures.

tionship to the real thing," wrote David Pagel.[60] Like those who assaulted the dissecting realism of Flaubert's era, these critics expressed a combination of concern with the aesthetic shift at stake in Sherman's work and fascination with the very fakeness they insistently read into these medical dummies.[61]

Sherman's own description of her work emphasized the same shock at the "realistic" body parts nevertheless "sculpted from clay."[62] At the same time, however, she explicitly positioned her work in the context of censorship debates raging since the late 1980s: "I thought that since less successful artists can't depend on getting funded anymore to do their work if they have sexual themes in it, the more successful artists should be the ones to make the more difficult work."[63] But even if, in her words, "nobody can cut [her] funding," reviews on both coasts summoned a censoring gaze always ready to cut short vision. Although this work explicitly staged confrontations between the historical uses of anatomical models in wax museums like that of the Dupuytren and the gazes that penetrated such spaces, it also put on display a series of fantasies about those gazes. For the critics who came to describe the contents of this show, these were always pictures one might want to avoid. If Sherman and her admiring reviewers managed to interrogate the censoring gaze of realism, they also found themselves caught up in its ricocheting devices. The gazes on display in this show were surely as much those of the censors as those of the pornographers who would find titillation in these disembodied anatomical models. But the precariousness with which one might display and interrogate such gazes reminds us how deeply embedded are the fears to which nineteenth-century realism gave a name.

In this essay, I have attempted to give a historical account of the ways looking came to be theorized in the nineteenth century as a way of making sense of the transformations of those theories in our own era. I have begun with the presumption that the "realistic vision" born out of the July Monarchy and early Second Empire was explicitly related to radical transformations in possibilities for looking. The optical instruments and wax anatomical models considered here in relation to that "realist gaze" were only two of the new ways the early nineteenth century gained access to what had hitherto been invisible. It should not be surprising that in an era in which something resembling a change of government came around every twenty years, in which something resembling a revolution transpired every quarter of a century, in which the territory of the French nation multiplied manifold with the colonialist expansion, and in which the time it took to cross France was divided many times over again by the creation of the railway system, that the ways people saw the world underwent radical disruptions. Our only access to those ways of seeing comes through the representations of the world willed us by those whose visual spheres were turned upside down. Through such representations, we can begin to tell how the nineteenth-century spectator imagined his or her own gaze working in the world, and how those representations of the gaze operated in the spheres of the everyday.

The rhetoric of realist vision we have examined here is one such representation of the gaze that gives us a privileged access to investments in looking in the mid-nineteenth century. The realist gaze summoned by critics, censors, and visual and literary texts themselves tells a story about fantasies about looking and the anxieties to which they gave rise. That such a gaze was always already accompanied by the censor, as I have tried to suggest here, tells us much about the powers attributed to looking in the mid-nineteenth century and about the growing appropriation of such powers by groups hitherto imagined invisible and without sights.

NOTES

I thank Margaret Cohen, Frédéric Cousinié, Georges Didi-Huberman, and Linda Nochlin for their generous feedback on drafts of this essay. I am also grateful to my research assistants, Paul Franklin, Elizabeth Galaznik, Sharon Haimov, and Marina Harss, for their help in sleuthing sources and images. Hannah Feldman and Vanessa Schwartz brought invaluable research suggestions. Thanks also to P. Petzel of Metro Pictures Gallery in New York City for help with Cindy Sherman materials. Research support for this project was provided by a J. Paul Getty Postdoctoral Fellowship in the History of Art and the Humanities and by a grant from the Milton Fund of Harvard University.

1. Eugène Maron, "Critique littéraire: Année 1846," *La Revue indépendante* 7 (January 25, 1847): 242. Unless otherwise noted, all translations are my own.

2. Eugène Poitou, *Du Roman et du théâtre contemporain*, 2d ed. (Paris: Durand, 1858), 16–18. I discuss these accusations in chapter 5 of my *Scenes of Seduction: Prostitution, Hysteria, and Reading Difference in Nineteenth-Century France* (New York: Columbia University Press, 1993).

3. Charles de Forster, *Quinze ans à Paris (1832–1848): Paris et les parisiens* (Paris: Didot, 1848–49), 1:124. On Dupuytren's career, see Russell Maulitz, *Morbid Appearances: The Anatomy of Pathology in the Early Nineteenth Century* (Cambridge: Cambridge University Press, 1987), 73–82.

4. Forster, *Quinze ans à Paris,* 1:124. Of some twenty-five travelogues from 1830– 70 in the Bibliothèque Nationale's Le Senne Collection on Paris history, only two—Forster and John Sanderson (*The American in Paris* [Philadelphia: Carey & Hart, 1839], 196) discuss the Musée Dupuytren, an indication of its inaccessibility. Though Poitou seems to have believed the pathological anatomy museum entirely closed to the public, some Paris guidebooks from the 1840s and 1850s suggest it may have been possible to get in—either by bribing the guard or during a few hours per week set aside for public visits. Tourist guidebooks are also confused about the accessibility of the other medical school museum, the Musée Orfila of Comparative Anatomy, established in 1844, which featured figures without pathological characteristics. By the 1860s, all guidebooks declare both museums completely inaccessible to the public. F. C. Stewart (*Hospitals and Surgeons of Paris* [New York: Langley, 1843]) informs visitors that "the public are admitted, gratuitously, on Thursdays, from eleven to three o'clock, and students, with tickets, daily during the same hours. Strangers may gain admission at any time by giving a trifle to the porter" (154). *Galignani's New Paris Guide for 1855* (Paris: Galignani, 1855) describes the pathology collection as open to the public on Thursdays, "to strangers daily on application, and to students on a professor's orders" (149–50), but even this guide adds caveats: "Admittance is obtained by a small fee to the porter. The unprofessional visitor must expect to see many disgusting objects" (429). Amédée de

Césena (*Le Nouveau Paris: Guide de l'étranger. Pratique, Historique, descriptif, et pittoresque* [Paris: Garnier, 1864], 108) and R. de Corval (*Paris monumental, artistique et historique* [Paris: Maillet, 1867], 110) suggest the Dupuytren museum was open only to students or doctors. Adolphe Joanne (*Paris illustré. Nouveau guide de l'étranger et du parisien* [Paris: Hachette, 1867], 731) claims neither museum was open to the public, though students and doctors could gain access to the Musée Dupuytren. On the Musée Dupuytren, see *Catalogue des pièces d'anatomie pathologique composant le musée Dupuytren* (Paris: Béchet, 1842); *Muséum d'Anatomie pathologique de la faculté de médecine de Paris ou Musée Dupuytren* (Paris: Béchet, 1842), 2 vols. plus atlas; Charles Houel, *Catalogue des pièces du Musée Dupuytren* (Paris: Dupont, 1877), 5 vols. plus 4-vol. atlas; Charles Houel, *Manuel d'anatomie pathologique génétarale et appliquée contenant la description et le catalogue du musée Dupuytren* (Paris: Baillière, 1857); René Abalanet, "Les musées d'anatomie pathologique de Paris. Le Musée Dupuytren," in *La Médecine à Paris du XIIIe au XIXe siècle,* ed. André Pecker (Paris: Hervais, 1984), 235–63; Michel Sakka, "Le Musée Dupuytren," *Histoire et archéologie* 97 (September 1985): 53–59; Nelly Dias, "Le corps en vitrine: Elements pour une recherche sur les collections médicales," *Terrains* 18 (1992): 72–79; and Michel Lemire, *Artistes et mortels* (Paris: Chabaud, 1990), 332–36. Access to the Musée Dupuytren continues to be most restricted. After persistent efforts over several months in 1992, I was told by the secretary of the current curator, René Abalanet, that the museum was not open —even to researchers writing on its collection. Like the critics I discuss here, I have thus been obliged to discuss the museum without any personal experience of its collections.

5. Poitou, *Du Roman,* 17–18.

6. Louis-Gustave Vapereau, *L'Année littéraire et dramatique* (Paris: Hachette, 1859), 55.

7. I discuss these critics and their accusations in *Scenes of Seduction,* particularly chapters 5, 6, 7, and 8. Bernard Weinberg's *French Realism: The Critical Reaction, 1830–1870* (New York: Modern Language Association, 1937) remains an excellent overview of critical attacks on the so-called realist novel.

8. Alfred Nettement, *Histoire de la littérature française sous le gouvernement de juillet* (Paris: Lecoffre, 1854), 242–54; Charles-Augustine Sainte-Beuve, "Madame Bovary par M. Gustave Flaubert," in *Causeries du lundi* (Paris: Garnier, 1851–62), 13:346–62; Armand de Pontmartin, "Les Fétiches littéraires, 1. M. de Balzac," in *Causeries du samedi,* 2d ser. (Paris: Michel Lévy, 1857), 32–103; Armand de Pontmartin, "MM. Edmond About et Gustave Flaubert," in *Nouvelles causeries du samedi* (Paris: Michel Lévy, 1859), 299–326. For further attacks on realism, see Weinberg's extensive bibliography in *French Realism* 202–54.

9. Although Auguste Luchet's *Nom de famille* (Paris: Souverain, 1842) was banned by the state in 1842, accusations against it revolved primarily around its subject matter—adultery—and its attitude toward the government. Its censorship, however, already prefigured battles over "realism." See my "The Limits of Reformism: The Novel, Censorship, and the Politics of Adultery in Nineteenth-Century France," in *The Cultural Institutions of the Novel,* ed. Deirdre Lynch and William B. Warner (Durham, N.C.: Duke University Press, forthcoming). For an overview of nineteenth-century French censorship, see Alexandre Zévaès, *Les Procès littéraires au XIXe siècle* (Paris: Perrin, 1924); and Yvan Leclerc, *Crimes écrits* (Paris: Plon, 1991).

10. Baudelaire's *Fleurs du mal* was also condemned in 1857 for its "vulgar realism, offensive to modesty." See G. Robert, "Le Réalisme devant la critique littéraire de 1851 à 1861," *Revue des sciences humaines* (1853): 14.

11. "Cour d'assises de la Seine, Présidence de M. Jurien. —Audience du 29 août, Affaire de *la Démocratie pacifique*," *La Démocratie Pacifique* (August 30, 1847). I discuss this case in chapter 7 of *Scenes of Seduction*.

12. Ibid.

13. "Cour d'assises de la Seine," *Démocratie Pacifique*, September 1, 1847.

14. Invented in Munich in the 1790s by Senefelder, lithography was introduced around 1814 in France by his student Lasteyrie and was widely used from the 1820s. See Beatrice Farwell, *The Cult of Images: Baudelaire and the 19th-Century Media Explosion* (Santa Barbara, Calif.: University Art Galleries, 1977).

15. See André Rouille, *Le Corps et son image* (Paris: Contrejour, 1986). An arrest register in the Archives de la Préfecture de Police of Paris, Bb-3, reproduces images of many of those involved in Second Empire underground pornographic photography and lists works confiscated—suggesting the enormity of this trade as well as the easy slippage for those involved between lithographic and photographic pornography.

16. Fernand Drujon, in *Catalogue des ouvrages, écrits, et dessins de toute nature poursuivis, supprimés ou condamnés depuis le 21 octobre 1814 jusqu'au 31 juillet 1877* (Paris: Rouveyre, 1879), lists dozens such prints banned by the state between 1814 and 1877.

17. These are the words of the prosecutor Bresson during the trial. "Cour d'assises de la Seine," *Démocratie Pacifique*, August 30, 1847.

18. Ibid.

19. Poitou, *Du Roman*, 17, 15.

20. "Réquisitoire, Plaidoirie et Jugement," in Gustave Flaubert, *Madame Bovary* (Paris: Garnier-Flammarion, 1966 [1856–57]), 373, 382. Translations are modified from the trial report in *Madame Bovary: A Tale of Provincial Life*, in Gustave Flaubert, *Works*, vol. 2 (Akron, Ohio: St. Dunstan Society, n.d.), 10, 26. All references to these editions of the trial reports will appear in the text by page number, noted as F (French) and E (English).

21. See Tamar Garb, "The Forbidden Gaze," *Art in America* 79, no. 5 (1991): 147–56. I discuss these issues in a book in progress, *Desires to Censor: Spectacles of the Body, Moral Vision, and Aesthetics in Nineteenth-Century France*. As I have suggested in the chapter titled "Exhibiting and Exposing: Historicizing the Gaze," presented as a paper at the annual meeting of the College Art Association in Chicago (February 1992), July Monarchy pornography frequently depicted women in art classes, museums, and looking through optical instruments.

22. Jean-François Bertrand-Rival, *Précis historique physiologique et moral, des principaux objets en cire préparée et coloriée d'après nature qui composent le muséum de Jean-François Bertrand-Rival* (Paris: Richard, 1801) opens: "I begin by saying that this book is not for the vulgar, or for children, or even for women; but only for careful, wise, and enlightened people."

23. Vapereau, *L'Année littéraire*, 54.

24. Another of the centerpieces of the popular pathological anatomy Spitzner collection (founded 1856) depicts a woman's pelvic region, with changing images of a pregnancy from conception through the ninth month. See *Cires anatomiques du*

XIXe siècle, Collection du Dr. Spitzner (Paris: Centre Culturel de la Communauté française de Belgique, 1980), 22.

25. "Le Lorgnon," *Aujourd'hui, Journal des Ridicules* (August 15, 1839): 2. The fashion of the *lorgnon,* as Figure 3.9 suggests, first belonged to "muscadins" and "incroyables," part of what Nicole Pellegrin has called an "epidemic" of myopia affecting young unmarried men of good families trying to avoid military service. It then became associated with high class standing and anti-Jacobin politics (*Les Vêtements de la liberté* [Paris: Alinea, 1989], 113). See also Jean-Claude Margolin, "Vers une sémiologie historique des lunettes à nez," in Pierre Marly, *Lunettes et lorgnettes* (Paris: Hoëbeke, 1988), 13; Mme Alfred Heyman, *Les Lunettes et les lorgnettes de jadis* (Paris: Leroy, 1911), 23; and Katell Le Bourhis, ed., *The Age of Napoleon: Costume from Revolution to Empire* (New York: Abrams, 1989), 49–69. See its significant appearance in the hand of Ingres's Madame Marcotte de Saint-Marie, 1826.

26. Delphine de Girardin, *Le Lorgnon* (Paris: Gosselin, 1832). The person with the magic lorgnon is male. By the 1840s, the use of a lorgnon seems to have become unmannerly, as notes the gossip column of *La Gazette des femmes* (November 25, 1843): 1: "We know that it is forbidden to honorable ladies:. . . To use a lorgnon." Why this may be so seems to relate to a further censorship of their gaze. It is also "forbidden" "to look assiduously around the room."

27. Caraccioli, *Dictionnaire critique* (Lyon, 1768), 1:384, cited by Pellegrin, *Les Vêtements,* 113; *Journal des dames et des modes* (April 20, 1823). The lorgnette's importance as part of the "new style" of the postrevolutionary period is emphasized by an engraving depicting new fashion confronting old fashion. The woman of the old fashion holds a fan (Châtaigner inventory no. 5.9, reproduced in Le Bourhis, *The Age of Napoleon,* 25); the new woman gazes at her through a lorgnette. An image I discuss in "Exhibiting and Exposing" from Gavarni's *Petits Bonheurs* (*Le Charivari* [April 8, 1837]) depicts the working-class girl trying a lorgnette, which is imagined to confer status to the aspiring worker.

28. Some clue to the appropriate way for a woman to wear a lorgnon might be gleaned from Ingres's *Portrait de Madame Marcotte de Sainte-Marie,* Paris, Musée du Louvre, where the woman decorously wears her looking glasses on a chain hanging nearly to her waist. Illustrations in *La Mode* (e.g., May 1836) depict women holding their looking glasses, like handkerchiefs or umbrellas, in their hands—never tucked between buttons of their blouses. A clue to the style Emma imitates—the way men may have worn their glasses—may be found in the Second Empire "Portrait de Laffièrere," in Louis Maigron, *Le Romantisme et la mode* (Geneva: Slatkine, 1989). Félicien Rops's charcoal (ca. 1860) of a woman with a lorgnon hanging around her bared neck suggests the "charms" of such an imitation; Jacques Derrida, *Mémoires d'aveugle* (Paris: Réunion des musées nationaux, 1990), plate 37.

29. Gustave Merlet, "Le Réalisme physiologique," in *Réalistes et fantaisistes,* 2d ed. (Paris: Didier, 1863 [1860]), 95, 96.

30. Ibid., 99. On the locked cabinet of the National Museum of Naples, known as the Museo Borbonico from the mid-eighteenth to the mid-nineteenth century, see Walter Kendrick, *The Secret Museum: Pornography in Modern Culture* (New York: Viking, 1987), 6–15. Kendrick points out that this "secret museum" of Pompeii was the referent for the meaning of the word *pornography* in the mid-nineteenth century (13). The first complete guide to the museum, M. L. Barré, *Herculanum et Pompei,*

8 vols. (Paris, 1875–77), compares the "untoward" parts of the museum to the cadavers before which an anatomist would not flinch (cited in Kendrick, 15). Daria Colombo's Harvard honors thesis research on nineteenth-century French tourist guidebooks to Italy confirmed that travelers knew of the locked cabinet but were prohibited admission until the late 1860s.

31. Merlet, "Le Réalisme physiologique," 114–15.

32. Ibid., 115, 141. Merlet's notion of that realism took root in the French language. *Le Petit Larousse,* 29th ed. (Paris, 1967), defines "bovarysme" as an "insatisfaction romanesque consistant à vouloir s'évader de sa condition en se créant une personnalité idéalisée, comme le fit l'héroïne de Flaubert *Madame Bovary.*"

33. "Il y a quelques années, une femme distinguée me posa la question suivante: *Chercher* les causes et les moyens qui donnent les apparences de la réalité aux oeuvres d'art." Champfleury, *Le Réalisme* (Paris: Lévy, 1857), 1.

34. Ibid., 2, 5.

35. See Roland Barthes, *S/Z,* trans. Richard Miller (New York: Farrar, Straus & Giroux, 1974; Leo Bersani, *A Future for Astyanax* (Boston: Little, Brown, 1976); Dorothy Kelly, *Fictional Genders: Role and Representation in Nineteenth-Century French Narrative* (Lincoln: University of Nebraska Press, 1989); and especially Naomi Schor, *Breaking the Chain: Women, Theory, and French Realist Fiction* (New York: Columbia University Press, 1985). Like Laqueur, I am interested in the way "the power of culture . . . represents itself in bodies, and forges them, as on an anvil." "Amor Veneris, vel Dulcedo Appeletur," in *Fragments for a History of the Human Body,* pt. 3, ed. Michel Feher (Cambridge, Mass.: Zone, 1989), 102. See also his *Making Sex* (Cambridge: Harvard University Press, 1990).

36. Thomas Haviland and Lawrence Parish, in "A Brief Account of the Use of Wax Models in the Study of Medicine," *Journal of the History of Medicine* (January 1970): 61, note that Bihéron was isolated from medical practices and forced repeatedly to leave Paris because of her gender. See also Lemire, *Artistes et mortels,* 80–85.

37. Haviland and Parish, "A Brief Account," 64–65.

38. Spitzner's popular and *public* "grand musée anatomique," at the Place de la République from the late 1850s, made its centerpiece the Venus whose 40 detachable pieces enabled viewers to explore a woman's internal organs. See Hervé Chayette, *Grand Musée Anatomique du Docteur Spitzner* (Paris: Nouveau Drouot, 1985), item 72; Hélène Pinet, "Cires anatomiques," in *Le Corps en morceaux* (Paris: Réunion des Musées nationaux, 1990), 51–56; and Lemire, *Artistes et mortels,* 341–45.

39. Fontana's Reale Museo di Fisica e Storia Naturale opened in 1775 with three life-size wax models: *Apollon of Belvedere,* an *Ecorché,* and the *Vénus de Médicis* (Figure 3.13), copied after a work by Bernini (1674) (Lemire, *Artistes et mortels,* 64). For further photographs of the Venus, see Sander Gilman, *Sexuality: An Illustrated History* (New York: John Wiley, 1991), 184–85, and Ludmilla Jordanova, "La donna di cera," *Kos* 4 (1984): 82–87.

40. Elisabeth Vigée-Lebrun, *Souvenirs* (Paris: Charpentier, n.d.), 236–38.

41. Ibid., 237.

42. I discuss theories of women's susceptibility to nervous disorders in *Scenes of Seduction,* especially chs. 4 and 5.

43. On Balzac's scalpel, see Forster, *Quinze ans à Paris,* 2:253: "Nothing escapes him in either Parisian or provincial life. His ruthless scalpel penetrates with boldness into all the miseries of humanity, making us see deep wounds, intolerable suffering,

vile trickery, there, where we were used to seeing happiness, the glamour of honor, and something of the chivalric." On Flaubert's dissections, see Sainte-Beuve, "Madame Bovary," 13:363; Charles de Mazade, "Chronique de la Quinzaine," *Revue des deux mondes* (May 1, 1857): 217–19; Albert Castelnau, "Le Roman réaliste," *Revue Philosophique et Religieuse* 8 (August 1857): 152–55; J. J. Weiss, "La Littérature brutale," *Revue Contemporaine* (January 15, 1858), 2d ser., 1: 144–85; Vapereau, *L'Année littéraire;* Merlet, "Le Réalisme physiologique."

44. Gustave Flaubert, letter of 24 April 1852, *Correspondence* (Paris: Gallimard, 1980), 2:78.

45. Sainte-Beuve, "Madame Bovary," 13:363.

46. Flaubert, *Correspondence,* July 27, 1852, cited in Robert, "Le Réalisme," 15.

47. Gustave Flaubert, *Le Dictionnaire des idées reçues* (Paris: Gallimard Folio, 1950), 550.

48. Paulin Limayrac, review in *Le Constitutionnel* (May 10, 1857).

49. Historian Colin Jones told me of eighteenth-century scandals surrounding women's viewing of medical school dissections. Female wax sculptor Bihéron was prohibited from participating in dissections (Lemire, *Artistes et mortels,* 80–85). Sanderson in 1839 depicted women in dissections of the École de Médecine, but these dissections were closed to the public, making viewing by anyone other than medical students extremely unlikely. For women's depiction on dissection tables, see William Stang, "The Dissecting Room" (Yale University Medical Library), reprinted in *Journal of the History of Medicine* (January 1970): 75; and Thomas Eakins, *The Agnew Clinic,* discussed by Marcia Pointon in *Naked Authority* (New York: Cambridge University Press, 1990), 35–58.

50. Baudelaire recounted how the prostitute Louise Villedieu accompanied him to the Louvre, where she "she set to blushing, covering her face, and pulling me at every moment by the sleeve, asking me, before immortal statues and paintings, how one could publicly expose such indecencies." *Oeuvres complètes,* 1:707, cited in Leclerc, *Crimes écrits,* 41.

51. I am indebted to Vanessa Schwartz for the reference that led to this image, originally published in Christiane Py and Cécile Ferenczi, *La Fête foiraine d'autrefois* (Lyon: La Manufacture, 1987), 104. We might wonder if this is the Musée Dupuytren referred to by Flaubert in the ironic *Dictionnaire des idées reçues* (composed in large part in the 1850s but not published until 1881) under the word "Musée." Flaubert mentions only three museums, the Louvre, Versailles, and the Dupuytren, which he describes as "very useful to show to young people" (541–42). One might imagine at the very least that Flaubert is here making reference to the controversy that surrounded his own resemblance to the original Musée Dupuytren. Nothing about this "definition" suggests that Flaubert assumes the Musée Dupuytren is actually open either to the public at large or to young people. Note, by way of comparison, that Flaubert cites the Louvre as "to be avoided for girls" (542).

52. Henri Marion, in *L'Education des filles* (Paris: Armand Colin, 1902), perpetuates a nineteenth-century assumption that girls become myopic from too much education: "With the same scholarly work, the danger of excess is thus greater for girls than for boys, whether because they have less resistance, or because their leisure hours are spent with books in their hands or in music exercises, rather than excercises outdoors" (160). Marion notes, however, the pleasures associated with this problematic gaze: "Myopia, it is true, is hardly to be seen as a serious disadvantage;

it lends itself to amusing games with an eyeglass, and one can make fun oneself of the little blunders that it occasions" (160).

53. For the full *X Portfolio* of "Robert Mapplethorpe: The Perfect Moment" (canceled at the Corcoran Gallery of Art, Washington, D.C., in 1989, and shown at the Cincinnati Contemporary Arts Center despite court challenges), see *Art Journal* 50, no. 3 (1991): 14–28. In "Is Art above the Laws of Decency?" an op-ed piece published in the *New York Times* (July 2, 1989), Hilton Kramer echoed language reminiscent of the prosecutor *and* defense in the *Démocratie Pacifique* trial: "I cannot bring myself to describe these pictures in all their gruesome particularities, and it is doubtful that this newspaper would agree to publish such a description even if I could bring myself to write one." According to Robert Storr ("Art, Censorship, and the First Amendment," *Art Journal* 50, no. 3 [1991]: 13), only Boston's PBS affiliate, WGBH, broadcast the entire *X Portfolio*. Other networks across the country, as well as the print media, left viewing of these photographs to museum-goers in cities where the exhibit did open (Philadelphia, Chicago, New York, Hartford, Berkeley, Boston), indirectly feeding fantasies that might have accompanied oral or written descriptions of visual material. During the Cincinnati trial, jurors were not shown the original photographs, but copies distorted in size and quality. For details of the Mapple-thorpe episode, see Steven C. Dubin, *Arresting Images: Impolitic Art and Uncivil Actions* (New York: Routledge, 1992), 170–92, especially 345 n. 64, 348 n. 130. Judith Butler, in "The Force of Fantasy: Feminism, Mapplethorpe, and Discursive Excess," *differences* 2, no. 2 (1990): 105–25, provides a fascinating analysis of the "representational violence" performed around the Mapplethorpe works.

54. This installation, called the "Cabinet des visages pâles," was the work of Jean-Marc Ferrari, director of La Maison de la Magie. The excellent exhibition catalog (*A Visage découverte* [Paris: Flammarion, 1992]), edited by Georges Didi-Huberman ("conseiller de l'exposition"), mercifully omits photographs of this installation.

55. "These are molds that you practice putting catheters in," Sherman explained to art critic Amei Wallach, "Tough Images to Face," *Los Angeles Times*, June 7, 1992, Calendar sec., 80.

56. *Splash Magazine* (Spring 1992), 24.

57. Wallach, "Tough Images to Face," 77.

58. "Sherman is more like a sex terrorist," wrote Elizabeth Hess in the *Village Voice*, May 5, 1992, 107. Sherman's images "have a horrific, Devil-Doll, Chucky's back quality that takes them into the horror genre," wrote Brian D'Amato in "Cindy Sherman: Limbless Hermaphrodites and Dismembered Devil-Dolls," *Flash Art* (Summer 1992): 107. "A sign posted by the door . . . warns parents that they might want to view the works inside before letting their children see them. The warning is understandable," began Charles Hagen's review in the *New York Times*, April 24, 1992, C32.

59. Hess, in the *Village Voice*, 107.

60. David Pagel, review of Sherman exhibition at Linda Cathcart Gallery, *Los Angeles Times*, May 28, 1992, F5.

61. Pagel wrote, for example: "The blatant fakery of Sherman's images battles with the nastiness of illicit subject matter. Although you know that you're looking at cheap props, artificial limbs and exaggerated theatrics, their effect is undeniably real." Ibid. Hess noted that each "dehumanized plastic doll" "divides into sections, as if ready for an autopsy. Sherman vaguely humanizes her puppets, . . . as if they

were once real" (107). Wallach also remarked on the paucity of reviews in terms resembling nineteenth-century critics' difficulties in *representing* what they saw as simultaneously horrifying and enthralling: "It's something of a trick to print the words you need to write about close-ups of plastic parts and repulsive sex acts after all." "Tough Images to Face," 77.

62. Quoted in ibid., 80.

63. Ibid., 77.

Realism without a Human Face

Judith L. Goldstein

Nothing less resembles a man than a man.

—Honoré de Balzac, "Traité de la vie élégante," 1830

The idea that the face is a primary visual focus of personal and social identity was central to the realist project. A description of each character's appearance generally accompanies his or her introduction in realist novels; consequently, such descriptions are numerous. We are so accustomed to these textual portraits—indeed, we are so much the inheritors of this tradition in the popular literature of our own time—that we have not sufficiently questioned the centrality of the face or the role it plays in the ascription of social identity. In this chapter, I consider the social cost of assuming that cultural difference takes a plastic form in the bodies of individuals.

I approach this issue through the processes of defamiliarization and comparison. I read together the work of two artists, in two different times and places, who experimented with received ways of looking by producing images of animal-human hybrids—images with human bodies and animal heads. I offer the following consideration of realism without a human face with the intention of complicating our understanding of realism with a human face.

Metamorphoses

J. J. Grandville published a series of lithographs in 1828–29 called *Les Métamorphoses du jour,* in which elaborately dressed human beings with animal heads were pictured in relatively ordinary, fully displayed, social situations.[1] The metamorphoses of the series title refer to the appearance of humans as animals, but it is possible to speak of another type of metamorphosis also clearly depicted in the series, and that is of human being to victim. Political prisoners, hungry children, exhausted workers, abased bureaucrats, and humiliated women are all portrayed as victims of a society that sacrifices them.

I will concentrate in this essay on Grandville's portrayal of his hybrid female victims. His sympathetic renderings of certain women make his work different from that of other popular illustrators of his time, who were generally more concerned with portraying women either as objects of desire or as objects of derision. What is the connection between Grandville's use of animal imagery and the sympathy he creates for the women he portrays? What kind of identification is created with people who are portrayed as animals? To pose the question more broadly, what pictorial conventions make it possible for us to care about people?[2]

It would be enough to pose this question for Grandville's oeuvre alone. *Les Métamorphoses du jour* made Grandville famous, and was sufficiently unique and important in its time to warrant examination. No one I know of has considered this work as a site for the portrayal of gender, which it most certainly is.[3] These lithographs of people with animal heads constitute an unusual body of work to think of in connection with the realist portrayal of gender and sexuality, and their message is, appropriately, also unusual. Grandville broke not only with the popular imagery of women, which might be interpreted as more realist/ic, but also with the artistic tradition of animal imagery. This double rupture, and the resulting new combination of the two pictorial modes in his work, produced a body of images whose goal was to portray the confining dimensions of contemporary social situations. The viewer's eye was moved, in an unaccustomed direction, away from the moral character of individual women. However, I would like the issues raised by Grandville's work to be seen not only in relation to his own time, but in relation to ours as well.

How are we to understand the current successes of *Maus* and *Maus II,* by Art Spiegelman, two books that tell the story of the Holocaust by portraying its human characters in cartoon form as animals? The critics who have reviewed the books have tended, with very few exceptions, to praise them for their accessibility. They claim that the animal imagery makes it easier to understand or to approach the events of the Holocaust and to identify with the characters portrayed.[4] Some reviewers even said they found it easier to sympathize with victims with animal faces than with victims with human faces. So I ask again, in this second context, what kind of identification is created with people who are portrayed as animals?

Thus, this essay poses questions about visualization and identification, and, in particular, about how displacement serves to facilitate or to block compassion. Animals are good to think, according to Claude Lévi-Strauss, and I will examine some ways in which animals are also good to visualize. Lévi-Strauss, in his discussion of "so-called totemism," analyzed how animal terms are used to mark social difference. In totemic societies, species differences interpreted as natural are mapped onto social differences seen as cultural. Animal terms and animal images are also used to embody and display social difference in Western societies such as those of nineteenth-century France and the twentieth-century United States, societies not usually identified with totemism, so called or otherwise.[5] Juxtaposing an early nineteenth-century experiment in the use of animal imagery with a later twentieth-century one allows us to see that the representation of cultural difference as visible difference has been an enduring problem for the realist project.

The Urban Jungle

In short, nature never copies herself; this is the difference between her and most modern authors.

—Louis Huart, *Muséum parisien,* 1841

The theme of human and animal resemblance was an important one in nineteenth-century French popular culture. In albums of lithographs and illustrated volumes, men and women were given animal names and animal appearances. These products of "animalomania" can be considered part of the larger corpus of popular literature devoted to the description of Paris and its inhabitants, an early realist project. How does the animal imagery—Grandville's as well as that of the writers who moved between animal terms and straight descriptions—transform the problematic of popular description? How did "realism" and "totemism" divide up the field of representation?

I will briefly consider one such product of animalomania to set up some comparisons between it and Grandville's work. In some fifty chapters and some four hundred pages, *Muséum parisien* by Louis Huart carries out the assignation of animal terms to social types with a rather daunting energy. It does this because the use of animal terms for the urban inhabitants of Paris was a contemporary fashion. "For some time now animals have become very fashionable. . . . Not satisfied with invading the theater, the animals have gone on to invade the dictionary of the Academie Française, and have imposed their name on a crowd of social classes."[6] However, although the volume adds a twist to the panorama literature, it does not substantively change the problematic of social description. The book's illustrations (a couple of which are by Grandville) are of people, not of animals or animal-human hybrids, and the animal terms do not really permit the identification of new social types. The mapping of animal names onto urban inhabitants adds another model of minute description to the panoramic literature. It is not, contrary to what we might assume (or wish to argue), primarily a mode of naturalization.

I do not wish to say that nothing is changed. *Muséum parisien* does offer a somewhat different vision of completeness than do better-known examples of the panoramic genre, such as the *Physiologies* or *Les Français peints par eux-mêmes*.[7] But (especially when compared with Grandville's hybrids) the animal terms function primarily as a new set of terms for familiar faces. The concierge becomes a hawk, the seducer is called a minotaur, the flaneur is a lizard; the dupe of speculators is a plucked chicken, and the old conservative is an antediluvian fossil.

Totemism, as represented by the literature that gave animal names to social types, is effectively absorbed by realism because the urban jungle is ruled by the same set of laws as is the urban metropolis. The same stable of writers generated both genres of descriptions. Louis Huart, who wrote *Muséum parisien,* also wrote a number of *physiologies,* including the *Physiologie du flâneur.* These writers participated in the realist project. Rosen and Zerner describe *Les Français peints par eux-memes* as "a socio-picturesque description of France . . . where each social type, each profession, is precisely and humourously described." They consider such literature "an important witness to the realistic element within Romanticism and hence to the continuity between the Romantic movement and Realism."[8] This description can be extended to *Muséum parisien* because that book should be classified with the panorama literature despite its animal analogies.

Fantastic as Grandville's illustrations are, and as far removed as they may seem from the later art movement officially termed realism, they should nonetheless be seen as an important contribution to the journalistic realism of the 1830s and 1840s. This popular descriptive realism experimented with animal terms, but it was Grandville who used animal imagery to change the way social facts were represented. Grandville turned the metaphors of the descriptive literature into the metamorphoses of his lithographic series *Les Métamorphoses du jour*. He did this by stressing what was unfamiliar, and not only what was familiar, in the tradition of animal portraiture.

Reading Grandville

A new world is born, may Grandville be praised.
—Max Ernst, *Un Autre Monde par Grandville,* 1963

If, as I am claiming, Grandville used totemic representation in a way different from other writers and artists of his time, then we need to construct an ethnographic guide to reading his work. The works in *Les Métamorphoses du jour* were first published as separate lithographs, with no explanatory text other than the captions and a short introduction by Achille Comte, and thus I turn to other Grandville illustrations to answer the question of what was entailed in making animals "good to visualize." Many of Grandville's pictures—his *"fantaisies,"* as they are sometimes called—were drawn for *Le Magasin Pittoresque* and appeared in that journal with generally unattributed commentary attached to them. These texts of the 1840s explain Grandville's methods by referring the reader to the principles of Lavater and Gall. In fact, it is not at all clear that the principles of physiognomy and phrenology can fully account for Grandville's fascination with the descent of man.

The principles through which we can read Grandville's work are embodied in two illustrations he did for *Le Magasin Pittoresque*. The first principle is that animal faces can be "read" in much the same way human faces can be "read." In *Physionomie du chat,* Grandville produced twenty sketches of a cat with different emotional expressions. As the accompanying text noted, they all had "a more or less sensible rapport with the signs of the passions which incessantly modify the human physiognomy. . . . For [Grandville], the principle of the physiognomists, that the face is the mirror of the soul, has, up to a certain point, always seemed applicable to animals."[9] The cat's expressions are labeled as if human: "philosophical reflection," "hypocritical envy," "digestive calm," and so on.

We can call the second principle "moral metamorphosis," and it is best illustrated in another pair of pictures—*The Man Descends toward the Brute* and *The Animal Ascends toward Man* (Figures 4.1 and 4.2). The first set shows five stages in a man's life, from a rather evil-looking (and rather mature) baby to his final "degradation." The second set begins with a sweet young puppy and ends with him as a wise old dog playing chess, with spectacles perched on his head. "He has approached human intelligence by his submission and the sweetness of his instincts."[10] This bespectacled dog sitting up and playing chess is close in appearance and posture to the fully clothed animal hybrids, and the examples of the cat and dog taken together analytically separate what Grandville combined in *Les Métamorphoses du jour.*

An examination of the artistic techniques Grandville used to transform animals to hybrids can, like physiognomic principles, take us only so far in reading his work (and in accounting for his innovativeness). Clive Getty's illuminating interpretations of Grandville's sketches from the museum at Nancy show how Grandville proceeded from naturalistic drawings of usually dead animals to the more hybrid man-animals by means of redrawing.[11] A lifeless supine rabbit, for example, would be stood up on its legs, and his posture progressively changed by degrees until he was standing like a man. Getty suggests that Grandville's pictures carried the impact they did in large part through the very realistic drawing of that which could not, in its final stages, be found in nature. Getty compares Grandville's technique of the realistic drawing of the unreal to later developments in surrealism.

Figure 4.1. Grandville, *The Man Descends toward the Brute*, lithograph from *Le Magasin Pittoresque*, April 1843.

Figure 4.2. Grandville, *The Animal Ascends toward Man*, lithograph from *Le Magasin Pittoresque*, April 1843.

A discussion of technique is important, especially as we know from the biographical accounts of the way Grandville worked that he took great care and a lot of time to produce his pictures. However, the technical skills that produced these transformations are performed on individual animals, and I would argue that the ultimate impact of Grandville's work does not result from the manipulation, skillful as it may be, of animals as isolated units. Instead, central to Grandville's oeuvre is the way in which animals are placed in *social* groups—I am thinking here of the illustrations for *Les Métamorphoses du jour*, the fables of La Fontaine, and the illustrations for *Scènes de la vie privée et publique des animaux*.[12] This is the third principle we need to read his work. The limitations of early illustrations of single animals (in human costume or not) are revealed by comparison with Grandville's pictures of interacting animals. Previous *animaliers* who concentrated on individual animals produced a body of work that is, I would argue, as discontinuous with Grandville's work as it is continuous.

Animal faces can be read like human faces in Grandville's work, as we have seen. But, more important, dressed animals can interact together just as humans do. These social situations can be read as narratives that carry moral points that are made clear either through explicit or implicit contrast. It is only by acknowledging the rupture with previous animal imagery that the social critique of Grandville's work can be understood. Its impact is not the result only of its technical mastery; rather, it is a product of Grandville's *transformation of the genre* of animal imagery. This genre of image becomes one that can carry a message about gender because it has been transformed into a genre that also carries a narrative line that is particular to each picture.

Earlier animal imagery could carry political meaning. In these caricatures, the faces of recognizable people of political renown were attached to animal bodies. Revolutionary cartoons represented Louis XVI as a pig and Marie Antoinette as a hyena.[13] This use of animal figures was, as Champfleury said of the tactics of revolutionary caricature more generally, "very close to symbolism."[14] Unflattering animal imagery was used persistently over the course of the nineteeth century. Animality meant political illegitimacy; to picture individuals as animals was to judge them unfit to rule.

In *La Ménagerie impériale,* Second Empire (1852–70) politicians were presented as hybrid figures whose faces were human and whose bodies were animal. The set of images that make up *La Ménagerie impériale* begins with Napoleon III pictured as a vulture ("cowardice," "ferocity") devouring France. The *Musée des horreurs* series appeared during the period of the Dreyfus affair. The carefully drawn faces of prominent Dreyfusards and Jews joined the bodies of such animals as pigs, donkeys, hydras, and cows.[15] In both series, the bestial hybrids took the form of individual portraits.

Grandville did not put recognizable human faces on animal bodies, as was done with the royal family in revolutionary caricature (a tradition that, as we have seen, was carried on in the political imagery of the Second Empire and the Third Republic), nor did he put anonymous faces on animal bodies as in the compendia of the

Restoration (as shown in illustrations in Grand-Carteret's volume on caricature).[16] He did not isolate his images on the page, as was also customary in the compendia. It seems fair to say that in relation to the Revolutionary cartoons, and to the simple animal images of the Restoration, Grandville was indeed a "Buffon d'un nouveau genre."[17]

The fact that this new genre can be read as saying something new about gender is related, I am claiming, in large part to Grandville's commitment to placing the dressed animals in elaborately drawn social situations. The pictures function as compressed narratives. It was only after Grandville had refigured the traditional decontextualization of hybrid figures that he could go on to use the animal genre to comment on the social consequences of gender.

Women of the *Juste Milieu:* The Art of Gavarni

It is not those beauties of popular prints,
Worn products born of a worthless century,
With slippered feet and castanettes for fingers,
Who can satisfy a heart like mine.

   —Charles Baudelaire, "L'Idéal," 1857

Grandville was not one of Baudelaire's favorite caricaturists. "There are some superficial spirits who are amused by Grandville; for my part I find him terrifying," he wrote, and this reaction of his to Grandville's "rearranged" world is often cited. Baudelaire, however, continued: "Doubtless Grandville produced some good and beautiful things, much assisted by his obstinate and meticulous habits; but he entirely lacked flexibility, and what is more, he was never able to draw a woman."[18]

Grandville "never able to draw a woman"? Why does this come to mind in consulting his oeuvre? It is indeed an odd comment to make about a man best known for his animal figures (*Les Métamorphoses du jour, Scènes du la Vie privée et publique des animaux*), and for the bizarreries of his later work (*Un Autre Monde*), in which so many human figures, male and female, are distorted or caught in the process of metamorphosing from one order of being to another.[19] To understand further Baudelaire's comment about Grandville, it is instructive to look at Bauderlaire's description of

Figure 4.3. Gavarni, *"Still beautiful!" "That's my condition!"* lithograph from *Les Lorettes* (Paris, 1841) (Bibliothèque Nationale, Paris).

Gavarni, "who is very much more important."[20] Gavarni, who achieved recognition at roughly the same time as Grandville— Grandville became famous with the publication of *Les Métamorphoses du jour* in 1829, and Gavarni's position as chronicler of Parisian life began with his appointment as fashion illustrator for *La Mode* in 1830—was most identified with his elegant and cynical drawings of women, particularly those women known as *grisettes* and *lorettes* (see Figure 4.3).

It would seem that Gavarni reflected a world, whereas Grandville turned it upside down. Baudelaire pointed to a certain realistic quality in Gavarni's pictures. He said of one, "You would really think that the lady must be a portrait." However, his idea of the real seems to be one that is always reproducing as well as reproduced. He continued, "but those rascals of Gavarni's are so engaging that young people will inevitably want to imitate them."[21]

Baudelaire described the movement between the women portrayed and the women who copy them as follows:

> Gavarni created the *Lorette*. She existed, indeed, a little before his time, but he *completed* her. . . . I said that Gavarni had completed her; and in fact he is so swept along by his literary imagination that he invents at least as much as he sees, and for that reason he has had a considerable effect upon manners. Paul de Kock created the Grisette, and Gavarni the Lorette; and not a few of those girls have perfected themselves by using her as a mirror, just as the youth of the Latin Quarter succumbed to the influence of his *Students,* and as many people force themselves into the likeness of fashion-plates.[22]

This assessment is not Baudelaire's alone; Champfleury picked it up again in his study of modern caricature. "Women of the world and dandies imitated the poses of Gavarni's heroes. His wit attracted followers and more than one actress has studied the French language from his captions."[23] In her autobiography, Rigolboche, a popular nineteenth-century dancer, goes Baudelaire and Champfleury one step further, by describing the influence of Gavarni on the dance she invented and from which she took her name. "Gavarni—our painter of history—has sometimes provided a reasonably complete image with his pencil. I have to admit that I borrowed certain stances from him. I wanted to realize his dreams. Have I succeeded?"[24]

In company with realist novelists, Gavarni leaned on the readability of his images, on what Harry Levin has described as realism's dependence on "an implicit intimacy between the novelist and his reader on certain attitudes and reactions to life."[25] Gavarni's *lorettes* are easily understood. For men, they are "fine" and "handsome," and therefore memorable. For women, they are models of appearance, gesture, nonchalance, survival. In either case, they present an ease of identification between viewer and image. The image, partly taken from life, partly an invented creation, functions as a fashion plate that women can copy. Reality suggests the image, which in turn affects reality and is incorporated in new images. Gavarni perfects the *lorette,* and the *lorettes* perfect themselves.

In the end, Baudelaire rejected Gavarni's portraits of women for failing to meet his vision of ideal beauty. This judgment should not, after the above discussion, surprise us. Gavarni's connection to the real world made him earthbound. Gavarni's beauties are *only* "those beauties of popular prints (*vignettes*)." Gavarni's ideal of feminine beauty can usefully be compared to that described by Leon Rosenthal as typical of the painters of the *juste milieu* (although Gavarni would not be expected to appear in such a discussion). According to Rosenthal, *juste milieu* painters were not looking for "an ideal beauty." The *juste milieu* painter "preferred pleasant and pretty faces, and since he did not claim to impose an ideal on his contemporaries, he espoused the idea of beauty found around him, of actresses, dancers, fashionable women. Thus the painter carried out his work by a series of concessions and attenuations."[26] Gavarni in drawing his *lorettes* also adopted the ideas of beauty around him. We seem to have come full circle: Gavarni assimilated the idea of beauty from the actresses, dancers, and women of fashion around him—he is praised as a great observer of women—and they in turn modeled themselves on his pictures.

Thus Baudelaire, "I leave to Gavarni, poet of chlorosis, / His murmuring flock of poor-house beauties."[27] Baudelaire rejects "these pale roses" for "a flower which resembles my ideal red." We can say, knowing his standards for the painter of modern life, that for Baudelaire, Gavarni only succeeds as a painter of the ephemeral beauty of his time; he fails as a portraitist of eternal beauty. Grandville's failure would appear, then, to be even more encompassing.

Grandville's Hybrid Women

I will not argue much longer with those who reproach me for putting clothes on animals and standing them up on their feet.

J. J. Grandville, "Au possesseur présent ou futur de cet album"

Where, then, does Grandville fail in his portrayal of feminine beauty? His drawings also depend on "certain attitudes and reactions to life."[28] The females in Grandville's *Les Métamorphoses du jour* often represent *lorettes* and *grisettes*. Their dress is fashionable, beautiful, and meticulously drawn. Grandville, like Gavarni, was a careful fashion illustrator. The clothing in Grandville's drawings, in fact, resembles the accuracy of fashion plates more than do the often sketchier creations of Guys or Gavarni. The situations in which the women find themselves are recognizable and have the narrative force and cynicism of much of Gavarni's work. And yet Baudelaire said that Grandville could never draw a woman. Champfleury again agreed, writing, "Grandville did not see woman as ugly, or faded, or ridiculous, or coquettish, as did certain satirists; he did not see her at all."[29]

Of course, something does get in the way of using Grandville's "women" as mirror images, and that is that they are pictured as animals. The drawings in *Les Métamorphoses du jour* may be easily read, but with a difference. Is one to read past the animals, or through the animals? The animals are not simply emblems, as so much of the Grandville criticism would have it. Although Grandville does make use of traditional physiognomic associations, there is no obvious repeatable code in which, for example, cats are always female or pigs are always greedy. Nonetheless, *something* about each picture is clear. I will argue that what is clear in the Grandville pictures is the *situation* pictured. The interpretability does not lie in the figures themselves, but in the relations among the figures and in the life narratives that make them readable. The legibility of the face is sacrificed to the legibility of the situation, which is to say, to the legibility of social factors. Thus, Grand-ville criticism that emphasizes the continuity between animals and humans and the human expression of the animals, to the exclusion of all else, is misplaced.

The Grandville drawings that place the two sexes together in some kind of relationship invite double readings. On one hand, we do seem to be reading the faces of the women. Contrary to their appearance in Gavarni, the women/animals in Grandville often appear as victims. The downcast eyes are not hypocritical; the fat-bellied suitors are not being led on by venial women who only appear to be innocent. The females are indeed lambs led to the slaughter. One in fancy dress and bonnet not only has a sheep's face, she also has a rope around her neck and a bird-man seems to be offer-

Figure 4.4. Grandville, "*Oh! that monster of a man is still following us!!*" lithograph from *Les Métamorphoses du jour* (Paris: Bulla, 1829).

Figure 4.5. Grandville, *The Dog-Days*, lithograph from *Les Métamorphoses du jour* (Paris: Bulla, 1829).

ing her to three lounging animal-headed males. Another lamb led to the slaughter is a young "woman" offered to an older crippled man in a marriage caustically captioned as one of convenience. Two animal-women, clearly identifiable as *grisettes/modistes,* with their Gavarniesque bonnets and packages, are followed by a goatish male, but they do not welcome his advances (see Figure 4.4). They would get rid of him if they could. The "woman" closest to the "man" ("Oh! that monster of a man is still following us!!") has her hand raised in protest and, perhaps, fear.

The décolleté dog of *The Dog-Days* followed by a canine pack (Figure 4.5) reminds me of nothing so much as Ruth Orkin's well-known 1951 photograph of a lone woman tourist being ogled by a crowd of men on a street in Florence.[30] One dog-man has his tongue hanging out, while another elbows a male competitor out of his way. The dog-woman looks frightened, and attempts to hold herself with dignity, trying in the stiffness of her body to indicate her lack of complicity in the situation.

These are not images that can be found with human faces, that can be found in the popular lithography of the time outside of Grandville's corpus. The positioning of the male and female figures in *The Dog-Days* is typical of the drawings in popular realist texts such as the *Physiologies*. In these illustrations, the man (the flaneur, for example) is often portrayed as following from behind a woman *whose face he cannot see.* In *The Dog-Days,* the canine males cannot see the face of the female they are following, but we, the viewers, can, and what we see is the "realistic" face of a woman pursued by aggression (and male competition) masquerading as desire. The subject position of the viewer is displaced from the male who owns the city to the female as urban victim.

Gavarni's *lorettes,* for example, are never victims. As Champfleury writes, "For Gavarni . . . life is a sort of carnival in which youth and love affairs triumph."[31] It could be argued, I suppose, that Gavarni portrays *lorettes* with some sympathy. He gives them a sort of life among themselves as coconspirators apart from their liaisons (as in *Les Partageuses*), and provides what appear to be ethnographic details about the standard of life they try to maintain through their economies. Baudelaire and Champfleury criticize Gavarni, in fact, for failing to condemn the immorality of their lives, for not identifying evil as evil. However, the sympathy of Gavarni's portrayals is attenuated by his assumption that the women are always in control. He limits his understanding of the codes that govern their relations to incidents between individuals (although these incidents have a form that repeats between partners and over time), and, unlike Grandville, it seems to me, avoids any representation of a larger social context. Much of the information we need to read the emotions of Gavarni's figures—both the women and the men—comes from the captions and the gestures and bodies of the figures. The human faces in Gavarni's images are not meant to carry the information that the animal faces do in Grandville's.

On the other hand, I would argue that it is precisely the semi-erasure of the face in Grandville's figures, insofar as it is an animal and not a human face, that makes sympathy possible. I think it can be said that the initial judgment in Gavarni as well as in the larger corpus of popular lithography of women (Deveria comes to mind here) is whether or not a depicted woman is attractive. It is a woman's attractiveness that is instantly read. This first judgment cannot be transferred so simply to Grandville's animal women, although a viewer can tell, and needs to know, whether or not a face is to be coded as attractive. (Does "never able to draw a woman" for Baudelaire mean "never able to draw an *attractive* woman"?) Two comparisons with other artists of the time clarify this point. For example, Philippon's series on female occupations is a set of eroticized portraits of female workers in public spaces (1827–29). Although distinguished by occupation such as salesgirl or baker, these nouns function as an excuse for the adjectives—the pleasant perfume-seller, the sweet candy-seller, the tender mattress-merchant, the piquant seamstress, and so on. All the women are pretty, and that is why they are worth looking at.

A second example of the salience of women's appearance is Daumier's series *The Bluestockings* (published in *Le Charivari* from January to August 1844) and *Socialist Women* (published in *Le Charivari* from April to June 1849). Philippon was Daumier's editor for these series. In them, all the women are unattractive, and that is why the morals of their stories are worth considering. Only ugly women are interested in the ideologies of women's issues. "Bad mother, bad wife, bad housekeeper, a cold, heartless monster, tyrannical, pretentious but without talent, dissolute and often spiteful, attempting to hide her pitiful ugliness behind lackluster jewelery, frumpy, but unaware of the ridiculous figure she cut—such was the *Bluestocking,* such were the *Socialist Women.*"[32]

Philippon's women are beautiful and Daumier's are ugly, and the viewers' knowledgeable response to each type is essential for the decoding of the images. With Grandville, I am arguing, the response is less complicitous and cannot hinge in any simple way on a woman's appearance. The (perhaps gendered) first question is not whether or not one desires the woman portrayed or whether or not one wants to look like that woman. It is the situation, instead, that immediately presents itself. The viewer is reading the situation while ostensibly being amused by animals dressed as humans, or by timeless human foibles, or whatever other shorthand is usually employed in the art historical criticism of animal/human pictures.

What is it that made Grandville's vision unique? I am not claiming that he was a feminist *avant la lettre* (any more than I think it makes sense to call him a surrealist ahead of his time). I am saying that Grandville tried to escape a pictorial rhetoric that was too thin and too transparent in its portrayal of women. His fellow caricaturists' depictions were essentially one-liners: a woman was desirable or she was not. In Grandville's women/animals, attractiveness is there as a signifier as much as a signified. A woman's attractiveness is one of the codes through which the picture is read; it is not, however, a particularly pertinent aspect of the female figure in herself. The female figures exist in narratives, in situations that can be read, but they are not ordinary objects of desire. A viewer needs to know if the female should be considered attractive in order to understand what is being said in the picture as a whole. With the other caricaturists, attractiveness is the beginning, the middle, and the end of the lives of women. In the case of Gavarni's aging *lorettes,* beauty is absent, but its former presence is the way in which the *lorettes* understand themselves and want others to understand them. As a woman in his series *Les Lorettes vieilles* says, "And of the beauty of the devil, this is what is left. . . [my] talons."[33] With Grandville, attractiveness is one sign, among others, to be read.

Françoise Parturier relates the message of Daumier's drawings of the 1840s to Jean Cau's recent, and notorious, 1973 comment: "You feminists are ugly, you are unlovely, unloved, unlovable."[34] She writes: "There is no contradiction in a radical republican being radically anti-feminist—it is almost traditional. . . . Indeed, the subject of women was the only one on which republicans and monarchists were agreed."[35] The image of women, she claims, is relatively stable across political divisions; I would argue that it is also so across genre divisions. The republicans inherited gender imagery from the monarchists just as the realists inherited it from the romantics.

This is why Grandville's women have to look different. "Realism" was without a human face in Grandville's work because, as I have been arguing, it had only one female face. That face could not be seen as a social fact, just as, in the clichéd image of the flaneur, the pursuing male could not see the face of the woman he followed. Put differently, it was the mask in the form of an animal head that allowed the unmasking of the woman's social situation.

I believe Grandville was trying to find a visual vocabulary that was not culturally compromised. He was using animals not so much as a clear code in the tradition of physiognomic readings, but as a way to interrupt cultural assumptions. It is through his portrayal of women, which is, in my interpretation, at odds with his fellows at *Le Charivari,* that we can see a larger struggle about social representation being enacted. The problem was how to say something recognizably true about a moment in time while also saying it in a different way. Grandville followed most of the conventions of the lithographic codes of his time, but replaced humans with animals, a replacement that displaced the other conventions.

Grandville interrupted cultural assumptions by breaking with the tradition of animal imagery, and by stressing the victimization of the hybrid humans he portrayed. This was particularly significant, in the context of the time, in his portrayals of women. Thus, he broke with the tradition of animal imagery and with the codes of representation of women in popular illustration. Our compassion for the victims in Grandville's illustrations comes from the awareness that the social situations in which they find themselves function as iron cages. As John Berger notes, "These animals are not being 'borrowed' to explain people. . . . Here animals are not being used as reminders of origin, or as moral metaphors. . . . The dogs in Grandville's engraving of the dog-pound are in no way canine; they have dogs' faces, but what they are suffering is imprisonment *like men.*"[36] This refusal to use animals as "moral metaphors" for people, but instead to move to the level of social interactions, and therefore to social constraints, makes Grandville's portrayal of women unique. It is hard, as I have said, to approach Grandville's animal/women directly as objects of desire. And it is equally hard, given the portrayal of the hybrid women in a social context (for example, a public space, as in *The Dog-Days*), to assume that her morality has determined her fate. Men may be the victims of other men in Grandville's illustrations, but women, in general, are the victims of individual men and of the cultural assumptions that support the types of male behavior that victimize women.

Of Mice and Men

The Holocaust was a crime committed by humans against humans, not—as Nazi theory held—by one biological species against another.
—Hillel Halkin, "Inhuman Comedy," 1992

Art Spiegelman's books *Maus* and *Maus II* combine the story of Spiegelman's relationship to his father Vladek with the history of Vladek's experiences as a Jew in World War II Europe. The text depends on hours of testimony from Vladek recorded by Spiegelman, and is largely told in Vladek's words. The text and accompanying illustrations depend on Vladek's experiences as well as on those of other Jews, and are very explicit. Vladek tells his son how to build a bunker and how to repair shoes, and the illustrations are technically specific and accurate. The books are in cartoon form, and all the characters have human bodies and animal faces. The Jews are portrayed as mice, the Germans as cats, and the Poles as pigs.

When the *New York Times* put *Maus II* under "fiction" on its bestseller list, Spiegelman sent a letter protesting this classification of the book. "To the extent that 'fiction' indicates that a work isn't factual," he wrote, it was an inaccurate and potentially dangerous way to classify "a carefully researched work based closely on my father's memories of life in Hitler's Europe and in the death camps." He added, "I know that by delineating people with animal heads I've raised problems of taxonomy for you."[37]

A year later, he described his fears about the reception of the books somewhat differently:

[*Maus*] doesn't try to simplify the complexities of interpersonal relationships and disastrous history . . . and yet it comes across in an easy-to-take tablet. The scary part to me is that *Maus* may also have given people an easy way to deal with the Holocaust, to feel that they've "wrapped it up," that reading *Maus* now makes it possible for them to feel that they understand it, and that's that.[38]

The danger is not only the support that classifying a historical memoir as fiction would give to people already ideologically prepared to deny the Holocaust, but the dismissal, on the part of people of goodwill, of the continuing need to examine and to try to understand genocide.

Spiegelman's two interventions are related to each other. The animal heads may make it hard to see the work as factual, but they also make the work "easy reading" for those who stop with this work on the Holocaust rather than go on to read more. This is not only because the books take a cartoon form. For people who find Holocaust events too painful to confront, the animal heads provide the distance that enables them to read *Maus*. At the same time, having read *Maus,* they then feel they have done their historical duty and can push away the events it describes.

There is yet another aspect to the animal heads that has come out in the reviews of *Maus*. A number of reviewers have implied or explicitly stated that the animal heads in fact increase the *human* dimensions of the characters. Two art critics, reviewing the Spiegelman sketches and memorabilia exhibited at the Museum of Modern Art in 1992, found it hard to identify with the photographs of Spiegelman's family. One reviewer remarked, "The bland faces of these lost generations suggest the difficulties of empathizing with the Holocaust."[39] Another critic, reviewing the exhibit for a major art journal, enjoyed Spiegelman's original sketches, but found that the other archival materials were "not so illuminating and were sometimes distracting. There was a photograph of the real Vladek, for example, and it was impossible to reconcile his handsomely chiseled face with the crotchety bespectacled anxiety-tormented mouse in Spiegelman's book, who seems far more human."[40] This is chilling; the mouse was *"far* more human"? Poor Vladek, whose humanity always seems to be in question for one reason or another. Both of these reviewers focus on the failure of the victims' *faces* to signify for them, to carry for them, as outsiders, some form of instant identification or understanding. The family members' faces are "bland," Vladek's is "handsomely chiseled"; these are the reasons given for the distance the viewer feels. These reasons constitute a physiognomic blaming of the victims. Both reviewers favor the animal faces.[41] What does it take for us to *see* the faces of others?

This is the dark side of displacement, the dark side, too, of children's books that also use animals to encourage empathy, to permit children to identify without being blocked, presumably, by the particulars of race or sex or ethnicity. The logic of this universalization/abstraction has it that making all the characters animals is an advance over making them all white. However, the logic also implies that it would be impossible to ask children to identify with individuals culturally defined as visibly different from themselves.

Both Spiegelman and Grandville succeed in placing a screen before the faces of stigmatized individuals that eases their acceptance as human beings for viewers who are perhaps culturally disinclined to empathize with them. I have argued that Grandville used animal symbols not to naturalize social relations so much as to make them accessible to viewers who would otherwise lack empathy because of entrenched social and political ways of seeing. The animal faces can call forth sympathy more directly, it would seem, than human faces.

We can say that the artists' success is society's failure. What does it mean culturally that we can have more empathy for a woman portrayed as a cat or a sheep than we do for a woman portrayed as a woman? When Grandville's hybrid women are placed in the context of the more "realistic" popular imagery of women of his time, it is the more realistic representations that seem to be lacking in humanity. Grandville's work startles by the sympathy it evokes, but also by the lack it illuminates in Gavarni's work. Gavarni's work has largely been taken by critics (writing in both the nineteenth and the twentieth centuries) as accurately reflecting the attitudes of the time, as the pictorial companion to Balzac's text of the *Comédie humaine*.

The reviews of the *Maus* volumes (more, again, than the "shock" of the cartoon form of the books themselves) pose a similar problem. What does it mean that putting Jews in nonhuman form makes them more human to some viewers? The issue is not just the obvious one of exploring the implications of portraying humans as animals. The issue is rather the struggle over forms of representation that the intersection of totemism and realism brings into view. The ultimate problem is not that of picturing humans as animals, but that of seeing humans as humans. Society's failure, in this sense, further tests the artists' apparent success. Perhaps it is best to see the artists' success as only partial. Critics praise Grandville and Spiegelman for portraying the universal in the particular. But these forms of representation instead prove that in our culture (modern and postmodern, early and late capitalist) the particular can be portrayed with sympathy only if it can be displaced onto something other than its cultural self.

NOTES

A longer version of this chapter will appear in my forthcoming book *Passions and Possessions* (Princeton, N.J.: Princeton University Press). An NEH summer stipend (1989) and research grants from Vassar College allowed me to travel to Paris to pursue the research on which this essay is based. With the exception of quotations from Baudelaire on caricature, all translations are my own. I thank Andy Bush, Margaret Cohen, and Brian Lukacher for helpful readings of this essay.

1. J. J. Grandville, *Les Métamorphoses du jour* (Paris: Bulla, 1829).

2. This question intentionally echoes the one Laqueur poses for English eighteenth- and nineteenth-century humanitarian narratives. He asks, "Under what conditions can we speak of other individuals so as to care for them?" Thomas Laqueur, "Bodies, Details, and the Humanitarian Narrative," in *The New Cultural History,* ed. Lynn Hunt (Berkeley: University of California Press, 1989), 202.

3. Important recent art historical work has been done on Grandville by, among others, Laure Garcin, *J. J. Grandville* (Paris: Eri Losfeld, 1970); Clive F. Getty, "The Drawings of J. J. Grandville until 1830: The Development of His Style during His Formative Years" (Ph.D. diss., Stanford University, 1981); Philippe Kaenel, "Le Buffon de l'humanité: la zoologie politique de J.-J. Grandville (1803–1847)," *Revue de l'art* 74 (1986); M. Mespoulet, *Creators of Wonderland* (New York: Arrow, 1934); Annie Renonciat, *La Vie et l'oeuvre de J. J. Grandville* (Paris: Vilo, 1985); and Judith Wechsler, *A Human Comedy: Physiognomy and Caricature in Nineteenth-Century Paris* (Chicago: University of Chicago Press, 1982). The Nancy catalog, *Grandville: Dessins originaux* (with introduction and catalog entries by Clive F. Getty and Simone Guillaume) (Nancy: n.p., 1986), and the reproductions of much of Grandville's work in the two-volume *Grandville: Das Gesamte Werk* (Germany: Manfred Pawlak, 1972) are important resources. Charles Blanc's *Jean Ignace Isidore Grandville* (Paris: Croquis biographique, 1855) is a central nineteenth-century review of Grandville's life and work.

4. Art Spiegelman, *Maus: A Survivor's Tale* (New York: Pantheon, 1986) and *Maus II: A Survivor's Tale: And Here My Troubles Began* (New York: Pantheon, 1991). Book reviews and articles in art journals on the subject of *Maus* and *Maus II* include the following: Paul Buhle, "Of Mice and Menschen: Jewish Comics Come of Age," *Tikkun* 7 (March–April 1992); Matthew Freedman, "When It's a Matter of Life and Death," *Arts Magazine,* October 1990; Hillel Halkin, "Inhuman Comedy," *Commentary* 93 (February 1992); Ken Johnson, "Art Spiegelman at MOMA," *Art in America,* March 1992; Kay Larson, "Of Mice and Men," *New York,* January 13, 1992; Russell Schechter, "Kat and Maus," *Communication Research* 16 (August 1989).

5. Claude Lévi-Strauss, *The Savage Mind* (Chicago: University of Chicago Press, 1968). Thus, from an anthropological viewpoint, this essay should be considered as

a contribution to the literature on the rethinking of totemism in the modern West. This not very extensive body of work includes James A. Boon, *Affinities and Extremes* (Chicago: University of Chicago Press, 1990); John Comaroff and Jean Comaroff, "Of Totemism and Ethnicity," in *Ethnography and the Historical Imagination* (Boulder, Colo.: Westview, 1992); Marshall Sahlins, "La Pensée bourgeoise," in *Culture and Practical Reason* (Chicago: University of Chicago Press, 1976); and Terence Turner, "Animal Symbolism, Totemism, and the Structure of Myth," in *Animal Myths and Metaphors in South America*, ed. Gary Urton (Salt Lake City: University of Utah Press, 1985).

6. Louis Huart, *Muséum parisien* (Paris: Beauger et Cie, 1841), 1–2.

7. Several authors have considered the *Physiologies* from historical, literary, and artistic perpectives; see, for instance, Walter Benjamin, *Charles Baudelaire*, trans. Harry Zohn (New York: Verso, 1989 [1969]); Judith L. Goldstein, "Social Classes and Social Classification: Descriptions of Nineteenth Century Parisians in the *Physiologies*" (unpublished manuscript, Wesleyan University, Center for the Humanities, November 1989); A. L'Heritier, *Les Physiologies 1840–1845*, ed. W. Hawkins (microfilm) (Paris: Service Internationale de Microfilm, 1966); Richard Sieburth, "Same Difference: The French *Physiologies*, 1840–1842, *Notebooks in Cultural Analysis* 1 (1984); Wechsler, *A Human Comedy*. James Cuno has written about their publishing environment in "Philipon et Desloges: editeurs des 'Physiologies,' " *Cahiers de l'Institut d'Histoire de la Presse et de l'Opinion* 7 (1983).

8. Charles Rosen and Henri Zerner, *Romanticism and Realism: The Mythology of Nineteenth-Century Art* (New York: W. W. Norton, 1984), 81.

9. J. J. Grandville, "*Physionomie du chat:* études par J.-J. Grandville," *Le Magasin pittoresque* 8 (January 1840): 12.

10. J. J. Grandville, "Fantaisie, par J.-J. Grandville. *L'Homme descend vers la brute. L'Animal s'élève vers l'homme*" (*Le Magasin pittoresque* 11 (April 1843): 109.

11. In *Grandville: Dessins originaux*.

12. J. J. Grandville, *Scènes de la vie privée et publique des animaux* (Paris: Hetzel, 1842).

13. *French Caricature and the French Revolution 1789–1799* (Los Angeles: University of California, Grunwald Center for the Graphic Arts, 1988), 190, fig. 82.

14. Cited in Michel Melot, "Caricature and the Revolution: The Situation in France in 1789," in *French Caricature and the French Revolution 1789–1799* (Los Angeles: University of California, Grunwald Center for the Graphic Arts, 1988), 28.

15. Norman Kleeblatt, ed., *The Dreyfus Affair: Art, Truth and Justice* (Berkeley: Jewish Museum/University of California Press, 1987), 244–52. Edouard Drumont (author of *La France Juive*) and the other anti-Semitic writers of his time used a large repertoire of animal terms—hyena, jackal, vulture, crow, octopus, monkey, pig, mole, serpent, grasshopper, and more—to describe Jews. "Blum appeared with the traits of a camel, a weasel, a mare and a dog, while Mandel was figured, for example, as a serpent or a spider, Pierre Mendès-France as an owl, Daniel Mayer as a 'black tadpole, quivering and viscous' and Laurent Fabius, most recently, as a monkey with hooked paws." Pierre Birnbaum, *Un mythe politique: la "République juive"* (Paris: Fayard, 1988), 202–3.

16. J. Grand-Carteret, *Les Moeurs et la caricature en France* (Paris: A La Librairie Illustré, 1888).

17. Ibid., 275.

18. Charles Baudelaire, "Some French Caricaturists," in *The Painter of Modern Life and Other Essays,* ed. and trans. Jonathan Mayne (New York: De Capo, 1964), 181–82.

19. J. J. Grandville, *Un Autre Monde* (Paris: Fournier, 1844).

20. Baudelaire, "Some French Caricaturists," 182.

21. Ibid., 183.

22. Ibid.

23. J. F. Champfleury, *Histoire de la caricature moderne* (Paris, 1865), 302.

24. Rigolboche, *Mémoires de Rigolboche* (Paris: E. Dentu, 1860), 70.

25. Harry Levin, *The Gates of Horn* (New York: Oxford University Press, 1963), 27.

26. Léon Rosenthal, *Du Romantisme au réalisme* (Paris: Macula, 1987), 207.

27. Charles Baudelaire, "L'Idéal," in *Oeuvres complètes* (Paris: Editions du Seuil, 1968), 53.

28. *Grandville: Dessins originaux,* 5.

29. Champfleury, *Histoire de la caricature moderne,* 290. Champfleury was writing about Grandville's allegorical figures in which women (Grandville's wife and her friend were models) represented France and Liberty. According to Champfleury, the images presented women as "cold and glacial dolls." It is probable that Baudelaire was also referring to these allegorical pictures. This itself is a problem of seeing—or rather of not seeing. It is significant that neither of these critics saw the pictures of metamorphosed animal-humans as being about gender. The female figures were apparently not female to them, for reasons this essay addresses.

30. In this photograph, the "American girl" (model Jinx Allen) runs a gauntlet, eyes downcast, one hand clutching a shawl to her bosom, between two rows of lounging men, all of whom are looking at her. I am sorry to say that Ruth Orkin's estate did not give me permission to reproduce the photograph for what was considered an "editorial" purpose. The formal parallels between it and *The Dog Days* are striking.

31. Champfleury, *Histoire de la caricature moderne,* 394.

32. Françoise Parturier, "Preface," in Honoré Daumier, *Lib Women* (Paris: Leon Amiel, 1974), 22.

33. Therese D. Stamm, *Gavarni and the Critics* (Ann Arbor, Mich.: UMI Research Press, 1981 [1979]), 156.

34. Quoted in Parturier, "Preface," 20.

35. Ibid., 7, 14.

36. John Berger, "Why Look at Animals?" in *About Looking* (New York: Pantheon, 1980).

37. Art Spiegelman, "A Problem of Taxonomy" (letter to the editor), *New York Times Book Review,* December 29, 1991.

38. Art Spiegelman, "Maus," *Tikkun* 7 (September–October 1992), 45.

39. She continued, "We are desensitized equally by the abstract numbers and the small traumas. When 10 million were lost, what are a dozen? Yet without those dozen, where are the 10 million?" Larson, "Of Mice and Men," 65.

40. Johnson, "Art Spiegelman at MOMA," 123.

41. I want to note what can be considered another form of denial. Many of the reviews take as their premise the history of the comics, and have devoted most of their space to this subject, mentioning the Holocaust, or even Spiegelman's relationship with his father, almost as afterthoughts. See especially Buhle, "Of Mice and Menschen"; Freedman, "When It's a Matter of Life and Death"; and Schechter, "Kat and Maus."

In Lieu of a Chapter on Some French Women Realist Novelists
Margaret Cohen

If English realism is unthinkable without English women novelists, the same cannot be said of realism in France. Where are the French Burneys, Austens, Charlotte Brontës, Eliots? During the July Monarchy, the period when men were writing the works that have come to constitute the foundations of the French realist canon, George Sand is the one woman novelist whose name comes down to us today. And both feminist theoreticians and more traditional literary historians agree that, with the exception of Sand's first novel, *Indiana,* her works were markedly hostile to key aesthetic and social facets of the realist project.[1]

Why did women writers not participate in the consolidation of French realism? The answer to this question promises insight into geocultural differences between traditions that previous moments of critical thinking have lumped together as one undifferentiated abstraction, "realism"; into differences between the French and English women's novelistic traditions; and into differences between the material status of women in general and women writers specifically in nineteenth-century England and France. But before we can explain the reasons for English and French women's asymmetrical relations to realism, we must make sure the problem is correctly posed. Does French women's absence from the canonical roster of realist writers indicate that women writers indeed were not writing realist novels, or are there forgotten works by women that literary histories do not include?

This essay fills in the blank of women's absence from the honor rolls of French realism by excavating women writers' novelistic production when men were laying the foundations of the French realist canon. Did women of the time write novels exploring the same subject matter as nascent realism, post-Revolutionary social relations?[2] If so, I ask, how do their treatments of such basic novelistic elements as plot, character, description, and narration compare with the treatments of these elements in the nascent realism texts? In this chapter, I will thus be using that loose, baggy monster, "realism," in local, descriptive fashion: to designate a set of historically specific narrative strategies. These strategies include extensive descriptions of physical appearance and social setting, omniscient, nondidactic narrators, and plots focused on ambitious quests for love and/or some form of social power working through suspense and revelation.[3] They are found in novels by Balzac, Stendhal, Charles de Bernard, and Félix Davin, and, to a lesser extent, in narratives by Prosper Mérimée and Henri Monnier.[4]

Returning to July Monarchy women's novels, we discover that women do represent post-Revolutionary social relations, but that Sand's ambivalent relation to realism is not the exception but the rule. The majority of her female contemporaries often polemically refused association with the novels of Balzac and Stendhal, and they wrote novels that handle some basic elements of narrative in substantially different fashion.[5] Their novels do, however, share an alternative set of narrative strategies that I will describe in this essay. These novels also share a common thematics. They focus almost exclusively on the ills women experience at the hands of a corrupted social order, what they term "suffering," although, as we will see, they differ concerning this suffering's content and cause.[6] That novels by women were preoccupied with the ills of the feminine condition was the (not always approving) perception of critics of the time. "These ladies (whom I will certainly refrain from naming) will carry on so much they will end up making husbands interesting," wrote Auguste Bussière in an 1843 article titled "Women's Novels." "Doubtless, marriage is a tyranny, and the tyrant must be slaughtered. . . . But as a result of slaughters of this kind, honest hearts, sensitive and gentle minds will eventually tire of seeing the sad head of what was formerly the family eternally dragged to be strung up by the levelers of community."[7]

From my description, the literary historian of the July Monarchy will recognize that women's forgotten novels on post-Revolutionary social relations belong to an important July Monarchy novelistic subgenre that critics termed the "social novel" at the time.[8] The most salient feature of the social novel is a thematics of "suffering." Social novels represent socially induced evils experienced by subjects in dominated social positions. The social novel has close ties to an eighteenth-century sentimental tradition and an explicit moral project; it seeks to put art in the service of social change. With this project, it challenges the classical liberal notion of the aesthetic sphere as separate from other arenas of social life.

It should be stressed that men writing social novels also produced what I shall henceforth be terming the *feminine social novel*.[9] Indeed, they wrote as many social novels on the feminine condition as they did on the sufferings produced by inequalities of class.[10] In this chapter, constraints of space prevent me from extending my description of the feminine social novel that emerges from my survey of July Monarchy women's novels to the feminine social novel as it was practiced by men. Because this comparison is critical to understanding the July Monarchy alignment of gender and genre, I want nonetheless to gesture to its content. There is, to make a long story short, less generic uniformity in works by men. A substantial number of feminine social novels written by men conform to the portrait of the feminine social novel provided in this chapter. Some novels by men, however, mix the generic features I describe with features that are not found in the feminine social novels by women but that are common in other novelistic subgenres of the time, notably what was called *le roman gai,* as well as nascent realism.

In characterizing the feminine social novel, I proceed, as in any generic description, through deduction rather than exhaustion; my generalizations are based on the novels enumerated in note 6. As is common in generic description as well, I begin by positing the generic identity that the argument subsequently describes. My heuristic starting point is a feature of these novels that is immediately striking on first reading: thematic attention to the feminine condition as a social problematic. As in any generic description, too, the relation among novels described will be that of family resemblance; not every feature isolated is found in every text.[11]

This essay, then, is a missing chapter in what might be called the underside of realism's history in France. And the resuscitation of the forgotten feminine social novel is of interest beyond the arena of French literary history. The feminine social novel, like the social novel more generally, is one of the first forms of literature qualified as avant-garde; the term *avant-garde* was itself an invention of French utopian socialism. That women were active in this form of aesthetic productivity is striking given their troubled relation to later avant-garde movements. What is the relation of the feminine social novel to the more celebrated early avant-garde works concerned with the injustices of class? How might female writers or feminine subject matter have helped shape the notion of the avant-garde, a conception of the aesthetic with major impact on twentieth-century art, literature, and radical politics?

A resuscitation of the feminine social novel is also of interest to a feminist archaeology of the liberal public sphere. Whereas women were officially excluded from much of public life, the feminine social novel was one manifestation of July Monarchy women's lively cultural production. What were the details of these women's participation in the public sphere, and how do we relate their participation to the institutional gendering of social space? What might this participation tell us about the way subjects live with dominant social formations, as they negotiate these formations with practices substantially more complex than reigning ideologicial accounts?

Learn, My Gabrielle!

The most obvious unifying feature of the feminine social novel is thematic. The feminine social novel portrays woman as *une victime,* women's "sufferings" wreaked by all manner of social pressures. "Learn, my Gabrielle, that a woman's life is one long suffering" is how a mother describes the situation to her daughter in Tarbé des Sablons's *Roseline.*[12] "Bah! it is only a lengthy fabric of novelized events.—Novelized! Ask those who have suffered if there is any misfortune, any crime that has been invented," runs the epigraph on the cover of Jenny Bastide's 1832 *La Cour d'assises,* a novel that tells the story of a Corinne-like heroine whose sufferings are inflicted by Napoleon, Restoration society, and an ambitious hypocrite named Julien.[13] But the term *thematic* is vague: the feminine social novel's concern with suffering extends from the text's thesis to the twists and turns of the action. We are here in the realm of "plot" as Peter Brooks defines the concept using narrative codes developed by Roland Barthes. "Plot, then, might best be thought of as an 'overcoding' of the proairetic by the hermeneutic, the latter structuring the former into larger interpretive wholes."[14] In the feminine social novel, women's sufferings traverse both the proairetic code (the code of actions) and the hermeneutic code: "The signified has a hermeneutic value: every action of the meaning is an action of truth: in the classic text (dependent upon an historical ideology), meaning is mingled with truth."[15] "Dependent upon an historical ideology": I privilege Barthes's account not only for its influential theoretical status but also because Barthes forged it through reading Balzac, that contemporary of the feminine social novelists long viewed by literary history as the single most important author in the genesis of French realism. The feminine social novel's problematic relation to realism underwrites my attempts to adapt Barthes's description to its practices, for this adaptation requires substantial modification.

Barthes understands the truth at stake in classic narrative to be endowed with a strong psychic component ("at the origin of Narrative, desire"; 88) and with a specific protocol of narrative revelation: "To narrate (in the classic fashion) is to raise the question as if it were a subject which one delays predicating; and when the predicate (truth) arrives, the sentence, the narrative, are over, the world is adjectivized" (76). In the feminine social novel, in contrast, the truth at issue is first and foremost moral, and this morality centers on women's relation to the social whole. At the origin of narrative is a pronouncement on women's social situation as it should and should not be. The novels proclaim this truth from their opening words, inscribing it on their covers, in titles, and in epigraphs, holding it up in tendentious prefaces where the narrator addresses the reader directly and/or uses scenes peopled by recognizable social types to do the didactic work. Caroline Marbouty's *Ange de Spola* opens with both. Marbouty follows a "Préface" structured as a drawing-room dialogue with an "Avant-propos" reiterating the sociomoral stakes of the work to come: "Women's education tends too often to disguise them, to mislead them. . . . If this moral mutilation of woman was doubtless necessary in former social periods, should it not come to an end with progress?—And should not and could not contemporary legislation remedy institutions which are so cruel and so opposed to the happiness of all?"[16] When the novel lacks a preface, the first paragraphs often present the kernel of the sociomoral truth to be elaborated in the subsequent work. Sophie Pannier opens *Un Secret dans le mariage* with a truth that is not universally recognized:

> In the life which Christian civilization has made for women, two types of duty are imposed on them which seem at first glance difficult to reconcile. Thus, on the one hand, modesty, this gentle instinct which would be a grace even it were not a virtue, separates their interior life from their social existence . . . while, on the other hand, marriage, here in accordance with duty, asks that woman have no kind of reserve for he who, becoming master of her fate, has on the interior movements of her soul rights that are not less legitimate, not less sacred, than those which marriage gives him over her actions.[17]

Opening with an overt proclamation of sociomoral truth, these texts interweave hermeneutic and proairetic codes in a fashion differing substantially from the classic text analyzed by Barthes. In the classic text, the hermeneutic and proairetic codes are in opposition, creating a tense forcefield where readerly suspense is produced and maintained: "The dynamics of the text (since it implies a truth to be deciphered) is thus paradoxical. . . . the problem is to *maintain* the enigma in the initial void of its answer; whereas the sentences quicken the story's 'unfolding' and cannot help but move the story along, the hermeneutic code performs an opposite action: it must set up *delays* (obstacles, stoppages, deviations) in the flow of the discourse."[18] Barthes associates the paradoxical overcoding characterizing the classic text with a characteristic protocol of reading. The classic text interpellates the reader through suspense and seduction. But what are the textual dynamics of a narrative whose truth, far from necessitating decipherment, is declared on the opening page?

In the feminine social novel, as in Barthes's classic narrative, narrative movement is occasioned by some form of disorder. The constitutive plot disorder, however, arises not as tension between proairetic and hermeneutic, an event posing an enigma requiring solution, but rather as their mutual reinforcement, an event instantiating the opening kernel of sociomoral truth. The heroine emerges from a private shelter at that age when she traditionally becomes worthy of narrative: when she becomes marriageable, or at least sexually desiring and desirable. In this emergence, which is synonymous with the novel's opening chapters if not opening lines, she encounters the larger social network in a formative trauma, a disastrous meeting with the social that, inflecting Lacan in Althusserian fashion, we might call the moment of *tuché*. Turning the heroine into a suffering victim, this constitutive encounter has determining value for the remainder of the plot. It is the underlying cause of each subsequent episode, and many episodes also repeat it in some form. Rather than delays, jamming, and revelation, the privileged hermeneutic gestures in the feminine social novel are annunciation, emphasis, and repetition, sometimes with variation. Instantiating hermeneutic truth, the proairetic code is ruled by the gesture of emphasis as well.

Caroline ou le confesseur, by the Baronne de Carlowitz, opens with two sociomoral truths: women's mistreatment at the hands of corrupt priests and women's more general brutalization by men. Carlowitz puts the second truth in the mouth of a doctor, a social type who often serves in these novels as the spokesman of correct morality: "If, like me, the apostles had studied anatomy . . . they would have taken pity on the perpetual sufferings which women are subjected to by their fragile physical organization. . . . They would have found in the lack of harmony which exists between women's moral and physical strengths the proof that they have not been created to be the slaves of our brutality."[19] True to the novel's opening theses, the *tuché* that precipitates the narrative is the seduction of Caroline, a pretty and innocent village girl, by an irresponsible priest. This seduction, resulting in an illegitimate child, marks the onset of Caroline's sufferings, starting her on a career that leads from one experience of social mistreatment, almost always by men, to the next. Caroline's misfortunes culminate when, unable to find work or even bread, she goes mad and tries to drown her starving infant son, who is miraculously saved but subsequently dies. Put on trial for murder, she is condemned to death by the father of the priest who seduced her.

Proairetic instantiates hermeneutic, hermeneutic emphasizes proairetic, but there is also some tension between the two codes.

The heroine, often with the support of a helper figure, also seeks to modify the truth of women's suffering as she struggles against her victimized lot. At these moments, the proairetic code resists hermeneutic enunciation, providing the closest equivalent in the feminine social novel to the paradoxical overcoding of the classic text. This equivalence, however, takes inverted form. It is not the hermeneutic code that jams the forward movement of the action, but rather the code of actions that endeavors to stave off the inevitable recurrence of narrative truth. This relation generates a weaker form of suspense than that found in classic narrative. What we might call resistant actions, actions working against hermeneutic emphasis, commonly not only fail but backfire, fatally producing precisely the consequences they were trying to avoid.

The feminine social novel's emphatic narrative overcoding finds one of its best supports in its typical narrator. These novels abound in first-person documents: letters, life stories both written and spoken, fragments of internal reflections, fragments of reflections noted down for others. But, with the exception of several purely epistolary texts, the feminine social novels surround their first-person documents with the commentary of an omniscient, sentimental, voluble, moralizing, and exclamatory third-person narrator who serves as hermeneutic guide. Occasionally underlining the significance of the first-person documents included in the text, the narrator is above all occupied with reiterating the content and significance of the actions depicted, employing a variety of tropes of hyperbole, emphasis, and foreshadowing. "Poor mother! . . . how she cries in seeing her daughter smile, her daughter who cannot yet foresee anything because she still has suffered nothing," the narrator laments as the heroine's mother watches her daughter embark on a *mariage mal assorti* at the opening to Abrantès's *La Duchesse de Valombray*.[20] Such foreshadowing helps generate the weak suspense previously described. How, the reader wonders, can the action to come possibly justify the hermeneutic buildup it has received?

In classic narrative, according to Barthes, there is a structural moment identified with closure: the moment when proairetic and hermeneutic codes meet. The feminine social novel lacks any such moment, and closure often poses a problem in these texts. The problem is in part a result of the nature of these novels' narrative work. If the overcoding of hermeneutic and proairetic creates an effect of emphasis, what standard determines when that emphasis is enough? Often, these novels are surprisingly short, as if, having reiterated several times the truth of women's sufferings, the narrative has no other task to perform. Sometimes, in contrast, they stretch in episodic fashion across two or three volumes. Whatever their length, the novels end abruptly. As the back cover approaches, the heroine either finds happiness or, more commonly, withdraws from society through retreat, madness, or death. There is at most a chapter serving as postmortem. In the last sentence of *Caroline,* Caroline has "just climbed onto the fatal cart" that is to take her to her place of execution (316).

The feminine social novel's emphatic overcoding solicits a different form of reader response from the seduction of the classic text. The actions narrated constitute concrete examples proving the opening kernel of narrative truth. At the same time, the detailing of these actions allows the reader to experience vividly the truth declared abstractly, to know it not only through the head but through the heart (these novels substitute a tripartite head/heart/senses distinction for the Cartesian mind/body divide). To appeal to both the head and the heart is an exemplary didactic gesture; "learn [*apprends*], my Gabrielle" serves as fit emblem for the readerly interpellation solicited by these texts. Tarbé des Sablons explicitly describes correct novel-reading as a process of learning in *Roseline*'s preface: "In painting some scenes from domestic life, we have had no desire other than to be useful and to pave the way for solid reflections. These reflections are born from experience enacted [*mise en action*]; experience we can profit from in a rather different way than from that derived through reasoning alone."[21] Throughout their commentary, the narrators reiterate that their stories have three goals: to demonstrate, to move, and to improve.

Soliciting the reader's emotional response in the service of instruction, these novels evince their continuity with the eighteenth-century aesthetico-moral discourse of sympathy.[22] In particular, they pursue a *topos* familiar from the sentimental novel that, in the first part of the nineteenth century, was linked with women both as writers and readers. Thus, Tarbé des Sablons's preface to *Roseline* echoes closely such statements as Madame Beccary's that the novel would offer "a 'tableau' which would always be 'a good example to represent to young people.' "[23] But Tarbé des Sablons's enunciation of the improvement that the reader gleans from the feminine social novel is uncommonly faithful to the past. July Monarchy feminine social novelists more often rework the didactic commonplaces of the sentimental tradition according to a characteristically post-Revolutionary understanding of the social function of the aesthetic.

This reworking is evident in the prefaces, where novelists put forth their ambitions in most concentrated form. While Tarbé des Sablons evinces her continuity with earlier aesthetico-moral discourse by presenting *Roseline* as aiming to educate the individual, feminine social novelists generally rather voice concern with improving the position of women as a collective social group. Stating their interest in soliciting sympathy, they justify this effort not as a means to stimulate the imitation of virtuous actions, but rather to help alleviate the pitiable sufferings they represent. The Countess Dash's opening to *Un Mari* is typical: "This is almost all women's fates. And they are accused and cursed! Oh! if people [*on*] were aware of their sufferings, if they were present at their battles, if they knew all the struggles they have to survive, the sympathies of pity would replace reproach, and they would say with Christ: let he who is without sin throw at them the first stone."[24]

The nature of the social intervention solicited by the novels differs from text to text. Whereas Dash is concerned with provoking that collective social *on* to abandon its stance of moral condemnation, Charlotte de Sor lays her emphasis on consoling women for their unhappy lots. In her preface to *Madame de Tercy,* she writes: "What belongs to me is the thought of throwing some consolation to the sharp sufferings of the heart. . . . I will say to us weak women: Let us have faith to withstand the betrayal of our generous illusions; to undergo the injustices and the demands of the society which has made us so wretched."[25] In the introduction to *Ange de Spola,* in contrast, we have seen Marbouty endow narrative with interventionary political function, as she calls for legal modification in women's condition. Whatever the nature of the intervention solicited, the feminine social novel recasts the sentimental understanding of literature's improving function in the direction of collective social change. In doing so, it transforms the sentimental tradition in the direction of the avant-garde understanding of the aesthetic concerned, as Peter Bürger points out, with overcoming the liberal distinction separating the aesthetic from other arenas of social production. The feminine social novel thus makes visible a conceptual continuum between pre-Revolutionary aesthetics and that post-Revolutionary notion of the aesthetic with arguably the single greatest impact in the nineteenth and twentieth centuries. This continuum is effaced by the avant-garde's subsequent rejection of sentimental discourse and its militant identification with aesthetic innovation and/or a social order that has yet to be made.

The feminine social novel was only one form taken by the "literature of ideas," as July Monarchy polemic also characterized literature in the service of social change.[26] Because the didactic quality of this literature is off-putting today, it is worth stressing that the "literature of ideas" enjoyed valorized aesthetic status at the time. In the arena of the novel, it constituted one of *the* major trends competing for dominance during a period when the novel was in a state of tremendous generic chaos. When Pierre Augustin Eusèbe Girault de Saint-Fargeau sketched the contours of the contemporary novelistic landscape in his 1839 *Revue des romans,* a two-volume work subtitled *Recueil d'analyses raisonnées des productions remarquables des plus célèbres romanciers français et étrangers contenant 1100 analyses raisonnées, faisant connaître avec assez d'étendue pour en donner une idée exacte, le sujet, les personnages, l'intrigue et le dénouement de chaque roman,* his introduction recognized two major novelistic trends:

> Writers are separated into two camps, march under two banners: here literature is treated as a means of distraction, there as a means of direction; the former are not concerned with any goal; the latter, under the influence of an idea, march towards a proof; the former are satisfied with entertaining, interesting; the latter claim to entertain, interest, and instruct.[27]

False Position, Woman's True Role, Two Types of Duty

Because the narrative truth at issue in the feminine social novel is sociomoral in content, the hermeneutic code is marked by tendentious ideological polemic. The nature of this polemic ranges across a spectrum that, for economy of discussion, I designate as running from left to right.[28] On the left end of the spectrum are the texts that cast women's suffering in explicitly feminist terms, saturated with the rhetoric of utopian socialism, and often sounding a call for legal and political change. Texts on the right end of the spectrum manifest allegiance to domestic ideology and Catholic morality; sometimes they speak approvingly of the church and of the monarchy. The range between the two positions is broad. Texts in the center attribute women's suffering to their gender-specific oppression, which must be alleviated, but they disassociate this concern from any overtly feminist position. Several social issues that are the subject of contemporary public discussion, however, run through the novels whatever their *parti pris*. These issues include women's education, the problems posed by women's legal and economic minority in July Monarchy society, and the difficulties of the *mariage mal assorti,* tied in many texts to the question of whether divorce should be reinstituted.

As a consequence of the mirroring relation between hermeneutic and proairetic codes, ideological tendentiousness plays an integral role in shaping plot. The heroine's opening disastrous meeting with the social takes one of three constitutive forms, depending on whether the novel is situated on the left, right, or center of the ideological spectrum. The *tuché* of the *false position* is typical of novels on the left, characterizing the onset of narrative movement in writings by Marbouty, Tristan, Stern, Monborne, and Dupuis, as well as in Arnaud's *Clémence* and Allart's *Settimia.* I take the phrase *false position* from *Une Fausse Position,* an 1844 novel by Marbouty. "My position is so difficult," Marbouty's heroine, Camille, laments. "Like all those that society tolerates and does not legalize," she is told by a benevolent doctor.[29] The doctor's reply evinces the accepted July Monarchy usage of the term: to designate a noncriminal but unsanctioned sociomoral position. In the novel of the false position, narrative movement starts when the heroine assumes "the position of women when they fatally leave the ordinary route" (1:96). A heroine who falls into this position may be seduced from or lose a happy parental home. She may be forced out of the domestic sphere when her husband dies, sometimes ruined, or when he commits a betrayal that itself draws the larger fabric of society into the home. Women actively choose the false position for only one reason: to follow an artistic career. This choice is made by Maréquita, Romantic singer of Spanish origins who is the heroine of Tristan's *Méphis,* and Clémence, the gifted painter of Angélique Arnaud's *Clémence.* And even these choices turn out to be the result of some disastrous *tuché* preceding the opening of the narrative. In the course of *Clémence,* Arnaud's heroine tells of being raped in her youth by the father of her best friend.

The *tuché* of the false position is the disorder both occasioning and maintaining narrative; the heroine suffers its bitter consequences to the end. She may try to right it in failed resistant actions, or simply to survive its psychological, moral, and economic toll. When *Une Fausse Position* opens, Camille has left a *mariage mal assorti* with a husband who does not love her for a lover, and has then been left by this lover for his career. Finding herself without economic resources in an equivocal moral position, Camille defiantly sets out to support herself. As she subsequently puts it, observing workers going off to their jobs: "And I, too . . . I will work—and like them, I will have, because it is necessary, the courage of my position" (1:242). But Camille quickly discovers that, in contrast to the worker whose social position is validated by his labor, seeking work places the bourgeois woman in a sociomoral catch-22. Camille is constantly refused work on the grounds of moral depravity; evidence of this depravity is the fact that she is seeking work in the first place.

In the course of her efforts to escape her false position, Camille passes from artist to woman of letters celebrated by high society and then disgraced, to nun, to suicidal, and back to rehabilitated woman of letters before a final plunge into madness. Both her peripatetic circulation and her end are exemplary of novels of the false position. These features are in part motivated by ideological concerns. Overwhelmingly, these novels stress that there can be no true position for women outside marriage, not because such a position is inherently evil, but because society accords women such a disempowered position that they cannot survive without the protection of men. Women's position becomes all the more desperate in novels where the "ordinary route" of marriage and children is itself depicted as one more false position. In these works, the "ordinary route" that women "fatally" leave turns out to be an ideological fiction to which *no* woman's lived experience corresponds (*fatalement* is a French word meaning both fatally and inevitably). *Une Fausse Position* is such a text; Marbouty puts her most trenchant analysis of the situation in the mouth of a battered working-class wife. "I have no more rights, and I still have responsibilities! Oh! Ma'am, suffering teaches many things to women. . . . I have suffered so much in the past four years that I ask myself what is this thing called law; if it has been created to help us or to mislead us, we poor women who know nothing about it" (1:297).

On the other end of the ideological spectrum are texts where narrative movement is occasioned by the *tuché* of a *woman's true role*. This form of trauma characterizes works by Dash, Tarbé des Sablons, Desves, Junot d'Abrantès, and Ancelot's *Gabrielle*. I take the phrase from an exemplary novella by Alida Savignac, *Le Rôle d'une femme: tout pardonner*.[30] Novels of a woman's true role begin when the heroine emerges from the private space of the family, often from a loving maternal education, to encounter the social as the pressure to conform to false femininity. This confrontation is usually catalyzed by entrance into marriage, generally *mal assorti*. With her marriage, Suzanne, the heroine of *La Duchesse de Valombray*, is launched on "a new existence, a worldly life, rich, noisy, with only this one safeguard [*sic*] . . . . her heart and her innocence" (1:10). The heroine's sufferings in the novel of a woman's true role consist in her efforts to resist the socially imposed pressure to false femininity, a pressure commonly exacerbated by her husband. The novel of a woman's true role, like the novel of the false position, is characterized by a negative representation of *le monde*. *Le monde* is a corrupt but powerful judge of sociomoral worth, and often encapsulates the abuses women suffer in society more generally. In contrast to the novels of the false position, however, the heroine's position in the novels of a woman's true role is not judged hopelessly false but rather only undervalued. The heroine is consequently more often able to reap some form of novelistic reward within this society and life.

The third type of disastrous encounter with the social structures novels from the middle-left to the middle-right of the ideological spectrum. It includes the remainder of the works listed in note 6. This encounter can be termed the *tuché* of *two types of duty*, echoing the opening lines of Pannier's *Un Secret dans le mariage*: "In the life which Christian civilization has made for women, two types of duty are imposed on them which seem at first glance difficult to reconcile." In the novels of two types of duty, the heroine usually emerges from the private into contact with society on the occasion of an impending marriage. This emergence catches her in a conflict between varying duties that can be schematized as opposing the values of the private to her public social role.

The novels of two types of duty generally represent the split between public and private duty in gendered terms. The values of the private are allied with that July Monarchy organ privileged as the site of feminine wisdom, the heart. The heroine has absorbed these values in her youth in a private sphere that these novels consistently code as feminine, constituted by the mother-daughter dyad, a happy convent education, or sometimes occupied by the daughter alone. The values of the social collective are most often introduced into this private feminized space through the intermediary of a man: the father or some father figure, who is a spokesman for collective social duty, and who usually presses the daughter into a loveless marriage that often coincides with his own ambition. "The will of my father" and "the affections for which nature had formed me" is how Merlin's heroine describes her two types of duty difficult to reconcile in the *Histoire de la soeur Inès,* a novel in which the masculine self-interest associated with the imperative to collective duty appears in starkest form.[31] Merlin's novel varies the standard terms of the opening *tuché* by transforming the heroine's loveless marriage into her entrance into a convent, which the father decrees in order to preserve his property for a male heir. *Un Secret dans le mariage* opens with another variation on the public/private conflict, where a woman's privacy of sentiment is opposed to her duty to tell all to her husband, "master of her destiny" according to the laws of the society in which she lives (1:4).

Le monde is thus portrayed in these novels, too, in negative fashion, often helping to hold the heroine in a loveless situation despite her private inclination to flee. Nonetheless, *le monde* is less unremittingly evil than in the novels of a false position or a woman's true role. Duty to the social collective is endowed with crucial moral value. The problem is defining its specific parameters and its relation to the duties of the heart. Feminine social novels of two types of duty are those that enter with greatest frequency into July Monarchy debate on whether to reinstitute divorce.

As in the other two types of novels, the constitutive *tuché* in the novel of two types of duty is the disorder determining narrative movement to the end. Throughout the novel, the heroine will struggle to resolve the two types of duty. This struggle generally ends in failure; the double bind of irreconcilable duties is the exemplary Hegelian tragic situation. Even when a happy ending occurs, it fails to reconcile the two terms of the double bind. Rather (this is the case for novels of the false position, too), some *deus ex machina,* generally a benevolent man, appears to facilitate the heroine's exit from social pressure in a more sentimentally fulfilled fashion than death or religious retreat. Tullie-Moneuse's *Trois ans après* tells the story of Marguerite Ruviès, locked by her ambitious father in a *mariage mal assorti.* As a result of her unhappy marriage, Marguerite will spend time in prison for adultery she did not commit. Nonetheless, the novel takes its title from its happy end, portrayed in a chapter titled "Conclusion," situated "three years later" in a pastoral, almost fantastic setting: "On the banks of the Génil, in the beautiful country of Grenada, not far from Baza, is a valley delightfully sown with some fairylike dwellings."[32] "You do not regret anything, my friend? your country, your family, your social position, am I then all that to you?" Marguerite asks her husband, Maurice, a man who has given up all other social ties to share with her an exiled life. Maurice answers: "Have I not united in you all my affections, are you not my treasure, my honor, my country and my family?" (362).

Still So Pure Despite Her Fault

Soliciting our sympathy and compassion, the suffering heroines in these texts are "interesting" according to the sentimental use of the term.[33] In *Virtue's Faults,* April Alliston suggests that the sentimental heroine lays claim to interest through exercising a very particular sort of virtue:

> The virtue of eighteenth-century heroines . . . does not consist, like manly virtue, in the performance of good deeds or serviceable actions, but rather in the avoidance of fault. The imperative to avoid fault . . . leads to the avoidance of anything resembling a deed, since actions necessarily involve consequences and the responsibility for them. Hence the classical virtue of agency is replaced with a feminine virtue of suffering both in the current sense and in the earlier

one of passively suffering the action of others. . . . heroines are interesting when they are victims.[34]

Another aspect of the sentimental heroine important for delineating her nineteenth-century descendant is her reluctance, particularly in France, to handle money. And although sexual chastity is not sufficient to define a sentimental heroine's virtue, it is a common necessary condition.

In the nineteenth-century feminine social novel, too, heroines are suffering victims. But their patterns of behavior have changed. The heroines in these texts constantly initiate action, whether to resist the demoralizations of the false position, to navigate the problem of conflicting duties, or to choose between true and false femininity. These actions, moreover, often backfire, putting the heroines at fault in the eyes of society and sometimes in the eyes of the narrator, and even occasionally leading to crime. Caroline tries to drown her son; in Bastide's *La Cour d'assises,* the Corinnian heroine stabs the Lucile-like woman her Lord Nelvil equivalent leaves her to marry (she inflicts only superficial wounds). In addition, heroines who lose their income, as is common in novels from the center to the left of the ideological spectrum, courageously confront the problem of supporting themselves, although they discover few choices at hand. The only path open to women with any ambition is that of artistic *gloire.* Alternatively, economic need may lead the heroine into a wealthy but ultimately unhappy *mariage mal assorti.* When these venues are not available, she adopts the traditional, sentimental pursuits of genteel poverty: sewing, private instruction, working as a governess or lady's companion. Should such activities fail to allow her to make ends meet, she may be forced to take a cut in class and work as a servant.

The heroine of the feminine social novel is not sexually innocent; these are not narratives of a young lady's entrance into the world. Rather, we are here in the realm of what the Harlequin Romances call "a second chance at love," more precisely a first chance at love, a second chance at sex. The heroine has in many cases achieved her initial sexual knowledge in an unhappy situation of disparate power relations, seduced, raped, or pressed by her father into a *mariage mal assorti.* Cases when she has been seduced are prime instances when the heroine is judged at fault by both society *and* the narrator. But, as Monborne's *Deux Originaux* demonstrates, this fault in no way makes her unworthy of "interest" (*Deux Originaux* is a rare novel of the false position that ends happily). The novel tells the story of the imaginative, naïve Léonie, seduced and made pregnant by her brother Gustave's scheming secretary. Horrified, Gustave casts her out of the house. Monborne, however, pointedly portrays Gustave as a philanthropist who, spending his time and money giving charity to men of the working class, is unable to extend his republican *fraternité* to his sister in need. The stance that Monborne rather condones is exemplified by a friend of Gustave's named Dulaur. "Moved, he contemplated the gentle and beautiful face of Léonie; this pale countenance filled with a charm which cannot be explained but which interests deeply. He thought with emotion that this young girl still so pure despite her fault, so humble and so frank in her repentance, could stand up again noble and strong to walk with assurance in life."[35]

Meditating on the case of Léonie, Dulaur indicates where these novels assign the principal responsibility for moral lapse: "Like the weak plant taken too soon from the protective hothouse, she withers prematurely; but soon gets back her sap and vigor under the benevolent care of an able gardener" (334). Blame falls on some aspect of the victim's environment, be it her education, her class position, the evil nature of *le monde,* current French law, or men's power over women in current French society (the last two factors are often related). And these novels are not shy about assigning blame. Passing judgment is part of the narrator's emphatic work. Characters within the text often reiterate this gesture as well. The tone of a lawyer addressing one of the multiple adulterous characters in Carlowitz's *Le Pair de France* is exemplary:

"Next to the coffin of Francesca, next to the coffin of the duke, I cursed the fanatical obstination which has refused to allow the reestablishment of divorce. You force me to curse it again; it is more guilty than you! How many existences has it already broken! How many people who would have been able to become virtuous husbands and wives have found themselves drawn into crimes!"[36]

"Still so pure despite her fault": If the heroine does not claim our interest for the same reasons as her sentimental predecessor, in what does her value consist? Does she occupy any positive moral territory of her own or does her appeal lie simply in her suffering state? The case of Léonie is instructive; Dulaur decides on her purity only after observing a scene between Léonie and her friend, Mina. Mina is Gustave's intellectual, virtuous ward who is engaged to him but who has put off their marriage until he revokes his condemnation of his sister. In the scene between the two friends leading Dulaur first to realize Léonie's worth, Léonie is telling Mina to forget about her and marry Gustave:

> Guilty sister, I have destroyed the peace and happiness of my brother! . . . Friend with neither courage nor virtues, I come to trouble your love for him! . . . No, I must not suffer this! . . . Let me take refuge in one of those solitary asylums where religion holds a helping hand out to repentance and comforts sorrow. . . . the picture of your happiness will be the recompense for my sacrifice. (332)

Despite her depiction of herself as a friend without courage, Léonie here displays what Marbouty calls "the courage of . . . [her] position" (1:242). Dulaur's interest is aroused at the moment that Léonie accepts her past actions and offers to take their painful consequences, rather than sacrificing Mina's happiness to her own. In addition, Léonie pardons Gustave for his behavior, as she smooths over Mina's position caught between estranged brother and sister.

The effect of Léonie on Dulaur is characteristic. The interest of the feminine social novel's heroine resides in what the novel points to as her moral authenticity, her efforts to refuse a reactive position, make choices independent of their consequences or success, seek the most suitable course of action under highly imperfect circumstances (the emphatic narrator often explicitly holds the heroine up for our admiration at moments of high moral effort). Virtue, although not to be sneered at, takes second place to a quality repeatedly termed "courage"; these suffering victims are in their own way *femmes fortes*. "Madame de Staël painted women dying for prejudices; our period, more advanced, paints women who bravely defy prejudices," Hortense Allart writes in the preface to *Settimia*.[37] Her statement proposes the courageous heroine as the principal modification that July Monarchy feminine social novelists work on the influential writings of their illustrious predecessor.

It is striking how often the word *courage* recurs to qualify these heroines' morally authentic stance. Even Caroline, who loses her reason for a good part of the novel, and hence her ability to make moral choices, will be granted the "courage" of her position before she dies. She recovers her sanity in time to realize the full consequences of her action and to denounce her inhuman judge. "I am only a weak woman! My *courage* here is like supernatural forces lent by the delirium of fever," she declares (293; emphasis added). And such moral authenticity is not synonymous with self-denial or denial of this world. In Tristan's *Méphis,* one test of Maréquita's courage is her ability to declare her sexual love for the hero, Méphis. Tristan comments on the difficulty of this behavior, "To give herself, a woman must feel very strong! In letting herself be taken as if subjugated by the power of the man, she reserves herself an excuse toward *le monde,* she persuades herself in her own eyes that she has been seduced."[38]

Tristan proceeds to project a better future, when woman will "free herself from the approbation of others" (2:145). In its fascination with courage, the feminine social novel tries to help women into such a brave new world. It struggles with how to make women into autonomous ethical subjects, ready to assume the same rights and responsibilities as men. This is an issue with evident political and legal implications, which are, however, made explicit only in texts on the left end of the feminine social novel's ideological spectrum. The word *courage* is well suited to capture the non-gender-specific notion of ethical value at stake. The term has its etymological roots in the feminized heart, *cor, coeur.* At the same time, the historical use of *courage* associates the term with the traditional masculine prerogative of bold initiative, audacious action.

Diverse Forms of Moral Beauty

The feminine social novel's interest in courage informs a recurrent feature of its narrative construction: the doubling or even tripling of its heroines. Through such doubling, these novels underline that the quality of courage is irreducible to any one feminine social situation or type. Arnaud makes explicit that doubling serves this function in her feminine social novel characterized by a pair of heroines, *Coralie l'inconstante.* Describing the effects of passionate, active Coralie and her bookish, melancholy, passively suffering, and sensitive cousin, Hélène, on the town society around them, Arnaud writes: "In showing themselves equally chaste, graceful and interesting for the soul and for the eyes, but so diversely charming, these young women seemed to have the mission to prove that physical beauty, like moral beauty, takes diverse and contrasting forms."[39] Paralleling physical and moral beauty, Arnaud underscores another recurrent feature of these texts. Feminine social novels often emphasize the diversity of moral beauty by drawing a sharp contrast on the physical plane. Coralie is dark haired and dark eyed, small and slender; Hélène is fair, tall, and buxom.

The doubling of heroines is found in novels across the ideological spectrum. In moral nuancing that may seem surprising given their confidence in the existence of a woman's true role, novels on the right end of the spectrum, too, stress that feminine moral worth is not reducible to any one type. Indeed, Tarbé des Sablons gives us not two but three heroines in *Roseline*. Whereas the frail, highly sensitive Amicie is receptive to the sentimental sufferings of others, the strong, energetic, practical Gabrielle is adept at doing material good works. The novel also includes in its pantheon of true womanhood the intellectual, artistic, self-controlled, self-sacrificing Valentine.

Such diversity of moral beauty, however, does not extend to the male characters who serve as the heroine's foils. Rather, three opposing types of men imbued with fixed moral value grace the pages of the feminine social novel across the ideological spectrum. The hero of Arnaud's *Coralie l'inconstante,* Abel Darcourt, exemplifies the slightly rigid "moral beauty" of the feminine social novel's ideal man:

> "How he showed himself gentle and benevolent, how he was discreet, good, and sensitive!" . . . Mr. Abel Darcourt was one of those rare young men who would be the subject of laughter in our mocking society if they did not force it to admiration. He worked incessantly, never gambled, and had never once been drunk; he spoke to a girl of the people with as much respect and courtesy as to a high lady; even his glances were discreet." (1:32)

The ideal man is opposed to two types of antiheroes. There is the cold, materialistic older man of *ancien régime* morality, skilled in the ways of *le monde* and often joined with the heroine in a *mariage mal assorti.* Lower yet on the moral scale is a frankly corrupt seducer who offers the heroine a wrong way to exit from unhappy marriage. A handsome, dissimulating, young *arriviste,* the seducer makes explicit all that is a woman's nightmare in that darling of much twentieth-century criticism on the realist novel, Julien Sorel (sometimes with emphatic allusion). Thus, the Corinne-like Laurentine in *La Cour d'assises* is led astray by Count Julien de Berville, adopted son of Beaumarchais whom the playwright found as a baby when he was returning from the opening night of "*Tarrare,* the least good of his plays despite the noble lessons of equality that he gives there" (1:109). These consummate hypocrites are the closest the feminine social novel comes to melodrama (aside from the hyperbolic, sentimental rhetoric that both share), for they are often endowed with an intense and seemingly unmotivated urge to persecute their suffering female victims. But this irrational urge to persecution is, in fact, a ruse of the social; the ambiguous paternity of Julien de Berville points to its unvarying source. These novels ground such evil behavior firmly in the corrupted modern values of the capitalist bourgeoisie. The seducer, then, has more affinity with the courageous heroine than at first it might seem. Both characters belong to the middle terrain of society, an entity made by men and that can hence be changed by men (and women?), rather than to a Manichean world of moral absolutes.

The only variations on these male types occur when their attributes are mixed. The mixing results in morally mixed characters, as the valences of these attributes would seem to be sufficiently fixed so as not to be susceptible to any modification. There are characters who mix the rectitude of Abel Darcourt with Julien-like ambition. They are exemplified by the heroes in novels on the left end of the feminine social novel's ideological spectrum who try, and inevitably fail, to enlist the heroine into their grand political schemes.[40] Sometimes these characters mix the Julien and Abel types in less favorable fashion. They often start off seeming like Abel but turn out to possess a large share of Julien-like ambition and hypocrisy, particularly after they have charmed the heroines into marrying them. The mixed Julien-Abel type often falls prey to the manipulation and/or seduction of the feminine social novel's female counterpart to the Julien figure, an older, corrupt woman embodying all that is shallow and empty in *le monde*. In Pannier's *Un Secret dans le mariage,* Ernest de Charmançay allows himself to be beguiled by the Baronne de Miremont, belonging to that category of "beings who are miserly, greedy, lazy, vain, and meticulous, and also women who are envious, jealous, and meddlesome" (1:124). Occasionally, however, the mixing of male types works as a vehicle of masculine redemption. The rich, older man to whom a young woman is married in a marriage of convenience can turn out to be endowed with a feeling heart.

A Light Touch

In a review of Virginie Ancelot's *Gabrielle,* the eminent critic Gustave Planche objected:

> We know too much about Gabrielle's physical person, we know too little about the heart that directs her conduct. It is unfortunate that Madame Ancelot, in sketching Gabrielle . . . felt obliged to insist on all the visual details of her model. . . . these details, which I find charming in a painting and pleasing in an English vignette, are of only mediocre interest to me in a narrative.[41]

Planche's reaction to Ancelot's emphasis on "the visual details of her model" belongs in part to July Monarchy polemic around nascent literary realism, whose defining characteristics critics already associated with extensive attention to external detail.[42] But his comments may also be the product of disappointed generic expectation. In dwelling extensively on the heroine's physical attributes, Ancelot transgresses the feminine social novel's standard treatment of sense impression in general and visual appearance in particular. In these novels, primary narrative attention is usually devoted not to the externals of the protagonists but rather to "the heart that directs" their conduct. When external details are mentioned, they are treated in restrained, impressionistic fashion. On the cover of *Deux Originaux,* Monborne placed an epigraph from Pope that well sums up the descriptive method that the feminine social novel prefers (I provide a prose translation): "To trace such pictures requires neither firmness of hand nor vigor of brush. It is enough to be able to place here shadow and there light, with a light touch [*touche légère*]." The feminine social novel manifests descriptive restraint in its treatment of social landscapes as well as in its treatment of characters.

The opening paragraph to Arnaud's *Coralie l'inconstante* exemplifies these novels' typical *touche légère*. I choose it in part because this novel's handling of description was praised by Sand.[43]

> The sun of the first day in April had risen pure and radiant on the small town of R. . . . It was a Sunday; mass was ringing out from the great parish, and the monotonous vibrations of the bell seemed to protect the innocent confidences which were being exchanged in a house neighboring the church.
>
> —You read only serious and sad works, Mister Abel, said a beautiful girl, blonde and calm, to a young man who had come to get some books from her *cabinet de lecture*. Well! you are the only one of our subscribers whose tastes agree with mine. I do not know if I should be glad, despite the charm one always feels in meeting sympathies; for to like the authors whom you choose, it is necessary to have suffered. (1:3)

In her first sentences, Arnaud calls a novelistic universe into being with a minimum of physical details. The details serve less to locate a highly individualized slice of social reality than to resonate with the moral and affective content of the scene evoked. Mention of the morning sunlight and the gravity of the bells serves to sanctify the melancholic solemnity of Hélène and Abel's nascent love. The physical presence of the hero is not sketched at all, but rather indicated metonymically, through his choice of reading. The physical person of the heroine is summoned up with stock adjectives that align her with a recognized "type" rather than specifying her individuality. And we will have to wait tens of pages for some further piece of visual evidence about the heroine's body, which, significantly, is provided through the eyes of an admiring man.

There is one exception to the feminine social novel's characteristically restrained treatment of the physical dimension. The novels enter into extensive description of striking, often sublime, natural scenes at highly charged narrative moments. Thus, Carlowitz precedes Caroline's attempt to drown her child with an extensive description of nature (which I quote only in part):

> A soft, melancholy light illuminates now the whole countryside; the bizarrely varied nuances of the pine forests and the birch woods, the sterile rocks and the enameled fields clash without running into each

other and seem to want to offer the image of the human heart which also unites the most opposing contrasts, for in this abyss whose depths the philosophy of so many centuries has not yet been able to measure, crime touches closely virtue, madness reason, fanaticism gentle confidence and divine goodness. (104)

In stating that nature offers "the image of the human heart," Carlowitz designates the narrative function of this treatment of nature, deviating from the feminine social novel's standard light touch. These descriptions function as one more tool in an arsenal of emphatic techniques, a way to intensify highly charged moral and affective moments that are also high points of narrative peripeteia. Such a use of natural description produces a specific narrative effect: it counteracts the weak suspense offered by the relation of proairetic to hermeneutic code. The brusque intrusion of natural sublimity jolts the reader, focusing attention just in time for the disaster to come.

Does the feminine social novel's refusal to engage in extensive external description have extraliterary stakes? These novels' thematic treatment of external appearance and above all the visual would suggest such a conclusion. Repeatedly, they condemn excessive attention to the external-visual dimension on moral, social, and epistemological grounds. This condemnation emerges clearly in *Coralie*. Arnaud has one pointed exception to her usual light touch, her portrayal of the town beauty, Adine Genevois, wife of the local district attorney. Adine is

a 28-year-old woman, beautiful and well built, but whose figure was starting to thicken with the flesh that is born from a comfortable and lazy life, and whose cheeks, like the flowers grown in a hothouse, lacked life and freshness; but this coloring, slightly livid and nuanced with blue veins, went well with her tired features, and set off strikingly the brilliance of her beautiful eyes; she was half leaning on the back of a small sofa, next to a mirror, and passed her hands slowly through the curls of her fine black hair, all the while casting on her graceful image a languishing and satisfied gaze. (1:41).

In striking contrast to Abel and Hélène, no aspect of Adine's physical person is left in doubt. It is also, however, striking that Arnaud leaves no doubt as to the heart that directs Adine's conduct. Adine is introduced as a *tableau vivant* of *vanitas,* her excessive attention to the visual dimension placed in a negative moral constellation including also gluttony and sloth. Arnaud gives this attention a class affiliation; the life permitting Adine to indulge her negative moral qualities is that of the idle *bourgeoise.* Arnaud also uses the character of Adine to condemn excessive attention to the visual on epistemological grounds. She points out a striking physical resemblance between Adine and Hélène, whose significance is explained by Abel. External appearance is deceiving: "These physical relations precisely where there was so much lack of resemblance between the hearts and minds even caused him [Abel] a painful feeling" (1:100).

A similar thematized critique of sense impression and above all the visual dimension runs throughout the feminine social novel, although it is never worked out in extensive detail. External, above all visual, aspect is implicated in women's harsh condemnation by *le monde,* by the courts, by society at large. Focus on the senses, and the gaze in particular, is often thematized as producing lascivious, improper male desire that precipitates heroines into their suffering state. The hypocritical Julien Sorel figure allows these novels to stress that physical appearances are deceiving. And the visual is sometimes located as the domain where men place women, to the neglect of the reality of their lives.

Such details imply that the feminine social novel's "light touch" has social, moral, and epistemological stakes reaching well beyond matters of literary technique. But to explain satisfactorily these novels' approach to external detail requires further inquiry. It entails looking theoretically at the literary function of description, at comments such as Philippe Hamon's that "description . . . risks compromising . . . the effectiveness of the demonstration. . . . the uncontrollable liberty of the descriptive can go along with the impossibility of controlling the reader's reactions."[44] Hamon's statement is suggestive, given the emphatic overcoding of the feminine social novel previously discussed. As rhetorical technique, description potentially threatens the narrator's control of the hermeneutic dimension and thus the feminine social novel's didactic project. In addition, description must be contextualized within the framework of literary history. What is the status and function of description in the preceding feminine novelistic tradition and in the sentimental novel more generally? How does the feminine social novel position itself in relation to nascent realism, a competing novelistic subgenre for rendering social reality pointedly attentive to the external-visual dimension? Finally, the feminine social novel's use of external description must be placed in relation to women's experience of the visual in other areas of July Monarchy social life, to such issues as how the visual dimension was implicated in the control of feminine sexuality.[45] I raise these questions as a way of returning to the problems with which this essay began. Having resuscitated the forgotten feminine social novel, the next step is to resituate it in literary history and in history more generally.

NOTES

This essay will appear in expanded form in *Why Were There No French Women Realists?* (Princeton, N.J.: Princeton University Press, forthcoming). It owes its existence to April Alliston, who, both in writings and discussion, has helped me to grasp what I initially found to be the opaque codes of a neglected feminine novelistic tradition. See, notably, her illuminating *Virtue's Faults*. Thanks also go to Jann Matlock, for sharing with me her panoramic grasp of the July Monarchy, and to Anne Higonnet, for inspiring dialogue on the contemporary relevance of genre.

1. On Sand and realism, see Naomi Schor's *George Sand and Idealism* (New York: Columbia University Press, 1993). On *Indiana* as a realist novel, see Sandy Petrey, "George and Georgina Sand," in *Textuality and Sexuality: Reading Theories and Practices*, ed. Judith Still and Michael Worton (Manchester: Manchester University Press, 1993).

2. Women novelists of the period also wrote large numbers of historical novels.

3. That these strategies characaterize July Monarchy realism is agreed upon by numerous critics (Auerbach, Lukács, Barthes, Jameson, Heath, and others) who disagree about just what realist novels are doing with them.

4. In associating this list of writers with realism, I follow both twentieth-century literary history and July Monarchy critics, although July Monarchy critics did not conceptualize resemblances among these writers' works as the constitution of a new novelistic subgenre. On the latter subject, see Bernard Weinberg, *French Realism: The Critical Reaction 1830–1870* (New York: Modern Language Association, 1937). Considerations of space force me to bracket a discussion of differences among the July Monarchy writers I have listed as "realist." They also force me to bracket questions about the relation of my local use of realism to more global critical articulations of the term.

5. The novels of Delphine de Girardin are an exception to this generalization.

6. Representative titles of novels by July Monarchy women concerned with women's suffering include Louise Maignaud's *La Fille-Mère* (1830); Jenny Bastide's *La Cour d'assises* (1832), *Pascaline* (1835), and *Elise et Marie* (1838); the Countess Merlin's *Histoire de la soeur Inès* (1832) and *Les Lionnes de Paris* (1842); Madame de Montpezat's *Natalie* (1833); Madame B. Monborne's *Une Victime: esquisse littéraire* (1834) and *Deux Originaux* (1835); Charlotte de Sor's *Madame de Tercy ou l'amour d'une femme* (1836); Aurore Dupin's *Marguerite* (1836); the Baronne Aloïse de Carlowitz's *Caroline ou le confesseur* (1833), *Le Pair de France ou le divorce* (1835), and *La Femme de progrès ou l'émancipation* (1838); Hortense Allart's *L'Indienne*

(1833) and *Settimia* (1836); Madame Tullie Moneuse's *Trois ans après* (1836) and *Régina* (1838); La Baronne de T***'s *Mystère* (1837); Madame Junot d'Abrantès's *La Duchesse de Valombray* (1838); Flora Tristan's *Méphis ou le prolétaire* (1838); Madame Charles Reybaud's *Mézelie* (1839); Mademoiselle Leroyer de Chantepie's *Cécile* (1841); Virginie Ancelot's *Gabrielle* (1836) and *Médérine* (1843); Mademoiselle Touchard-Lafosse's *Les Trois Aristocraties* (1843) and *L'Homme sans nom* (1844); Hermance Lesguillon's *Rosane* (1843); Angélique Arnaud's *La Comtesse de Servy* (1838), *Clémence* (1841), and *Coralie l'inconstante* (1843); Sophie Pannier's *Un Secret dans le mariage* (1844); Madame Tarbé des Sablons's *Roseline, ou de la nécéssité de la religion dans l'éducation des femmes* (1835) and *Zoé, ou la femme légère* (1845); Caroline Marbouty's *Ange de Spola, études de femmes* (1842) and *Une Fausse Position* (1844); the Countess Dash's *Un Mari* (1843); Daniel Stern's *Nélida* (1846); and Alexandrine Desves's *Marie de Kervon ou les fruits de l'éducation* (1847). Among the forty-five novels I have read, I have found only four that do not focus on the feminine condition: Louise Maignaud's *Les Etudians, épisode de la Révolution* (1831); Anne Bignan's *L'Echafaud* (1832), against capital punishment; Sophie Pannier's *L'Athée* (1836), about religious faith; and Clémence Robert's *René l'ouvrier* (1841), about the sufferings of a noble proletarian. In some cases, novels by women portray women's sufferings along with the sufferings of subjects who are in other ways victims of dominant social institutions. Thus, Flora Tristan's *Méphis* compares the vicissitudes of workers and women, showing the differences as well as the similarities between these two kinds of suffering.

7. Auguste Bussière, "Les Romans de femmes," *Revue de Paris* (October 1843): 349. Unless otherwise noted, all translations in this chapter are my own.

8. For a discussion of this nomenclature, see Margaret Iknayan, *The Idea of the Novel in France: The Critical Reaction 1815–1848* (Geneva: Droz, 1961). Karlheinrich Biermann states that "the designation 'social novel' appeared for the first time in 1838, as subtitle to the novel *Méphis ou le prolétaire* by Flora Tristan" (81). The subtitle was not present in the 1838 edition I consulted at the Bibliothèque Nationale. See Biermann's *Literarische-politische Avant-garde in Frankreich* (Stuttgart: W. Kohlhammer, 1982), 81.

9. The only previous critical consideration of the feminine social novel is found in David Owen Evans's *Le Roman social sous la Monarchie de Juillet* (Paris: Presses Universitaires de France, 1930). Performing the invaluable work of keeping these novels' memory alive, Evans approaches them largely in thematic terms.

10. Examples of novels by men on the feminine condition include Ernest Desprez's *Un Enfant* (1833), Etiennez's *Un Droit de mari* (1834), and Louis Couilhac's *Pitié pour elle* (1837). Works by men focusing on the sufferings of men in subordinate class positions include Michel Masson's *Daniel le Lapidaire, contes de l'atelier* (1832), Emile Souvestre's *Riche et pauvre* (1836), and Auguste Luchet's *Le Nom de famille* (1841).

11. A full discussion of this issue would require a theoretical consideration of the enterprise of generic classification as well as a historical examination of July Monarchy readers' horizon of generic expectation. I undertake this discussion in my forthcoming *Why Were There No French Women Realists?* where I also describe men's feminine social novels and situate the feminine social novel in the more general novelistic landscape of the period.

12. Madame Tarbé des Sablons, *Roseline, ou de la nécéssité de la religion dans l'éducation des femmes* (Paris, 1835), 2:235.

13. Jenny Bastide, *La Cour d'assises* (Paris, 1832). Bastide takes her epigraph from Sterne.

14. Peter Brooks, *Reading for the Plot* (New York: Knopf, 1984), 18.

15. Roland Barthes, *S/Z*, trans. Richard Miller (New York: Farrar, Straus & Giroux, 1974), 62.

16. Caroline Marbouty, *Ange de Spola, études de femmes* (Paris, 1842), 1:9.

17. Sophie Pannier, *Un Secret dans le mariage* (Paris, 1844), 1:4.

18. Barthes, *S/Z*, 75.

19. Baronne Aloïse de Carlowitz, *Caroline ou le confesseur* (Paris, 1833), 19–20.

20. Junot d'Abrantès, *La Duchesse de Valombray* (Paris, 1838), 1:2–3.

21. Tarbé des Sablons, *Roseline*, x.

22. On the use of the discourse of sympathy in eighteenth- and early nineteenth-century efforts to expose collective social ills, see Thomas Laqueur, "The Humanitarian Narrative," in *The New Cultural History*, ed. Lynn Hunt (Berkeley: University of California Press, 1989). The feminine social novel differs from the later nineteenth-century naturalism discussed by Lacqueur in treating the suffering body in restrained rather than detailed fashion. A detailing of physical reality is subordinated to an analysis of the suffering *heart*.

23. Cited in April Alliston, *Virtue's Faults; or, Women's Correspondences in Eighteenth-Century Fiction* (Stanford, Calif.: Stanford University Press, forthcoming).

24. Countess Dash, *Un Mari* (Paris, 1843), 1:5.

25. Charlotte de Sor, *Madame de Tercy ou l'amour d'une femme* (Paris, 1836), 1:xi.

26. Describing the "mission of the novel" in the 1836 preface to *Riche et pauvre,* Emile Souvestre writes: "To it [the novel] falls the task to popularize [*vulgariser*] ideas of progress, to personify them, and to make them act, to give them in some measure the authority of example." Emile Souvestre, "Du Roman," *La Revue de Paris* 34 (1836): 121. July Monarchy discussions of the literature of ideas sometimes blur into July Monarchy aesthetic debates on the ideal; for a careful and nuanced representation of the latter debates, see Schor, *George Sand and Idealism*. Schor's account of Sand's idealism can usefully be supplemented by situating Sand against the background of the July Monarchy feminine social novel. As we will see, this instance of the literature of ideas frequently does not conform to an important feature of idealism: feminine social novels often do not idealize in their portrayals of heroines and rarely idealize in their plots.

27. Pierre Augustin Eusèbe Girault de Saint-Fargeau, *Revue des romans* (Paris, 1839), 1:vi.

28. As the history of the French Revolution shows, gender issues are only imperfectly accommodated by such liberal political distinctions.

29. Caroline Marbouty, *Une Fausse Position* (Paris, 1844), 2:224.

30. This tale is found in the 1833 six-volume *Les Heures du soir.*

31. Comtesse Merlin, *Histoire de la soeur Inès* (Paris, 1832), 18, 17.

32. Madame Tullie-Moneuse, *Trois ans après* (Paris, 1836), 359. The conclusion to Sand's *Indiana* constitutes the prototype of this happy end through exit from society.

33. As Alliston writes, "To be 'interested' in the sympathetic sense to come to mean the opposite of to be 'interested' in another equally current, but more strictly self-directed sense, the sense in which one might act from 'interested' motives." *Virtue's Faults.*

34. Ibid.

35. Madame B. Monborne, *Deux Originaux* (Paris, 1835), 333–34.

36. Baronne de Carlowitz, *Le Pair de France ou le divorce* (Paris, 1835), 3:366.

37. Hortense Allart de Méritens, *Settimia* (Paris, 1836), 1:ix.

38. Flora Tristan, *Méphis ou le prolétaire* (Paris, 1838), 2:145.

39. Angélique Arnaud, *Coralie l'inconstante* (Paris, 1843), 2:220.

40. The exceptional proletarian, Méphis, from Tristan's *Méphis,* tries to turn Maréquita into the Woman Messiah, whereas the brooding *carbonaro,* Horace Gramond, attracts the ill-fated love of Arnaud's artist, Clémence. Refusing to fulfill this love, Gramond rather advises Clémence to work on her painting as an instrument of social revolution, but the unhappy Clémence ends up throwing her body in the path of a bullet aimed at Gramond on the barricades of 1830.

41. Gustave Planche, review of *Gabrielle, Revue des Deux Mondes* 17 (1839): 834.

42. On early critical debates around realism, see Bernard Weinberg, *French Realism: The Critical Reaction 1830–1870* (New York: Modern Language Association, 1937).

43. See George Sand to Angélique Arnaud, Paris, beginning of June 1843, in Sand, *Correspondance,* vol. 25 (supplement), ed. Georges Lubin (Paris: Garnier, 1991), 414.

44. Philippe Hamon, *Introduction à l'analyse descriptif* (Paris: Hachette, 1981), 15.

45. For a penetrating discussion of the July Monarchy nexus of realism, the gaze, and the social control of feminine sexuality, see Jann Matlock, *Scenes of Seduction: Prostitution, Hysteria, and Reading Difference in Nineteenth-Century France* (New York: Columbia University Press, 1993).

S/Z, Realism, and Compulsory Heterosexuality
Diana Knight

Is mimetic writing necessarily complicit with the value systems of the society it represents? This is a question that several critics, familiar with the argument of Barthes's *S/Z*, have directly addressed. Christopher Prendergast, for example, in *The Order of Mimesis*, oscillates self-consciously between negative critiques of realism's inherent conservatism—naturalization of the status quo, vehicle of ideological control—and the more optimistic suggestion that mimetic narratives, in explaining the world, offer an important tool for reshaping it.[1] For Naomi Schor, on the other hand, Prendergast's careful overview of mimesis is subsumed as part of a wider problem. Wishing to account for the toppling of George Sand from her original position as a major figure of nineteenth-century literature, Schor blames the overevaluation of Balzacian realism in canonical accounts from Lukács to Barthes, and in such commentators on this tradition as Prendergast. Recent critiques of the legitimating function of representation stop short of questioning the hegemony of the realist paradigm. Schor's own strategy for unsettling the received narrative of nineteenth-century realism is to recuperate Sand's radical idealism as "the only alternative representational mode available to those who do not enjoy the privileges of subjecthood in the real." Thus, it is the excessive preoccupation with realism as a whole, rather than this or that rhetorical device, that reinforces "the phallo- and ethnocentric social order we so often confuse with reality."[2]

Schor is concerned with the gendering of the aesthetic value judgments that shape literary history, and realism emerges as a "masculine mode" in league with a sexist society.[3] Clearly, her repositioning of Sand in these terms is an original and important argument. However, I am less persuaded that sexism is more than a historically contingent feature of the realist paradigm, or that mimesis actually obliges its readers to confuse reactionary social orders with reality. Although it is true that the politically optimistic strand of *The Order of Mimesis* is relatively silent on the nature of the politics that it might enable, I cannot see that Prendergast's lack of attention to gender issues (for example) invalidates claims that mimesis can unsettle the world it represents.[4] It is, after all, the politics of readers and critics—as in the case of feminism at work on perceived phallocentrism—that determine views of what is being constructed or demystified in the first place. Thus (as another example), critiques of the ethnocentrism that Schor mentions in passing would doubtless produce their own evaluation of realist representation. My own chosen perspective, however, is the heterocentrism that Adrienne Rich, addressing the historical naturalization of female heterosexuality, has so usefully labeled "compulsory heterosexuality." If the point of this coercive order is to channel women's emotional and erotic needs away from other women and into marriage and motherhood within the family, it is clear that men, whatever their sexuality, will be positioned very differently in relation to it. Nevertheless, they are just as likely to have internalized it, in ways affecting not just their behavior but their interpretive frameworks.

My starting point is the final section of a book dealing with a subject at the heart of compulsory heterosexuality: Tony Tanner's *Adultery in the Novel*.[5] In linking his ambitious discussion of marriage and adultery to the "contract and transgression" that form the subtitle of his book, Tanner refers in some detail to two passages from *Roland Barthes by Roland Barthes*.[6] The first is Barthes's consideration of the ambiguous values attaching to the contracts that regulate social exchange. Whereas he is always ready to denounce the get-something-in-return accounting of the bad bourgeois contract, Barthes is simultaneously attracted to the neutrality that contracts can introduce into human relationships: "Since the body intervenes directly here, the model of the good contract is the contract of Prostitution. For this contract, declared immoral by all societies and by all systems (except the most archaic), in fact removes the burden of what might be called the *imaginary embarrassments* of the exchange" (59). Tanner proceeds to link this passage somewhat inappropriately to his own argument about adultery:

> Which would seem to leave us, in Barthes's terms, with the perverse ideal of the good contract of prostitution (the reverse mirror image of the bourgeois ideal of a good contract, but arguably the very structure of its bad conscience)—or that something in between contract and prostitution, which I have called adultery or transgression—for an adulteress is a wife who is not a wife, a prostitute who is not a prostitute, the keeper and breaker of the insecure security of the contract of marriage. (375)

But this is a misreading that actually reverses Barthes's point, for the zero-degree bodily exchange of his "good" contract (neither selfish nor self-sacrificing) would be free of transgression and bad conscience. Moreover, Tanner's conflation of wives, prostitutes, and adulteresses fails to recognize that, when read in the context of other fragments of *Roland Barthes,* this contract almost certainly alludes to male homosexual prostitution.[7] It therefore makes little sense to *equate* it with an argument about the complicity of the marriage contract and its transgressions in adultery. That both form part of the heterosexual paradigm, Barthes would agree. But he is trying to situate that paradigm as historically contingent and, in the second passage quoted by Tanner, to pinpoint its naturalization in realist narratives:

> The relation to Narrative (to representation, to *mimesis*) has something to do with the Oedipus complex, as we know. But it also has something to do, in our mass societies, with marriage. . . . Thus marriage affords great collective excitations: if we managed to suppress the Oedipus complex and marriage, what would be left for us to *tell?* With them gone, our popular arts would be transformed entirely. (121)

Tanner's claim, that this comment is "aimed in particular at contemporary mass entertainment" (377), trivializes Barthes's attempt to think *beyond* the complicity of today's collective representations with the social and sexual structures that they represent. Worse, Tanner associates Barthes with his rather trite concluding words, that without the subject of adultery, the history of the novel would have been very different, "and much poorer." His suggestion that adultery introduces a new story into a tired life betrays vicarious approval of the very television interviewer whose attempt to force a hint of infidelity ("the seed of a story") out of a well-known actor had motivated Barthes's comments in the first place. I take Barthes's point to be that without the heterosexist obsession with marriage and adultery, cultural forms might have been very different, and possibly richer rather than poorer.

Tanner's sophisticated reading of Barthes therefore goes astray because he takes a heterosexual frame of reference for granted. Yet Barthes warns against this in the very same text, when he connects clichéd language with denial of the speaking subject's body. He is referring to his analysis of the passage in *Sarrasine* where Zambinella offers to be "a devoted friend [un ami dévoué]" for Sarrasine, thereby unmasking his gender by the use of a masculine form. Sarrasine, misled by the stereotypical formulation, fails to understand. From this retrospective allusion to *S/Z*, Barthes moves to the more general observation: "How many subjects repressed, refracted, blinded as to their true sexuality, *from refusal to let go of a stereotype*" (89–90). The stereotype here can refer only to heterosexuality. But is this what Barthes originally meant in *S/Z*? Given that *Sarrasine* is the singular text from which Barthes draws a very influential account of the workings of realist representation, the answer could have far-reaching effects. I want, therefore, to pursue the implications of viewing *Sarrasine* as a story about the misreading of sexuality, rather than engaging with the more familiar critical narrative of a misreading of gender.[8]

Barthes's point of reference for those who cling to a stereotype was Valéry's allusion to people who die in accidents rather than let go of their umbrellas. This appealing image is an appropriate starting point for another look at the issue of Barthes's supposed "castration reading" of *Sarrasine*, the single-mindedness of which, according to Barbara Johnson, castrates the text itself of its writerly potential.[9] In *S/Z*, Barthes repeatedly links the hermeneutic code with the question-and-answer structure of the Oedipus story. But what *was* the final predicate of the hermeneutic sentence of *Sarrasine*? In Balzac's text the answer is a gap—a foregrounded ellipsis as the narrator's final explanation, "Now you can readily see what interest Mme de Lanty has in hiding the source of a fortune which comes from . . . ," is cut short by Mme de Rochefide's imperious "Enough!" But Barthes leaps in with the missing answer, drawn from his symbolic code: "*SYM. Taboo on castration" (209–10).[10] Despite his original claim not to establish any hierarchy among his five codes, Barthes admits, in his summary of the three "points of entry," that he may appear to have privileged the symbolic field, saturated as it is by the human body (214–16). His attempt to unsettle the ideological plenitude of the readerly text depends upon the general collapse of economies identified here: the loss of a founding origin for economic wealth, the undermining of sexual difference, the falling apart of the orderly antitheses that determine the stability of meaningful representation. Without stable points of reference, the realist system falters—in Barthes's unraveling of *Sarrasine* the body becomes the crucial mediator of that economic and linguistic uncertainty.

The specific focus of Barthes's reading is necessarily the narrator of *Sarrasine,* who operates the would-be stable system of representation, only to see it fall away from him as an effect of the story he tells. Insofar as Barthes is laying the ground for the symbolic castration reading that appears to triumph at the end of *S/Z,* he early on establishes a critical perspective on this narrator by constantly labeling him with the seme of "asymbolism." This interpretive rivalry is set up by Barthes's reading of the set-piece rhetorical antithesis with which Balzac's narrator opens the text. As he sits in his window recess at the Lanty ball, the crucial system of oppositions that the narrator elaborates is held together by his ironically foot-tapping *body.* With his superficial analysis of the atmospheric conditions prevalent at Parisian balls, the narrator tries to deny to himself that he risks catching anything more than a chill:

> The narrator's participation in the profound symbolism of the Antithesis is here ironized, trivialized, minimized by reference to a causation which is physical, vulgar, contemptible: the narrator pretends to reject the symbolic, which in his eyes is a "matter of drafts"; moreover, he will be punished for his disbelief (SEM. Asymbolism). (26)

Even in the face of Mme de Rochefide's distressed reaction to the end of his story (her withdrawal from their supposed amorous contract), the narrator still attempts to pass off his story as a reassuring tale of Italian moral progress ("Those unfortunate creatures are no longer created there"). Again Barthes glosses this as a last, somewhat pathetic, injection of "asymbolism" ("Let us return to earth, to 'reality', to history: there are no more castrati"). So sure does Barthes seem of his reading here that the narrator's rejoinder is dismissed with sweeping sarcasm: "*The disease has been wiped out,* it has disappeared from Europe like the plague, like leprosy; petty proposition, unlikely rampart, absurd argument against the torrential force of the symbolic" (213–14).

However, it is not true that Barthes frames castration by the symbolic code alone, for he variously insists on the overdetermination at work in the conjunction of the symbolic and the hermeneutic codes. In the digression "And/or" he refuses to make a choice between a psychoanalytic code of the symbol (taboo on castration) and an Aristotelian code of poetics (answer held back in the interests of suspense) (76–77). Later, he decides that it is the symbolic reading, if any, that is superfluous, because any latent symbolic castration in this story is already manifest in the literal tale of a physical castration (163–64). Not only does Barthes rehabilitate the reputation of the readerly hermeneutic code here (thus undermining the superior writerly values attaching to the symbolic code), he occasionally adds details to the "nauseous" and outdated cultural codes on the narrator's behalf. Immediately after his ironic attack on the narrator's attempt to seek asymbolic refuge in the solidity of the real world, Barthes elaborates upon the historical code of castrati, thus providing, through his dates, places, and proper names, a fine example of the reality effects that he analyzes (101–2) as the stock-in-trade of the realist novelist:

> . . . REF. History of castrati. The historical code to which the narrator refers informs us that the last two famous castrati were Crescentini, who was given the Order of the Iron Crown after Napoleon heard him in Vienna in 1805 and brought him to Paris, and who died in 1846, and Velluti, who gave his final performance in London in 1826 and died just over a hundred years ago (in 1861). (214)

Other elaborations on castrati are less pedantic. An early digression on the voice, while again filling in information, carries an intertextual reference to Stendhal: "The star castrati are cheered by hysterical audiences, women fall in love with them, wear their portraits 'one on each arm, one at the neck hanging from a gold chain, and two on the buckles of each slipper' (Stendhal)" (109). Later, he exploits the semic code ("SEM. Star") to motivate a mininarrative of the fortunes of Farinelli, "*il ragazzo*":

> Farinelli ("*Il ragazzo*") left England (where he had caused problems for Handel) covered with gold; proceeding to Spain, he cured the mystic lethargy of Philip V by singing to him daily (always the same song, moreover); and for ten years received from the King an annual pension of 14 million old francs; discharged by Charles III, he built himself a superb palace in Bologna. (187)

In a haphazard list of Barthes's everyday tastes, Renaud Camus, a gay French writer who is an astute commentator on Barthes, includes the following: "That he found the word *ragazzo* irresistibly appealing, and that if he had to find a single definition of his sentimental ideal, this was the word he always came back to."[11] That the *ragazzo* is an erotic ideal, and not merely a pleasing signifier, is spelled out by Camus in an earlier allusion to Barthes's preferences: "This is how R. B. would define the ideal object of his desires: 'a *garçon* (but I mean in the strongest sense of the word).' And if pressed a little he would add: 'No, not a *gars,* I'm thinking more of an Italian *ragazzo.*'"[12]

Camus himself makes no connection with Barthes's discussions of Zambinella. However, since discovering this intriguing revelation (whatever its status), I am now unable to read *S/Z* as I used to. Barthes specifically claims that the unmasking of the castrated *ragazzo* behind Zambinella triggers a spectacular blocking of desire: the metaphorical castration that passes from Sarrasine through Mme de Rochefide to the narrator. It is difficult, however, not to feel that the discovery of Zambinella's "identity" must have liberated Barthes's own desires as reader of this text. Take a key moment of Barthes's analysis: the kissing of Zambinella by Sarrasine, upon which Barthes disingenuously dwells in the supposed interests of the theoretical status of first and second readings:

> This retrospective reading bestows inestimable significance upon Sarrasine's kiss: Sarrasine passionately kisses a castrato (or a cross-dressed boy); castration is transposed onto Sarrasine's own body and we ourselves, second-time readers, receive the shock waves. (165)

Castrato or cross-dressed *garçon*? The status of the alternative becomes interesting once we consider that the reader does not have to share Sarrasine's subject position, and that the destruction of Sarrasine's illusory perfect woman could be positive rather than catastrophic.

I want to look in some detail at Barthes's handling of the crucial recognition scene in which Zambinella, in male dress, sings at the ambassador's concert. Here Prince Chigi, Zambinella's first protector, reveals the facts of Zambinella's sexual status to Sarrasine in such a way that he finally understands: "I am the one, monsieur, who gave Zambinella his voice. I paid for everything" (185). Indeed, the truth strikes Sarrasine in suitably castrating fashion: "A horrid truth had pierced his soul. It was as though he had been struck by a thunderbolt" (187). How, at this point, does Barthes handle the naming of this "truth"? In the digression "*Dénouement* and disclosure," he exploits a favorite rhetorical device of endlessly repeating a syntactic structure to generate different readings:

> For the anecdote, the truth is a referent (a real object): *Zambinella is a castrato*. For psychology, it is a misfortune: *I have loved a castrato*. For the symbol, it is an enlightenment: *In Zambinella, it is the castrato whom I have loved*. For the narrative, it is a prediction: *having been touched by castration, I must die*. (187–88)

But this is also a neat device for keeping one's options open. "In any case," Barthes lamely concludes, truth if the finding of the final predicate. However, the digression that precedes this is in fact a lengthy gloss on the first (and supposedly most trivial) possibility on the list. This is the anecdotal, *referential* reading, sparked off by Chigi's confidences: a little speech that is "fatal," according to Barthes, on account of the images it unleashes: "For a start, by designating the boy in Zambinella, it forces Sarrasine to descend from Superlative Woman to the urchin (the crinkly haired Neapolitan *ragazzo*)" (185–86).

Thus the idealized Superlative Woman (end point and foundation of Art), gives way to "a dirty and ragged young lad, on the loose in the poverty-stricken streets of Naples." Barthes is unusually defensive about his elaboration of these images of Zambinella as *ragazzo*, insisting that they are connoted by the text:

> By evoking the time prior to Zambinella's castration (this is not specu-
> lation on our part but merely a development of the connotation),
> Chigi releases a scene, a whole little novel of what went before: the
> *ragazzo* taken in and kept by the old man who takes charge of both
> his operation (I paid for *everything*) and his education, the ingratitude
> of the protégé on his way to stardom, cynically taking a richer, more
> powerful, and visibly more amorous protector (the Cardinal). (186)

According to Barthes, this "little novel" has a sadistic function: forcing Sarrasine to see that his mistress is actually a boy, it constitutes
the only note of pederasty in the whole story. It also vulgarizes castration by reducing it to a "perfectly real" surgical operation, and
denounces Chigi, the Roman prince who paid for it, as the literal
castrator of the story. If Chigi's trivial gossip mediates the symbolic
structure that leads to Sarrasine's "castration" and death, the prince
nevertheless remains a "colourless mediator, lacking symbolic
scope, engulfed in contingency." Chigi therefore reenacts (*en
abyme*) the narrator's function—he is an asymbolic narrator if ever
there was. By drawing attention to Chigi, and by elaborating a homosexual scenario on his behalf, Barthes is surely complicit in this
"vulgarization" of more noble symbolic castrations.

Even as Barthes glosses his final "SYM. Horror of castration," he
keeps in play three competing reasons for the disgust attaching to
the origins of the Lanty fortune. If we bracket out the tautologous
"horror inseparable from castration" that is foregrounded by
Barthes as the main reason (210), we are left with the legacy of
blood (Sarrasine's murder by a jealous protector) and the unambiguous fact that the fortune originated in prostitution (the *ragazzo*
kept by Chigi and later by Cardinal Cigognara). Which of these upset Mme de Rochefide so severely that she called off her deal with
the narrator? According to Barthes, what distresses her is "the story
of a terrible and irresistibly contagious disease; carried by the narrative itself, this disease finally contaminates the lovely listener and,
withdrawing her from love, stops her from honouring her contract"
(213). Barthes claims to be very interested in *Sarrasine* as a "con-
tract-story"—"the narrative is exchanged for a body (it's a prostitution contract)"—and wants to argue that the real subject of the text
is not "a story about a castrato," but rather the effect of the exchanged story on the storytelling contract (88–89). Yet Barthes's
decision to link the two story levels through castration strangely

bypasses another connection. The inner story is also the narrative of a contract—a second prostitution contract, but one in which male sexuality is exchanged between men. As long as Mme de Rochefide believes that she is listening to a tale of heterosexual attraction, financial protection, and rivalry she betrays no moral scruples. However, she reneges on her own heterosexual contract once she realizes that the contract on which the narrator's mystification turns is a homosexual one. The beautiful young man whom she had desired in the Adonis painting has not only turned into the very same old man who had frightened her on the previous evening; the beautiful model was in fact always a homosexual prostitute. In other words, the blocking of desire that is represented in this story is a blocking of heterosexual desire, and the narrator, with a fair degree of irony, presents himself as its victim.

If Mme de Rochefide's reaction is simply a homophobic one, then the more worldly narrator is right to chide her for treating the aged and coquettish Zambinella as some horrible apparition: "You are being ridiculous, taking a little old man for a ghost" (67). Although the narrator has clearly contrived his narrative so as to make Mme de Rochefide, along with Sarrasine, a victim of the Roman hoax, and although he appears to have done this as a mildly malicious revenge for her desire for the portrait, homophobia is perhaps the effect he had underestimated. But has his story provoked a more profound disturbance to Mme de Rochefide's internalization of heterosexuality? And what was the attraction of the Adonis painting?

Barthes's own references to the sexual status of the Adonis figure are a curious feature of his frequent allusions to the chain of artistic representations. On the basis of Mme de Rochefide's happy exclamation, "Does such a perfect creature exist?" Barthes launches into a digression titled "Au-delà et en-deçà" (that which lies beyond something and that which falls short of it). Vien's painting was copied from a reproduction of the statue that Sarrasine had fashioned from his entirely illusory perception of Zambinella as Essential Woman (the normally scattered perfections of Woman miraculously assembled in one model). Now beauty, in Barthes's analysis, is in fact a catachresis, whereby the beauty of woman could only ever be figured metaphorically through an ever-receding code of masterpieces. Sarrasine, of course, believed that he had found the origin of the code in Zambinella. But as Zambinella is "really" a castrato, Barthes considers his point proven that there is no founding origin for the code of artistic representations. What I find bizarre, despite its relation to the theoretical point Barthes wants to make, is the very negative language through which he equates Zambinella with an absence—on the one hand, the painting figures perfection and *the* Female Masterpiece (the *au-delà* or beyond); on the other, it inscribes the execrable "subman" (*sous-homme*) of the *en-deçà* (that which falls short): "castrato, deficiency, definitive *minus*" (71–72).

This is in keeping with Barthes's tendency to reinforce the view of both Sarrasine and Parisian society, that a castrato belongs to some subspecies of humanity. When the narrator introduces the "strange character" of Zambinella with a perfunctory "It was a man," Barthes denounces this as a lie on the part of the hermeneutic code: "The old man, in fact, is not a man" (41). Similarly, when the narrator deflates the wild Parisian rumors about Zambinella's quasi-supernatural status with the bald statement "The stranger was merely an old man," Barthes leaps in with accusations of tautology ("*The old man was an old man*") and the now familiar charge of asymbolism (43). At the same time, Barthes persists throughout with the notion that Zambinella is of undecidable gender, lamenting that the French language has no gender-neutral article. Yet once we know that Zambinella is simply a castrated male, the hesitation between linguistic genders is subsumed under the rhetorical skill of a narrator manipulating his narratee. I appreciate that Barthes pursues his argument to suggest that the text undermines the stable oppositions upon which linguistic representations are founded. What the argument curiously omits, however, is the possibility of representing Zambinella not as a horrible castrato but as a beautiful *ragazzo*. It is a referential possibility that is also excluded from Barthes's reading of the Adonis painting.

Yet Barthes acknowledges that the text of *Sarrasine* registers a moment of erotic accord between the young woman and the painted Adonis, as she examines, "with a gentle smile of contentment, the exquisite grace of the contours, the pose, the colour, the hair; in short, the entire picture" (72). According to Barthes, Mme de Rochefide's pleasure is overdetermined, and derives from three different but superimposed objects:

(1) *a man*: Adonis himself, the mythological subject of the painting; the narrator's jealousy will be aroused by this interpretation of the young woman's desire; (2) *a woman:* the young woman perceives the feminine nature of the Adonis and feels herself in harmony, complicity, even Sapphism, in any event once again frustrating the narrator, who is denied access to the prestigious field of femininity; (3) *a castrato*: who obviously continues to fascinate the young woman.

Mme de Rochefide's comment that the Adonis is too beautiful for a man is simply reduced by Barthes to "is not a man," and he reiterates his stark alternative: the painting represents either Woman (perfection) or a castrato (a subman) (72–73). The possibility that Mme de Rochefide might desire a representation of the real-life Zambinella is simply bypassed in Barthes's account—if she desires "a man" it can be only the mythological figure of Adonis, object of the narrator's "jealousy."

If we move backward along the chain of copies from painting to statue, we find Barthes making the same argument: that Sarrasine's statue of Zambinella is one of the links in the long chain that duplicates the body of Essential Woman (194). Yet *no one* in the story shares Sarrasine's illusion; every other mediator of the artistic chain perceives its referent to be a beautiful young man. For the cardinal, who has the statue copied in marble, it is quite simply a statue of Zambinella, the young man he loves. As Barthes himself puts it, Cicognara has no scruples about appropriating his victim's work of art and contemplating the effigy of his *mignon* through his rival's eyes (207). Vien copies that statue as an Adonis, not as a woman, and Girodet's painting of Endymion, which Barthes uses in *S/Z* as an ironic photograph of Zambinella, is the last of the beautiful boys in the chain.[13]

However, Barthes insists on glossing the collapse of Sarrasine's grand illusion from the sculptor's own point of view: "The statue is ironically true, dramatically unworthy: the emptiness of the model has invaded the copy, communicating to it its sense of horror" (199). Yet if Sarrasine's statue is reduced to an empty and useless ruin, it is only because of the sculptor's homophobic conviction that a castrated boy is literally "a nothing." The "ironic truth" is surely that Sarrasine has produced a beautiful statue of a desirable *ragazzo* despite his private, social, and artistic ideology. Because

Sarrasine's attempt to destroy his statue fails, "something," in Barthes's words, will be transmitted to the Adonis, the Endymion, the Lanty family, the narrator, and the reader. Barthes's something is clearly "castration," a negative disturbance of desire. My own view is that the story does represent a disturbance to heterosexual desire. However, this is achieved not through a negative contamination with castration, but through forcing an acknowledgment of homosexual desire.

Barthes appears to claim that Sarrasine is punished for his "bad" realist aesthetic: "The 'realist' work must be guaranteed by the integral truth of the model which the copying artist must know through and through" (198–99). Sarrasine's manic sketches of Zambinella after his first evening at the theater are glossed by Barthes as the realist artist's obsession with uncovering appearances: "always to get *beyond, behind,* according to the idealist principle which identifies secrecy with truth: one must thus go *into* the model, *beneath* the statue, *behind* the canvas." This, he insists, is the error of realist writers and realist critics alike, who want to go *behind* the paper, and discover, for example, the "*exact* relationship between Vautrin and Lucien de Rubempré." Their attempt, however, is doomed to failure—just as there is no reality, no referent, behind this paper (but only "Reference," a receding code), so there is nothing under or inside Zambinella but castration, of which Sarrasine will die, "having destroyed in his illusory statue the evidence of his failure" (122).

The first point to note is Barthes's bizarre *lapsus.* The statue is not in fact destroyed; it lives on to tell a tale. Second, Barthes's example of critical naïveté is itself intriguing. The desire to seek out what lies behind a representation is later labeled a form of "indiscretion" (208)—only an indiscreet and foolish critic, it seems, could want to know the exact nature of the relationship between Vautrin and Lucien de Rubempré. In fact, Barthes is wrong to say that Mme de Rochefide reads the Adonis painting for its mythological referent. Rather, she wants to know if such a perfect being *exists,* and (indiscreetly) she wants to identify the real-life model: " 'But who is it?'. . . 'I want to know,' she added sharply" (74). In short, the represented narratee of *Sarrasine* is a referential listener. That the identity and sexuality of the referent take Mme de Rochefide by surprise is no reason to take apart her aesthetics, for the realist illusion of the painting did have a referent in the represented real life of the story. Desire is not contained by the symbolic code, and a homosexual *ragazzo* would seem to be a legitimate starting point for realist art.

My conclusion to this reexamination of *S/Z* is a simple one: that the missing final term of the hermeneutic code be labeled "taboo on homosexuality" rather than "taboo on castration." If we want to find reasons for that taboo, we could turn, for example, to Luce Irigaray's well-known analyses of the homosocial contract—a contract that underpins the occlusion of same-sex relationships between both women and men. If female homosexuality cannot be conceptualized by an order in which women may function only as objects of exchange, explicit male sexuality is marginalized or proscribed for a related but different reason. The homosocial exchange of women grounds a sublimated homosexuality, but as the secret motor of the system, male homosexuality must precisely remain hidden. If men are supposed to make the system work by maintaining their subject position and exchanging women, they cannot allow themselves to become objects of exchange.[14] Zambinella, who is both homosexual and, as a male prostitute, a visible object of exchange, therefore represents an overdetermined taboo. The explosion of this taboo, so splendidly figured in *Sarrasine,* could well open up a reading of the structures that have positioned Zambinella as such. Extended to the wider social and psychological canvas of *The Human Comedy,* such a reading would need to examine the relative positions of male and female homosexuality within a compulsory heterosexuality that, as the ideological prop of a patriarchal society, might be expected to disadvantage women more severely than men.[15]

The aim of this essay, however, has been far narrower in scope. Restricting myself to *Sarrasine,* I hope to have shown that heterosexist assumptions are both foregrounded and unsettled by this realist text. Proust, of course, had no qualms about identifying homosexuality (male and female) as one of the motors of Balzac's psychological universe, linking the origin of the Lanty fortune—"the love of the cardinal for a castrato"—to other examples of "mysterious laws of the flesh and of feeling."[16] Yet Proust also notes that Balzac never discussed his work in this way. Similarly, many critics of Balzac have tended to steer clear of the representations of homosexuality in this supposed champion of family values.[17] Even Barthes, as we have seen, has played hide-and-seek with his audience by denying his own investment in the referential "asymbolic" reading, while taking euphemistic refuge behind the supposedly more prestigious symbolic code. "In *Sarrasine*," Barthes seems to say, "it was castration I loved, rather than a Neapolitan *ragazzo*." Yet it is Barthes's own step-by-step method that reveals that the body is woven into all threads of the text, not just that which he has labeled the symbolic code. In trying to restrict the territory of the body in this way, is Barthes in bad faith, or has he too been misled by a stereotype?

To recall that Barthes twice claims that the hermeneutic code subsumes the symbolic code—rather than vice versa—may be considered theoretically regressive. Doesn't such an argument undermine Barthes's more powerful and influential claim that *Sarrasine* both portrays and initiates a disturbance of representational art? Yet this is precisely my quarrel with *S/Z:* that Barthes appears to ally the symbolic castration reading to a "progressive" aesthetic (the sapping of representation) while the uncovering of the inner story line of homosexual prostitution is devalued as reactionary realism. If any stereotype is at work in Barthes's reading, it is not, then, heterocentrism—rather, it is the claim that realism as artistic form is inherently reactionary. Paradoxically, it is Barthes's own inconsistent critical practice in *S/Z* (his brilliant burrowing under every buried assumption of the practice of mimetic fiction) that leads me to claim against him that there is an important role for realist readings that aspire to force out the details "behind" a text, and that might thereby alter our ideological perceptions of both contents and forms. Mimetic narratives may well, as Barthes claims in the passage of *Roland Barthes* quoted by Tanner, be tied up with patriarchal structures such as the Oedipus complex, heterosexual marriage, and its transgression in adultery. The rhetoric of realist discourse may also, as he claims in *S/Z*, conflate secrecy with truth. But what if this contingent truth is precisely a social secret, such as the taboo on homosexuality that grounds that heterocentric order in the first place? In that or in similar cases, unearthing the final predicates of the hermeneutic code cannot be dismissed as naive.

NOTES

1. Christopher Prendergast, *The Order of Mimesis: Balzac, Stendhal, Nerval, Flaubert* (Cambridge: Cambridge University Press, 1986).

2. Naomi Schor, *George Sand and Idealism* (New York: Columbia University Press, 1993), 54.

3. Ibid., 45.

4. Ibid., 228 n. 60. See also my review of Prendergast's *The Order of Mimesis* in *Poetics Today* 8 (1987): 709–13.

5. Tony Tanner, *Adultery in the Novel: Contract and Transgression* (Baltimore: Johns Hopkins University Press, 1979).

6. Roland Barthes, *Roland Barthes by Roland Barthes,* trans. Richard Howard (New York: Hill & Wang, 1977).

7. See the following fragments of *Roland Barthes:* "The Goddess H" (63–64), "Active/Passive" (133), "Abu Novas and Metaphor" (123), and "Overdetermination" (170). For a discussion of the homosexual subtext of Barthes's later writing, see Diana Knight, "Roland Barthes: An Intertextual Figure," in *Intertextuality: Theories and Practices,* ed. Michael Worton and Judith Still (Manchester: Manchester University Press, 1990), 92–107.

8. For important readings of *Sarrasine,* see Terence Cave, *Recognition: A Study in Poetics* (Oxford: Clarendon, 1988); Ross Chambers, "Seduction Denied: *Sarrasine* and the Impact of Art," in *Story and Situation: Narrative Seduction and the Power of Fiction* (Minneapolis: University of Minnesota Press, 1984), 73–96; Barbara Johnson, "The Critical Difference: BartheS/BalZac," in *The Critical Difference: Essays in the Contemporary Rhetoric of Reading* (Baltimore: Johns Hopkins University Press, 1985 [1980]), 3–12; Dorothy Kelly, *Fictional Genders: Role and Representation in Nineteenth-Century French Narrative* (Lincoln: University of Nebraska Press, 1989), 106–17.

9. See Johnson, "The Critical Difference," especially 11–12.

10. I have occasionally modified Richard Miller's translation (New York: Hill & Wang, 1984) of Roland Barthes, *S/Z* (Paris: Seuil, 1970). Page numbers appearing in the text correspond to the 1984 translated edition.

11. Renaud Camus, "Inventaires," *La Règle du jeu* 1 (1990): 59 (my translation).

12. Renaud Camus, *Notes achriennes* (Paris: Hachette/P.O.L., 1982), 126 (my translation).

13. See Barthes's fantasy that if we were to go into an art shop in the rue Bonaparte and ask to see a reproduction of the Girodet painting, this would effectively be a photo of Zambinella. *S/Z,* 71.

14. See Luce Irigaray, "Commodities amongst Themselves," in *This Sex Which Is Not One,* trans. Catherine Porter with Carolyn Burke (Ithaca, N.Y.: Cornell University Press, 1985), 192–97. On "homosociality," see too, of course, Eve Kosofsky Sedgwick, *Between Men: English Literature and Male Homosocial Desire* (New York: Columbia University Press, 1985) and *Epistemology of the Closet* (Berkeley: University of California Press, 1990). D. A. Miller's study of the Victorian novel, *The Novel and the Police* (Berkeley: University of California Press, 1988), places its policing of characters and readers in a broadly homosocial framework. Although Miller engages with sexual politics in a way that Prendergast tends to avoid, his very negative view of the function of realist narrative strikes me as less convincing than Prendergast's

cautious rehabilitation. Finally, for a particularly suggestive exploration of the relationship between homosexuality and the social repression of male homosexuality, see Ross Chambers, "Messing Around: Gayness and Literature in Alan Hollingshurst's *The Swimming-Pool Library*," in *Textuality and Sexuality: Reading Theories and Practices,* ed. Judith Still and Michael Worton (Manchester: Manchester University Press, 1993), 207–17.

15. See Diana Knight, "Reading as an Old Maid: *La Cousine Bette* and Compulsory Heterosexuality," *Quinquereme* 12, no. 1 (1989): 67–79. That article, together with the present essay, represents the starting point of a long-term project to investigate the ramifications of compulsory heterosexuality in Balzac's fiction. An excellent Balzacian example of sublimated homosexuality, linked to the homosocial exchange of wives, mistresses, and daughters, is the friendship between Hulot and Crevel, the "rival" adulterers of *Cousin Bette*. It is comically figured in the scene where the the two men, temporarily ousted by their shared mistress, spend a night together in Crevel's secret love nest. The explicitly homosexual Vautrin (a key figure of *The Human Comedy*) graphically illustrates, on the other hand, the proscription of homosexuality through his status as master criminal. Indeed, Vautrin's eventual co-optation into the secret police could be seen to confirm the hidden function of that homosexuality in the social order of nineteenth-century France.

16. Marcel Proust, *Against Sainte-Beuve and Other Essays,* trans. John Sturrock (Harmondsworth: Penguin, 1988), 69.

17. See, however, Leo Bersani, *Balzac to Beckett: Center and Circumference in French Fiction* (New York: Oxford University Press, 1970), especially 47–49. On critical unease with the theme of lesbianism in *Cousin Bette,* see Knight, "Reading as an Old Maid."

Real Fashion:
Clothes Unmake the Working Woman
Anne Higonnet

There is a delicate form of the empirical which identifies itself so intimately with its object that it thereby becomes theory.
—John Berger, quoting Walter Benjamin quoting Goethe[1]

Patterns

Two seamstresses pose for a photographer (Figure 7.1). The photographer has recorded his identity as M. de Charly, dated the image 1862, and labeled it *Dans l'atelier.*[2] He has also recorded the seamstresses' identity, as they have presented it to him. He might have brought his equipment to their workshop, but technical reasons argue instead that they have come to his studio.[3] Dressed in fine products of their skill, the seamstresses have surrounded themselves with tokens of their trade: scissors, tool basket, cut fabric in front of them, pattern pieces behind them to the left, assembled dresses to the right. We know nothing else about these women: no names, no dates.

The image knots form, class, and gender into a historical meaning. But when I say "historical meaning" I beg my own question. This essay on one photograph is also an essay on the problem of visual historical meaning, which I will argue is never purely visual. Let me begin with the idea of the *combinatoire,* which translates from French only very awkwardly as "combinator" or too familiarly as "combination." In 1980, Michel de Certeau introduced his idea

Figure 7.1. M. de Charly, *Dans l'atelier*, photograph, 1862 (Eastman House Museum of Photography, Rochester, N.Y.). Reprinted with permission.

of culture as "combinatoires d'opérations,"[4] and in 1975, Fredric Jameson, himself citing Charles Mauron and Tzvetan Todorov, explained: "The *combinatoire* aims at revealing, not the causes behind a given form, but rather the *conditions of possibility* of its existence."[5] If an image, in this case the photograph *Dans l'atelier,* can be thought of as a *combinatoire,* then what is it combining, how, and why? How do the aspects of one image's meaning fit together at one moment? And then how do its visual and verbal components slip out of alignment, jolting into new combinations with other meanings?

Any investigation of an image's historical meaning is necessarily—I believe—an investigation into what has been called *realism*. What effect of the real does any image produce, and how do visual and verbal modes of realism interact? In what sense is any image a form of history, and what place can its material factuality occupy in narratives written always after the fact? In contrast to a specifically literary realism, what interests me are the forms of realism produced by images, not merely considered as a question of their subject matter's optical verisimilitude, but rather as a mode of realism always playing against, supplementing, complementing, or contradicting textual modes of realism. What interests me are modes of realism that work not only through subject, but also through visual form and cultural conditions of sight, modes of realism that imply a history not just of subjects, but of visual culture. Charly's photograph draws my attention to these issues both because its unusual subject seems to give it a privileged place among images within social history and because its medium seems so realistic.

It would be easy to say that Charly's *Dans l'atelier* simply records how a visually underrepresented sort of person—the woman worker—really looked. This response would be the standard social historian's. Yet social historians do not, in practice, take photographs like *Dans l'atelier* very seriously. By and large, they consider images only to illustrate prior meanings. According to such a procedure, the social historian, having investigated the production of class and gender in mid-nineteenth-century France, would then invoke *Dans l'atelier* to show the appearances of a history that can be, has been, written already. If *Dans l'atelier* is construed to show how seamstresses actually—really—looked, it could only be because their identity had been produced prior to the photograph. For most social historians, images do not produce meaning, and therefore cannot function as integral elements of history.

Art historians dismiss photographs like *Dans l'atelier* in their own way. The methods that have dominated art history have no place for such images. Charly is not a known author, he belongs to no canon either on his own merits or by association, and his photograph is somewhat inert formally: banal in its composition, light effects, and printing. Basically, *Dans l'atelier* does not qualify as art. At best, an art historian would compare *Dans l'atelier* to a painting of seamstresses by some famous artist in much the same way a historian uses photographs: to reinforce the conclusion of a prior argument about something else. The history of photography has included some remarkably supple and innovative essays,[6] but this work has been marginal within a formalist photographic history that patterns itself on the history of painting and that ignores in photographs exactly those factors of class and gender that would constitute *Dans l'atelier's* realism for social historians.

Painting, sculpture, and architecture have histories, albeit histories that are limited by an unquestioning acceptance of those media's boundaries. Some other media, notably photographs and prints with artistic intentions, have received the same treatment in subordinate versions. Historians of painting have long been engaged in studying popular imagery as a function of issues pertinent to painting. We have, however, very few historical studies of reciprocal relationships among image types. Which is to say that we have no clear or comprehensive histories of visual culture, let alone histories that mesh visual culture with social and literary history. The method by which we could write the historical meaning, the realism, of an image like *Dans l'atelier* will have to be invented.

It should already be clear that I believe such a project entails studying how the image that materializes a historical moment unites the meanings so disparately treated by the fields of history and art history. The object forces us to see how meanings function in a real object at one moment in relation to each other. It forces us to see how meanings act as functions of each other, with no independent significance, as elements of *combinatoires*. In the *combinatoire*, no meaning can be prior to any other, privileged over any other. The only origin is the object itself, yet none of its meanings is inherent to the object. Each of the *combinatoire's* elements refers to past meanings that themselves are just the most recent links in an endless regression of citations. As Barthes writes in *S/Z*, invoking images: "Thus realism . . . consists . . . not in copying reality, but in copying a (painted) copy of reality."[7] Neil Hertz identifies this regressive process as the "irreduceable figurativeness of one's language," which he derives from Sigmund Freud's psychoanalytic concept of "repetition compulsion."[8] Nonetheless, the object and its moment are constituted by a particular intersection of these regressions. The configuration of that intersection, the pattern formed by different vectors of meaning, their respective velocities, their capacity to deflect or even absorb each other, together constitute the *combinatoire*. That pattern determines the *combinatoire*'s function, temporarily. The very energy of the elements that enter into it and the transformation of those energies by their mix guarantee that the *combinatoire* can neither last nor reproduce itself exactly, but rather constantly mutates into unprecedented forms and functions.

Petits Metiers

Neither art history nor history has dealt much recently with genre. Yet genre, I believe, is where a history of visual culture must begin. Art historians have long since given up the rigid hierarchies of subject matter promulgated for painting by *ancien régime* art academies and called "genres." Yet in many ways art historians have substituted for this defunct hierarchy a new one, which passes as a description of medium. Supposedly neutral, classification by medium allows an exclusive concentration on the internal organization of its categories.[9] It thereby suppresses the historical meanings inherent in relationships among media, for it masks the ways in which the location, character, and function of media boundaries interact with subject matter to produce genres—not in name but in effect. History, meanwhile, has been so concerned with the illustrated meanings produced within genres that it has ignored the historical significance of genre's material conditions. For historians, the existence, origins, and lineages of image types seems to fall within art history's formalist province. Genre is assumed.

Jameson, following Claudio Guillén, has proposed that genre's apparent neutrality only testifies to the success of its cultural work. By calling genre "institutions of social life" "based on tacit agreements or contracts," Jameson suggests that genres produce meaning by their use of signs that already fulfill cultural functions for their intended audiences.[10] If we extend Jameson's definition of literary genres to include visual analogues, then we are dealing with contracts drawn in terms of reproduced visual conventions whose histories designate their new spectators.

Charly's photograph of seamstresses belongs to a genre called *petits métiers*. To understand the photograph, we have to work our way back along the regression chain of the *petits métiers* genre. The purpose of this exercise is not to provide anything like a complete history of the *petits métiers* genre, but instead to articulate some of *Dans l'atelier*'s 1862 contract clauses.

The genre of the *petits métiers* dates back to about 1500.[11] It was a genre that represented people plying their trades or commerces, almost always in the street, where they advertised their goods and services with shouts or calls, hence their other common name, of *cris*. More pointedly, they were often called *cris de Paris*, regardless of where they were produced or sold, thus indicating that they represented what was imagined to be a specifically urban, and hence modern, form of labor. With very few exceptions, *petits métiers* images took the form of prints, usually a series of prints, each depicting a different trade, or else as single sheets showing a variety of trades in rows and columns (see Figure 7.2). They were executed in a range of styles and prices. The more crudely drawn and colored, cheaper, end of the *petits métiers* range assures us that they were available to those they represented, at least marginally. The more expensive, sophisticated end of the range indicates another audience, wealthy and leisured, for whom even these relatively refined images would have contrasted sharply with the truly elite images to which they also had access.

The *petits métiers* genre conceptualized modern urban labor. In her essay on Annibale Carraci's seventeenth-century *métiers* prints, Sheila McTighe has proposed that such representations of work act as "ideations" of labor in relation to an emerging concept of leisure.[12] McTighe shows how prints like Carracci's participated in the "devaluation of manual work and the link between intellectual métiers and social mobility,"[13] a function they still fulfilled two centuries later in France. Early-nineteenth-century *métiers de Paris* images continued to allow the urban artisanal class a very rare representation of themselves and their work. And they continued to cast a measure of social distance between working and nonworking

Figure 7.2. *Petits métiers de Paris,* estampe de pillot, 1827 (Musée des Arts et Traditions Populaires, Paris).

classes as a form that confirmed that distance, the form of instructive amusement enjoyable for a literate, leisured class.

Time had passed, but *petits métiers* images had hardly changed. The workers who were represented were the workers a middle-class person might encounter in the public domain of the street:

Figure 7.3. C. J. Traviès, *Tableau de Paris no. 14*, lithograph, c. 1835 (Musée Carnavalet, Paris). Copyright 1995 Artists Rights Society (ARS), New York/SPADEM, Paris.

knife grinders, cocoa vendors, flower girls, teeth extractors, used-clothes traders, and the like. *Petits métiers* images represented workers not as individuals with work experiences but as vehicles for signs of work. They classified labor into "types," which al-

Figure 7.4. V. Ratier, *Les Signalements no. 1,* lithograph, c. 1835 (Musée Carnavalet, Paris). Copyright 1995 Artists Rights Society (ARS), New York/SPADEM, Paris.

though seeming to individualize labor, in fact objectified it as costumes and accessories. Looking more closely at one *métier,* published around 1835 (Figure 7.3), our identification of the laundress depends on her apron, kerchief, and especially her basket, rather than on the process or the products of her labor. We are given to know nothing of her working conditions or her relationships to her employers, to other laundresses, or to her customers. Similarly, in *Les Signalements* (Figure 7.4), published in roughly the same period, a *lingère* (linen maid) and a *modiste* (milliner) are both shown delivering their goods (and not even to anyone) rather than producing them, despite the tiny portion of their careers they would have spent in the street. This depersonalizing effect was emphasized by the production of *petits métiers* images in series or on sheets in grid formats, even more so when, as was frequent, the *petits métiers* illustrated the letters of the alphabet. Workers in these images become a function of organizational schemata, so that the confusion of urban streets can be visually managed by the printed page—so that labor can be recognized yet not acknowledged.

The stasis itself of the *petits métiers* genre acquired a new significance in the context of the July Monarchy. During this period, no workers became more politicized than Parisian artisans, yet the images of their labor remained resolutely depoliticizing. And far from becoming obsolete because it was archaic, the genre became more popular than ever. Nor did the industrialization of the image market entail the representation of industrial labor. On the contrary, that industrialization, by the sheer volume of *petits métiers* images it could produce, crowded industrial labor out of visual consciousness.[14]

Mass Production

Charles Blanc, art publisher and critic, recalled that in the 1830s a song had circulated "everywhere: in drawing rooms, on the street" in Paris that celebrated a new craze. The invention of lithography, along with the discovery of cheap wood-engraving techniques, had in less than fifty years so rapidly expanded the print market that by the 1830s it had created the first modern mass visual media.[15]

> Hooray for lithography
> It's the rage everywhere
> Tall, short, ugly, pretty,
> The crayon retraces everything.
> Our boulevards all along
> Are now salons
> Where, even without posing,
> Everyone finds himself exhibited.[16]

So it seems that lithography was clearly understood by Parisians in the 1830s to be a medium whose significance lay in its difference as a democratizing street medium from the elite art of the salons, from the paintings for which one had to pose. When the *métiers* image verged on the grotesque, as in the case of our laundress (Figure 7.3), as in the case of many *métiers* series, that difference was all the more perceptible. "Si tu gueules comme ça tu n'iras pas voir guillotiner [If you go on bawling you won't get to see the guillotining]," warns the parody of bourgeois maternal discipline. The nineteenth century's contribution of the abject *chiffonier* (ragpicker) to the *métiers* genre's repertoire added yet a further effect of distance. (Whose garbage, after all, did the ragpicker collect?)

As the print market expanded, it became increasingly diversified. Existing genres were also developed and amplified, including the *petits métiers* genre. If we return to images previously discussed, for instance, we easily see how by the 1830s *métiers* images had become more urbane, both stylistically and thematically. Around the laundress, the *lingère,* and the *modiste,* a bit of street has been adumbrated, as well as a relationship to others on the street.

It is in these amplified *métiers* scenes that we can see the single greatest change in the genre: the sexualization of female labor. *Métiers* images before about 1820 did not gender labor; male and female *métiers* were represented in the same way. After about 1820, however, that changed. To return to our examples, both *lingère* and *modiste* display their ankles, while captions tell us the *lingère* has a "*minois futé* [pretty little minx look]," the *modiste* an arched back and short skirts. Most important, these two types have been placed on either side of a male student type "*regardant les femmes,*" and in his background his counterpart has picked up a smaller version of the *modiste.* Once out on the streets, where they are represented by the *métiers* genre, women workers become the sexual objects of a middle-class masculine gaze. Images of laundresses, milliners, and seamstresses proliferated during the Restoration and July Monarchy, precisely because the fact that these tradeswomen did not actually make or sell anything on the street allowed interpretation of their presence there the scope of fantasy.

Meanwhile, a documentary impulse both abetted the conventions governing the representation of female labor and opened up a marginal possibility for their transformation. The urge to investigate, classify, and quantify social conditions so widespread in the July Monarchy included the invention and deployment of documentary photography. Overwhelmingly, photographs of *petits métiers* both male and female duplicated the conventions of the print genre.[17] And by duplicating them in a supposedly mechanical medium, they ratified those conventions visually. Charly intended to do the same in his photograph of two seamstresses, but his intentions were led astray by the possibilities for change inherent in the medium itself. Someone had to pose for the camera. Existing objects had to be used as accessories. Agency within the visual institution of the *petits métiers* genre was thereby altered. The appearances that had always been constructed might now, perhaps, be devised by the one whose photograph was taken. If, perhaps, the one taking the photograph believed firmly enough that his medium would confirm his preconceptions, he might not notice or quite understand that the appearances he confirmed told a slightly different story. The *petits métiers* genre contract could become something more like an exchange than it had been before photography, or at least could turn out to contain an escape clause.

Confusing Signs

The two seamstresses in Charly's photograph have availed themselves of their opportunity to an exceptional degree. Nothing in the tradition of the *petits métiers* genre leads us—or led M. de Charly—to expect the appearances they brought to their image. Elaborately coiffed, the two women wear meticulously fitted, intricately ornamented dresses, dresses at the height of fashion for 1862, yet eminently respectable: buttoned high and neatly smooth. These decorously fashionable dresses should, according to visual expectation, have been the products of their labor destined for those who pay for that labor, whereas the seamstresses themselves should have been identifiable by signs of difference, deference, or sexual availability like those Traviès attributed to his laundress or Ratier to his *lingère* and *modiste*. Instead, the seamstresses have, as it were, fashioned the self-image of their choice. They have presented to the camera the appearances that genre attributes to the bourgeoisie.

To have created this discrepancy between expectation and image, the seamstresses had to have been aware of class difference as it was played out visually. They knew the terms of the *petits métiers* contract and chose not to honor them. To some extent, therefore, it would be possible to say that these women have manifested a class consciousness, and even resistance to the conventions that place them in an inferior and sexualized position. They refuse to play the socially subordinate role assigned to them and instead play one that puts them in a more advantageous, respectable bourgeois position. The role they play makes them appear to belong to the same class as does the photographer. The imbalance of power between subject and author, moreover, might seem to be further redressed by the aggression of their move itself. They have, to some extent, seized control of the production of the image, expanded the role of the subject at the expense of the author's. Mapped onto that shift, of course, is gender. The author (as usual) is masculine, and in this case the feminine subject seems to usurp some of his prerogatives, or at least deflect his sexual privileges. At this point an exclusive attention to subject matter would imply that the conventions of genre had been contradicted by reality. In a simplistic Marxist scheme, now would be the moment to assert that the seamstresses have unmasked the false consciousness of the bourgeoisie and revealed that its status is nothing but fetishized appearances—class as costume. A dogmatic feminist could add that gender conventions have trumped class conventions, inasmuch as the women have realized the photographer cannot object to the signs of respectable femininity no matter how dismayed he might be by their social motivations.

Yet the image itself, or rather the image's reference to itself as an image, contradicts any such easy interpretation. The seamstresses have brought along a fashion print with the rest of their professional paraphernalia. (And we know from textual sources, such as Margaret Oliphant's 1895 *Kirsteen*, as well as from visual sources, such as caricatures in *Le Charivari*, that such prints did indeed hang on the walls of workshops and were taken as stylistic inspiration by workers.) The print has been attached to the wall directly behind them, so that we look beyond them to it. Not only have the seamstresses recognized that an image constitutes a sign of their trade, but they have chosen to duplicate that sign. The clothing they wear looks just like the kind of clothes represented in the print, and furthermore they have adopted the poses and gazes of the plate's figures. This *mise en abyme* completely unsettles the reality effect of the photograph, for it occurs not in a mirror, which would tempt us to speak of truth, or even another photograph, which might tempt us to talk about mirroring, but in an image notorious for its artificiality. The seamstresses have not replaced the conventions of the *petits métiers* genre with the reality of a self-conscious agency, but rather joined one set of conventions to another. Far from revealing the reality behind one genre, the camera pushes us back along another genre's archaeology of reference, along the trajectory of the fashion plate.

Figure 7.5. J. D. de Saint Jean, *Homme de qualité allant incognito par la ville,* colored engraving, 1689 (Bibliothèque Nationale, Paris).

Fashion Looks

Prints dedicated to costume first appeared in France under the reign of Louis XIV.[18] Themselves descended from illustrations of exotic foreign costumes, these first prints (Figure 7.5) announcing changes in European clothing styles coincided with the establishment of the guild of couturiers in 1675.[19] Together, prints and guild

Figure 7.6. Gavarni, *Toilettes de visite du matin,* colored wood engraving from *La Mode,* October 1830 (Bibliothèque Historique de la Ville de Paris).

launched the modern concept of "fashion." Early fashion prints associated the wearing of a new style with a social status based on birth and breeding, hence the title of the print, *Homme de qualité.* By the beginning of the nineteenth century, fashion prints had loosened their ties to a fixed aristocratic hierarchy and instead positioned themselves—literally—as parts of luxury magazines that purported to create a cultural (as opposed to an ostensibly economic) elite through the promulgation of fashions diversely sartorial, theatrical, and literary. Fashion in clothing was meanwhile being gendered, as the number of fashion prints representing women began to outnumber those representing men. The genre had drifted toward the transformations that would radically alter its meaning in the 1830s.

In 1830, Honoré de Balzac announced the birth of a hybrid. In the October issue of a new periodical called *La Mode,* he heralded the appearance of Gavarni's fashion prints (Figure 7.6). Gavarni, Balzac claimed, had "conceived of fashion illustration as a specialization," and as an "artist and even a superior artist," he depicted

Figure 7.7. Jean Gigoux, *Satisfaction,* lithograph from *L'Artiste,* 1832 (New York Public Library). Reprinted with permission of Art and Architecture Collection, Miriam and Ira D. Wallach Division of Art, Prints, and Photographs, The New York Public Library, Astor, Lenox, and Tilden Foundations.

women who were "really truly women."[20] In one succint declaration, a new genre had been named, legitimated with authorship, and designated as the representation of female reality.

Gavarni's innovation consisted in merging the existing conventions of the fashion print with those of the domestic genre print

(Figure 7.7), yet another "specialization" made viable by the expansion of the print market. Domestic genre prints represented the daily lives of middle-class women. Their settings, actions, and costumes expressed the domestic, emotional, familial ideal of early nineteenth-century femininity. Gigoux's *Satisfaction* takes as its theme the pleasure a woman derives from the image of herself wearing a new hat, fashionable sign of femininity. The difference between painting and her fashion self-image (as well as the entire print that contains her look) is emphasized by the relative positions of the central mirror and a framed painting disappearing off the side.

Moreover, prints such as Gigoux's that both represented and urged women's identification with specific kinds of images other than high art painting in turn referred to another genre's conventions, those of feminine amateur picture making. Especially during the first half of the century, many European women painted and drew extensively but unprofessionally; Gigoux's painting-within-a-print shows a woman standing at an easel holding a palette; she is probably exactly such an amateur artist. In their amateur work, women themselves had developed an iconography of nineteenth-century domesticity.[21] Feminine amateur imagery therefore not only provided domestic genre prints with a set of cues that signaled domestic femininity, but also guaranteed the claims to women those cues could make for self-representation.

Gavarni's plates for *La Mode* explicitly tapped into those established references. The amply upholstered chaise of Figure 7.6, for example, metonymically indicates a feminine domestic interior, and the costume of the two women, one hatted, the other bareheaded, evokes the feminine ritual of the afternoon visit to a woman who is, to use the English expression, "at home" (scheduled to receive such visits). Gavarni further urges women's identification with his genre of image by depicting women looking at fashion plates. Moreover, Gavarni equates looking at fashion prints with the feminine literary practice of reading novels. A novel-sized book lies open on one woman's lap, ready to be taken up again when the fashion print is laid aside.

Whether or not Gavarni can be credited as individually as he was by Balzac with the creation of a genre, all fashionable fashion prints from about 1830 onward adopted the hybrid conventions Gavarni had demonstrated. The domestic references back through domestic genre prints to feminine amateur self-representation were being invoked just as the production of fashion prints entered the realm of mass industrial production, and as fashion prints urged women to identify with the consumption of industrial commodities. Balzac described Garvarni's formula as "satisfying at once the demand of the artist and the taste of high society, producing itself as a thing of art and of fashion, both a necessity and a luxury."[22] His euphemisms allude to, without admitting, the culture industry that bound the artist to the consumer tastes of moneyed society, that governed art with fashion, and that conflated necessity with luxury.

Fashion prints advertised products for sale. Indeed, fashion prints were the first advertisements that consistently enlisted images. It seems appropriate that advertisements not just for particular products, but for the very concept of fashion that drove the mechanisms of consumption, should be the first to harness scopic drives. But what of the fact that the first advertisements to use images should be of and for women? This coincidence corroborates what many cultural historians have been telling us, namely, that consumer culture organizes itself around a revision of women's roles, establishing new gender polarities that align femininity with the display and consumption of commodities. The conditions under which the fashion print emerges as a modern genre, and the conditions of subjectivity the genre fosters, show us how very much a *revision* this was. Fashion prints deliver the domestic references of their antecedents to the mechanisms of capitalist production and commodity fetishism. The print, itself an industrially marketed, mass-produced product, conflates both its gender ideal and the possibilities of feminine self-representation with a desire to become a spectacle of commodity consumption. A reification of desire, the fashion print casts femininity as fetishistic image.

Take My Word for It

If the fashion print provides us with a paradigmatic example of consumer culture's strategy and its effects, the genre also demonstrates the work in between—the work that produces the effects of strategy—for the visual meaning of the image that figures feminin-

Figure 7.8. Heloïse Leloir, fashion plate, colored wood engraving, from *La Mode Illustrée,* 1865 (author's collection).

ity functions together with verbal meanings. Though only the visual centers of fashion prints tend to be reproduced, the genre always includes both an image and words. The absence of any psychological contact between the female figures in fashion prints, as well as of any apparent gestural or narrative exchange within the image, allows our attention to be drawn to the more intimate contact between the image and the text beneath it.

A typical print, like the one in Figure 7.8, includes three signatures in the traditional place of the painter's signature: "Heloïse Leloir," the woman who made an initial pencil and watercolor version of the image; "Bonnard," the man who translated the image into a wood engraving plate from which to print; and "Gilquin Fils," the printer of the entire page. Larger than any of these three is the name of the couturieres who made the costumes depicted, "Mlles Rabouin." Largest of all are the words "La Mode Illustrée," the name of the magazine that published the page. The authorship of the page has not only been transformed according to an industrial division of labor and the methods of mechanical reproduction, but that authorship includes an incitation to buy—to buy both *La Mode Illustrée* and Mesdmoiselles Rabouin's clothing. If at the center the image figures an ideal, we find that ideal framed by the economic conditions of its production and acquisition. Lest the consumer remain in any doubt, the printer, the clothes designers, and the magazine are all named along with the exact places where she may conduct her purchases: "3, rue St. Jacques; 56, rue Jacob; 67, rue Neuve des Petits Champs."

Endowed with primary ontological status, the image naturalizes gender. Visuality immobilizes references to what by the middle of the century had come to be regarded nostalgically as an innate femininity. An identification of women with home, garden, children, and each other is thus maintained intact and apart from the signs spelled out in words of women's transformative forays into the worlds of business and technology. By urging women to become active consumers yet remain passive spectacles, the fashion print in its entirety makes contradictory meanings not only coexist, but reinforce each other. It accomplishes this through perceived distinctions between visual and verbal meanings, which allow image and text to be understood separately though they cannot be understood separately.

Fashion's ability to alter conventions, however, became subversive rather than reassuring when it raised the possibility that difference might disappear. Fashion prints and the magazines that included them appealed to European women of all classes and promoted a visual ideal of gender uniformity. It has become a truism of nineteenth-century cultural history that middle-class men and women felt a rising anxiety about what they perceived as diminishingly reliable visual signs of class. Which was the prostitute and which the respectable woman? Which was the seamstress and which the seamstress's client? Their clothes might mislead rather than guide, for fashion—that is, the visual conventions formulated and propagated in and by the fashion print—upset a social hierarchy dependent in considerable part on its visibility.

Even the scattered information we have suggests that fashion plates were identified with all along a class spectrum. In 1866, *La Mode Illustrée* alone claimed a circulation of 52,000, and it had a half dozen strong competitors. Print runs of fashion plates far outnumbered those of the magazine's text, for French fashion prints were sold loose as well as to women's magazines in other countries.[23] Magazines were passed around, so that even supposing a considerable overlap in readerships, we can estimate the number of women looking at fashion prints at easily half a million just in France, a number that indicates an audience extending well beyond an elite upper and middle class. The nascent fashion print genre, moreover, quickly developed a variant in the form of advertisements for department store clothing. The first recorded illustrated department store catalog took the form of a fashion magazine called *Les Nouveautés*. It was produced in 1839 by the Maison Popelin-Ducarré and mailed to what the store management considered an elite clientele.[24] But the clientele for ready-made clothing proved to be far from elite. Narratives like Zola's *Au Bonheur des dames* make it quite clear that the department store appealed to all classes of women, and that only working-class or very lower middle-class women bought dresses there. A professional interest need not alone, therefore, explain the identification of the two seamstresses with their fashion print. Certainly they could see it as a model for their professional products, but its role in Charly's photograph shows that they also, like other women of their class, took it as a model for their self-presentation.

The resulting tension in the photograph between gender and class signals reminds us that in the middle of the nineteenth century these signals were always contending for dominance, and are never reducible one to the other. The configuration produced at any one moment in any one image varies as a function of existing class and gender conditions, and also as a function of concurrently historical image technologies. Fashion improved the possibilities for self-representation available to the seamstresses in Charly's photograph. Had their class position been initially better, this might not have been so. Moreover, the seamstresses' opportunity depended on the medium of photography. Like fashion, photography introduced a mode of visuality that lodged meaning in surfaces. Both promised the reality of the seen. Charly presumably intended to enhance the reality effect of the traditional *petits métiers* genre, and thereby to ratify its social contract, by transposing it into photography. His intentions, however, have been subverted by the very effect on which he relied. The seamstresses presented the "wrong" appearances to his camera, and his production of the photograph only makes them look more right. According to beliefs contemporary with the medium, the photograph reveals how the seamstresses "really" looked. But *Dans l'atelier* reveals something quite different. Far from guaranteeing realism, photography's promise of a transparently significant visuality allows opaquely referential visual meanings to disrupt the previous social contracts that constitute a perceptual "real."

As it happens, we know what Charly's intentions were for his photograph. He used it as one among eleven images assembled into an album. The album was intended to teach women the truth about themselves. Each page taught a lesson about a supposed reality of gender, class, and respectability that underlay supposedly false values. Charly relied primarily on photography's reality effect to convince his audience. He called the album *Pérégrina-tions d'un objectif* (The wanderings of a lens) and expanded on the implications of his title in an inscribed preface.

> Everything I see in passing
> to my pictures serves as model.
> And it's known that a faithful mirror
> Is by turns ugly or charming:
> Without relying on tales,
> I might even become adorable
> If, when you see me there
> You don't hide yourself.[25]

But of course that preface is in words, so that from the very start Charly does "rely on tales." And on every page of the album, the photograph that was going to reveal the truth visually has been textually framed by explanatory captions above and moral axioms below. On the first page, the image of a bourgeois woman reading a letter while her maid reads over her shoulder is titled *À la Ville* (In the city) and accompanied by the warning "Méfiez-vous des soubrettes [Beware of easy working-class girls]"; the stage for class antagonism has been set in the city. On the last page, the image shows a moderately middle-class woman having her future predicted by a lower-class fortune-teller, the two distinguished from each other by their clothing. Charly called this picture *Où manque la confiance en Dieu* (Where faith in God is lacking) and smugly concluded, "carte de malheur [card of woe]." Visual meanings were assumed to be natural and self-evident, yet textual meanings are here invoked to speak the "truth."

Visual and textual meanings together set the terms for realism's contracts. If at any one moment either kind of meaning claims to represent truth or nature or reality more effectively than the other, that claim will always, as in the case of *Dans l'atelier*, facilitate an ideological work whose unexpected consequences will eventually require the intervention of its putatively more artificial semiotic counterpart. Nor can configurations of visual and textual meanings be replicated or controlled any more reliably than any other aspect of *combinatoires*. Charly maintained an evenly authoritative tone throughout his album, with one exception—page 8, the page that includes *Dans l'atelier*. When it comes to this photograph, he cannot draw any conclusion. All he can write, confounded by the conflicting signs of his subjects' appearance, is "petit travail grande toilette [small craft grand dress]." We are left with a contradiction he cannot resolve into moral prescription, with an apposition of words unconnected grammatically. *Dans l'atelier*'s *combinatoire* of gender, class, and formal meanings has caused its genre to mutate onward beyond Charly's control.

An Allegorical Object

It might be objected that *Dans l'atelier* is too exceptional an object to sustain any argument larger than itself. Though this photograph has never been deemed of any consequence by the field of history or that of art history, it may seem unusually replete with imploded meanings. I would first respond that many apparently banal images would prove to be equally complex if anyone seriously attempted to begin a history of visual culture. I would also argue that any essay with methodological intentions requires concentration on a few exceptional objects. In work with a broader scope, it would of course be preferable to deal with patterns of objects evolving over time in different ways for different audiences. The limited scope of an essay calls for single objects that carry within themselves, *mise en abyme,* the signs of their own conditions. To recognize and value such objects, finally, requires an understanding of the object or document as allegory. Michel de Certeau wrote that his goal was to "faire de l'analyse une variante de son objet [make analysis into a variation of its object]."[26] Fidelity to the material object forces a relational analysis of its references. Yet the recognition that those references are intrinsically relational makes the object into their merely transient meeting place, into an isolated historical moment. The object's significance lies not in being itself paradigmatic or exemplary, but in acting poetically as the sign of a historical reality our writing can never attain but only evoke. The material object, this photograph of seamstresses, by its obdurate materiality, by the fact of its survival, stands allegorically for the lived human experience.

NOTES

Margaret Cohen and her landmark work on the July Monarchy feminine realist novel inspired this entire essay. Thanks also to Patrice Higonnet, Margaret Higonnet, Deborah Cohen, and Jann Matlock, and to Aggie's.

1. John Berger, "The Suit and the Photograph," in *About Looking* (New York: Pantheon, 1980), 28.

2. Collection of International Museum of Photography at George Eastman House, Rochester, New York.

3. In the 1860s, photographic equipment was still too cumbersome and artificial lighting still too unreliable for most indoor sites other than a photographer's studio. On this subject in relation to photographs of work sites, see Michael Hiley, *Victorian Working Women: Portraits from Life* (Boston: David Godine, 1980), especially ch. 5, " 'Honest Labour bears a lovely face.' "

4. Michel de Certeau, *L'Invention du quotidien. I. Arts de faire* (Paris: Gallimard, 1990 [1980]), xxxvi.

5. Fredric Jameson, "Magical Narratives: Romance as Genre," *New Literary History* 1 (Autumn 1975): 158.

6. Most pertinently, these include some excellent investigations into gender, class, and the place of the photographic medium in nineteenth-century visual cul-

ture, including André Rouillé, "Les Images photographiques du monde du travail sous le Second Empire," *Actes de la recherche en sciences sociales* 54 (September 1984): 31–44; Abigail Solomon-Godeau, "The Legs of the Countess," *October* (Winter 1986): 65–108; Leonore Davidoff, "Class and Gender in Victorian England: The Diaries of Arthur J. Munby and Hannah Cullwick," *Feminist Studies* 5, no. 1 (1979): 87–141.

7. "Ainsi le réalisme (bien mal nommé, en tout cas souvent mal interprété) consiste, non à copier le réel, mais à copier une copie (peinte) du réel: ce fameux réel, comme sous l'effet d'une peur qui interdirait de la toucher directement, est *remis plus loin*, différé, ou du moins saisi à travers la gangue picturale dont on l'enduit avant de le soumettre à la parole: code sur code, dit le réalisme." Roland Barthes, *S/Z* (Paris: Seuil, 1970), 61. All translations in this chapter are my own.

8. Neil Hertz, "Freud and the Sandman," in *The End of the Line* (New York: Columbia University Press, 1985), 97–121. Significantly, this concept stages Hertz's very unusual skill in meshing visual and verbal meanings.

9. Chiefly, this has consisted of an obsessive attribution of paintings to authors and the organization of authored paintings by date and provenance.

10. Jameson, "Magical Narratives," 135.

11. An excellent local history of *petits métiers* images, abundantly illustrated and rich in anecdotal information, is found in Massin, *Les cris de la ville: commerces ambulants et petits métiers de la rue*, 2d ed. (Paris: Albin Michel, 1985 [1978]).

12. Sheila McTighe, "Perfect Deformity, Ideal Beauty, and the *Imaginaire* of Work: The Reception of Annibale Carracci's *Arti di Bologna* in 1646," *Oxford Art Journal* 16, no. 1 (1993): 75–91.

13. Ibid., 81.

14. On these issues of artisanal identity and the political paradoxes of archaic self-representation, see Michael Sonenscher, *Work and Wages: Natural Law, Politics and the Eighteenth-Century French Trades* (Cambridge: Cambridge University Press, 1989); and William H. Sewell, Jr., *Work and Revolution in France: The Language of Labor from the Old Regime to 1848* (Cambridge: Cambridge University Press, 1980).

15. See Beatrice Farwell, *French Popular Lithographic Imagery, 1815–1870*, vol. 1 (Chicago: University of Chicago Press, 1981); and Jeff Rosen "The Political Economy of Graphic Art Production during the July Monarchy," *Art Journal* 48 (Spring 1989): 40–45.

16. "Vive la lithographie / C'est une rage partout / Grand, petit, laide, jolie, / Le crayon retrace tout. / Nos boulevards tout du long / A présent sont un salon / Où, sans même avoir posé, / Chacun se trouve exposé." Cited in Ségolène Le Men, *Les Abécédaires illustrés du XIXe siècle* (Paris: Editions Promodis, 1984), 33.

17. See *Atget. Géniaux. Vert. Petits métiers et types parisiens vers 1900* (exhibition catalog, Musée Carnavalet) (Paris: Musées de la Ville de Paris, 1984); Hiley, *Victorian Working Women;* Rouillé, "Les Images photographiques"; Molly Nesbit, *Atget's Seven Albums* (New Haven, Conn.: Yale University Press, 1992).

18. See Raymond Gaudriault, *La gravure de mode féminine en France* (Paris: Editions d'Amateur, 1983); Vyvyan Holland, *Hand-Coloured Fashion Plates, 1770–1899* (London: Batsford, 1955).

19. See *La Mode et ses métiers: du XVIIIe siècle à nos jours* (exhibition catalog, Musée de la mode et du costume) (Paris: Ville de Paris, 1981).

20. Honoré de Balzac, "Gavarni," *La Mode*, October 1830, 20.

21. See Anne Higonnet, "Secluded Vision," *Radical History Review* 38 (1987): 16–36; reprinted in *The Expanding Discourse,* ed. Norma Broude and Mary D. Garrard (New York: HarperCollins, 1992), 170–85.

22. Balzac, "Gavarni," 20.

23. Françoise Tétart-Vittu and Piédade Da Silveira, *Dessins de mode: Jules David et son temps* (Paris: Mairie du VIe arrondissement, 1987), 10–11. See also Anne Higonnet, *Berthe Morisot's Images of Women* (Cambridge: Harvard University Press, 1992), 84–99.

24. Tétart-Vittu and Silveira, *Dessins de mode,* 17.

25. "Tout ce que je vois en passant / A mes tableaux sert de modèle. / Et l'on sait qu'un miroir fidèle / Est tour à tour laid ou charmant: / Sans avoir recours à la fable, / Je deviendrai même adorable / Si, quand vous me verrez là-bas / Vous ne vous cachez pas."

26. De Certeau, *L'Invention du quotidien,* xxxiii.

Figura Serpentinata:
Visual Seduction and the Colonial Gaze
Emily Apter

> Her great serpent, the black Python, was wasting away; and for the Carthaginians the serpent was both a national and private fetish. It was believed to be born of the earth's clay, since it emerges from the earth's depths and does not need feet to move over it; its progress recalled the rippling of rivers, its temperature the ancient, viscous darkness full of fertility, and the circle it describes, as it bites its own tail, the planetary system, Eschmoûn's intelligence.
>
> . . . From time to time Salammbô approached its silver-wire basket; she drew aside the purple curtain, the lotus leaves, the birds' down; it stayed constantly rolled up, stiller than a withered creeper; and from looking at it she ended by feeling a kind of spiral in her heart, like another serpent slowly coming up into her throat to choke her.[1]

In this passage from *Salammbô,* Flaubert's striking image of the doubled serpent portrays a creature coiled listlessly on itself to signify an ailing national fetish, unwinding in reverse iterability into the body of a woman whose contorted dancing will exorcise "the spiral in her heart" now threatening to choke her to death from within.[2] This reverse iterability takes the form of a jackknife image if one sees the juncture where national and female fetish cross as opening out into mirror trajectories of signification.[3] The line of fate that inscribes the threat to Carthage posed by the rebellious Barbarians shadows the twisted line of fate belonging to Salammbô, daughter of Carthage's king Hamilcar, and victim of ravishment by Mâtho, the colossal Barbarian captain. Together these lines describe a pattern of serpentination linking, allegorically and conceptually, the classic scene of seduction in colonial narrative to the whorls and circuities of the colonial gaze.[4]

I intend to look specifically at descriptions of Oriental dancing that seem designed to compete with the allure of visual representations promising direct access to the colonial real. Recent theoretical work on the real has introduced the problem of how to negotiate analytically among the interconnected though epistemologically distinct categories of realism as a literary genre (typified in the French tradition by Flaubert's historical novels), the Lacanian real of our desire,[5] and social, historical, or economic reality—the real or "reals" of everyday life. The colonial real, as it slides toward the literary genre of colonial realism, designates the place where tourist narrative and realist Orientalism (as featured in Balzac's *La Fille aux yeux d'or* or *La Peau de chagrin*) not only join each other, but also coincide with the sign of the real that interpellates the subject at the blindest spot of his or her identity in national space. Though there are obviously many ways to ramify this notion of the colonial real, for now it must stand as an experimental term mediating between psychoanalytic and historical accounts of the colonial subject (colonized and colonizer alike), whose positionality is a phantasmatic construction of literary texts, themselves firmly anchored in the sociopolitical history of nineteenth-century French colonial life in North Africa.

The representation of exotic dance scenes in French realist and naturalist literature provides fertile ground for examining the way in which the female subject of colonial domination was used to figure a visual fantasy of direct contact or physical touch with the real. From the trotting out of *bayadères,* to ceremonial performances by daughters of the court, to the commercialized acts of belly dancers and striptease artists, such scenes have always served to structure the formulaic spectacles of opera, ballet, cabaret, and film. In the novel, as well as in painting, sculpture,[6] and photography, these production numbers or entertainment set pieces are particularly susceptible to psychoanalytic dissection because of the way in which they reveal the reification of cultural attitude in psychical, phantasmatic space. What interests me is the way in which the rhetorical repetitions of undulation and serpentination encrypt what Lacan would call the "line of desire" cathecting colonial looking to its exoticist visual object. Scopophilia, cultural voyeurism, and the market-propelled techniques that produce canonical images of colonial "reality" seem commonly driven into the shape of the "interior 8" that, in this instance, maps out an aesthetic of colonial desire. I want to investigate the bizarre formalism of this colonial desire as a way of understanding the seductive call within the history of colonialism and postcolonial theory alike, of a "re-enchantment industry" (the expression is Ernest Gellner's) that continues to seem profoundly reliant on late-Orientalist figurations of eroticized tourist attractions.[7]

Decadent Formalism

I draw my fascination with the serpent-figure not from any hackneyed psychology of the serpent-phallus, or from the even more overused repertory of biblical images of evil, but rather from the art historian Leo Steinberg's analysis of Picasso's "Women of Algiers" paintings of 1954 and 1955.[8] I will dwell extensively on the terms of Steinberg's interpretation because his language, though ostensibly more concerned with aesthetic rather than cultural questions, provides highly suggestive categories for rethinking cultural vision.

Steinberg begins by exploring Picasso's "life-long obsession with all-sided presentment," his appropriation of techniques "developed within the Renaissance system of focused perspective . . . of harmonizing an ideal of omnispection with the logic of a fixed point of view."[9] Among these techniques he notes the *figura serpentinata:*

> In a note to Vasari acknowledging the gift of a drawing, Aretino (1540) praises a certain nude which, "bending down to the ground, shows both the back and the front." He was describing a figure of hairpin design, a variant of the *figura serpentinata*. Its elastic anatomy serves Mannerist art for the simultaneous display of front and back without recourse to repetition, external propos or the aid of witnesses. It incorporates both views at once in a jack-knifing spine lengthened only by one or two extra vertebrae. (S 183)

I have already noted a similar kind of hairpin kineticism characterizing the love dance performed by Salammbô and her serpent:

> The python fell back, and putting the middle of its body around her
> neck, it let its head and tail dangle, like a broken necklace with its
> two ends trailing on the ground. Salammbô wound it around her
> waist, under her arms, between her knees; then taking it by the jaw
> she brought its little triangular mouth to the edge of her teeth, and
> half closing her eyes, bent back under the moon's rays. (F 174)

This obvious paroxysm of feminine *jouissance,* at once kitschy and
high art in its decadent aestheticism, curiously imbricates perspecti-
val twists and mirror effects, suggesting that desire pictures itself
through waving, bending lines. The python circles the woman's
neck and is coextensively wound by Salammbô around her waist;
this inverted and self-inverting encirclement, in which snake slides
into female body and vice versa, is compounded by the jackknife
image of the arching back: the snake "falls back" to initiate the ritual
and at its closure Salammbô "bends back" under the moon's rays.

The wavy line of movement that Steinberg identifies as a motif
of Picasso's modernist Orientalism, as seductive as the snake
charmer's meandering melody or the curls of smoke rising from the
hashish smoker's narghile in nineteeth-century Orientalist tableaux,
is of course grounded in the long and complex decorative history
of the Moorish arabesque, but it also possesses yet another aesthetic genealogy that may help to explain the psychology of colonial visual pleasure, with all its attendant ideological consequences
for skewing the iconographic power relations of East and West. As
Ernst Gombrich reminds us in *The Sense of Order: A Study in the
Psychology of Decorative Art:*

> It was William Hogarth who first suggested that the pleasure he
> found in what he called the "line of beauty," the wavy line, derived
> ultimately from our searching mind and eye: "The serpentine line by
> its waving and winding at the same time different ways, leads the
> eye in a pleasing manner along the continuity of its variety, if I may
> be allowed the expression; and which by its twisting so many differ-
> ent ways, may be said to inclose (tho' but a single line) varied con-
> tents."[10]

There is a "having one's cake and eating it too" aspect to Hogarth's
line of beauty, for it satisfies epistemological hungers ("the searching mind and eye") *and* the appetite for visual seduction ("leads
the eye in a pleasing manner") at one and the same time. The same

conjunction of intellectual curiosity and visual drive can be found in Lacan's appositely formulated notion of the "interior 8" or "line of desire," which he claims emerged from his attempt to draw the "topology of the subject":

> You can obtain it [the topology] from the interior 8. Bring the edges together two by two as they are presented here, by a complementary surface, and close it. In a way, it plays the same role as complement in relation to the initial 8 as a sphere in relation to a circle, a sphere that would close what the circle would already offer itself as ready to contain. Well! This surface is a Moebius surface, and its outside continues its inside.
>
> . . . This image enables us to figure desire as a locus of junction between the field of demand, in which the syncopes of the unconscious are made present, and sexual reality. All this depends on a line that I will call the line of desire, linked to demand, and by which the effects of sexuality are made present in experience.[11]

Lacan's Möbius surface loops the loop of inside and outside, recursively intertwining the unconscious with the sexual real, knotting the pulsation of demand with the sinuations of mediated looking so that they fuse into a common thread of desire whose path reiterates yet again the *figura serpentinata.*

Though an abstract, logically abstruse way of characterizing an optical trick for capturing all-seeingness or subjective multisidedness in a single line, Lacan's line of desire, concerned as it is with making manifest the "effects of sexuality," may be brought "down to earth" so to speak, as a depiction of the form of the scopophilic gaze as it targets the object of seduction. This seems to be part of what Leo Steinberg is getting at when he locates the *figura serpentinata* in the art of the pinup, itself derived from the conventional, age-old posture of the sensual (usually female) figure rotated on its axis, projecting, as he puts it, "well-being, self-admiration or erotic enticement" (S 185). "Pin-up models posing for calendar art," Steinberg affirms, "tend to work up a *figura serpentinata,* and their photographer, if he has a sense of craft, knows just how much expository rotation is wanted to meet the terms of an 'eyeful' " (S 185–86). A still version of the dancing body, which likewise seeks to expose itself simultaneously from front to back, the pinup model as "eyeful" underscores how the image of sensuality gathers itself up and delivers itself over as a "filling" repast for the scopophilic gaze. And epistemologically, this gaze often perceives itself self-consciously as a serpentine construction.

Global Vision

Let us go back for a moment to Flaubert's dancers, specifically to the Salomé of his short story "Hérodias," in which the Tetrarch's temptress performs for the price of John the Baptist's head: "Her eyes half closed, she writhed her body above her waist and undulated her belly with a wave-like motion that shook her breasts; and her face remained impassive, and her feet never stopped."[12] Salomé finishes this medley of serpentinas by spreading her legs and arching her body back so far that her chin brushes the floor. As critics have long surmised, this scene was inspired by the "bee dance" or striptease of Flaubert's favorite courtesan, Kuchuk Hanem, of whom he wrote to his mistress Louise Colet:

> To go back to Kuchuk. You and I are thinking of her, but she is certainly not thinking of us. We are weaving an aesthetic around her, whereas this particular very interesting tourist who was vouchsafed the honors of her couch has vanished from her memory completely, like many others. Ah! Traveling makes one modest—you see what a tiny place you occupy in the world. (FE 220)

This passage is interesting for a number of reasons: first, it illustrates the way in which the serpentine figure goes from being a rather literal evocation of the gyrations of a dance to a metaphorical way of talking about the epistemological limits to knowing culturally "other" subjects. "We are weaving an aesthetic around her" says Flaubert to Louise, thereby making transparent the process by which the appearance of the seductive object is attached, as if by a figure 8, to the hermeneutics of aesthetics and sexual fantasy.

A second interesting aspect of Flaubert's statement lies in his taking cognizance of "the tiny place you occupy in the world." Flaubert's tourist seems situated here in a frustratedly fixed Occidentalism that is nonetheless in the process of insistently trying to wrap its vision around the world. Here the serpentine figure seems to embody the yearning for global perspectivalism, the tourist's hunger for an "eyeful" of cultural alterity balanced on the head of a Eurocentric pin. Once again Steinberg's language, in relation to Picasso's "cutting loose" of vision through the use of "circumspicuous or circumambient sight, of visual rays bent around corners," seems uncannily apt in its unwitting conjugation of visual curiosity with colonial desire (S 189–90). Depicting Picasso as an image-fetishist who "paints a figure as though he had toured it to collect impressions of its various aspects" (S 190), Steinberg then goes on to place him, "entwined with his passions," in a cartographic imaginary replete with a kind of narrative coda describing the history of colonial conquest:

Closer still [to Picasso's radical simultaneities] are those splendid projections whereby geodesists, cosmographers, and mathematicians have for centuries rendered the world's sphere on a plane surface— gnomonic, quincuncial, and homolographic projections, discontinuous and kidney-shaped map projections with their distortions, repeats, and disjunctions. These ingenious summaries of the sphere on the plane are the natural analogue for Picasso's manipulations of the human image. Granted that Picasso's heuristic impulses are not pure but entwined with his passions, he treats the body as those maps treat the globe, treats it like a cartographer processing data, and again like the global ruler in the Age of Discovery whose *mappa mundi* unfurls a circumnavigated world. (S 192)

The cosmographer-cartographer, like the colonial observer of Orientalist dancing, seems to steer a serpentine course between the desire for *dépaysement* (the loss of fixed national self-reference) and the will to dominate and domesticate foreign territory through unitary (Western) perspectivalism.

In Flaubert we see some of this effect in the opening of "Hérodias," where the female body is displaced to the landscape. In this passage, Salomé's dance of seduction is foregrounded by a panoptical, geomorphic survey of the ground itself:

The citadelle of Machaerous rose up toward the east of the Dead Sea, on an outcrop of basalt in the form of a cone. Four deep valleys surrounded it, two on the sides, one in front, the fourth behind. Houses were piled up against its base, in the circle of a wall that undulated, following the unevenness of the terrain, and by means of a zigzag route through the rock the town was connected to the fortress, whose walls were one hundred and twenty cubits high with numerous corners, crenellations on the edge, and here and there towers that appeared like fleurons on this crown of stones suspended over the abyss.[13]

It is not just phallic towers and plunging valleys that code this vision of the Oriental world in a field of sexual desire, but more specifically the belly dance in the territory: the undulating wall, the zigzagging path that sculpts the rock face (the verb *taillader,* "to cut," encompasses the word *taille,* in turn connoting the undulating waist of the dancer)—these figures of speech point to the way in which Orientalism, through the figure 8 of serpentination, plants a palimpsest of seduction inside the viewer's craning outlook toward the east.

Corporeal Translocation

Though I have been deliberately taking Steinberg's topic-specific discussion of Picasso's serpentination out of context, bending his rhetoric to frame a theorization of the colonial gaze, I feel somewhat justified in doing so because of the rich implications of Steinberg's apparently throwaway analogies between global visual projection and Picasso's representational strategies for treating the female nude. Commenting on Picasso's nudes of the 1940s, Steinberg deploys tantalizing concepts of corporeal "vagrancy" and "translocation," as if the woman's body constitutes a world map of nomadized territories, encampments of exile, and ambient land masses:

> The female body undergoes new kinds of revision. Its "commonplaces" serve as exponents of vagrant aspects. A dotted bosom becomes the prefix to any aspect soever, so that frontal figures as they bend over sprout breasts at the shoulder blades. . . . Yet the body coheres; there is neither Cubist dismemberment nor schematic disjunction. These figures work, and Picasso's draughtsmanship makes their irrational translocations seem genuinely informative about the rotundity of the object observed. Could a cartographer do it? Could he make the world's other side present to the imagination by entering Pacific islands on the Atlantic? (S 207–8)

Steinberg's omnipotent cartographer remaking the world according to whim by "entering Pacific islands on the Atlantic" parallels the privileged spectators of Oriental dance numbers who "translocate" portions of the female anatomy, as if in an effort to map their bodies according to their own inner topographies of exoticist longing. Flaubert characterizes Azizeh (one of Kuchuk Hanem's rivals), as a corpus whose head might break off from her skeleton and float away like some imperiled peninsula: "Her neck slides back and forth on her vertebrae, and more often sideways, as though her head were going to fall off; terrifying effect of decapitation" (FE 121). Even more to the point is Edmond de Goncourt's description of belly dancing at the Universal Exposition of 1889, in which the lower quarters of the dancer's body migrate like pieces of relocatable urban fabric from one "quartier" (pun intended) to the next.[14] "The belly dance performed by a naked woman interests me," Edmond writes, "making me aware of how her feminine organs move house [me rendrait compte du déménagement des organes de la femme], of how the parts of her belly change neighborhoods"[du changement de quartier des choses de son ventre] (J 290). This nomadism of the female sex is anticipated in a prior scene where de Goncourt recounts how he came to see Gustave Courbet's pornographic sketch of a truncated vagina titled *The Origin of the World* (the work was putatively commissioned by a Turkish bey for private delectation and eventually ended up, as Linda Nochlin recently discovered, in the personal collection of Jacques Lacan):[15]

> [The art dealer] de La Narde says to me: "Do you know this one?" And he unlocks a painting whose exterior panel shows a village church in the snow, and whose hidden panel is the picture painted by Courbet for Khalil-Bey, a female belly with a black and prominent mons Venus, over the narrow opening of a pink cunt. Faced with this painting, which I had never seen before, I was obliged to make honorable amends to Courbet: this belly is as beautiful as the flesh of a Corregio. (J 287)

In this episode, the suspension in space of a disembodied "origin of the world" recalls Steinberg's analysis of Picasso's formalist nudes whose "task is to make exiled space present in effigy" (S 208). The "romance" of exile (tourism) and fetishized erotic display (the effigy) come together in Steinberg's phrase, which could serve as the caption to a cultural interpretation of de Goncourt's translocated belly, itself a fetish symbol for the spellbinding visual appeal of the colonized female sex.

Like the world of the Sultan's jealously guarded seraglio, turned out of its private quarters for European viewing, Courbet's exposed, depersonalized genitalia affords Edmond de Goncourt a vision "bent around corners"; a line of perception leading directly to the most exciting recesses of colonial desire. It is perhaps for this reason that he uses the pretext of a sociological *flânerie* through the mock "rue du Caire" at the exposition to unveil a number of saucy revelations about his personal experience with "Moorish" prostitutes.

> Here a remark suggested by my nights with Moorish women in Africa. It is hardly explicable, this dance, with its furious unleashing of the belly and bum, in women who in coitus have the least pronounced movement, a barely perceptible *rolling,* and who, if you ask them to spice this movement up with some of the *pitch* of our European women, reply that you are asking them to make love like dogs. (J 290)

Edmond's deception over the lovemaking capabilities of Arab women implies that their dancing offers better sexual value for the money: coitus emerges as low-energy choreography, it is dance minus the serpentination (not enough "tangage" or pitching about, he complains). A similar idea can be found when he praises a Saxe porcelain chamber pot on view at the "exposition des Arts de la femme" for its "snaking form" [une forme plus contournée, plus serpentente], "more amorous even than the secret parts of woman" (J 753). With characteristic misogyny, de Goncourt ingeniously and perhaps unwittingly inverts the traditional interpretation of belly dancing as a thinly masked performance of the sex act, by configuring the sex act as a poor second to the dance.

Dance Numbers

Edmond de Goncourt's privileged ranking of dance may be more fully understood when one recalls the erotic value of money as it was used in the staging of belly dance numbers either on site in North Africa or in European music halls and brothels. Catering to male tourists who would presumably make an evening of it by trysting with a prostitute, the dance would invariably reach an "interactive" climax when spectators would come forward to "reward" the performers. Théophile Gautier records this moment in his *Voyage pittoresque en Algérie* (published in 1845) after describing "la danse moresque" in what by now has become a familiar language of serpentination—"perpetual undulations, twisting loins, shaking hips, body in an impossible spiraling rotation, body like a caterpillar upright on its tail, neck bent back."[16] The scene continues with the appearance of a black factotum who holds a candle up close to each part of the dancer's body, as Gautier says, to "face, throat, arm, or something else." This inspection, reminiscent of the slave-market painting by Gérôme, has the effect of assigning a financial rating to each lineament, and there is a strange erotic frisson that comes of turning people into property that may be part of the secret "kicks" inherent in even the most bureaucratic form of colonial domination. Like the ghostly agent of colonial mimicry in Homi Bhabha's ascription, the attendant shadowing the dancer encourages her purchase with obsequious grins.[17] And as this figure of doubled serpentination loops its loop, we have the "interactive" finale: spectators plaster gold pieces on the sweaty body of Zorah (the most African of the dancers, and therefore the favorite among Gautier and his companions), "on her forehead, on her cheeks, on her chest, on her arms, and finally, on the spot that they admired most."[18] This "money shot" was and continues to be a stock-in-trade convention of the belly dance. In 1919 we find a similar scene in Elissa Rhaïs's best-selling colonial novel *Saâda la Marocaine:*

> One heard the clicking of the gold and silver coins which the spectators made ring for the *bayadères.* One saw handsome *caïds* rise to their feet, pull glittering louis from their pouches, moisten them with saliva and stick them onto the dancers who were lucky enough to please them.[19]

For the spectator normally confined to voyeurism because of the distance from the stage conventionally required by the dictates of spectacle, this ability to touch a live performer with coin affords a particularly transgressive thrill (it remains today a standard trope of striptease acts worldwide). I would argue that the promise of such a touch—a magical Midas touch rendering transparent the transmogrification of sex into money—provides a key to understanding the peculiar attraction of the belly dance as performed under Western eyes. In addition to serving as an objective that motivates the serpentine visual foreplay of the colonial gaze, and in addition to "dangerously" confusing art, ethnographic spectacle, prostitution, and erotic performance, this "on the money/on the body" moment in the dance holds out what every colonial traveler or modern-day tourist seems to desire, namely, the chance of being "touched" by what one sees, of experiencing a palpable collision with the real. It was this vital though bitter-tasting touch of the real that Flaubert seemed to be after with the dancer Kuchuk Hanem (as he explained didactically to Louise Colet):

> You tell me that Kuchuk's bedbugs degrade her in your eyes; for me they were the most enchanting touch of all. Their nauseating odor mingled with the scent of her skin, which was dripping with sandalwood oil. I want a touch of bitterness in everything—always a jeer in the midst of our triumphs, desolation even in the midst of enthusiasm. (FE 220)

Evoking the erotics of disgust—the "nausea" of archaic (anal-erotic) drives—Flaubert's encounter with the colonial real matches up with Maupassant's equally acidulous pleasure in the spectacle of women dancers performing "unnatural acts" on members of their own sex. Intrigued with the dance as a visual translation of crypto-lesbian sensuality (much like Walter Benjamin in relation to the sinuous forms of art nouveau), Maupassant added the serpentination of sexual deviance to the Flaubertian idealization of cultural eccentricity.[20]

Theory's Belly Dance

To conclude, I would simply argue that there is something about the way in which serpentination is recapitulated in the discourse of postcolonial theory that makes one wonder whether a "wavy line" of disavowed colonial desire haunts even the most rigorous, well-intentioned efforts to unmask the colonial gaze. A case of this eerie return of the repressed within theory itself can be found in Malek Alloula's provocative, original analysis of early twentieth-century harem postcards. *The Colonial Harem* (published in France in 1981 with the subtitle *Images d'un sous-érotisme*) is avowedly an exploration of the "multiform violence" buried in what Alloula ascertains was "a right of (over)sight that the colonizer arrogates to himself."[21] Alloula wants "to return this postcard to its sender" by theorizing the hidden history of colonial domination unconsciously recorded in the cards. But with all due respect to Alloula, there is something about the layout of his book that retraces the sinuous path of the colonial gaze even as it is being dismantled intellectually. As the text moves along with its accompanying images—women shrouded in heavy muslin up to their eyes, women behind bars, women taking tea, women smoking pipes, women lounging, women dancing—there is progressively more nudity. First a breast is partially exposed, then by the middle of the book the *poitrine* is fully bared, and finally by the end the striptease of the torso is complete. Round, tattooed breasts are compared with untattooed pendulous breasts (as if once again in the slave market), and the final image, perhaps most disturbing of all, is a picture titled *Arabian Woman with the Tachmak,* in which the breasts, bifurcated by a long black veil, become entirely aestheticized, placed in a formal arrangement around the garment. The woman's eyes stare directly into the camera, as if to say "Terminus, the *figura serpentinata* stops here." This book, like so much postcolonial theory at the moment, proceeds recursively, like a dance of seduction—a critically sophisticated one, no doubt, but a teasing, undulating dance nevertheless that makes of the critic a colonial tourist.

NOTES

I would like to thank Tim Clark and Ann Wagner of the University of California, Berkeley, for inviting me to present this essay to their discussion group on French visual culture in the spring of 1992. Unless otherwise noted, all translations in the text are my own.

1. Gustave Flaubert, *Salammbô*, trans. A. J. Krailsheimer (New York: Penguin, 1983), 166. Unless otherwise noted, all further references to this work will be to this edition. Citations will appear in the text, abbreviated F.

2. Gustave Flaubert, *Salammbô*, in *Oeuvres* (Paris: Gallimard, 1951), 869.

3. In 1925 the woman travel writer Myriam Harry would echo this idea of the belly dance as serpentinated national fetish when she described women dancers in Tunis: "At each movement, the long ribbons of her silver belt unfolded like serpents; her arms twisted, voluptuous swans' necks, and her long hair was either trailing on the ground or apparently coiling itself around an invisible, beloved body. . . . After the Circassian woman, the others took their turn, shaking their flanks, dancing

and redancing the eternal dance of the Arabs, the dance of the sex and the belly, which is perhaps a national symbol." *Tunis la blanche* (Paris: Arthème Fayard, 1925), 63–64.

4. For a pointed characterization of the Lacanian "gaze" (distinguished from Freudian scopophilia or the Sartrean look), see Elizabeth Grosz, "Voyeurism/ Exhibitionism/The Gaze," in *Feminism and Psychoanalysis: A Critical Dictionary,* ed. Elizabeth Wright (Oxford: Basil Blackwell, 1992), 447–50.

5. In evoking the category of the "colonial real," I am aware of the multiple slippages and ambiguities surrounding the notion of the real in Lacanian theory. Definable as a term that marks the haunting of the subject by a dream of subjective plenitude or nonseparation with the maternal body (the "lack of the lack," in Lacan's words), immersed in the traumatic moment of the splitting of the subject, identified in its retroactive function in fantasy as the "object-cause of desire" (Lacan) or the "psychic reality of desire" (see Slavoj ⊡i¥ek), the real in psychoanalytic terms presents itself linguistically and visually on the sly. Intruding itself on the subject at a moment least expected, the real is that sudden and terrifying flash when the subject perceives the gaping hole in subjectivity tenuously papered over by repression. On the relationship between the real and reality, see Slavoj ⊡i¥ek, *Looking Awry: An Introduction to Jacques Lacan through Popular Culture* (Cambridge: MIT Press, 1991), chs. 1–2. See also Elizabeth Grosz, *Jacques Lacan: A Feminist Introduction* (New York: Routledge, 1990).

6. In sculpture I am thinking specifically of Rupert Carabin's art nouveau rendering of Loie Fuller performing "La Danse du serpent."

7. Ernest Gellner, "Ethnomethodology: The Re-enchantment Industry or the Californian Way of Subjectivity," in *Spectacles and Predicaments: Essays in Social Theory* (Cambridge: Cambridge University Press, 1991 [1979]). "The pre-packaged ready-cooked and so very contingent subjectivity is similarly convenient; is, so to speak, an industrial, supermarket, ready-to-eat subjectivity. You just warm it up. When Max Weber spoke scathingly of the intellectuals who furnished their private chapels with spiritual exotica and indulged in intellectual antiquarianism, he clearly had in mind an élite hobby, which presupposed privileged access to leisure and resources. It was hand-made Re-enchantment for the Few. But one of the advantages of the affluent society, of the further advance in the equalisation of conditions, is that re-enchantment itself is now mass-produced, standardised, and rationalized. Subjectivity, like the Mexican peasant's meal, is no longer produced in the mud hut of the pueblo; specialists will prepare and package for mass-consumption a variant of it which, when all is said and done, is almost as palatable and perhaps much more hygienic. So let us welcome the day when we can be reassured of the existence of our own subjectivity, and be supplied with tools for locating or erecting it, in a way which is no longer restricted to a privileged elite, nursing its nostalgia for enchantment like a badge of rank; but, on the contrary, which is supplied so as to make both the nostalgia and its solace available to *all*" (64).

8. T. J. Clark has pointed out to me that the dates of Picasso's Algiers paintings coincide, perhaps not accidentally, with the beginning of the Algerian Revolution. It would be interesting to explore in another context an interpretation of the paintings that would take the specific historical backdrop of the revolution into account.

9. Leo Steinberg, "The Algerian Women and Picasso at Large," in *Other Criteria: Confrontations with Twentieth-Century Art* (New York: Oxford University Press,

1979), 177. All further references to this piece will appear in the text, abbreviated S.

10. Ernst H. Gombrich, *The Sense of Order: A Study in the Psychology of Decorative Art* (New York: Columbia University Press, 1979), 137.

11. Jacques Lacan, "Sexuality in the Defiles of the Signifier," in *The Four Fundamental Concepts of Psychoanalysis,* trans. Alan Sheridan, ed. Jacques-Alain Miller (New York: W. W. Norton, 1978), 155–56.

12. Gustave Flaubert, *Flaubert in Egypt: A Sensibility on Tour,* trans. Francis Steegmuller (Chicago: Academy Chicago Limited, 1979), 221–22. Steegmuller excerpts and translates this section of "Hérodias" in a note to the passage in Flaubert's Egyptian journal where he describes the "bee dance." All further references to *Flaubert in Egypt* will appear in the text, abbreviated FE.

There are multiple literary, cultural, and psychosexual interpretations of the bee dance in recent literary criticism. See Edward Said, *Orientalism* (New York: Random House, 1978); Dennis Porter, *Haunted Journeys: Desire and Transgression in European Travel Writing* (Princeton, N.J.: Princeton University Press, 1991); Charles Bernheimer, *Figures of Ill-Repute: Representing Prostitution in Nineteenth-Century France* (Cambridge: Harvard University Press, 1989); Lisa Lowe, *Critical Terrains: French and British Orientalisms* (Ithaca, N.Y.: Cornell University Press, 1991). Most recently, in an essay titled "Vacation Cruises, or the Homoerotics of Orientalism" (unpublished manuscript, 1994), Joe Boone reminds us, through a critique of Said's discussion of the bee dance, that the *"first* exotic dancer to catch Flaubert's eye is not the female Kuchuk but a *male* dancer and well-known catamite, Hasan el-Belbeissi, whose sexualized pantomime, female garb, and kohl-painted eyes, as Flaubert writes home to his friend Louis Bouilhet, 'put additional spice into a thing already quite clear in itself.' " Stressing Flaubert's connections among Hasan's bee dance, the availability of boys, and his own sense of obligation to sample sodomy while on tour in the Orient, Boone avoids concluding, as one might, that Kuchuk's bee dance is simply a surrogate for the homoerotic template, but points out "how contact with different cultural attitudes opens one's perception of *the possible*—and *this* possibility, as references throughout Flaubert's papers reveal, becomes a newly welcome source of stimulation" (8).

13. Gustave Flaubert, "Hérodias," in *Trois contes* (Paris: Garnier-Flammarion, 1986), 109.

14. In Edmond de Goncourt and Jules de Goncourt, *Journal: Mémoires de la vie littéraire,* vol. 3 (1887–96) (Aylesbury, Great Britain: Editions Robert Laffont, 1989). All further references to this work will be to this volume and edition and will appear in the text, abbreviated J.

See as well the analysis of this passage of the Goncourt journal in Zeynep Celik and Leila Kinney, "Ethnography and Exhibitionism at the Expositions Universelles," *Assemblage: A Critical Journal of Architecture and Design Culture* 13: 35–59, especially 46. These authors situate the fashion for belly dancing in relation to the broader culture of popular Parisian dance forms (the cancan, the quadrille, the chahut, and so on) in addition to theorizing the "exhibitionism" of Orientalism in the staging of Universal Expositions during the nineteenth and early twentieth centuries.

15. Linda Nochlin, "The Origin without an Original," *October* 37 (Summer 1986): 76–86. See also Nochlin's chapter in this volume.

16. Théophile Gautier, *Voyage pittoresque en Algérie* (Geneva: Librairie Droz, 1973 [1845]), 76.

17. Homi Bhabha, "Of Mimicry and Man: The Ambivalence of Colonial Discourse," in *October: The First Decade, 1976–1986,* ed. Annette Michelson, Rosalind Krauss, Douglas Crimp, and Joan Copjec (Cambridge: MIT Press, 1987), 317–25.

18. Gautier, *Voyage pittoresque,* 76.

19. Elissa Rhaïs, *Saâda la Marocaine* (Paris: Plon, 1919), 163.

20. See Guy de Maupassant, *Au soleil* (1884), in *Maupassant au Maghreb* (Paris: Le Sycomore, 1982), 112. "Elles vont ainsi, l'une vers l'autre. Quand elles se rencontrent, leurs mains se touchent; elles semblent frémir; leurs tailles se renversent, laissant traîner un grand voile de dentelle qui va de la coiffure aux pieds. Elles se frôlent, cambrées en arrière, comme pâmées dans un joli mouvement de colombes amoureuses. Le grand voile bat comme une aile. Puis, redressées soudain, redevenues impassibles, elles se séparent; et chacune continue jusqu'à la ligne des spectateurs son glissement lent et boitillant."

21. Malek Alloula, *The Colonial Harem,* trans. Myrna Godzich and Wlad Godzich (Minneapolis: University of Minnesota Press, 1986), 5. Alloula's book can be easily criticized, indeed has been criticized, for its lack of historical precision and blinkered sexism. The female models are left anonymous and undocumented: no mention is made of their vastly differing facial expressions (mutinous and resentful of the camera's eye in one collective harem picture [p. 33]), and nothing is made of the fact that many of the same models reappear, some in vastly different contexts and guises (e.g., the chaste young girl in a "scènes et types" lovers shot [p. 43] is astonishingly reincarnated later on as the lasciviously smiling, bare-breasted, tattooed model of "la belle Mauresque" [p. 124]). Individual photographers are amalgamated into a composite figure of *the* colonial photographer whose gaze is assumed to be homogeneous and whose camera seems to operate according to a common point of view that uniformly embodies colonial ideology (see Alloula's note 26). The albums and photographic agencies from which the cards were selected are insufficiently described. The messages on the cards are haphazardly reported (with little attention to the class, gender, or geographic status of addressees). A colonial phantasm is put on the *divan* as if it were an anonymous, poststructuralist subject, and no explanation is given for the absence of male, homoerotic counterparts to the female models (for which there was a corresponding photographic archive, though perhaps more underground). On the other hand, Alloula's brilliant configuration of psychoanalytic interpretations of scopic eroticism and the politics of decolonization (prefigured in Frantz Fanon's chapter "Algeria Unveiled," in *A Dying Colonialism,* trans. Haakon Chevalier [New York: Grove, 1967] must be recognized as a kind of landmark in cultural studies, particularly in light of when the book came out in France [1981] under the shadow of Roland Barthes's *Camera Lucida,* trans. Richard Howard (New York: Hill & Wang, 1982 [1980]).

Flaubert and Realism: Paternity, Authority, and Sexual Difference
Roger Huss

Although Flaubert complies scrupulously with many of the conventions and presuppositions of realism (rules of cause and effect are respected, behavior is carefully motivated, subjective constructions of the world are relativized, and characters are placed in specific social contexts), his narrative voice, often difficult to locate precisely, fails to endorse the various orders that guarantee realism, among which figure most prominently paternal authority, the related order of sexual difference, and language itself. This absence of endorsement does not, however, challenge realism directly, as Flaubert's favored mode is ironic.[1] The text remains readable both in terms of classic realism and in terms deriving from the analytic habits of psychoanalysis and structuralism that denaturalize the text. Two examples of this ambivalence that are implicit in the analysis of *Madame Bovary* that follows concern the status of individual persons and the foregrounding of language.[2]

Flaubert's characters are painstakingly individualized, but a suspicious reading will pick up the fact that the details of their definition are constantly migrating, cutting across the supposed separateness of fictional selves in realism. Discreet textual displacements imply equivalences that contradict commonsense distinctions of character and even gender (Homais = Bovary *père* = Larivière, for example, or Charles = Justin = Hippolyte, or Charles = Emma), but these fantastic traces are contained within the realist fiction; one might even say they require the camouflage of realism to attain any kind of expression. Similarly, Flaubert constantly emphasizes language in a manner consistent with realist convention (language seen as an objective part of social reality), but when the text offers us what is, in this respect, a perfectly legitimate thematization of, for example, puns, it also turns us away from a prosaic, realist reading of its own language as transparent and encourages us to place an unusual emphasis on the signifier.[3]

The Delayed Report of a Father's Death

The scene through which I have chosen to explore Flaubert's ambivalent realism is taken from the second chapter of the third part of *Madame Bovary*. I start with a conventional summary of what is a particularly complex piece of text, stressing sequences of events and the psychological explanations typically foregrounded in realism. This is not only intended to make the subsequent analysis easier to follow; it also gives primacy to an order within which Flaubert is uncomfortably contained and that, as I hope to show, he places indirectly under strain.

The chapter begins with Emma returning to Yonville, after making love with Léon for the first time, to find Félicité waiting for her in the street with a message, which she delivers "with an air of mystery" (233): Emma must go urgently to the pharmacist's. She arrives to find a scene of disorder: Homais's favorite chair has been upturned and he is berating his assistant Justin for having dared to enter the pharmaceutical sanctuary he calls the Capharnaum (a dignified term for glory-hole) to fetch a receptacle for the jam that the whole Homais family is busy making. For Homais this confusion of the pharmaceutical and the domestic (which may also be read as a confusion of male and female domains) is a serious transgression. Emma is unable to interrupt the chemist's angry recriminations in order to find out why she has been summoned; as she waits, he reaches a climax of indignation, describing in polychromatic detail a bottle marked "Dangerous," blue in color, sealed with yellow wax and containing a white powder, arsenic, placed hazardously close to the bowl misappropriated by Justin.

As Homais, asserting his authority but less and less in control of himself, rages on, imagining the terrible consequences for himself and his family of the poison escaping his vigilance, Emma tries, and fails once more, to obtain enlightenment, this time from Madame Homais. The chemist's wife, like Félicité earlier, seems unauthorized or unable to give information, referring only to "a calamity" (237). Her husband is now shaking the hapless Justin, an action that reveals a new horror as *Conjugal Love,* an illustrated medical textbook of sexual difference, falls from the boy's pocket. In a second fit of indignation (which implicitly sets up a parallel between the anatomical fact of sexual difference and the danger-ous arsenic that motivated the earlier outburst), Homais expands on the dangers of this corrupting object falling into the wrong hands, prevents his wife from touching it, and banishes his chil-dren from the room (236).

Only now does Emma learn that her father-in-law is dead, a piece of information that Homais, in his distraction, delivers abruptly, with none of the tact that, we are told, Charles had hoped he would bring to the announcement of "the horrible news" (237). The authorial voice here provides a psychological explanation for Charles's mysterious delegation of responsibility to Homais: his concern for Emma's feelings. The implausibility of the whole ellip-tical motivating sequence that brings Emma to the pharmacy, and therefore to knowledge of the exact site of the arsenic, is here re-cuperated by a familiar topos readily available in this context (the cuckold's ignorance of his wife's desires and actions) and by our sense (established at the beginning of the novel and since repeat-edly confirmed) of Charles as one who does not understand. Naively he has exaggerated Emma's sensitivity by imagining that his father occupies a special place in her thoughts. In its explana-tion of Charles's motives, the authorial voice borrows ironically from the inflationary excess of Homais's own discourse to mock Charles's misplaced concern: "the horrible news," which in any case overstates the son's feelings, sits bathetically with the prosaic circumstances of Bovary's death "from an apoplectic stroke, as he was leaving the table" (237). The effect is to devalue the father and any mourning associated with him. Nevertheless, even if for Homais the death of Bovary's father is of little importance, the placing of the news in the context of his angry outburst has the ef-fect of attaching the "horror" of the father's death to the two pre-ceding horrifying revelations, Justin's invasion of the sanctuary containing the poison and his precocious misappropriation of sexual knowledge; this connection will be explored presently.

Emma, having learned nothing more than the simple fact of Bovary's death (and, indirectly, the place of the poison), now returns home to a tearful Charles, while Homais resumes his lecturing of Justin, in a more moderate, "fatherly" mode this time, acknowledging that the scientific aspects of *Conjugal Love* (the author was a doctor after all) are something that it will be useful, indeed necessary, for Justin to know when he eventually becomes a man.

Léon Bopp, reading *Madame Bovary* with an eye to the kinds of realist motivation of plot and individual psychology that we know Flaubert also to have been exercised by, is troubled by this scene.[4] He finds a lack of verisimilitude in Charles's belief that the news will be a blow to Emma and sees her visit to Homais as a subterfuge on the part of the novelist: Emma must learn the exact whereabouts of the arsenic with which she will kill herself, and the announcement of Bovary *père*'s death by Homais is merely the means to this end.

Although Bopp's reading is often shortsightedly literal (he is an indefatigable calculator of times and distances), his focus on moments of the text at which realist motivation appears to be under stress stimulates us to consider what other kind of motivation can be so important as to bend the text in the direction of *invraisemblance*. The nature of such a motivation is suggested by the repeated foregrounding, in the short space of this scene, of wild fluctuations in the status of Bovary *père*. The mocking words "horrible news" already contain traces of such fluctuation, because their irony depends on a retreat from a falsely epic evaluation of the importance of Charles's father's death.[5] Similarly, the place of Bovary *père* in Homais's thoughts is both central (in that Homais has spent time preparing an elaborate rhetorical announcement of the death) and marginal (as this masterpiece can be so readily eliminated by the rage that possesses him: "Anger had swept away rhetoric" (237). For the (first-time) reader, too, Bovary *père*'s death is both incidental to the scene (arresting Homais's colorful outburst only for a brief and bathetic moment) and central (unspoken, it keeps the reader, like Emma, in suspense; when announced, it answers the mystery introduced by Félicité at the outset). As for Emma herself, although the status Charles imagines for his father in his wife's thoughts is such that his death should trouble her profoundly, in reality it is a matter of indifference to her, occupied as she is by thoughts of her new lover. Finally, the contradictory character of these assessments is taken up in a delayed reference to Charles's own feelings toward his father later in the same chapter: he "was surprised to feel so much affection for one whom up till then he had thought he loved but little" (239). Charles's astonishment rewinds the process of relegation signaled by the authorial "horrible news" and reinstates Bovary *père* in an affection he patently has not deserved.

What Flaubert is suggesting obliquely here is a son's disavowal of hostility toward his father. Charles fails to conceive of a more negative emotion toward his father than loving him "but little." This in spite of the fact that the history of their relationship would amply justify feelings of resentment: as a child, Charles is unable to measure up to his father's "virile ideal" (7),[6] remaining more attached to his mother, who for her part suffers in a loveless marriage; he feels obliged to conceal his examination failure from his father, who discovers it five years late; visiting his son and daughter-in-law, Bovary *père* is as parasitic as a feudal lord, abusing his paternal authority and even seizing Emma playfully, or not so playfully,[7] in front of Charles. Still, Charles remains filial in his bereavement: the deliberate omission that is the only sign that his feelings toward his father are problematic—the decision not to declare in person that his father is dead (thus avoiding the danger of discovering that the constative utterance is but the repetition of a previously repressed and dreamed-of performative?)—can equally and quite simply pass for a sign of grief. In any case, the authorial commentary, as we have seen, steers clear of elaborating on Charles's feelings toward his father and chooses a quite different tack involving a clearly inappropriate displacement onto Emma of the burden of feeling for Bovary *père*.[8]

We can read this as an effect of censorship operative when the father-son relationship is directly at issue. It is significant that hostility or irreverence is admitted when expressed not by the son but by the "impersonal" authorial instance. The creature that is Charles cannot be shown mocking the "author of his days," but the author that is Flaubert can mock his creature, Charles-Denis-Bartholomé: paternity has its privileges.

This is not to say that the authorial instance is free of the self-censorship I am attributing both to Charles and to Flaubert when writing any insufficiently distanced father-son relationship. If Flaubert's presentation of Charles expresses (without analyzing or explicitly understanding) a son's resentful thralldom to a father, Flaubert's irony at Bovary *père*'s expense is not truly the lifting of censorship—the son's settling of accounts with the father is too indirect. Instead, what Flaubert gives us to fill Charles's silence is, through Homais, a garrulous enactment, displaced and coded, of everything the son cannot say about the father, a performance that, as will also be seen, at the same time reveals the substance of paternal authority to consist of control over language and the knowledge of sexual difference.

The scene of Homais's tirade at Justin's expense, far from being dictated merely by the needs of the plot and only contingently connected with the news of the father's death, is discreetly tied in with the person of the deceased and pervasively overdetermined by the thematics of paternity. A particularly uncanny connection is established when the apoplectic anger triggered in Homais by the actions of his pseudo-son and favorite victim Justin metamorphoses barely fifteen lines later into the apoplectic attack that kills Bovary *père*.

If the prime motivation of the apoplexy motif is its connection with the paternity theme, we will not be surprised later to see Emma's father, Monsieur Rouault, contracting, if only metaphorically, what is by now a textually transmissible disease, with Homais as the carrier. Writing the news of Emma's poisoning to Rouault, Homais is as concerned about the father's feelings as Charles was earlier about Emma's; but again his message misfires, this time by being too unclear. However, in a significant reversal, what causes Rouault to collapse "as though stricken by apoplexy" (316) is not anger (Homais) or self-indulgence (Bovary *père* dies after lunch), but the thought that Emma is dead. Here the paternal figure undergoes a compensatory and exceptional transformation that conveys the ambivalence of the relation toward the father in *Madame Bovary* and points to one of the meanings that overdetermine Emma's suicide. Resentment of the father may produce murderous fantasies, but it does not remove the desire to be loved by him at last, with all the passion of despair, when murder has been redirected by the child against itself.[9] That the death of the father can be thus linked in one emotional complex with the suicide of a child is one sense of the strange placing in our scene of Charles's delegated message. It enables Emma to learn on one occasion two things that are implicitly related, one "intended" by Charles—his father's death—and the other the means to suicide. This reading, of course, cuts uncomfortably across the conventional separateness of fictional characters in realism and requires us to assimilate Emma's predicament to that of Charles, overlooking sexual difference in the process.

As for Homais, in this scene very much the paterfamilias with wife and children in attendance, not only does he share the apoplexy that kills Bovary *père,* but the death of the whole Homais family at the hands of Justin is imagined by Madame Homais—"You might have poisoned us all!" (235)—while Homais evokes the accidental death of a patient by arsenic poisoning and sees himself, branded a murderer, mounting the scaffold. The reference to capital punishment appropriately reactivates an earlier event in which Homais bears a heavy responsibility, the club foot operation and resulting amputation, which produced a lugubrious atmosphere in Yonville "as though it were execution day" (172). That episode combined, in a compromise formation, a fear of paternal power (amputation as castration)[10] and a resentful refusal of paternal prestige (we know that Doctor Flaubert experienced failure in attempting to correct a club foot), but in a way that is totally inaccessible to readers lacking very specific biographical information.[11]

It should be clear by now that filial resentment is present, similarly censored, at the center of the Capharnaum scene: a father is imagined as poisoned, poisoning, and executed. The cause of this is not, say, Napoléon or Franklin, one of Homais's natural sons, but Justin, whom he claims to have treated *as* a son: "That's how you repay me for the father's care I've showered on you!" (235). In fact, the "father's care" is a diet of browbeating and humiliation. However, because, in Justin's case, Homais is only a pseudo-father, any indictment of the excesses of paternal authority is mitigated and deflected from its mark.

Thus far I have stressed ambivalent feelings toward the father. I want now to examine more closely the content and significance of the figure of paternal authority in this episode. The theme of Bovary *père*'s attempted and failed reproduction of himself through his Spartan upbringing of his son (introduced in the novel's opening chapter) reappears, parodically displaced, in the Homais-Justin relationship. By restaging the relationship between Charles and his father in Homais's treatment of Justin, Flaubert manages not only to elaborate on abuse of authority (Justin is silently defenseless, the imbalance of forces evident), but to suggest connections between the father's *word* and the order of sexual difference, so important for the novel as a whole.

A transgression of difference is at the root of Homais's anger against Justin. The boy's invasion of Homais's sanctuary is doubly an infringement of difference: not only is the place itself set apart, but this theme of separation is overdetermined by the activities Homais undertakes there, precisely those of ordering, naming, and labeling—actions based on separation.[12] Justin is defined in terms that emphasize his exclusion from such a place: "You haven't the makings of a scientist! You're scarcely capable of sticking on a label!" (356). The gulf between Homais's values and Justin, who will never be able to repay Homais's "fatherly" care adequately by embodying these values, no doubt explains a strange breach of verisimilitude, registered, disapprovingly but without further inquiry, by Bopp: Homais accuses Justin of "sheer laziness" (234) in taking the key to the Capharnaum even though the action seems rather to require effort and initiative, particularly since the room is at the top of the house.[13] The logic of Homais's inappropriate interpretation is to be found in a pervasive economy of sexual difference: in the French text, Justin's "laziness" is paired with the noun *mollesse* (literally softness, limpness), a term whose feminizing connotations are foregrounded in this novel, and that relegates Justin to a place with women and children, this side of science. The complement and antithesis of *mollesse* appears a page later in the image of the callus, which, Homais asserts, comes from experience and is metaphorically prerequisite to the performance of a public (masculine) role in society: "You've got to bend your back to the oar—get some calluses [*du cal*] on your hands" (235). The overdetermined character of the callus-masculinity-paternity connection is confirmed by its echoing of an earlier reference to Emma's lack of sensitivity: "She was anything but tender-hearted or sympathetic to other people's troubles. (In this she was like most sons and daughters of country folk: their souls always keep some of the horniness of their fathers' hands [*la callosité des mains paternelles*].)" (62). The chiasmus that deprives sons of their masculine inheritance (Justin is not yet a man, Charles is a poor one, defined by the refrain *pauvre homme* five times in the French text) but settles it with ironic inappropriateness on a daughter is just one expression of the anxiety of gender at the center of *Madame Bovary*.[14]

Homais's constant affirmations of the order of gender can be seen as an expression of the same anxiety: his name echoes the diminutive *hommet* (little man) and needs only the slightest dislocation to become an emblem of masculine self-doubt (*ho[mme] mais*), but the point is sufficiently made by Homais's own repetitions: *homme* three times in as many lines, as he remonstrates with Justin: "It [*Conjugal Love*] deals with certain scientific aspects that it does a man [*homme*] no harm to know about—aspects, if I may say so, that a man [*homme*] *has* to know about. But later, later! Wait till you're a man [*homme*] yourself" (237). One may even speculate that one of the attractions of the word *capharnaüm,* for Flaubert and for Homais, lies in its final syllable, phonetically identical in French with *homme*. Homais's outpourings are, for all their incoherence, obsessively centripetal: whatever he says bears on or implies sexual difference or is led in that direction by Flaubert's textual relays. Take the example Homais uses to convey the scandal of Justin's confusion of the separate domains of pharmacy and kitchen: "It's like carving a chicken [*poularde*] with a scalpel" (234). This produces some satisfying immediate meanings (we notice Homais's self-ennobling assimilation of pharmacy to surgery and perhaps enjoy the implicit cannibalistic logic of his analogy: take a scalpel to a fowl, or a knife and fork to a patient), but above all his comparison lugubriously echoes the earlier words of the surgeon Canivet to Homais on preparing to amputate Hippolyte's leg: "It's all the same to me whether I carve up a Christian or any old chicken [*volaille*] they put in front of me" (173).[15]

What Homais has presented as a disorder (analogous to Justin's failure to make the appropriate distinction) is in fact revealed by Canivet as the (hidden) truth of medical authority: the carnivore surgeon's obscene mastery of his patient's inert body. Remembering Baudelaire's analogy of surgeon and lover,[16] we may choose to perceive the surgeon's object as symbolically feminized, not just by the inertia that is explicitly associated with femininity in this novel but also by the castrating act of amputation and by the linguistic gender of the birds involved (*volaille* and *poularde* are feminine forms, preferred to the masculine *poulet*). This dark fantasy of the surgeon's authority thus takes in the fact of sexual difference.

It becomes all the clearer that the associations activated by Homais's outlandish analogy are not casual textual effects if we remember what brought Emma into Charles's life: her father's broken lower limb. Although Charles only puts the father's leg in a splint, reference to the surgeon's knife is introduced with uncanny menace into the text as the novice *officier de santé* calms the older man "with all kinds of facetious remarks—a truly surgical attention, like the oiling of a scalpel" (14). Rouault celebrates his recovery from his humiliating position by presenting Charles with a turkey: the gift, repeated regularly (62, 161) and promised even after Emma, the link between the two men and herself a gift (in marriage) from the father to Charles, has disappeared from the text (321), functions as a reassertion of this father's mastery (Rouault raises these fowl) and an exorcism by transference of the victim status Flaubert associates with both patients and the animal world in this novel.[17]

More complex connections are made by Flaubert's strategic placing of the bizarrely overdetermined *pilon* twice in this chapter, once at the beginning of the Capharnaum scene and once immediately afterward. The signifier *pilon* requires some initial commentary. Its first meaning here is "pestle," which evokes both pharmaceutical and culinary uses (thus reinstating a confusion that is anathema to Homais);[18] the pestle/mortar couple also provides a familiar analogy for the complementarity of male and female. Another meaning, although not literally present, readily springs to mind because of the proximity of the fowl image: *le pilon* is part of a chicken's anatomy (the drumstick) when the bird is considered gastronomically. But the word can also be used to describe a wooden leg and appears as such in this chapter, when Hippolyte, setting Emma's cases down for her after she returns from the pharmacy, swings his *pilon* around in an awkward quarter circle (238).

We are thus invited to see him as the living embodiment of the very disorder (scalpel on chicken) that Homais fears and has nevertheless brought about by his desire to impose order (the club foot operation was supposed to normalize Hippolyte). In fact, the imposition of order, the attempt to correct the club foot—described as a "patriotic idea" (164), a phrase in which the dead metaphor of paternity stirs chillingly—has led to mutilation and symbolic castration.

In this respect, the placing of the earliest reference to Hippolyte's *pilon* is highly significant, for it occurs in the immediate context of the young Justin's fetishistic attempts to imagine sexual difference. Contemplating the clothes Félicité is ironing he asks her whether Madame Homais is "a lady, like Madame [Emma]" (177) and, when she mocks his beardlessness, insists on cleaning Emma's boots (muddied by her racing across the fields to Rodolphe). The text, after stressing that Emma has many pairs of boots (the familiar multiplication of the absent phallus), shifts to the wooden leg she has given Hippolyte, naturalizing the symbolic motivation of this move in the realist camouflage of psychological consistency: just as the submissive Charles never criticizes her spending on boots, so he readily provides the money for Hippolyte's leg.

With uncanny appropriateness, the signifier *pilon,* with its connotations of sexual difference, figures prominently in the scene of disorder upon which Emma intrudes. Homais's armchair, attribute of his *ex cathedra* authority and metonymy for the man himself, has been knocked over, and the *Fanal de Rouen* (the local newspaper for which Homais writes) is lying on the floor "between the two pestles [*pilons*]" (233). The definite article reminds us that the pestles are presupposed objects, as much part of the furniture as the armchair with which they are automatically yet bizarrely linked (an earlier scene has Homais testily instructing Justin to replace the armchair in its proper position and, in the same breath, not to knock over the mortars; 157). The topographically alert Bopp sees a lack of motivation here: How could Homais's outburst in the kitchen have produced an effect elsewhere, knocking over the chemist's favorite armchair?[19] In fact, what Bopp identifies as a failure of realistic motivation is also a significant overmotivation. The cast-down pestles, divorced from their mortars, reinforce the image of challenged masculinity presented by the upturned chair. Moreover, they strangely frame the *Fanal,* vehicle of the chemist's self-importance. The contiguity of *pilons* (the "masculine" pestles) and *Fanal* (a "beacon" of [masculine] enlightenment) is partly motivated by an *analogy* between two symbols of the masculine position in the sexual order. However, the tableau's suggestiveness is compounded by the echoes of Hippolyte's wooden leg in the signifier *pilon* and by the strange application to Homais's favorite organ of the adjective *tendu,* a term that has been "normalized" out of the English translation; it refers awkwardly to the fact that the paper is "extended," "opened out" between the pestles, but it also has the connotation of erectness, which helps transform Homais's *Beacon,* the organ in which he deploys his verbal potency, crucially placed between the *pilons* (with their ghostly echo of absent legs), into the male member, conceived not so much as part of the body but as a symbol of the paterfamilias's word, of reason, of everything that separates the man Homais from passive, feminized, amputated beings like Justin, Charles, Hippolyte, the blind beggar, and even Emma, characterized as they all are by their silence or by their inadequate relationship to language. For the moment, Homais's verbal splendor lies on the floor (threatened by the specter of amputation), but we have no doubt that, when Homais recovers his composure order will soon be restored, the chair returned to its upright position, the pestles put back in their mortars, and the printed word rescued from the dust. Indeed, toward the end of the novel Homais's articles in the *Fanal* will be sufficiently potent to have the beggar permanently removed from public sight. Given this reading of the displacement of the chemist's chair, his organ of information, and his pestles as a questioning, albeit fitful, of masculine authority, it is not surprising that sexual difference, and its policing by the paterfamilias, should be at issue in what now follows.

When *Conjugal Love* falls to the ground from Justin's pocket, it does so with a clear ironic point, as its title's apparent reference to sexual harmony in marriage clashes with the recent adulterous act that is still occupying Emma's thoughts. Homais's articulation of the title—"*Conjugal* . . . *Love*! he cried, placing a deliberate pause between the two words" (236)—by dislocating love from marriage, reinforces this point. But his introduction of a separation into the title is also overdetermined by the context I have been discussing and makes the point that what the book signifies is not so much the complementarity of the sexually different in marriage as the principle of distinctness itself. The knowledge of sexual difference that the book and its engravings communicate is not common knowledge: it proceeds from a masculine source and is addressed to adult males. For beardless adolescents, women, and children it presents risks of contamination, is poisonous knowledge (thus Homais can describe it both as "wicked" and as useful). Accordingly, the words with which Homais holds his inquisitive wife at a distance ("No! Don't touch it!") echo his earlier exclamation to Justin: "Arsenic! and you go meddling [*toucher*] with that!" (235). This, Justin's second transgression of distinctness, is such a direct challenge to the segregation of sexual roles that it is difficult not to see the physical transformation Homais now undergoes ("rolling his eyes, choking, puffing, apoplectic") as a pathologically displaced tumescence ("puffing," in Steegmuller's skillful but normalizing translation, skirts the French *tuméfié*), a swollen reassertion of masculine authority: he is the phallus that makes all the difference and imposes order. Appropriately, this vision of Homais as an unhealthily engorged member (*tuméfié*) echoes Hippolyte's swollen limb before the amputation, with its "livid tumescence [*tuméfaction*]" (169), and thus keeps before us the idea of (the sexual) order as itself a pathology.

There remains one central detail in the Capharnaum episode whose relation to the thematic network of sexual difference, paternal authority, filial resentment, and death has not been fully explained. By this I mean the arsenic itself. Realist convention is clearly under strain here: the arsenic is too evidently a "plant" brought into Emma's ken to prepare a subsequent plot development. Motivated by a future event (Emma's suicide), the foregrounding of the arsenic disturbs the narrative's logic of cause and effect and reminds us of an authorial presence plotting backward against the temporal sequence.

Yet, as we have found with other instances of suspect motivation in this episode (Charles's having Emma sent to Homais, Justin's being called lazy, the upturned chair), the arsenic's presence here is amply motivated on the symbolic level. I have already mentioned the parallel, set up by Homais's anger at Justin, between the knowledge of sexual difference and knowledge of the place of the poison. One can see how, acting as a metaphor for sexuality, poison can signal, and even naturalize, the strong prohibitions set up by society around the sexual. But why arsenic and not some other poison? Here the appropriateness of Flaubert's choice of poison becomes clear, for arsenic is, etymologically, male (from the Greek *arsenicon*); this poison is, therefore, not just a sign of the danger attaching to sexuality but, more specifically, an indication of the part played by masculinity in Emma's death. By making this masculine substance the instrument of her death and placing her discovery of it in a context saturated by the assertion of masculine power and repressed signs of filial resentment at the fathers who hold that power, the text implies that what is at issue in the adultery that leads to Emma's suicide is her infringement of the terms of sexual difference, her attempts to appropriate masculinity, and not her taking of illicit sexual partners as such.

Emma's death is aptly brought about by the symbolic ingestion of the masculine, which the novel shows her persistently attempting and failing to appropriate; the oral route by which the unassimilable male poison enters her body is overdetermined by the associations made in the novel between orality and masculinity. Whether through the assumption of authority in speech (Homais's tirades, the speeches at the Agricultural Fair, the persuasive eloquence of Rodolphe and Bovary *père*) or the satisfaction of appetite in eating and drinking (in Emma's mind a man can "*feast on* [*mordre aux*] the rarest pleasures"; 85, translation and emphasis mine), orality is persistently gendered masculine in *Madame Bovary;* the focus on Emma's orality is a rule-confirming exception, because what it expresses in her case is lack, or desire—her mouth thus appears as the main site of her gender trouble.[20]

Entering the Capharnaum passage through points at which realist verisimilitude and motivation seemed under strain has made it possible for us to appreciate the extent to which sexual difference is here tied into the issues of paternal authority and language and is presented not simply as part of the natural order, but as a problem. It can, admittedly, be shown that, despite some extremely complex textual moves, Flaubert's novel implicitly reaffirms the sexual order.[21] Yet even if Emma's story is read as finally conservative,[22] the nature of its contextualization or framing within Charles's story suggests an unusually complex authorial relation to masculinity and a different way of understanding Emma's "androgyny." It is possible to read Emma's story, following the order of Flaubert's narration, as a continuation of Charles's story by other means. By this I do not simply mean that there is a shift in viewpoint, that after the husband we get the wife and that this gives us a "fuller" sense of their joint and several realities. This is no doubt true and works well enough within realist convention: the framing introduces Emma through the male gaze and also makes the social point that, whatever Charles's limitations, Emma, as his wife, depends on him. I mean rather that the issue of the appropriation of masculinity central to Emma's story is already present in the novel's opening chapter.

The theme adumbrated there (a boy growing up, his sexual and intellectual initiation and difficult passage to manhood) is commonplace, though insistent enough to require at least three versions (to Charles we must add Justin and Léon).[23] Yet, unlike the more canonical manifestations of the theme (*Manon Lescaut, La Dame aux camélias*), in which evacuation of a male protagonist's perceived unmanliness is achieved vicariously through the heroine's death, *Madame Bovary* presents this *Bildung* from the point of view of its impossibility or incompleteness: not just by reference to Charles, the *pauvre homme* who dies "overcome with emotion, like an adolescent" (330), and Justin, whose adulthood falls outside the novel (while Léon's maturity is questionable and pusillanimous), but by the uncanny displacement of the story into the feminine, the only context in which accession to the masculine becomes, *realistically* and without fear of argument, absolutely impossible. This is what Emma's story expresses, but with greater pathos and potential for reader identification than would have been possible in a text directly centered on a man's failure to appropriate masculinity.

NOTES

1. The radical nature of the aporias this produces is camouflaged by the narrative chain, emerging only upon reflection; it does not strike the reader with the immediacy of more compressed aporias such as the Cretan liar paradox, with which, as Christopher Prendergast has shown, Flaubert's narrative logic has strong affinities. *The Order of Mimesis: Balzac, Stendhal, Nerval, Flaubert* (Cambridge: Cambridge University Press, 1986), 180ff.

2. Gustave Flaubert, *Madame Bovary,* trans. Francis Steegmuller (New York: Random House,1993). All page numbers cited are from this translation.

3. Puns are stressed at Charles's wedding (28) and both Bournisien (106–7) and Larivière (305–6) produce them. In the French original, Larivière's is particularly significant, being an imperfect one for the ear (between *sens* and *sang*) and accessible only to the reader who is thus constituted as one alert to meanings hidden in signifiers.

4. Léon Bopp, *Commentaire sur "Madame Bovary"* (Neuchâtel: A la Baconnière, 1951), 387ff.

5. For the central role of the mock epic, see Michel Crouzet, "Le Style épique dans *Madame Bovary,*" *Europe* (September–November 1969): 151–69.

6. Bovary *père* prefigures Homais as arbiter of gender.

7. "Monsieur Bovary was a man to whom nothing was sacred" (87).

8. This burden is inappropriate in terms of psychological verisimilitude but less so if, as I suggest later, we read Emma's story as a displaced version of her husband's.

9. Significantly, responsibility for the suicide is shared by a child and a father: it is Homais who, unwittingly, directs Emma to the arsenic, but Justin who unlocks Homais's sanctuary a second time, giving her access to the poison.

10. Hippolyte's name itself evokes the theme of a death sentence pronounced by an angry father (Theseus) on a supposedly incestuous son. Significantly, Flaubert chose to exclude from his definitive text a far more direct reference to the Hippolytus story that he had placed, well before the mock epic Hippolyte appears, at the moment when Charles presents himself as a suitor before another father, Emma's. After his inarticulate request for her hand (he stammers "Père Rouault" repeatedly without really delivering his message), Charles awaits the verdict and passes the time trying to remember "the death of Hippolytus" (Théramène's famous lines in *Phèdre*), which he has learned by heart. Gustave Flaubert, *Madame Bovary: Nouvelle version,* ed. J. Pommier and G. Leleu (Paris: Corti, 1949), 170.

11. See Gustave Flaubert, *Madame Bovary,* ed. Claudine Gothot-Mersch (Paris: Garnier, 1971), 459 n. 75.

12. The sanctuary image has already been used with connotations of exclusion to convey Charles's first uncomprehending encounter with the language of the medical syllabus, "names of unfamiliar etymology that were like so many doors leading to solemn, shadowy sanctuaries" (9).

13. Bopp, *Commentaire sur "Madame Bovary,"* 388.

14. One of the several connotations of the drawing of Minerva (an idealized self-portrait?) that Emma dedicates to her father (15) is precisely the exclusion of the maternal inheritance.

15. After his death, Charles too will come under Canivet's scalpel: the autopsy will, of course, reveal an overdetermined nothing, corresponding to the absence of a physical cause of death (the broken heart motif), but also to Charles's more general lack, his symbolic castration.

16. Charles Baudelaire, *Oeuvres complètes,* ed. Claude Pichois (Paris: Gallimard, 1975), 1:651. The text implies a similar confusion when Charles examines Emma after the poisoning: "Very gently, almost caressingly, he passed his hand over her stomach. She gave a sharp scream" (299).

17. See Hippolyte's cry "like the howling of some animal being butchered" (175) and the discussion in Roger Huss, "Nature, Final Causality and Anthropocentrism in Flaubert," *French Studies* 33 (1979): 294–96.

18. On the occasion of the amputation, Canivet patronizes Homais with the same confusion: "You pharmacists are always cooped up in your kitchens" (172). When Homais blushingly claims to be too sensitive to witness the operation, Canivet, in another prolepsis of the Capharnaum scene, counters that he seems "more like the apoplectic type" (172).

19. Bopp, *Commentaire sur "Madame Bovary,"* 388.

20. She pricks her fingers and sucks them (14), bites her lips when silent (15), licks the last drops of curaçao from the bottom of her glass (21), drinks vinegar to lose weight (63), gulps down brandy (118), spits blood (118), and so on.

21. Roger Huss, "Masculinité et féminité dans *Madame Bovary* et *Ulysses,*" in *James Joyce 2: Joyce et Flaubert,* ed. Claude Jacquet and André Topia (Paris: Minard, 1990).

22. See Michael Riffaterre, "Flaubert's Presuppositions," *Diacritics* 11 (1981) 2–11.

23. Hippolyte, manipulated and patronized like a child, could be regarded as a fourth.

The Adulteress's Child
Naomi Segal

In Evelyn Waugh's novel *A Handful of Dust* (1934) there is one scene that sticks in everyone's memory. Brenda Last, the adulterous wife, is in London; her lover has just taken a plane to France and she is anxious about his safe arrival. Meanwhile, her son, whose first name is the same as her lover's, has been killed in a riding accident. A friend hurries down from Hetton, the family estate in the country, to break the news.

> "Jock Grant-Menzies wants to see you downstairs."
> "Jock? How very extraordinary. It isn't anything awful, is it?"
> "You'd better go and see him."
> Suddenly Brenda became frightened by the strange air of the room and the unfamiliar expression in her friends' faces. She ran downstairs to the room where Jock was waiting.
> "What is it, Jock? Tell me quickly, I'm scared. It's nothing awful, is it?"
> "I'm afraid it is. There's been a very serious accident."
> "John?"
> "Yes."
> "Dead?"
> He nodded.
> She sat down on a hard little Empire chair against the wall, perfectly still with her hands folded in her lap, like a small, well-brought-up child introduced into a room full of grown-ups. She said, "Tell me what happened. Why do you know about it first?"
> "I've been down at Hetton since the weekend."
> "Hetton?"

196

"Don't you remember? John was going hunting to-day."

She frowned, not at once taking in what he was saying. "John . . . John Andrew . . . I . . . Oh, thank God . . ." Then she burst into tears.[1]

Women in the novel of adultery are doubly mothers.[2] First, they function in the phantasy triangle that brings the adultery story out of the oedipal motive, and second, more literally but no less complicatedly, they actually have children in the texts, through whom they suffer and sin. I want to look at a number of aspects of the relations in the nineteenth-century novel of adultery between mothers and their children. My texts are all by men: Stendhal's *Le Rouge et le noir* (1830), Flaubert's *Madame Bovary* (1857) and *L'Education sentimentale* (1869), Maupassant's *Pierre et Jean* (1888), Tolstoy's *Anna Karenina* (1873), Hawthorne's *The Scarlet Letter* (1850), and Fontane's *Effi Briest* (1895). In none of them are the mother-child relations casual or tangential; rather, they work within a motivated structure that is at once filial and paternal, in which the woman stands between generations and between the positions of the implied author and the intended reader, in the place where the mother stands in the oedipal triangle, at a point that has to be surpassed. How is she used by her author as a version of that textual reproduction by which he intends to evade the use of the body? How does her desire and its punishment function in his structure of desire, designed according to the masculine mode to win pleasure out of failure? What difference does it make to all this if the text is hominocentric or feminocentric, or if the desired mother in the text has a daughter or a son? Why must Brenda's son John be misloved and die because he has the same name as her lover?

The male-authored novel of adultery can be placed at a particular moment in the family romance that brings realism out of romanticism. My texts are dated from 1830 to 1895, across sixty-five years, but they all seem to me to belong to a later stage of phantasy than the confessional *récit*, with which I should like to begin my discussion. The *récit* is written as the confession of a young man to an older man—frame narrator, retrospective editor, or older self— who receives and sanctions the narrative, acknowledges the boy's failures, and accepts him into the literate society of men. The tale the boy tells is the oedipal tale: desire of a woman who is stronger, older, the unique object, but somehow inadequate to him so that, whether she loves too much or too little, is his sister or someone's wife, an heiress or a saint, she will prove the dyadic bond impossible, and die.

Women in the *récit* tend to die not only because mortality for females is generally higher than for males in fiction (what is more poetical?), but for a specific reason. These texts are premised on the childbed death of the mother giving birth to the desiring hero. "I cost my mother her life when I came into the world,"[3] so René begins his narrative. From then on he hounds his sister Amélie with a desire for which she must take total responsibility and that will end by killing her. René's self-pity takes refuge in the understanding arms of two older men, one of whom sympathizes while the other criticizes, but neither of whom arraigns him for the real crime, which is other-directed: the destruction of the woman, in which, as patriarchs, they of course have a part.

At the other end of the century we find another son's narrative, *Dominique* (1863), in which the mother dies a few days after weaning but the hero suffers agonizing pangs only when made to leave the paternal estate, an Eden he has freely plundered as a child. When he falls in love with his friend's cousin, Madeleine, he too pursues her mercilessly until she first admits his passion, then begins to express her own. At the point where, virgin to vamp, she suddenly flings herself at him, he "drops his prey" and abandons her, nursing the nostalgia of a story of renunciation forever after from within a mediocre marriage. But a few days before this climax, Madeleine takes Dominique to see a dead child whom her sister Julie had nursed. "On the way home, she wept a great deal, repeating the word 'child' in a tone of acute distress that told me much about a secret sorrow that was eating away at her life and of which I was pitilessly jealous."[4] This pitiless jealousy, directed toward a baby that is not even allowed to exist, is the first principle for the representation of the mother-child pair in the novel of adultery.

If I have called the *récit* the son's story this is because, in the oedipal structure, it stands most clearly at the moment before resolution. The end of the young man's speech is the beginning of the reinterpretation of his failure to love as an ability to renounce, a response to the castration threat that will eventually allow manhood to emerge out of enmity. The older man stands ready to receive an almost inert child who may yet be capable of rescue. What comes most clearly out of this negotiation is that the oedipal drama is premised not on a murderous attitude of son to father but on one directed by both of them toward the mother and that is the movement of refusal that marks the emancipation from immaturity to maturity. For a boy to resolve his Oedipus complex and grow up, to change from son to father, winning the right to make and terrorize other little boys, is a temporal step, the move required to stride across the isosceles base—that step must be taken across the body of the mother. And this gesture both temporal and spatial that makes son into father is also the basis of the pattern of negotiations that is realist narrative. Narrative is a plot contracted between men over women.

The *récit* is the son's story also because of a first-person structure that presents narrative as application: as in Foucault's *scientia sexualis,* one confesses, the other hears (chastises, absolves). With the novel of adultery, something happens to put the muscle and hair of a bourgeois genre onto the slim frame of its predecessor. Authorship becomes something literary historians are prone to call mature: texts get bigger, heroes less wimpish, subject matter more manly, and the author starts pretending to be either God or a scientist. And triangular desire seems to take on more angles. Mediation is more complex (as René Girard distinguishes them, the *romantique* displays its mediation, whereas the *romanesque* hides it),[5] and a third-person voice is made to do something rather more guarded than the first-person voice did. Two phantasies inform the assumption of realist authorship. One, embodied in the protagonist, is the wish to be the hero of the family romance, deliciously weak, absurdly hopeful, the Tom Thumb of the gold-paved city; the other, disembodied in the narrator, is the wish to control that child rather like the banal cotton reel we throw out beyond the pleasure principle in a repetition that can never have enough. Thus the author can play at being two alternative himselves who will battle it out before our reading eyes, and win, and lose, and all the while he can float out of sight paring his fingernails, leaning, hovering, and understanding "the language of flowers and silent things."[6]

Baudelaire's "Elévation," from which I have just quoted the last line, represents most exactly the double fantasy of authorship, in which the phallic desire of the poet moves from a filial zooming— he takes off repeatedly, but never goes off (and the castration image cannot be casual here)—to a sudden assumption of the paternal position of the "subject presumed to know," hovering out of sight. The latter is the implied author's position, most fully exemplified in Flaubert, and the former is the fantasy given narrative flesh and adventures as the hero of the novel of adultery.

He goes out on his fairy-tale quest to win public success and consequent sexual gratification. If he is Julien Sorel, he wins both, but the order is reversed and then rereversed, and both come disguised as failures, for Julien Sorel is the nearest thing to flesh made out of the desire to have worldly fame and the love of women not despite but because of a boyish foolishness that misspells this, falls off that, sobs at the wrong moment, and then finds he reassures rather than annoying by his temporary impotence. Julien as hero cannot lose because his losing is the sweetest mode of winning. "Stendhal" as narrator is equally blessed: he whispers over the boy's shoulder in accents we are grown-up enough to understand, plays fairy godfather, guides him, mocks him, strokes him on his way.

With unsubtle directness I have suggested the pleasure of the implied author's phantasy of control: how nicely the hero plays phallus in a world for him. But if the phantasy is to hold good there must be something more, a further limb to keep the phallus masculine. (After all, King Kong, that organless body, is logically a girl, because he has not what he is; and it is clear that if Freud describes the little boy as "the small bearer of the penis,"[7] all men are metonym to a metonym, and therefore never safe.) That last limb is the little boy, beloved and threatened, as if in the widest stretch of the parenthesis, by the implied author who is God enough to hold the rights of life or death. The woman begins to desire: the boy falls ill; he survives, but only just.

In the novel of adultery it is still not the father figure who is most to be feared. Fathers are husbands merely: cuckolds, comic in the very stupidity or vulgarity of their power. Like a Molière protagonist, Arnoux is all bluster, Rênal a gullible fool, Karenin saintlike perhaps but irredeemably ugly. Mothers in the novel of adultery tend to be done to death as they are in the *récit,* but a little more indirectly—they die through their children.

They tend to have either daughters or sons, taking up thereby one of two positions in a genealogy they cannot fully escape. The mothers of sons are in what I shall call the *patrilinear* position. Framed as icons, they play Mary, Venus, Jocasta; they stand where they are put, as the channel or seedbed that, once itself transferred from father to husband, carries "the name of the father" from husband to son. Into this conventional idyll irrupts the desiring hero— all boy, wanting and hating her in equal measure, determined to bring sexuality out of the maternal pose—and for a moment it seems that a dyadic structure of desire might replace the function of the legitimate couple. But around the time that they begin sleeping together, her son (or her youngest son) falls ill. When this happens, the dilemma of husband versus lover, the parenthesis in which she seemed caught, changes into another: beloved child and paternal God. Where her desire may go from here, along with the foolish hero's, will depend on the individual mode of the paternal phantasy taken up by the author of the novel.

Mothers of daughters—the matrilinear alternative—are already chastised, and whether the child is born before or during the adulterous liaison, whether she is the offspring of lover or cuckold, the very fact of self-reproduction in a mother seems a scandal that can be read only as punishment. Women in fiction don't have daughters unless they are transgressive: prostitutes keep their mothers or daughters by the effort of their sin, murderesses like Thérèse Desqueyroux, mad things like Nadja, and a host of adulteresses from Atala's mother to Alissa's can produce nothing but what Sartre calls "a virgin *with* a stain."[8] There is, it seems, something so disturbing in this willful doubling of the gendered other that it appears in fiction framed within a cell, a garden, some sort of *oubliette*. If the son as subject of desire is (as we shall see) never quite there, the daughter with her mother is always quite precisely there. Where "there" is, is a secret place that does not bear looking at— so the voyeur-author cannot help but peep, and when he does he of course does *not* see nothing. What he envies after all is not the icon whose distribution he controls but the site where he is not, where only a feminized effigy of himself is possible. In representing such a pairing among females across the genealogical divide, in representing matrilinear love, the male author makes what his body cannot make. Like lesbianism in Proust, this is the place where masculine authorship stops.

Sick Sons

I want now to turn to the novels to examine in some detail the different modes of maternity and authorship that they present. Rather than try to be inclusive, I shall take a stepping-stone route through, beginning by setting out more fully the terms of the patrilinear plot in the "sick son" texts. I will then take as a contrastive instance *Anna Karenina,* the novel (so Lionel Trilling tells us) in which readers most commonly identify the pleasures of realism: "We so happily give our assent to what Tolstoi shows us and so willingly call it reality because we have something to gain from its being reality."[9] It is also the text in which patrilinear and matrilinear modes most clearly vie within the focalization of the fiction and the female central character, for Anna has a legitimate son and an illegitimate daughter and is the desired object of both women and men. After that, I shall go back to the case of Flaubert, who, in one hominocentric and one feminocentric novel of adultery, uses irony to divide and rule not just according to a classed hierarchy from the divine down to the stupid but also by a gendered politics of discourse to do with the dread and the compulsion of copying. And finally I will end with the gruelling *Scarlet Letter,* and try to suggest in conclusion how patriarchy makes scarlet letters of us all.

The son falls ill, I have proposed, because he is what the mother may and must love if she is to remain the good beloved, the maternal virgin of the icon. But he must also fall ill because, if he is the phallus of the phallus, how near to castration, how far from safety he must be. *Le Rouge et le noir* is a text that begins and ends with mothers and sons. At the end, Mathilde is still carrying a child everyone insists is male—that is, too good for her—and for him to stay unborn is both his temporary saving and the way to keep the space clear for *Julien* to return to the womb of death, not quite a father yet and evading even being a son. At the opening of the text, Mme de Rênal has three sons, of whom we see only the elder two, cavorting dangerously on a wall erected by their father the mayor; and Julien is the overliterate youngest of his motherless home, foundling, changeling, or cuckoo in the all-male nest. When they meet, she first takes him for a girl. As he enters the edenic scene of a loving family with her children, she finds him more and more exactly the image of a man she has never known before.

Then she sleeps with him, and the favorite son, the one who occupies Julien's family position, falls ill.

It is here that the challenge of the mother's son as rival becomes clear. Mme de Rênal discovers apparently for the first time that what she has been doing is a sin, a "crime in the eyes of God."[10] At the boy's bedside, she flings herself at her husband's feet, claiming that she has killed their child; he, fortunately, is too stupid to understand. Julien's consolations and entreaties seem to her "the blandishments of the devil" (107). Then he has the inspiration to take up the first of a series of Christlike attitudes: " 'Oh, if only I could take his illness upon myself!' 'Oh, you love him, at least!' cried Mme de Rênal, getting up and throwing herself into his arms" (110). At this moment, we see the benignity of Stendhal's divine position: all three protagonists will survive, to pass through more vicissitudes and end up reaffirming the *Liebestod* of desire.

Flaubert is less kind to his stupid hero. Frédéric's love is infinitely patient: it is the woman's fetishes—the arc of her dress, her lace, her black hair, her daughter—that he worships her by, and to cross these would be as unthinkable as to leave her alone. This text too offers a double mother-son structure: we remember Rosanette's poignant and hideous maternity, the child no sooner born than rotting away and laid, purple, in a frame of camellia petals. Both the sons in this novel have peculiar gestations: Rosanette's takes inordinately long to be born, and Mme Arnoux's is four years old when Frédéric returns to Paris after two years at home. The brat is snotty-nosed and dirty-fingered, but the young man can bear him if it will ensure the confidence of his beloved. Regular visits to inquire after the health of this or that family member make him "the parasite of the household."[11] Then one day the boy has a sore throat, and in her distress and gratitude (Frédéric offers some platitudes about his being better in no time) Mme Arnoux agrees to meet her admirer the following Tuesday in Paris, on the corner of the rue Tronchet.

But the author has something else in mind for his hero. Tuesday happens to be the first day of the 1848 Revolution. At the same time, little Eugène wakes his mother (with a sound she dreams as a dog barking),[12] displaying the horrible symptoms of croup. Mme Arnoux, unlike Mms de Rênal, suffers the whole crisis alone. In a rare piece of viewpoint narrative from her, but entirely behavioristically presented, she performs her absurd agony before no audience and with the sole aid of the author's pitiless scalpel. After pages of detail, the boy coughs out the croupous membrane and is saved; his mother offers up "like a holocaust the sacrifice of her first passion, her one moment of weakness" (282).

The difference between these two scenes underlies the different modes of power the author may have over the world in which he is to take pleasure. Stendhal creates a vale of happiness dependent on the greater bliss of romantic death; Flaubert sets up a dialectic of overmaterial world and undermaterial author, the one a fistful of dust, the other hovering, hovering—and how this affects his female protagonist we shall see in a moment.

In Maupassant's novel *Pierre et Jean,* the whole story takes place a generation after. Pierre is the black-haired, wayward elder son, just settled down to a career as a doctor; Jean is fair and pliable, and in love, like his brother, with the pretty widow next door. Then a family friend, Maréchal, dies and leaves all his money to Jean. The novel consists of Pierre's gradual discovery, Hamlet-like, of his mother's long-buried sexual passion, which originated unsurprisingly when, as a little boy, he caught scarlet fever—"and Maréchal, whom we hardly knew at that time, was such a help . . . he'd go to the chemist's and fetch your medicine. . . . And when you got better, you can't think how pleased he was and how he hugged and kissed you."[13] Even before his suspicions start growing, Pierre is outraged at this, and utters the complaint of our whole list of insufficiently loved legitimate boys: "If he knew me first, and was so devoted to me, if he loved and hugged me so much, if I was the cause of his great friendship with my parents, why did he leave all his fortune to my brother and none to me?" (97).

In romanticism, the "gods stand up for bastards." It is, after all, always a question of who inherits, how much, and from whom. Let us not forget that it is not only in folktales that the youngest child ends up inheriting something bigger and better than the older, legitimate brothers. In the Bible, too, the privileged genealogy passes down from Abraham to Ephraim and Menasseh, each time through a younger son favored by his mother and the authorial God. In the protest of Pierre we see the righteous anger of the child who is, after all, the favorite only of convention and not of passion, whose inheritance will evade the narratives we really like to read, the desires we dream by.

The Two Anna Kareninas

These texts of the patrilinear mother are in the masculine mode not only because of the bind in which the mother finds herself but also because they are (closer in this respect to the *récit*) told from the viewpoint of a desiring man; the matrilinear texts, in a variety of ways, are feminocentric rather than hominocentric. In *Anna Karenina* we find a woman split conventionally between husband and lover, more cruelly between lover and legitimate son, but also in a less overt way between the patrilinear and matrilinear and the hominocentric and feminocentric modes. If Lionel Trilling admires the text for its fragrant everyday values and its comfortable paternity, he has not looked too carefully at the heavy inexorability with which Tolstoy strips Anna of the charm that, in the opening pages, makes her what Virginia Woolf once called "central . . . the whole thing," that is, the mother.[14] Like Mrs. Ramsay, we lose Anna with a shock during the course of the narrative, but we lose her long before her death.

Camus's cynic Clamence offers a good definition of charm: "a way of making people say yes to you without ever having asked a direct question."[15] At the start of the novel Anna arrives as good fairy to a household in turmoil: her sister-in-law Dolly has discovered her husband's adultery and Anna, through sheer sympathy, induces her to take him back. Anna shares her charm with her brother Stiva—but we see how unforgiving a double standard operates here when, for passion rather than good-natured appetite, she does once what he has repeatedly done. From the moment of the first embrace an iron divinity watches and pursues her, and she is never allowed to be "really" happy again. The son whom she loved without rival in his infancy continues to pull her back, whereas the daughter conceived in the fullness of desire "somehow never quite grips the heart." Anna's patrilinear dilemma is clear-cut; she represents it thus to Dolly:

"Do you see, I love . . . equally, I think, but both more than myself, two beings—Seriozha and Alexei.

. . .

I love these two beings only, and the one excludes the other. I cannot have them both; yet that is my one need. And since I can't have them, I don't care about the rest. Nothing matters; nothing, nothing! And it will end one way or the other, and so I can't—I don't like to talk of it."[16]

Such is the inexorability of the either/or economics of the patri-linear bind. Anna's clarity of understanding, forced into the moral lacing of her author's concept of right, fails at the end of this state-ment; "it must end one way or the other," she stammers, and so it does. Her son Seriozha is presented more tenderly and carefully than the other sons—and he never falls ill, though it is at his bed-side that she famously visits him on the morning of his birthday. While Vronsky's viewpoint is very rarely taken, on one of the few occasions it is, he is intuiting Seriozha's confusion of choice: "What does it mean? Who is he? How ought I to love him?" (203), the boy wonders, and it is in response to his gaze that both Anna and Vronsky get "a feeling akin to that of a sailor who can see by the compass that the direction in which he is swiftly sailing is wide of the proper course, but is powerless to stop" (203–4). The stop comes with Anna's suicide at the local station; and the last time we see her lonely son he is playing the dangerous "railway game" he has learned at his all-male school.

If Anna's charm is first presented in her encounter with Vronsky's mother, in which they exchange a mutual sympathy as the mothers of sons, this is actually the first of several woman-woman relations that shape her initial impression. Both the Countess Vronsky and Dolly's little sister Kitty are described in the opening pages as falling "in love" with Anna. And it is this that leads me to suggest that, where the hazy certainty of Anna's mater-nal value seems to be unexpectedly viewed without the viewpoint of any specific man's desire, where we might be inclined at first to call it (as many critics have) the author's desire coloring the whole value system of her world, I think its atmosphere rather resembles that of Mrs. Ramsay's world, the unpredatory, only dimly sexual desire of daughter for mother. Vronsky's attitude toward Anna never takes the undestructive gazelike form of Kitty's. And the clever plotting of the author-God insists of course that Kitty's love should change into horror when she sees before her very eyes that the two people she adores are falling in love with each other.

Kitty grows up, through this and other useful humiliations, and marries the sensitive, oafish Levin—whose probity is shown by his inability to respond to Anna's charm except briefly, drunkenly, and as a lapse he would never live by. And Kitty has a legitimate, loved, healthy son, whereas Anna's daughter is none of these things. When she is born, Anna nearly dies; she is given the same name as her mother, as if only one of them may survive; and for a while, the world is turned upside down while Anna seeks her husband's forgiveness, Vronsky is driven to attempt suicide, and Karenin, alone of all the household, takes care of the innocent baby. Later, after Anna and Vronsky have left and are living together with Ani, we see through Dolly's viewpoint how incomplete their not-quite-domestic scene appears to a "real mother."

Anna refuses both to get a divorce and to give Vronsky any further children. In using contraception, she is choosing not to satisfy his wish for paternity (of sons?) and the chance to pass on his name. In this text, as in many of the others, parenting by choice rather than by blood is marked with favor over the genetic relation that breaks down. We have seen Karenin's selfless impulse to nurture his wife's illegitimate daughter; at the point where all her patrilinear relations are flawed by the sanction of social judgment, Anna herself fosters a red-haired English girl by the name of Hannah. "'You'll end up being fonder of her than of your own daughter,'" her brother comments. "'How like a man!'" Anna responds. "'In love there's no such thing as more or less. I love my daughter with one love, and this girl with another'" (731). But Anna is held tight in a bind of either/or. In the end, a quarrel with Vronsky over this girl precipitates Anna's suicidal crisis; she visits Dolly and finds her starry-eyed over the icon of Kitty and the baby; as she falls under the train, she thinks of her own childhood, no one else's. But after her death, it is Karenin who takes the infant child of his rival and alone is permitted to unite the son and the daughter of Anna Karenina in one family.

Flaubert and the Fall

Anna Karenina is one negative version of the matrilinear text. Another is *Madame Bovary,* published twelve years before the mature *Education sentimentale* but, in terms of my rhetoric, a more complex version of Flaubert's obsession with the unbodied reproduction of the text.

He began the novel that he loved to hate, so the anecdote goes, after his friends Bouilhet and Du Camp advised him to drop the unwieldy *Tentation de Saint Antoine*. Comparing the two texts, he later wrote: "*Saint Antoine* did not cost me a quarter of the intellectual tension that *Bovary* demands. It was an outlet; I had nothing but pleasure in the writing; and the 18 months it took me to write its 500 pages were the most deeply voluptuous of my whole life. Consider then, every minute I am having to get under *skins* that I find antipathetic."[17] If the saint's pained continence lets Flaubert pour forth, this novel of adultery is repressive precisely as it represents the entry "inside the skin" of the woman. Everything in *Madame Bovary* is a sexual relation: the author refuses the very entry he desires.

His godlike position (hovering, not touching) is a refusal of incarnation because that would feminize. The implied author Flaubert must be what Emma is not. She consumes, is watched, fails, and can only read; he is pure creativity, "present everywhere and visible nowhere,"[18] pouring forth and unseen; above all, a writer. Emma can only take in the linguistic matter of others, predigested cliché, and (in a move copied by Joyce in his silly females Eveline and Gerty MacDowell) she is represented in *style indirect libre* by an exact computation we work out, obedient creatures of irony, as the coefficient of knowing author to stupid character. Where foolishness is, in one of those passages, there is Emma; where control, unbodied desire, and "style" are, there is Flaubert. In doing this we think we are catching up with him, but the author, like God, can never be caught up with; and after all our effort (as similarly in the *Dictionnaire des idées reçues*) we find ourselves in the character's position after all, only consumers, feeding on our own vomit, readers.

For Flaubert, then, the gender politics of the text is a mode of paternal control. But after all he exists in it also as his own daughter. Critics kindly assure him that identification has not made him girlish; from Baudelaire onward, they exclaim at the "masculinity" of Emma Bovary. But Baudelaire, as usual, sees what this means. What is this powerful dandyish woman, he warns, but the "poet as hysteric."[19] A hysteric, nowadays, is a woman who does not know whether to be a woman or a man. The poet as hysteric is the man who does not know how to reproduce himself.

Flaubert plagued Louise Colet with letters raging at the thought of her being pregnant: "Me—a son! Oh no, no, sooner be knocked down by a bus and die in the gutter."[20] But, against this horror of self-reproduction in the body via the woman, he viewed textual creativity as "the real thing": "We're good at sucking, we tongue a lot, we pet for hours, but can we fuck? can we discharge and make a child?"[21] If the child is the book, it must be the detached phallus: "a book about nothing, . . . without attachment to anything outside, that would stand up by itself by the internal force of its style."[22] This disguise, this anti-incarnation as the phantasy of divinity, is the extreme opposite of the woman's self-reproduction. Emma Bovary must have a female child—and fail to love her, as her daughter mimics and reveals her fall, like Effi Briest's, by tumbling and cutting herself—because she is capable only of copying. Flaubert must have no child but a text, a text in which all that is body is readerly, female, and despicable, because he above all will not copy. The copiers are Bouvard and Pécuchet, or the younger codgers Deslauriers and Frédéric, or the readers of the *Dictionnaire des idées reçues*. But the phantasy of textuality is never stable against ironies beyond authorship. Flaubert, like Homais, accepted the Légion d'Honneur.

Scarlet Genealogies

I turn finally to the American archetype of the matrilinear text, *The Scarlet Letter*. Hester wears, her daughter is, the illuminated capital of disgrace. When they first appear, poised at the prison-house door, the narrator identifies this couple as the anti-icon, marking by contrast that other maternity that existed "to redeem the world."[23] From this moment we know the baby must be female. Pearl is the beginning and end of Hester's transgression. Less sexual than almost any other novel of adultery, this fiction is all in a fever of interpretation, fixed in a townscape of cannibalistic eyes that would eat up the matrilinear pair whose own nourishment is all mutual. On the masculine side, the pseudonymous husband, a doctor of course, penetrates and probes the body of the priest-lover by psychoanalytic means, waiting and waiting until confession comes. No one sees the obvious, because otherwise there would be no story. And the moral story is about the saving of the girl by the discovery of paternity.

Freud's first version of the superiority of the visible over the invisible is a little boy's tale: in the *Three Essays on the Theory of Sexuality,* children of both sexes agree that what you see is better than what you don't. His second version, that of an old man, reverses the evaluation while retaining the valency of gender: in the section of *Moses and Monotheism* subtitled "The Advance in Intellectuality," he prefers the more subtle truth of paternity, which can be inferred, not seen, over the blatancy of maternity, demonstrably visible to the naked eye. *The Scarlet Letter* is a book about the "advance in intellectuality," when paternity is discovered and polytheism gives way to the Judaic disincarnation. If it is America's founding myth of boyhood, giving birth to lines of good bad boys from Huckleberry Finn to the Sundance Kid, it is also strictly genealogical, putting fathers in the place where mothers might be. Pearl and Hester are everything to each other, and we are shown a powerfully everyday grind of domesticity that anticipates all the tales of single parenthood that present-day feminism lives by; but Pearl and Hester are divided by the man they must discover and uncover, and who wears his scarlet letter on his flesh. When he exposes himself, abandons the mother, and dies, we are told, the child's spell is broken: "As her tears fell upon her father's cheek, they were the pledge that she would grow up amid human joy and sorrow, nor for ever do battle with the world, but be a woman in it" (256). Pearl enters the genealogy by leaving the matrilinear cell where Hester remains. She is no longer scarlet. As Chillingworth shrivels up and dies, cheated of his prey after so much work in the underground darkness, he leaves all his worldly goods to Pearl, fostering perhaps not so much Hester's as Dimmes-dale's child, but again ensuring that legitimacy has not lost its rights to bequeath.

Dimmesdale, first described in terms of the Christ child, cannot take up his place on the adulteress's bosom. His suffering is internal and fraught, constantly contrasted negatively with her drama of modest exposure. Only she can be purified by the public show, for they have made her the public show, and therefore scarlet. Castration is your dream, not ours. The scarlet of Hester's social sin has to do with an overbodiedness that is never only textual. Unlike the torture victim of Kafka's *In der Strafkolonie,* Hester is not just a written page. Her redness is the sign of a bleeding that is whole, not castrated; there is no wound in her.

Men's part in reproduction begins with alienation and ends in appropriation.[24] At the beginning of the process, he enters the woman, gasps and leaves her his seed; the phallus emerges no longer a phallus; what has he given her? At the end of the process, he co-opts the child from the women who give it birth; if it is male, he marks it again with a socially prescribed bleeding and gives it his name; but the female child remains unmarked and will bleed in her own irregularity.[25] Under this genealogy, daughters can only be copies of a fault. Not castrated but rather castration itself, the mother's daughter bears witness to what the boy child risked: she is a thing utterly removed from the man's body.

The son is nearly there: he cries to reenter but enters only text. The daughter is so much there that when she is textualized the letters all become scarlet. We have seen the dilemma of the patrilinear woman in terms of the impossible choice between two men; the matrilinear mother is centered outside the social in her marginalized cell. Finally and familiarly, this comes back to a question of economics. Patriarchy reasons by an economics of scarcity: masculine desire, in its hydraulic mode, is a thing to be spent, measured out, channeled, a fluid that can flow only one way, like logic. But actually we know this is not true. Semen, like breast milk, increases in supply along with demand; desire and nurturance are things of plenty rather than scarcity. However risky it may be nowadays to speak in favor of the narrative of penetration, this is what is at stake in the novel of adultery. In these texts, an internal event (love, gestation, the doubly desiring womb, the moment of shared pleasure) is also an external one (marriage, politics, the visible phallus, the once-born child)—a movement that, let us insist, may not be equivalent to the sad economics of alienation and appropriation.

NOTES

All translations from French, unless otherwise attributed, are my own, and reference is given to the original text. Page numbers for further references to cited texts appear after quotations; passages without page references are from the last-cited page. Unless otherwise stated, all italics are in the original works and all ellipses are mine.

212   Naomi Segal

1. Evelyn Waugh, *A Handful of Dust* (Harmondsworth: Penguin, 1951), 117–18.

2. This chapter is based on my book *The Adulteress's Child: Authorship and Desire in the Nineteenth-Century Novel* (Cambridge: Polity, 1992); the material on the *récit* is taken both from there and from my *Narcissus and Echo: Women in the French Récit* (Manchester: Manchester University Press, 1988).

3. François-René, vicomte de Chateaubriand, *Atala, René, Les Aventures du dernier Abencérage,* ed. F. Letessier (Paris: Garnier, 1962), 185.

4. Eugène Fromentin, *Dominique,* ed. B. Wright (Paris: Garnier, 1966), 274.

5. René Girard, *Mensonge romantique et vérité romanesque* (Paris: Livre de poche, 1961).

6. Charles Baudelaire, "Elévation," in *Oeuvres complètes,* ed. M. Ruff (Paris: Seuil, 1968), 46.

7. Sigmund Freud, "The Dissolution of the Oedipus Complex," in *The Pelican Freud Library,* vol. 7, trans. James Strachey et al., ed. Angela Richards (Harmondsworth: Penguin, 1977), 321. The original German is *"der kleine Penisträger."* "Der Untergang des Ödipuskomplexes," in *Gesammelte Werke,* vol. 13, ed. Anna Freud (London: Imago, 1940), 401.

8. Jean-Paul Sartre, *Les Mots* (Paris: Gallimard, 1964), 18.

9. Lionel Trilling, "Anna Karenina," in *The Opposing Self* (Oxford: Oxford University Press, 1980), 61.

10. Stendhal, *Le Rouge et le noir,* ed. P. Castex (Paris: Garnier, 1973), 107.

11. Gustave Flaubert, *L'Education sentimentale,* ed. P. M. Wetherill (Paris: Garnier, 1984), 171.

12. In the first *Education sentimentale,* completed in 1845, another dog barks out of turn, signifying in an unclear way a paranoia that the male protagonist must outgrow. Critics have debated this scene uncomfortably, but without making the connection with Mme Arnoux's dream. In the latter, on the lines of Freud's first category of dream narratives based on external sensory stimuli, the demands of maternal duty drag her away from a scene in which she is literally streetwalking.

13. Guy de Maupassant, *Pierre et Jean,* ed. P. Cogny (Paris: Garnier, 1959), 97.

14. Virginia Woolf, "A Sketch of the Past," in *Moments of Being,* ed. J. Schulkind (St. Albans, England: Triad/Panther, 1978), 96.

15. Albert Camus, *La Chute* (Paris: Gallimard, 1956), 62.

16. Leo Tolstoy, *Anna Karenin* [sic], trans. R. Edmonds (Harmondsworth: Penguin, 1978), 671–72. The first ellipses in this quotation are Tolstoy's.

17. Gustave Flaubert, letter to Louise Colet, April 6, 1853, *Correspondance,* vol. 2, ed. J. Bruneau (Paris: Gallimard, 1980), 297.

18. Gustave Flaubert, letter to Louise Colet, December 9, 1852, *Correspondance,* vol. 2, ed. J. Bruneau (Paris: Gallimard, 1980), 204.

19. Charles Baudelaire, "Gustave Flaubert," in *Oeuvres complètes,* ed. M. Ruff (Paris: Seuil, 1968), 452.

20. Gustave Flaubert, letter to Louise Colet, April 3, 1852, *Correspondance,* vol. 2, ed. J. Bruneau (Paris: Gallimard, 1980), 67.

21. Gustave Flaubert, letter to Louise Bouilhet, June 2, 1850, *Correspondance,* vol. 1, ed. J. Bruneau (Paris: Gallimard, 1973), 628.

22. Gustave Flaubert, letter to Louise Colet, January 16, 1852, *Correspondance,* vol. 2, ed. J. Bruneau (Paris: Gallimard, 1980), 31.

23. Nathaniel Hawthorne, *The Scarlet Letter,* centenary ed., vol. 1, ed. W. Charvat and F. Bowers (Columbus: Ohio State University Press, 1962), 56.

24. See Mary O'Brien, *The Politics of Reproduction* (London: Routledge & Kegan Paul, 1981), 47.

25. For the significance of blood to life-cycle rituals, see, for example, Bruno Bettelheim, *Symbolic Wounds* (London: Thames & Hudson, 1955); Thomas Buckley and Alma Gottlieb, eds., *Blood Magic* (Berkeley: University of California Press, 1988); and Chris Knight, *Blood Relations* (New Haven, Conn.: Yale University Press, 1991).

The Body and the Body Politic
in the Novels of the Goncourts
Patrick O'Donovan

The Body Social

Modern civilization tends progressively to efface the body, such that to find traces of its history, one must think to look for them: "Civilizations are not merely transformations of beliefs, of habits, of the mentality of a given people; they are transformations also of the habits of the body."[1] In the novels of the Goncourts, there is hardly any aspect of the text that cannot be related to the incorporation of the body into a network of social relations; the chief phases of the action, almost without exception, are plotted in accordance with the changing state of the body, but also its numerous metonyms: the room, the street, a person's clothing, the city itself as an endless series of metonymically related sites.[2] The situation of the characters oscillates between isolation and sociability, mobility and morbidity. So, in *Madame Gervaisais,* the singularity of the heroine, apparently too cultivated to be susceptible to the demonic appeal of religion, gives way to a paradoxical condition of the body, a lethargy that is in fact a highly active, if perverse, state, an anomie that is palpable. The body is the focus also of an inquiry into the violence of the social order. The Goncourts use the body, in effect, to apprehend—on occasion, to challenge—the symbolic foundation of social and political attitudes. The reasons, then, why one should write on the body are numerous. It functions in fact both as a means of structuring the representation of the modern world and, more especially, as a way of rationalizing the protean enterprise of the inquiring writer; and, as we shall now see, it is the occasion of an attack on other, politically prestigious, representations of society.

If the wider plot of the novels seeks to embrace the whole social fabric, how are we to obtain a purchase on so vast, yet so intricate, an entity? This is a key question in the political thought of the nineteenth century as well as in its literature. The response of a figure such as François Guizot is, interestingly, to construct a vision of social life predicated on the wholeness of the body: "Made of men, society is made just as man is."[3] This epigrammatic sentence is the statement of a project, part political, part intellectual, that "of making the nation known to itself,"[4] which is the prime article of faith of nineteenth-century French liberalism in its most dynamic and intellectually fertile phase, that is to say, in the period between the Restoration and the arrival of liberals like Guizot in power in 1830. Guizot's exploitation of the classic metaphor of the body politic is heuristic. As distinct from a political order that is enshrined in the person of the king, he envisages a system that will come to terms with the complexity of modern mass society. The notion of making the nation known to itself is identified by Guizot and by associates such as Rémusat as a means of revealing to the bourgeoisie the prospects for positive political action generated by the new regime of the Restoration; it also posits an understanding of society as the condition of such action. The body is used here for its cognitive value: it points beyond itself to the imminent creation of legitimate structures of order, based on the whole body politic.

The political project that Guizot expounds can tell us a certain amount about the realism of the 1850s and the 1860s. If authority is to be derived from a claim to a proper understanding of the body politic, then such understanding immediately becomes contentious. Realism can be seen both as a further, more skeptical, version of the attempt to understand the social world and also as a critical response to a now tainted political venture, voiced from within the disaffected bourgeoisie. This response is, moreover, not primarily political in its motivation, but rather derives its vehemence from an extreme sense of intellectual alienation. So, one might conclude, the work of the Goncourts amounts to a repudiation of the liberal adaptation of the metaphor of the body politic, and their realism might be regarded as the expression of a determination to write on, and of, the body as such, and to exploit the narrative potential of the body in fictional discourse that places political authority in question.

The effect, paradoxically, is to defamiliarize the body, in part because thus to conceive of it is to obscure its own contours and to stress its inseparability from the context in which it is inscribed. Now Guizot's remark strives to secure the anatomical and physiological unity of the body, for this is the quality that he seeks to emulate in his rehearsal of a viable political theory. Guizot's model seeks either to efface what we would today term difference, by raising citizens to the point where they are capable of political action, or to rationalize it, by controlling the lives of those who are excluded from the *pays légal,* the body of the electorate qualified by wealth. The Goncourts follow a counterpremise, one that stresses the vulnerability and the particularity of the body: theirs is a realism founded on an extraordinarily intense apprehension of the real as a mass of particularities, of fleeting sensations that must be brought within the control of writing, but that, by the same token, exceed the reach of received notions of representation.[5] Their attention turns to the heterogeneity of the body politic; thus they explain the motivation of much of the historical work that precedes their fiction. In the preface to *Les Maîtresses de Louis XV,* they remark on how the inclusion of women revolutionizes the practice of history:[6] a new form of history, what they term "social history," results from the recognition of difference. In the novels, the body— as subject of *moeurs*—is a central structuring element and the object of a massive symbolic investment. The focus oscillates between objects and relations, between the body and the body politic; as such, the body provides a strong novelistic impulse for the writing of the Goncourts and partly accounts for their abandonment of history for the novel.

The defamiliarization of the body is the effect of a narrative process that molds itself to the vicissitudes to which the body is prone in a modern society. In *Germinie Lacerteux* there is a movement from a phase where the dirt of the city leaves its trace on Germinie and becomes part of her substance to one where her every action is the result of her complete subjection to the maniacal drives of the body. Thus, her first acts of theft mark a turning point: "It was then that Germinie's humiliation, her degradation, began to appear in her person, began to stupify her, to stain her" (*GL* 184). Later, after her break with Gautruche, her depraved *amours* denote a further point in her degeneration: "She no longer needed to wait for the arousal of desire. . . . She lit hungrily on the first person she met, scarcely looking at him. . . . Her eyes, in all men, saw only man: the individual mattered nothing to her" (*GL* 226). Speaking of Germinie's sexuality amounts to a challenge to orthodoxies of taste and of feeling. The Goncourts claim in the preface to this novel that the modern writer is entitled to avail himself of the freedom and the frankness of modern science. They are advertising a commitment to an understanding of the body. The crucial point to grasp is that it is not merely the substance of the body that is in question, not merely its anatomy, but its habits, its changing appearance, its location in space and in time, all issues that extend far beyond the scope of the scientific model and beyond the terms of reference of those prevailing political models, such as liberalism, to which the brothers also refer (they highlight the contentiousness of their portrayal of extreme degradation in an era "of universal suffrage, of democracy, of liberalism"; *GL* 55). The scientific model, it has been argued, promotes a form of understanding that strives always to move productively between the poles of the particular and the general.[7] What the Goncourts invoke, as one element of a discourse that makes serious claims on the reader's attention, is the *language* of science, rather than its claims to generalization. But their project is closer to a kind of ethnography, in which the body figures not as subject of an anatomical construction, but as the object of a many-sided descriptive endeavor.[8]

The Goncourts argue that what they term social history will reveal "the prime characteristic of nations, those manners that dictate events."[9] They place manners, the sometimes minute particulars of social practice, before other forms of historical data; the character of a given social group is, then, to be seen as an abstract reconstruction of processes that directly affect the body. The Goncourts' use of this as a model for their historical writing and, ultimately, for their kind of realism is idiosyncratic. By contrast with mainstream liberal intellectuals of an earlier generation, they attend to the most ephemeral of historical data, rather than to the emergence of the social and intellectual institutions of modern secular states. And, by contrast with mainstream nineteenth-century anthropology, which is dominated by "physicalist" approaches concerned with the description of racial characteristics, their method acquires a dimension that is markedly nonscientific in character.[10] The Goncourts' writing, which originates in a certain dissidence with regard to prevailing norms of historical writing, moves between the poles of science and an unorthodox kind of ethnography. It uses the scientific mode to signal its aggressive self-demarcation from other kinds of knowledge, and the more uncertain, more fluid mode of ethnography to promote a dynamic exploration of its own rationale as writing.

The Body in Its Field

The setting and the structure of *Soeur Philomène* give the clear impression of a narrative outline dedicated to a certain conception of the body's condition as a determining factor: its clinical plot keeps the body, and attitudes toward the body, at the center. Thus, to begin with, the young nurse Philomène is enchanted by the seeming order of the hospital, which she apprehends as the result of an impersonal process: "The laughter of the interns brought an echo of youth to the room. From murmuring beds, the babble of convalescence could be heard. . . . the pangs of death made so little fuss that the sister was astonished to find herself reassured and calmed by the reality" (*SP* 100). The personae of the inmates are kept at a distance: bodies are identified with abstractions, as synecdoches and metonymies (*laughter, convalesence, pangs of death*) combine to convey a picture of medicine as a force that transforms and controls the corporeal.

The closed setting of the novel shifts in its value, however. Philomène's first impressions change, as she confronts illness more directly: "Now everything spoke to her, right to her entrails" (*SP* 103). She is compelled to mediate between the suffering of the patients and the regime of the hospital. The outcome of this dialectic process is a provisional state of harmony, which is established by the middle of the novel. Yet, as the action moves from the ward to the operating room, from depersonalized *malades* to the erotically charged, but fatally threatened, body of Romaine, the harmony of the working environment is broken: with the arrival of the doomed prostitute, the particularity of setting, of clinical process, is used to signify the failure of medicine to wield control over the body.

The potency of the body, and the demands it makes of writing, are revealed in the structuring and in the language of the novels. Its many secret meanings also feed the imaginary identification of the writer as the true forensic visionary. *Germinie Lacerteux* illustrates this point abundantly, in that it is a novel that is open to a world subject to change, in contrast to *Soeur Philomène,* where the relative closure of the setting is a decisive factor, or *Madame Gervaisais,* where the progressive hermetic seclusion of the heroine charts her movement from an inquiring engagement with the history and the life of Rome to her seeming inertness in the face of the will of God (she ceases, in effect, to be a surrogate ethnographer). *Germinie Lacerteux* moves between the past (the period of the Revolution) and the present. The novel opens with an account of signs of the body's condition, both material and moral. Rites of passage are marked by bodily afflictions: when Germinie arrives for the first time in Paris, she is covered in lice. At a later point, it is Germinie's person that is exposed to the taunts of other women, who ridicule her jealous custody of Jupillon. The turbulence of the setting itself becomes an allegory of the changes that social development imposes on the person. Germinie, who initially appeared as an accessory to the action, as the servant to Mlle de Varandeuil, now dominates the novel; yet the inquiry into her destiny equally takes the novelist into uncharted spaces, the *café-concert,* the hospital, the street, the *banlieue,* as each part of the world becomes permeable to the commotion of the whole.

The extreme transformations undergone by each of the characters in *Manette Salomon,* and of Anatole in particular, point to a different version of this process. Anatole's mobility in the face of the real ultimately affords him, by way of contrast with Germinie, a salvation of a sort, despite his abandonment of his career as an artist. It exposes the novel to the persistent threat of distraction from any predictable paradigm of plot or single predetermined path toward discovery: the mobility of each of the characters results in an ever greater proliferation of particularities. It is not only the body that is at issue, in that the metonyms through which we can apprehend its immersion in the social world are also essential to the construction of a fragmentary plot. More and more, the novel becomes parasitical on the heterogeneous materials it un-covers. Anatole's sensitivity to the picturesque appeal of impover-ishment and randomness equips him to deal with the world and enables him to preserve his freedom. He revels in his *misère* and comes to incarnate the body politic, paradoxical as such an out-come may seem: "Anatole presented the curious psychological phenomenon of a man who has no sense of his own individuality. . . . His temperament drew him to every assembly, every gathering, every meeting, occasions that blend and dissolve the initiative, the freedom, the person of each one who is there" (*MS* 356). This is as positive a view of the social process as it is possible to have—a radically contingent one.

The effect of the body in the text is in part a matter of poetics: the very task of mediation is inconceivable without a poetics founded on multiplicity, variability, fragmentation. To the fragmen-tation and the multiplication of bodies, there corresponds a frag-mentation of the narrative, a fluctuation between states and events, between wholeness and dissipation. The mobility of the text forces itself on the reader's attention. The question that follows is how to measure the strategic magnitude of the ethnographic turn that fur-nishes it with both its substance and its effect. The program of the Goncourts affects not only the practice of reading (by virtue of how the reader's processing of the text is conditioned by the use of abstraction and ellipsis), but also the object of reading, the out-come of which is left in the balance. The reader's bearings on the text continuously shift. Thus, the last pages of *Manette Salomon*, which are written in the present tense, are distinctly euphoric in character: they present a vision of man's quasi-primitive natural condition—in the very center of Paris. Closure is achieved by means of an imaginary, indeed, a mythologizing identification with the primitive Other perceived as the object of an impossible desire: "The former Bohemian now relives the joys of the Garden of Eden, and it is as if he experiences something of the happiness of the first man in the face of virgin Nature" (*MS* 426). The body serves, in this novel and in the others, to crystallize the topoi of modernity: the problematic relationship between the body and its environment and its concomitant exposure to transformation; hygiene and filth, health and disease; alienation (here thrown into relief by its para-doxical metamorphosis into a state of primeval bliss). These topoi, in turn, feed a form of writing that derives much of its energy from its ongoing pursuit of self-understanding, but that on occasion generates its own myths in order to advertise its own singularity.

The Body Desired, the Body Destroyed

The novels' articulation of the experience of the body hinges on the variance between the perspective of the observer, the narrator or indeed the reader, on the one hand, and a figure such as Germinie, who exists as an agent in the world under representation, on the other.[11] This variance calls into question the possibility of neutral scientific scrutiny: neither the writer nor the reader comes to the portrayal of, say, the *basses classes* without a set of beliefs articulated with reference to the body conceived of as something that is low, that is vulnerable to accident and to drives that precipitate those who succumb to them into irrationality. The novels—herein lies much of their distinctiveness—set out both to exploit these terms and to indicate something of their relativity.

The treatment of the body, and its bearing on the plot, are governed alike by paradox. Thus, for instance, Germinie's body is repellent, yet attractive: "From this ugly woman, there came a harsh and mysterious sense of seduction" (*GL* 97). Germinie's enigmatic allure sets off a series of events: she becomes the unwitting object of the duplicit attentions of others, her expectations of fulfillment are confounded, her banal misadventures unleash extraordinary forces. The veiled erotic quality of everyday life in the city becomes a distinct strand in the novel. When Germinie arrives in Paris, she discovers a sense of her own *pudeur*, as she becomes aware of the constant contact with the bodies of men to which the city exposes her. When she tries to come between the eager Jupillon and the unscrupulous Adèle, she finds that "she was drawn into their embraces, she shared in the desires triggered by their contact" (*GL* 109). Whenever the action takes the characters into public spaces, bodies become entangled. Each part of the body is the object of the interest of others: "Hands touched, mouthes brushed each other, coarse talk was whispered from ear to ear, the arm of a shirt would suddenly slip round a waist" (*GL* 205). The presence and the action of other bodies are signified by means of synecdoches: hands, eyes,

mouths represent the wholes of which they form part. The use of
synecdoche accentuates the rapidity and economy of notation for
which the Goncourts characteristically strive. Yet the parts that are
invoked do not belong merely to individual bodies. These words
function also as metonymies, in that the parts that they designate
here figure as the instruments of the world as it acts first upon
Germinie's eye, then upon her person. These actions connote occulted rituals, where bodily practice is the sign of habituation, of
involuntary participation in the rites of urban life. This is a kind
of realism that largely suspends the cognitive value of images of the
body, in order to bring into view those bodily practices that are con-
ducive to the performance of social ceremonies.[12]

Germinie's meeting with Gautruche, in the course of the picnic
in the Bois de Vincennes, serves moreover to mark a distinct phase
of her misadventures. The debauchery that unites this desperate
pair is itself the culmination of a malign pattern of contact, their
chance meeting is a sign of the perverse fitness of each partner to
the other. Here desire precipitates destruction: their lovemaking—a
series of "caresses that were marked by the brutality and the anger
of wine"—all but transforms their bodies into cadavers (*GL* 220).
The language that describes this entanglement is remarkable for its
compression and density; it underscores the significance of the affair as part of a socially determined process, in that it indicates how
the intensity of the characters' pursuit blinds them to the forces to
which they are subject.

From the programmatic air of the Goncourts' writing there is a
significant inference to be drawn: the text seeks to claim a right to
be read and received in the extratextual world. Of particular importance to this effect is the handling of closure in the novels: closure points to how the reader can reconcile the fragmented parts
with the whole. It is a prime characteristic of the novelistic discourse of the Goncourts that plot tends always toward an overtly
symbolic resolution, as the explanatory pretensions of the novelist's inquiry are thrown into manifest relief. This tendency is to be
interpreted as the final repudiation of, rather than a compensation
for the absence of, forms of telling that are more linear and more
complete: the *envoi* is often more trenchant, more violent, than the
narrative it brings to a close, and it thus propels us back into a consideration of the text, rather than away from it. In *Germinie*

Lacerteux, the problem adumbrated in the preface, namely, how to conceive of the experience of the *basses classes,* is directly confronted in what amounts, in effect, to an epilogue to the action. The ferociousness of the process that leads to extinction points to the gravity of the covert plot, in which the corruption of Germinie's body, lying in a common grave, permeates the body politic as a whole. The story culminates in an ending yet more abject than that which Germinie's sordid decline might have led us to expect. Yet the ending also gives her death a heretofore unexpected sacramental dimension. One paradox begets another: death brings on a rite that transforms the *coupable* into a martyr. Here as elsewhere, the Goncourts use the figure of the survivor to communicate to the reader something of the bewilderment that is the residue of the narrative. The sense of abjection continues even beyond the point of physical extinction: Germinie's body disappears, but will never be resurrected, and Mlle de Varandeuil is left absolutely bereft, the antithesis of the women who find Christ's body providentially missing from the tomb on the third day.

This is the final merging of the person and the material world, a process that has been under way since Germinie's arrival in Paris. Why this absolute obliteration, why this epilogue? In part, it stands as the reversal of the opening scene. At the beginning, Mlle de Varandeuil's deliverance from illness renews the bond between mistress and servant and prompts the lengthy comparison of their past lives. This analeptic movement serves a number of purposes: it establishes a dialectical relationship between the two main characters, the servant Germinie and her mistress, who is a remnant of the *ancien régime;* it conditions our reading of the narrative in that it presents each protagonist as a figure embedded in history and subject to social processes, domestic and public.[13] The novel culminates in a vision of the enduring, but pestilential, modern city, and of the radical social and human disorder that it generates: Germinie's annihilation becomes all the more potent for being set against this horizon. The ending is reminiscent of that of *Le Père Goriot,* but bleaker by far. Here, the roles of victim and witness are reversed: the older character (like Goriot, a survivor of the period of the Revolution) outlives the younger; and Germinie is destroyed by the world in which she finds herself, whereas Eugène returns to the city and sets out to overcome all adversity. This intertextual transformation triggers the symbolic resolution of the narrative: the level at which the reader must realize the full bearing of the text is that of the multiplicity of competing models for the understanding of modern experience. The plot feeds off, but also feeds afresh, our conception of the body and of the processes to which it is subject; and, as it disappears from view, these improvised rituals of death take its place as the object of ethnographic inquiry.

The novel achieves this effect by adopting a stance with regard to the reader that is in essence aggressive, sometimes implicitly so, sometimes explicitly. Both the project and the mode are foreshadowed in a document such as the preface to *Germinie Lacerteux,* where the claim to understand society, but also to reveal its contradictions and flaws, is explicitly asserted. Yet the matter of how this assertion can be given substance is more difficult to resolve. The role of the witness figure, at the end of several of the novels, is of crucial importance. In *Germinie Lacerteux,* Mlle de Varandeuil's discovery of Germinie's past results in an extreme sense of shock, followed by a powerless recognition of the maid's predicament. In *Manette Salomon,* as the threads of the story must be drawn together, the narrative moves, by contrast, into what one might term a positing phase, where the model of scientific exposition is loosely followed: a segment of observation is followed by a segment of explanation. Thus, we read that Coriolis "reaches that state of disenchantment that is the fatal climax to the life and the career of great painters of modern life in this century" (*MS* 343). The truest sign of Coriolis's failure is the fact that he becomes a simple bourgeois. In *Renée Mauperin,* Renée's death, and that of her sole surviving sibling, who dies in childbirth, proclaim the end of the line to which each belongs, an ironic outcome to the project of bourgeois self-aggrandizement on which the plot turns.

The novel's overt exploitation of novelistic devices of parallelism, coincidence, and reversal is at once the rhetorical expression of its claim to be received in the world beyond its own limits and, perhaps more important, the means of its largely covert subversion of the claims of authoritative discourses other than literature. Thus, *Germinie Lacerteux* is presented as "the clinic of Love" (*GL* 55). What is the sense of this claim? Like *Renée Mauperin* and *Soeur Philomène,* this novel gives a highly negative portrayal of clinical medicine: there is an unstated, but powerful, conflict between the novelistic *étude* and its ostensible model. The "clinic of Love" can only be a pathology, not just of love, but of the entire body (hence its absorption into a network of eroticized social relations). The claims of medicine, both to cure and to aid understanding, are confounded by the very plot of the novels, by seemingly inexplicable deaths, which can be rationalized only by invoking the symbolic power of the text. The novel is the occasion of the scrutiny of generalized pathology in which medicine is complicit: in this text, in particular, medicine is an emblem of corruption. The insidious subversion, here, of medicine and science, and elsewhere of religion, reveals a brutal dialectic at work, whereby literature annihilates the claims of its own models, ostensible or implicit, and establishes the novelistic *étude* as the resulting problematic synthesis. The body is an inexhaustible topic—both as an object of the analytic gaze and as something that stands beyond the grasp of established discourses. This inexhaustibility, so visibly highlighted by the endless centrifugal movement of the Goncourts' texts, points to the inexhaustibility of literature itself, and to its crucial role in a process of mediation that, these novels tend to suggest, has barely been initiated. The aggression that is constitutive of writing in modern bourgeois society is applied to the subversion of those forms of knowledge that seek to establish themselves in and give order to civil society: this attitude is an essential part of the Goncourts' self-image as writers and is reflected in the heterogeneity of their corpus. Novelistic discourse strives after closure, but remains, paradoxically, open to a continuing engagement with the problems of modern experience.

The novels of the Goncourts are dedicated to harnessing something of the chaotic power that the protean body politic unleashes. This enterprise places the writer-figure in an equivocal position. The analytic gaze of the writer as observer is directed at others as agents, from whom he remains distinct; yet the articulation of the experience of the Other alienates the writer from those to whom his work is addressed. The Goncourts are as remote from the position of a Germinie as they are from that of a Guizot. Edmond himself, in the preface to *Les Frères Zemganno,* calls for a naturalist scrutiny, not merely of the *basses classes,* but of more educated and more distinguished sections of society: to confront that society with a "cruel analysis" of its own contradictions will be to put an end to a set of values (those that are representative, in Edmond's phrase, of "classicism and its tail") that are ill adapted to the new body politic.[14] These values are not merely aesthetic ones, but represent also intellectual and social attitudes. These, in turn, are what trigger the novel's antagonistic engagement with a culture whose self-understanding is inadequate. The texts that result are addressed to those who are in greatest need of them, the bourgeois *citoyens capacitaires* on whom liberal political ideology depends. The effect is to preserve the distinctiveness of the observer, whose identity depends on the singularity of the poetic dimension of the work, more specifically, on the power writing derives from its countering of norms of style, of narration, and of taste.

The Goncourts' writing exemplifies a realism that is sensitive above all to the extraordinary difficulties that beset mediation and incorporation, whether at the conceptual or the practical level. In *Des moyens de gouvernement et d'opposition,* Guizot attempts, as we have seen, to build a political order that gives a voice and a place to those interests within public life that can be said to be worthy of concern. But, he argues, society cannot be atomized. Effective political action cannot repose on arbitrary distinctions between informed and freely held opinions, on the one hand, and the interests on which members of a given class can be expected to act, on the other; rather, "a sort of nervous sensibility is common to both and serves to unite them. . . . Power acts on each element at once, for, in the body social just as in the human body, there is no element that is insensitive and each element depends on all of the others."[15] Guizot is concerned to develop a vision of political power founded on the accommodation of newly emergent interests, rather than on the perpetuation of the social order of the *ancien régime.* This passage of argument as a whole is structured in such a way as to give prominence to the closing, lapidary statement, where the equation of the body and of society is reiterated. Guizot's liberal political theory does not involve a reformulation of the concept of society (as, for instance, in a contractual model); he seeks rather to organize relations in such a way as produce a form of political life whose claim to legitimacy would lie in its social dynamism.[16] Creating effective social contact is the essence of the claim to political power, on the explicit understanding that such contact remains subject to the controlling vision of an ordered body.

This vision of the body reveals something of the potency of mediation as a question that must be answered afresh: social relations predicated on its wholeness must somehow connect. The cause of the failure of liberalism lies here: where liberals failed, when they came to hold power, was in the attempt to bend inherited institutions, such as the Catholic church, to their essentially Protestant conception of a polity founded on positive intellectual values.[17] The collapse of the political experiment precipitated the liberals' conservative turn. In the fiction of the Goncourts, the abandonment by the emancipated middle classes of the principle of the creation of a political class from within a broadly based social movement generates much satirical interest, notably so in *Renée Mauperin,* where Bourjot, for instance, turns his back on his earlier, more militant, convictions ("All of a sudden 1848 erupted; the carbonaro of the Restoration, the liberal of the reign of Louis-Philippe, abruptly gave way to the property owner. . . . His ideas were transformed overnight, and his political sensibility was turned on its head"; *RM* 123). The Goncourts posit a moral and intellectual vacuum; against this background, writers themselves eclipse politicians and political thinkers (as well as doctors and scientists). The self-sufficiency of the bourgeois vision is aggressively denounced: the Goncourts bring into the open the world that lies beyond the fiction of the *pays légal,* subject to its own processes of regulation and retribution. Thus, the violent destruction of Germinie is the effect of a harsh set of ethical and social values, those of the *rue.* The response of the ethnographic observer is one of shock, as is revealed in the closing pages by the sudden eruption of the extraordinary caustic counterhymn to the city: "O Paris! you are . . . the great charitable and fraternal city!"—but Paris exposes its poor to "the promiscuity of worms" (*GL* 260–61). The observer's inquiry lays bare the contradictions that the rites of sanitization conceal. The fact of writing on and of the body enables the Goncourts to articulate an acute and complex awareness of change. But their sense of alienation is so extreme that it amounts almost to fear. Thus, their attack on liberalism does not amount to an act of political engagement: by the 1860s, liberalism is quite moribund. The novels become ambiguous, in that they represent an attempt to develop a symbolic language of the body with a stronger political charge, no doubt, but also a negative one, and one that fosters a sense of spectacle that points in turn to the complicity of writer and reader alike with the structures of power that subsist.[18]

The Body of the Other

Writing on and of the Other is a continuous factor in the Goncourts' self-discovery as writers. It is a spur to stylistic experiment and it leads to the invention of new novelistic paradigms structured according to the inscription of social practice within bodily performance. The analysis of the Other itself generates an ethnography of writing, in the *Journal,* albeit one that is fragmentary and distinctly prone to imaginary projections: witness the frequent emblematic intimations of the writer's own alienation and morbidity. But the pursuit and, as we have seen, the annihilation of the Other is as much a pretext for writing as it is the object of writing. The fact of writing on the body points to the impossibility of purity, for the ethnological impulse that I have posited is by no means innocent. It is rooted in a profound ambivalence toward modern experience. The ethnographical model is used to articulate not a claim to discovery, but a claim to recognition: it points to the disorder of society, which it seeks also to contain, precisely by linking it to the failure of political systems. The ethnographic study of the Other in modern, as opposed to primitive, society points to the impossibility of progress.[19] This impulse is equally subject to the reproduction of racial stereotypes reminiscent of mainstream nineteenth-century anthropology. Thus, a prototype of Manette Salomon is perceived, in a notebook devoted to *La Fille Élisa,* as a model in two senses of the word: "A *model,* child of comfortably off workers, with no need to pose for a living, pride in her body. . . . A *model* Jew, a different moral sense from ours, for her, in the end, the Christian is an enemy."[20] This skeletal notation summarizes much of the plot of *Manette Salomon:* it is already marked by a tension between an attempt to relativize moral attitudes, on the one hand, and, on the other, a transparent partiality on the part of the observer, denoted by the disjunctive pronoun (in the French, *nous*). Knowledge of the body of the Other is, in the last analysis, problematic. A form of writing that proclaims its resistance to the political naturalization of society itself becomes vulnerable to stereotypes of race and of sexuality.

The figure of Manette generates a certain defensiveness on the writer's part. This response points to a sense of equivocation at the core of the Goncourts' writing. The relativizing stance adopted by the Goncourts in their ethnographic mode generates anger in the face of orthodoxy. But here the loss of relativity triggers a different kind of rage, a latent hatred of the Other. What I have termed the Goncourts' anger is a means of rationalizing the conflicting pressures to which the writer is subject, a tactical device to articulate opposition to orthodoxies of taste and civility, and, notably in the *Journal,* the path to a certain liberating extremity that it is not necessarily open to works of literature themselves to assume. Anger is consistently antiendoxal and hence represents the radicalization of the dialogic disposition characteristic of ethnography. The alternative to this anger may be nothing other than a self-deceiving acceptance of the prevailing political order. Anger is liberating, in that it is characterized by a prodigal disregard for acceptability; it is problematic, in that it is the liminal and fictive component of a marginality that cannot simply be assumed and a gesture toward the creation of an identity that is not given, that of the writer. It is the symptom by which today we might discern, within realism, a loss of faith in the centering power of human subjectivity: if this is its source, then the anger that fuels realism, and the hatred it generates, must indeed be unmasterable.

NOTES

1. Edmond de Goncourt and Jules de Goncourt, *Journal: mémoires de la vie littéraire,* 3 vols., ed. Robert Ricatte and Robert Kopp (Paris: Laffont, 1989), 1:242.

2. Reference will be made in the body of the essay to the following editions of novels by the Goncourts: *Soeur Philomène* (Paris: Flammarion—Fasquelle, n.d.) (*SP*); *Renée Mauperin,* ed. Nadine Satiat (Paris: Flammarion, 1990) (*RM*); *Germinie Lacerteux,* ed. Nadine Satiat (Paris: Flammarion, 1990) (*GL*); *Manette Salomon,* ed. Hubert Juin (Paris: Union générale d'édition, 1979) (*MS*); *Madame Gervaisais,* ed. Marc Fumaroli (Paris: Gallimard, 1982) (*MG*); all translations are my own.

3. *Des moyens de gouvernement et d'opposition dans l'état actuel de la France,* ed. Claude Lefort (Paris: Belin, 1988), 149. This text dates from 1821, before the period of Guizot's own political eminence.

4. Charles de Rémusat, cited by Pierre Rosanvallon, *Le Moment Guizot* (Paris: Gallimard, 1985), 181. Rosanvallon's study and Pamela M. Pilbeam's *The 1830 Revolution in France* (London: Macmillan, 1991) are indispensable works of reference for an understanding of the intellectual ambitions of French liberalism, its fortuitous emergence as a political force, and the causes of its failure. The Goncourts themselves frequently comment caustically on the prestige of liberalism: "Libe-

ralism, a party that will always be strong. It has all the grandeur of human stupidity and human hypocrisy" (*Journal*, 1:540).

5. For an incisive analysis of this aspect of the Goncourts' realism, see Michel Crouzet, "Rhétorique du réel dans *Manette Salomon*," *Francofonia* 21 (1991): 97–119.

6. Edmond de Goncourt and et Jules de Goncourt, *Préfaces et manifestes littéraires*, ed. Hubert Juin (Paris: Slatkine Reprints, 1980), 178.

7. David Baguley, *Naturalist Fiction: The Entropic Vision* (Cambridge: Cambridge University Press, 1990), 59.

8. On the emergence of this distinction, see Michèle Duchet, *Anthropologie et histoire au siècle des Lumières* (Paris: Maspero, 1971), 233–34.

9. Goncourt and Goncourt, *Préfaces et manifestes littéraires*, 177.

10. On this matter, see Elizabeth A. Williams, "Anthropological Institutions in Nineteenth-Century France," *Isis* 76 (1985): 348. Williams points out that the concept of ethnography emerges in its current sense in France only in the 1920s, as "a reformulation of anthropology along lines suggested by Durkheimian sociology." On the approach of liberal historians of the 1820s and 1830s, see Marcel Gauchet, ed., *Philosophie des sciences historiques* (Lille: Presses universitaires de Lille, 1988). On the rise of nationalism in the nineteenth century and on the perception of ethnography as a "residual form of knowledge that defines itself in opposition to the history of Western Europe," see François Furet, *L'Atelier de l'histoire* (Paris: Flammarion, 1982), 93.

11. The distinction between agent and observer is based on anthropological usage; Carlo Ginzburg remarks that "the essence of what we call the anthropological attitude—that is, the permanent confrontation between different cultures—rests on a dialogic disposition." *Myths, Emblems, Clues*, trans. by John Tedeschi and Anne C. Tedeschi (London: Hutchinson Radius, 1990), 159.

12. On this important distinction, see Paul Connerton, *How Societies Remember* (Cambridge: Cambridge University Press, 1989), 74, 104.

13. On the dialectical relationship between servant and mistress, see Naomi Schor, *Breaking the Chain: Women, Theory, and French Realist Fiction* (New York: Columbia University Press, 1985), 127–34.

14. *Les Frères Zemganno*, ed. Mario Petrone (Naples: Liguori/Paris: Nizet, 1981), 25.

15. *Des moyens de gouvernement et d'opposition*, 112.

16. See Rosanvallon, *Le Moment Guizot*, 40.

17. On this point, see ibid., 239–40 and passim.

18. On this point, compare Amy Kaplan, *The Social Construction of American Realism* (Chicago: University of Chicago Press, 1988), 1–14.

19. See Claudie Bernard on the acute sense of perplexity that results from the quasi-ethnographic scrutiny of Otherness in novels of *chouannerie*, in *Le Chouan romanesque: Balzac—Barbey d'Aurevilly—Hugo* (Paris: PUF, 1989), 267–75.

20. Cited by Robert Ricatte, *La Genèse de "La Fille Élisa"* (Paris: PUF, 1960), 193 n. 2; emphasis added.

Experimenting on Women: Zola's Theory and Practice of the Experimental Novel
Dorothy Kelly

Gender and Science

If Zola's essay "Le Roman expérimental" has long been studied as his theory of naturalism, the rhetorical nature of Zola's discourse in that essay and the relation of that discourse to gender and science have not been investigated.[1] One might believe that a scientific treatise would be the last place to look for questions of gender and sexuality, but, as we shall see, that belief is far from the truth. Perhaps the one sentence that most clearly introduces the gender question into the theory of the experimental novel can be found in Zola's praise of Claude Bernard: "I will adress to the young literary generation, which is now developing those great and strong words of Claulde Bernard. I know of no others as *virile*."[2] Bernard's, and thus Zola's, scientific method is virile, masculine, strong, as opposed to the weak, soppy, effeminate "art" of medicine and the novels of romanticism. As we shall see, this cultural cliché contrasting masculine and feminine has a profound effect on the direction taken by Zola's naturalist texts, which, in their quest for the "pure" truth, carry out their project at the expense of women.

The very general link between masculinity and science is explored by Evelyn Fox Keller in her important book, *Reflections on Gender and Science*.[3] She shows how, from Plato to quantum mechanics, science has been intricately linked to definitions of gender and issues of sexuality, how men, women, and science have been constructed in an interlocking network. Her analyses strike a remarkable chord when read in conjunction with Zola's "virile" experimental project: "For the founding fathers of modern science, the reliance on the language of gender was explicit: They sought a philosophy that deserved to be called 'masculine,' that could be distinguished from its ineffective predecessors by its *'virile'* power, its capacity to bind Nature to man's service and make her his slave (Bacon)" (Keller 7; emphasis added). After first reviewing some of the thematic elements of gender in Zola's theory while accompanying this analysis with concepts from Keller, I will turn to a study of the ways in which these gendered elements structure two of Zola's related novels, *La Faute de l'abbé Mouret* and *Le Docteur Pascal.*

As noted above, the word *virile* marks Zola's scientific project as masculine, and this category of the masculine is defined by very conventional, clichéd qualities. The most elementary quality of the masculine is objectivity, as it opposes feminine subjectivity and sentimentality. In "Letter to Young People," Zola maps out this zone of degraded female sentimentality and contrasts it with virility as follows: "To applaud rhetoric, to become enthusiastic over the ideal, these are but nervous emotions: women cry when they hear music. Today we need the virility of the true in order to be glorious in the future, as we have been in the past" (*Roman* 60).

In order to remain clear of contamination by sentimentality, the scientist must steer clear of emotions and, by association, women. This leads to a myth of isolation and autonomy, to a belief that the scientist is totally divorced from the object studied, and from others around him (Keller 70). In Zola, this need for the male scientist to isolate himself from woman's dangers is suggested in the theory in the above quote in which the new, strong scientist must be different from the tearful woman.[4]

Keller goes on to show how this isolation is also related to an avoidance of sexuality. Historically, this developed in the seventeenth century as a linking of chastity with objectivity (Keller 59). Keller also describes how psychological studies reveal in scientists a "personality profile that seems admirably suited to an occupation seen as simultaneously masculine and asexual" (91).

This need to keep science objective and masculine does not seek simply to separate man and science from woman and subjectivity; it seeks also to dominate both woman and nature. Keller emphasizes that the domination of nature is tied to gender and power: "It is important, however, to see how deeply Bacon's use of gender is implicated in his conception of mastery and domination. The fact that mastery and domination are, invariably, exercised over nature as 'she' can hardly escape our attention, and indeed has not gone unnoticed" (Keller 35). This notion of mastery is expressed most often in Zola's theoretical texts as mastery over nature: "Our true task is there, for us experimental novelists, to go from the known to the unknown, to make ourselves the master of nature" (*Roman* 25).

Finally, the feminine area of sentimentality is considered to be filthy as well as dangerous. In speaking of Hugo's *Ruy Blas,* which he uses as an example of romantic and effeminate idealism and error, Zola says of the historical plot of the play: "This story is not only crazy, it is filthy [*ordurière*]; it does not push one to good deeds, since the characters commit only coarse acts [*saletés*] or trickery [*gredineries*]" (*Roman* 64–65). This filth can corrupt the pure and objective person: "It is time to prove to the new generation that the true corrupters are the rhetoricians and that there is a fatal fall into the mire after each rise to the ideal" (*Roman* 60).

Male Purity

Let us turn now to a study of *La Faute de l'abbé Mouret* and *Le Docteur Pascal* in order to see how the genderization of science plays itself out in the novels. Although separated in time of composition by nearly twenty years, the two novels have male protagonists who are remarkably similar, particularly in their gender identities and their relations to women. Indeed, Serge Mouret, the priest, and Pascal Rougon, the scientist, seem to link together their two disparate occupations.

It may, in fact, seem contradictory to claim that the life of a priest and that of a scientist could share any similarities, particularly because *La Faute de l'abbé Mouret* was written in part as a kind of condemnation of celibacy. However, the similarities between Mouret and Pascal, similarities both superficial and profound, belie the surface condemnation of religious celibacy and link the two professions at a deeper, almost mythological level in Zola's texts.[5]

The superficial link between religion and science appears most frequently in *Le Docteur Pascal* in the very rhetoric of the description of the scientist Pascal's life. Here, religious terms used by Pascal to describe science link his path with Mouret's, a path in which science becomes the new religion: "Do you want me to recite you my *Credo,* my own, since you accuse me of not wanting any of yours? . . . I believe that the future of humanity lies in the progress of reason through science. I believe that the pursuit of truth through science is the divine ideal which man must give himself."[6] Pascal's and Clotilde's love affair is also described in biblical, religious terms when Clotilde draws a picture of them as the elderly David and the young Sunamite, a comparison dreamed of earlier by Pascal. Finally, the only remaining fragment of Pascal's lifework is described as a saint's relic left over when all his other work was destroyed by his mother (*Pascal* 1203).

At a deeper level, the life histories of the two men, Serge and Pascal, repeat each other in almost uncanny ways. As Pascal and Clotilde walk by the Paradou (the very garden paradise where Serge and Albine, the protagonists of *La Faute de l'abbé Mouret,* loved each other, and where Albine died), Clotilde is reminded of the love affair Pascal had previously that was like Serge and Albine's. Furthermore, Pascal loves Clotilde in an endless garden similar to the Paradou. In order to bring home the equivalence, the narrator calls Clotilde "Albine" at the moment when Pascal and Clotilde walk by the Paradou: "The vision of Albine had arisen, Pascal had seen it flower again like the spring. . . . Clotilde, having sensed the vision pass between them, lifted her face toward him, in a renewed need for tenderness. She was Albine" (*Pascal* 1081).

However, the most important similarity involves the chastity of the priest and the scientist (a chastity Zola seemingly condemns in *La Faute de l'abbé Mouret*). Mouret's struggle is to keep himself away from Albine, to keep himself chaste for his duties. Pascal's life has been the same: "Since his definitive installation at Plassans, he led a Benedictine monk's existence, cloistered in his books, far from women" (*Pascal* 1027). As we recall, Evelyn Fox Keller shows the relationship between chastity and science: the scientist must flee woman and her contamination, he must remain objective and avoid feminine sentimentality, he must be asexual in his search for the truth.

These three elements—the religious cast given to science in *Le Docteur Pascal,* the similarity between Pascal and Mouret, and the importance of chastity in religion and science—call for a reading of *La Faute de l'abbé Mouret* with *Le Docteur Pascal* and an investigation of Serge's life in *La Faute de l'abbé Mouret* as one that parallels that of the life of a scientist, that shares its rhetorical battles. We study *La Faute de l'abbé Mouret,* and not just *Le Docteur Pascal* alone, because of the above similarities, and also because it displays the clichés described by Keller so much more vividly than does *Le Docteur Pascal,* where they appear in sketchier form. Our next step is to study these clichés in both novels, and then to see how the conclusions of the two books offer two different interpretations of these clichés and of the naturalist project.

Female Contamination

In *Le Docteur Pascal* and in *La Faute de l'abbé Mouret,* women are considered to be dangerous. Mouret harbors a rather ridiculous fear of his powerless servant, La Teuse. This fear is linked to the need to keep women away from the clergy and from the ceremony of Mass. When there is no one else to serve Mouret during morning services, La Teuse offers to help him, but he refuses, and La Teuse gives this explanation for his refusal: "The priest is afraid I'll soil the good Lord."[7] There is a fear of ruining science and religion if they are contaminated by women.

In *La Faute de l'abbé Mouret,* this fear of ruination is acute, and is embodied in the sadistic Brother Archangias. He feels that religion is being "feminized" and ruined, and that the cult of Mary practiced by Mouret is particularly dangerous: "It softened souls, put skirts on religion, created an entire pious sensibility unworthy of the strong" (*Faute* 118). Here the sentimentality and subjectivity feared by scientists and embodied in women show up in Archangias's hate for Mary. Archangias cannot tolerate the fact that women are allowed in church near the altar.

One of the reasons women should be kept away from the altar is because the men find them literally dirty. (As we have seen, Zola viewed the plot of Hugo's effeminate romantic play as figuratively "dirty": it is "filthy" and contains "coarse acts." The link between figurative and literal filth permeates Zola's work and can be seen most clearly in the character of Gervaise in *L'Assommoir.*) The most spectacular example of this is Serge's sister, Désirée, who is constantly associated with manure: "Désirée arrived running, all red with joy, bareheaded, her black hair tied tightly at the nape of her neck, with her hands and arms covered with manure up to the elbows" (*Faute* 55). It is stated several times that she grew up in the manure pile, and she is always associated with the odors found there, and with odors in general. It is Archangias who most succinctly ties together women and odors: "They have the devil in their bodies. They stink of the devil, they stink of him in their legs, their arms, their belly, everywhere" (*Faute* 109). This filth and odor of women is contrasted with the purity and rites of purification of the male priest: "And, having prayed again, Mouret came back to pour himself water in thin streamlets on the extremities of the thumb and index finger on each hand in order to purify himself of the least bit of stain from sin" (48).[8]

Albine, too, is associated with odor, although not of the disgusting kind. Her odor is that of the metaphor that defines her in this text, a flower, "a great bouquet with a strong odor" (*Faute* 83). Similarly, Clotilde in *Le Docteur Pascal* is associated with odors in "her fresh odor of youth" (*Pascal* 1138). Thus woman's odor links her to the physical, sometimes to filth.

Her odor also links woman to an animal state, particularly in the case of Désirée, who is always in her courtyard with her animals and her manure. Désirée is herself an animal in this text: "She had grown up in the middle of manure, her head empty, with no grave thoughts of any kind; she benefited from the plush soil, from the open air of the country, developing all in the body, becoming a beautiful beast, fresh, white, red-blooded, with firm flesh" (*Faute* 93). Because of their odors, women, animals, and the animal nature of humankind are associated: "A human odor rose from that pile of rickety houses. And the priest thought himself still in Désirée's farmyard, faced with the pullulation of animals ceaselessly multiplying" (*Faute* 104). Women are described as smelly animals, whereas men in the church are all soul, pure, and bodiless in their religious attire: "He closed the door of his senses, sought to liberate himself from bodily necessities, was nothing other than a soul ravished by contemplation" (*Faute* 60).

Sex is at the root of all of these images. Women, odor, and sex are personified in Rosalie, the pregnant woman whom Mouret tries to marry to her lover. Here Archangias links woman to manure, sex, and contamination: "Go on, you can pull their ears until they bleed, the woman still grows in them. They have damnation in their skirts. Creatures good for throwing in the manure pile, with their poisonous filth!" (*Faute* 66). Odor represents fornication in the Paradou, in a scene that is so packed with reproduction as to be hallucinatory:

> An animal odor arose, hot with the universal rut. All this pullulating life gave off a shiver of childbirth. Under each leaf an insect conceived; in each tuft of grass a family grew; flies in flight, stuck to each other, did not even wait to land before copulating. Little parcels of invisible life that populate matter, the atoms of matter themselves, loved, mated, gave to the ground a voluptous shaking, made of the garden a great fornication. (*Faute* 247)

This fornicating nature is dirty, like the women who are associated with sex: "Nature presented him only with traps, with filth; he prided himself on doing her violence, in despising her, in disengaging himself from human mire" (*Faute* 60). Perhaps the most remarkable passage of the book is the final few paragraphs, in which all of these rhetorical elements—woman, woman's exposed body, sex (reproduction), animals, and manure—are brought together to conclude the text:

> A frightening din arose from the farmyard, behind the wall. The goat bleated. The ducks, geese, turkeys clicked their beaks, beat their wings. Chicks sang out as they laid their eggs, all together. The wild cock, Alexander, threw out his bugle crow. Even the rabbits could be heard hopping, shaking the boards in their hutches. And, beyond this noisy life of the small animals, a great laugh rang out. There was a rustling of skirts. Désirée appeared, her hair down, her arms exposed to her elbows, her face red with triumph, her hands resting against the top of the wall. She must have climbed up to the top of the manure pile. . . . "Serge! Serge!" she cried louder, clapping her hands. "The cow had a calf!" (*Faute* 373)

Man is thus represented as pure soul and mind, and he must separate himself from smelly, dirty, female reproductive nature. Man's chastity alone can keep him from being contaminated. This chastity of Mouret and Pascal is also linked to the notion of autonomy and isolation. As Keller shows, the need to be separated from women and subjectivity leads to the illusion of autonomy and independence of the scientific self. Similarly, in *La Faute de l'abbé Mouret,* the object that best symbolizes Mouret is the lone tree, significantly named "the Solitary One," that grows near the graveyard. In *Le Docteur Pascal,* the doctor lives "alone" with a maid and a young niece, two people "below" his stature, and is fascinated and horrified by the life of the solitary man who lives next to him. The lone man represents the ideal of autonomy and objectivity that Pascal cannot attain because he falls in love with Clotilde.

The entire plot of *La Faute de l'abbé Mouret* centers on Serge's struggle to remain autonomous and to avoid the feminine: he first successfully separates himself from women, he then succumbs to Albine, and finally he is able to separate himself completely from her at the close of the novel. In *Le Docteur Pascal,* the scientist's need to keep away from women originates from the threat that women will destroy his work: Clotilde, Martine, and Pascal's mother all want to burn his notes on heredity, the results of his medical experiments, and the records of his family that he has been keeping for years. The woman represents the thing that could destroy science.

The Site of Mastery and Experimentation

If we turn to this construction of clichés in terms of naturalism, we see once again Keller's description of the chaste, objective, virile scientist who distances himself from sentimentality and female nature. We see the scientist (represented by Mouret) as guarding his objectivity even as he must "treat" nature: Mouret must deal with Rosalie and the fecund townspeople, he must "treat" their souls, just as the objective scientist must observe nature, experiment on her, "treat" her. Mouret's and Pascal's celibacy represents their attempt to confront nature without being contaminated by her. In a remarkable choice of quotation, Zola cites Claude Bernard precisely on this topic of the scientist who must come into contact with the smelly, dirty, fetid aspect of nature, must "treat" nature, in order to emerge into the pure light on the other side:

> One will never arrive at truly fecund and enlightening generalizations on vital phenomena until one has done experiments oneself and has moved about the hospital, the amphitheater, and the lab, the

fetid ground where life palpitates. . . . If it were necessary to make a comparison that could express my feelings on the science of life, I would say that it is a superb drawing room, sparkling with light, which one cannot reach without passing through a long and hideous kitchen. (*Roman* 25–26)

The purity of the scientist is not manifested simply as a need to keep oneself away from contaminating femininity, however. It becomes a battle against women, it becomes a need to master women and nature, just as Keller describes the new virile, masculine science as one that needs to master and conquer. This battle between the sexes takes on the form of a battle against dangerous and threatening women. Several women pose a serious threat to the men in *Le Docteur Pascal*. Pascal's mother stands and watches as Macquart burns to death, and thus she essentially murders him; Dide watches, powerless to help, as the young, feebleminded Charles slowly bleeds to death. Clotilde's brother is done in by the women allegedly sent to him by his father. In the battle between Pascal and Clotilde, however, Pascal wins in the end; Clotilde gives up the fight, and then becomes his lover and "slave." Because her capitulation to him in their battle coincides with her giving of herself sexually, there is a kind of equation between mastery and man's sexuality. The same is true in *La Faute de l'abbé Mouret*, when, immediately after they make love for the first time, Mouret can dominate his attraction for Albine and return to the church.

The battle is not just between Pascal (or men) and women, but between science and women. The women wish to destroy Pascal's scientific project, and two of them do so in the end. There must be either love or science: when Pascal is with Clotilde, he gives up his work. When Clotilde leaves to care for her brother, he can take up his work again. Women and scientific thought do not mix.

The battle in *La Faute de l'abbé Mouret* becomes very physical and literal. Archangias gleefully tells of the "spankings given that morning to the little girls" (*Faute* 283), and Serge, as he looks over the land around the church one night, imagines Archangias spanking young women, with a specifically sexual overtone: "He heard Brother Archangias raise up the skirts of the girls and whip them until they bled, he heard him spit in their faces, himself stinking of the billy goat that could never be satisfied" (*Faute* 140). Here man's sexual attraction to women gets turned into a desire to hurt them, to dominate and humiliate them physically. Indeed, several times Archangias says that "it would be good riddance if they strangled all girls at their birth" (*Faute* 66).

This sadistic relation to women is not the sole province of the rather hyperbolic character of Archangias, however. Mouret, too, displays certain sadistic traits. In his religious zeal regained, in his need to remain chaste and separate from women so as to be pure and chaste enough for his duties, he finds himself sadistically smiling at his mistreatment and abandonment of Albine, an abandonment that leads to her death (*Faute* 320).

Thus, we see that in *Le Docteur Pascal,* and allegorically in *La Faute de l'abbé Mouret,* the scientific ideal necessitates mastery over women, and in order to achieve this goal, it enters into a violent battle with women in which women are physically harmed or even killed (Albine commits suicide because of Mouret's change). Women are seen as spoilers of the scientific or religious project, and as dangerous seducers who can "poison" man and lure him from his work. In both texts, the two women who "seduce" the scientist and the priest are rejected by the men and separated from them ultimately by death.[9]

The desire for purity and for separation from women seems to originate in an ambivalent relation to procreation manifested by the male characters in these works. We have seen already the disgust and loathing for procreation shown by Archangias in particular. But the characters in the novels show simultaneously a distinct fascination with fecundity and birth. Mouret, in his flight from procreation, still manifests an intense sensitivity to it, and the language in which his fascination and disgust are described is lavish and itself "fecund":

> From the flower bed came odors of swooning flowers, a long whisper that told of the marriage of the roses, of the sensual delights of the violets, and never had the solicitations of the heliotropes had a more sensual ardor. From the orchard there came whiffs of ripe fruit brought by the wind, an odor thick with fecundity; the vanilla of apricots, the musk of oranges. The fields sent up a deeper voice made up of the sighs of millions of plants kissed by the sun, the large sigh of an innumerable crowd in rut. . . . The forest breathed the giant passion of oaks. . . . And, in this coupling of the entire park, the roughest embraces could be heard from afar, there on the rocks, there where

the heat made the stones burst as they became swollen with passion, where spring plants loved each other tragically, and the nearby springs could not comfort them, set all aflame themselves by the sun that descended into their beds. (*Faute* 246–47)

It is in particular in this fascination with procreation that Zola's scientific naturalism reveals the way in which it is driven by gendered concerns. The fascination with procreation is a fascination with the woman's body and the way in which she produces her offspring. The descriptions of Désirée and her constantly reproducing animals are rich in carnal imagery and point to a fascination and disgust with the way animals are born—fascination in the hyperbolic nature of the description, disgust in the ever present manure pile: "From the piles of manure, from the copulation of animals, came a flood of generation in the midst of which Désirée tasted the pleasures of fecundity" (*Faute* 95).[10] But it is in particular the mother who is the center of interest and of disgust, as when Désirée makes the reluctant Mouret look at the rabbit hutch, which teems with mothers and babies: "Then, it was in a hutch, a hole of fur, at the back of which swarmed a little pile, a black mass, indistinct; it had a heavy breath, as if it were all one body" (*Faute* 96). It is not surprising that Désirée, who presides over all this reproduction, should be called the communal mother, responsible for all this generation (*Faute* 95).

The above quote reveals one of the motivating forces behind this fearful fascination with the mother and birth: the baby rabbits and the mother seem to be one body, unseparated, "indistinct." There is a fear of incomplete separation from the mother, from femininity here, a fear that one is still a part of the mother's body (the study of heredity, in fact, shows how much one *is* one's mother). In *La Faute de l'abbé Mouret,* the priest's fascination with conception, immaculate and not, is also his interest in the *interior* of the mother's body and in himself being *in* that interior. It can take the religiously symbolic form of his desire to be inside Mary's chest, near her heart, when he contemplates her image, her chest opened in a "red hole": "It was like a panic of his whole being, a need to kiss that heart, to melt himself in it, to lie down with it in the depths of that open chest" (*Faute* 24). This desire to be inside the woman's body takes on more sexual overtones in the following words of Mouret: "Then I will rise to your lips like a subtle flame, I will enter you through your open mouth, and our marriage will take place" (*Faute* 147).

The image of the interior of the woman's body as womb and as sexual organ is the most vivid in the image of the *trou;* this metaphor of the hole appears in many of Zola's texts, and in each one it takes on a slightly different meaning. In *La Faute de l'abbé Mouret,* it takes on first of all the metaphorical meaning of the very place where birth happens, the symbolic womb and birth canal. The *trou* is used to name Désirée's courtyard, which symbolizes, as we have seen, female reproduction: "She owned a farmyard, a little spot [*trou*] that they let her have, where she could let her animals grow as she wished" (*Faute* 95).

These *trous* are also places of fear, however, as they reflect the negative aspect of procreation. They represent the possibility of being buried alive, of never being able to be born, of being stuck inside the mother (of being incompletely separated from her). Mouret uses this image when he speaks with Albine in the Paradou about his previous life, before he was "born" to his affair with her: "It is strange that before being born one dreams of being born. . . . I was buried somewhere. I was cold. I heard the life outside stirring above me. but I blocked my ears, I despaired, I was used to my *hole* of shadows" (*Faute* 179; emphasis added). When Jeanbernat describes the Paradou as being made of *trous,* he speaks of the danger of death and of being poisoned by the air, in a kind of contagion: "It is stupid, these trees go on forever, with moss everywhere, broken statues, *holes* where one risks breaking one's neck at every step. The last time I went there it was so dark under the leaves, it was so poisoned with wild flowers, with strange breaths that blew down the paths, that I was afraid" (*Faute* 81; emphasis added). One wonders if this fearful image of intrauterine existence appears in Zola's recurrent nightmare of being a plant stuck underground, fighting to break through the soil. Indeed, Ripoll associates this plant imagery with the mystery of origins.[11]

The fear of poisoning or contagion is also linked to the fact that *trous* are holes in walls and in containing structures, holes that let separated areas mingle together, that hint of the impossibility of clearly defining boundaries between self and mother. They are the windows in Mouret's room that let nature and the outside in (*Faute*

129), they are the holes in the dilapidated church that let nature (the birds) in (*Faute* 49). In another way, the hole is that in the wall of the Paradou that lets Archangias into the "female" paradise of Albine (*Faute* 254). The hole, associated with the inside of the mother's body, with being inside the mother's body, is also associated with the possibility of inadequate boundaries, of contamination, and of the death of the individual. The fascination with and desire for unity with the mother's body are combined with fear of incomplete separation from her, from woman.[12]

So we are back to the need to separate man from woman, to keep these two spheres walled off from each other with impenetrable barriers. At the end of the novel, Mouret blocks up those holes that have allowed nature/woman into his church: "He gave himself the task of gluing paper windows on the broken panes in the nave" (*Faute* 279). Mouret expels Mary from his church: "He chased woman away from religion, he took refuge in Jesus" (*Faute* 324). Albine, too, blocks up the holes in her room, blocks out the masculine by using nature/woman itself before she poisons herself with her own symbol, flowers, before she shows that she dies because she is a woman: "She gathered fragrant greens: citronella, mint, verbena, balsam, fennel; she twisted them, bent them, and made plugs of them, and with their help she plugged the smallest cracks, the smallest holes in the door and the window" (*Faute* 360).

This desire for and fear of the inside of the mother's body have profound implications for Zola's naturalist and scientific project. Given that Mouret and Pascal represent the scientist's quest to "treat" nature, study her, learn her secrets, and dominate her, this quest is shown to be one for sexual secrets of female reproduction, and it is carried out in the aim of mastery over woman and nature through this knowledge. In *Le Docteur Pascal*, naturalism manifests a kind of morbid curiosity with just how women conceive and give birth, just what happens inside the woman's body, how a person is conceived and born.[13] This context of the enigma of reproduction elucidates one of the most important and surprising literary passages in Zola where the naturalist project that is described. It reveals in a rather incredible way these hidden drives behind the naturalist quest for pure truth. Here, the celibate scientist, Pascal, is quite literally interested in woman and *reproduction*. This passage of *Le Docteur Pascal* makes clear that the Naturalist investigation into heredity is the investigation of woman, sex, and reproduction. It is a science that literally experiments on the woman:

> What had led Doctor Pascal to concern himself in particular with the laws of heredity was, in the beginning, his work on gestation. As always, chance played its part by furnishing him with a whole series of corpses of pregnant women who died during an epidemic of cholera. Later he checked over the dead bodies that came through, completed the series, filled lacunae, and succeeded in familiarizing himself with the formation of the embryo, then the development of the fetus in each day of its intrauterine life, and he had thus compiled the clearest, most definitive observations. From that moment, the question of conception, at the heart of everything, posed itself to him in all its irritating mystery. Why and how a new being? What were the laws of life, that torrent of beings that made the world? From then on, as facts accumulated and were classified in his notes, he attempted a general theory of heredity that might suffice in explaining them all. (*Pascal* 944–45)

Here, in his attempt to master nature, to arrive at the truth, the scientist triumphs as he investigates the inner regions of a dead woman's body. Through Pascal's investigation of the origins of human life, Zola provides us with a certain interpretation of his own hereditary project, the study of various generations of a family with a woman at its origin. Through Pascal's and Mouret's relations to women, we see naturalism as an investigation of man's relation to woman, an investigation of the mystery of the origin of the self[14] and the mystery of the woman's body. We see the experimental project as one that attempts to separate man from woman, man from nature, and a desire to dominate in this separation. The quest for pure, uncontaminated truth pursued by naturalism shows itself to be, in fact, contaminated by the very thing it seeks to avoid: fear (emotionalism) and blindness to its own ideology and subjectivity. Perhaps the excessive desire for pure, uncontaminated objectivity arises because of the fear of incomplete differentiation from the mother.

In the network of rhetorical constructions provided by these two novels, the experimental novelist must investigate smelly, dirty, sexual woman and reproduction in order to emerge into the light of truth beyond, in order to reveal her secrets. But in *La Faute de l'abbé Mouret,* he must do so by remaining "celibate," by not allowing himself to be seduced into joining with woman and nature, into losing his male identity and objectivity. Although *Le Docteur Pascal* manifests this same rhetorical structure, its ending perhaps points to a different, revised understanding of science and woman. *La Faute de l'abbé Mouret* ends with the death of the woman and her unborn child and the continued existence of the living but emasculated male (Mouret's impotence and Archangias's castrated ear). It ends by showing the tragedy of the separation of male from female, of the domination of man over nature and woman. *Le Docteur Pascal,* however, ends with the death of the scientist who so radically separated himself from Clotilde, who desired to dominate and control nature and woman. At the end of that novel, the woman and her child live on, are not purged. The novel ends in a tragedy of death, of lost love and work, but that tragedy is shown to be a product of the desire for separation and mastery, and the living woman and child point to a hope for the future.

NOTES

1. Bernadette L. Murphy has, however, studied the use of the derogatory category of the feminine in Zola's argument against Hugo in "Zola critique de Hugo: les enjeux d'une polémique," *French Review* 61 (March 1988): 531–41.

2. Emile Zola, *Le Roman expérimentale* (Paris: Charpentier, 1880), 39; emphasis added. Page numbers for further references to this work appear in the text, with the abbreviation *Roman.* All translations from Zola are mine.

3. Evelyn Fox Keller, *Reflections on Gender and Science* (New Haven, Conn.: Yale University Press, 1985). All further references to this work appear in the text.

4. Janet Beizer studies a similar theme in the novel when she notes the importance of difference (not just gender difference) in its structure in "This Is Not a Source Study: Zola, Genesis, and *La Faute de l'abbé Mouret,*" *Nineteenth-Century French Studies* 18 (Fall/Winter 1989–90): 186–95.

5. Françoise Gaillard also ties Pascal to religion in "Genèse et généalogie (Le cas du *Docteur Pascal*)," *Romantisme* 31 (1981): 181–96. The link between *La Faute de l'abbé Mouret* and *Le Docteur Pascal* has been noted previously by Chantal Bertrand-Jennings, in "Zola ou l'envers de la science: de *La Faute de l'abbé Mouret* au *Docteur Pascal,*" *Nineteenth-Century French Studies* 7 (Fall/Winter 1980–81): 93–107.

6. Emile Zola, *Le Docteur Pascal* (Paris: Pléiade, 1967), 953; emphasis added. Page numbers for further references to this novel appear in the text, with the abbreviation *Pascal.*

7. Emile Zola, *La Faute de l'abbé Mouret* (Paris: Garnier-Flammarion, 1972), 44. Page numbers for further references to this novel appear in the text, with the abbreviation *Faute.*

8. Mieke Bal investigates the relation of women's guilt to religion in her article "Quelle est la faute de l'abbé Mouret? Pour une narratologie diachronique et polémique," *Australian Journal of French Studies* 23, no. 2 (1986): 149–67.

9. Although in *Le Docteur Pascal* the scientist sends Clotilde away as a generous and selfless act, the result is the same cruel rejection of the woman.

10. One might also see an infantile explanation of birth in the linking of manure (anal instinct) and animal birth, and in the figurative oral presence of tasting (*goûtait*).

11. R. Ripoll, "Le Symbolisme végétal dans *La Faute de l'abbé Mouret*," *Cahiers Naturalistes* 31 (1965): 11–21. See also Colette Becker, "Introduction," in Zola, *La Faute de l'abbé Mouret,* 20–21.

12. Bernadette Murphy also sees a theme in Zola's works of a desire to separate oneself from the mother. See Murphy, "Zola critique de Hugo."

13. I address this quest for the origin of the self as the primal scene in my book *Telling Glances: Voyeurism in the French Novel* (New Brunswick, N.J.: Rutgers University Press, 1992).

14. Françoise Gaillard, too, investigates this quest for the origin so often found in naturalism. See "Histoire de peur," *Littérature* 64 (December 1986): 13–22.

Temples of Delight: Consuming Consumption in Emile Zola's *Au Bonheur des dames*

Barbara Vinken

Realism's, especially late nineteenth-century realism's, approach to questions of gender seems to have the advantage of thematization. Emile Zola's "gynomythology" is "an obligatory stopping place" for such a thematics of gender.[1] In this essay I am less interested in the modes of thematization offered by realist fiction than in the quasi-"mythological" nature and outcome of realism's approach to coping with gender questions. There is no other feature of Zola's naturalism that could be more telling than its regressive gender politics; and there is no better explanation for this tendency than the fetishism grounding Zola's naturalism. This fetishism itself is thematized in Zola's work to such an extent that it illuminates the growing importance of that term between Marx and Freud. It is as if with fetishism realism gave away its secret, both in its attitude toward reality and in the secret mechanizations that kept this attitude working. In Zola, the clash between the descriptive, not to say revealing, value of fetishism's exposure on the one hand and the subsequent return to an ultraconservative politics of gender on the other is especially crass. No deconstruction of the exposed attitude is achieved in Zola's text. Zola's naturalism relapses into the mythic schemes that it thought to have left behind. It "shows" itself unable to overcome its fetishistic predicament.

In the novel of the same name, Au Bonheur des Dames is the name of a department store whose marketing principle is the arousal of feminine desire. Women's addictive consumerism leads to an ever greater accumulation of capital for the store. From the first page, the novel stresses the interdependence of the economic and sexual orders. It delivers this message emblematically, through the juxtaposition of the department store's logo with that of the family-owned boutique. The logo of the Bonheur des Dames shows two laughing, bare-breasted women unrolling the name of the house that promises an erotic paradise on earth. The logo of the doomed fabric store spells, in yellow letters bleeding onto a greenish background, the name of the owner and his patriarchal affiliation: "Baudu, successeur de Hauchecorne" (45; 9).[2]

The threat offered by the meteoric rise of the department stores to specialized trade is a fact of the Second Empire. Zola dramatizes this vertiginous ascent with a procedure akin to time-lapse photography, concentrating a process that took decades into a few years, and thereby making the change seem all the more dynamic. Zola's main character is the Bonheur, a cross between the two biggest Parisian department stores at the time, the Bon Marché and the Louvre; his novel describes "le commencement d'un grand magasin, allant toujours en s'amplifiant, jusqu'à ce qu'il emplisse toute une partie de la ville."[3] The reason for such incredible success is explained coolly in the novel: the accelerated flow of capital allows an always increasing profit by multiplying the turnover. Walter Benjamin's *Das Passagenwerk* patiently assembles contemporary sources describing the invention of mass consumption and its success, owing to an incredible acceleration of the turnover.[4] Zola's description is thereby confirmed in detail. His realism consists, as these sources reveal, last but not least in participating fully in the contemporary phantasmagoria that brought a new element of spectacle to business.[5]

Zola does not present as mere fact the triumph of the department stores that ruins specialized trade—he glorifies it. The forces Zola sees in operation are not only contemporary and modern and therefore the forces of the future, they are as staggeringly unstoppable as the forces of nature, they are the forces of Life itself. To live, Life must kill. Denise, the heroine, who, in her "woman's heart" (402) cannot deny her compassion and her tears to the sanctified victims of raging Life; Denise, "so reasonable" (299); Denise, in her "instinctive love for the logic of life" (220), summarizes the novel's final moral: "This invincible work of life . . . requires death as its continual seed" (402; 345). The triumph of Octave Mouret, the owner of the Bonheur des Dames, lies in the logic of things, which is the fatal logic of Life itself. Not to live and let live, but to eat in order not to be eaten is the new motto. Charity is nothing but a helpless anachronism. The social reforms initiated by Denise in the Bonheur do not throw a monkey wrench in the wheels of Mouret; they serve in the end the smoother functioning of the machine. Even when they appear to be social reforms they are in the service of Life, and that means in the service of the "patron": "And she pleaded the course of the wheel-work of the colossal machine, not from any sentimental reason, but by arguments appealing to the very interests of the employers" (370; 315).

Why is this interest celebrated as the cause of Life? Denise gives one answer to this question: the misery of today is a precondition of the health of tomorrow's Paris. According to this vitalist-utopian discourse, the victims suffer for some public happiness to come. They are martyrs despite themselves in a general historical plan that, like the triumph of Christianity, takes a toll (390). In a more global perspective, the ruin and suffering of the victims is justified as a necessary sacrifice and thereby legitimated. This discourse believes in the possibility that a state of general happiness can be achieved. It stems from the ideology of free trade and is guided by the idea that nobody loses and everybody wins. Such an optimism is intrinsically at odds with another discourse informing the novel, social Darwinism. For social Darwinism there is no qualitative historical change, and thus no teleological development, that one day will bring a balance of forces and an amelioration for everybody. Two incompatible ideologies clash.

A struggle, however, runs deeper than the clash of these incompitable discourses, a struggle that has allegorical traits: a fight for Life against Death. The department store represents Life, whereas the specialized trades represent Death. What Life finally kills are the already dead, who maintain nothing of life but its appearance. The specialized trades are not depicted as living competitors, defeated in the struggle for existence, but rather as an already corrupted, fissured organism. Death nests behind its facade and lives on the already half dead, from whom he has sucked all blood. The caste of small business people, irreversibly bearing the mark of death, stubbornly keeps up the facade of life. Mouret's triumphant march hardly does more than show the creviced facades that collapse without resistance for what they are: graves inhabited by the living dead. Mouret does not bring death, he forces it into the open and thereby exorcises it.

Consuming Femininity; or, How to Exorcise Vampirized Vampires

The trouble is that the victory of Life stands on shaky feet. It is undermined from within, as this new department store resembles more than anything else a self-destructive artifice. Its foremost product is destruction: unrequitable, sterile, consuming desires for vain trifles that pitilessly destroy everything. For vanities huge fortunes vanish in this voracious machine without a trace—and the profit the department store owner gets out of this ruinous spending has to be reinvested in the insatiable monster. All passions spent, nothing but ruins and ashes remain. But a new voracious Moloch reemerges phoenixlike from these ashes in all its resplendent, seductive glare. In such an economy nothing solid or lasting can be created. The sheer overflow paradoxically engulfs everything. Capitalism, in the end, feeds on itself. It consumes itself after devouring everybody else; it ends up destroying itself, because it depends on the consuming addiction of women—thus the moral of Zola's novel.

The department store is a Moloch that eats human flesh, a machine developed to devour the flesh of women, who, consumed by desire, throw themselves into its deep throat. Something feeds on them and they cannot stop consuming. But the more they consume, the more consuming is their desire.[6] Femininity is, like capitalism, a vampirized vampire. The lecherous department store that consumes female flesh and consumed/consuming femininity live on each other in a parasitic dependence. They oscillate between the extremes of mania and depression. Vampirized melancholically by a desire from within, capitalism and femininity devour maniacally the objects of the world. The forces that consume them make them consume. The figure of the vampire lives on this double lack. The department store Au Bonheur des Dames sells the stuff that dreams are made of: the fetishized female body. Her flesh is transformed by Zola's description into fabric: the tights are velvet, the bosom satin, the arms silk. The department store itself is nothing but a huge alcove where this body can be consumed over and over again. No wonder capitalism is connoted as feminine.[7] The women consume intoxicating femininity; they function as the medium for the flow of money, as subject and object of desire. What they ruin in this consuming overflow is not only themselves, but, more devastatingly, men.

Mouret's revolution uncannily turns out to rely on the very principle it set out to overthrow: Death in Life. Rather than dramatizing the triumph of the department store over an older form of trade, the novel seeks to redeem capitalism from itself. The true revolution, turning everything upside down, can happen only through a radical break that must appeal to forces not entirely of this world. Denise is the antidote administered; the New Woman is incarnated in this virgin child-mother who is not consumed by the demon of consumerism. She can spend herself completely for others and deliver men from the nightmare of intoxicated femininity. Zola's *Bonheur* is the redemption of capitalism from its inherent structure of consuming femininity. Mankind is mythically restored by the introduction of a new economy. The capitalistic vampirized vampire, eaten by death and transmitting death, is saved by an ever flowing, nourishing source of motherly love that the manchild can suck without ever being in danger of being sucked. Despite its meticulous documentation of the economic facts, despite all its realism, the novel is informed by a mythical plot: the momentary redemption of the man-eating monster by a fairy-tale princess, who is also a saint.

Capitalism as Subversive Force; or, The Free-Floating Woman

Zola's capitalism follows a logic that destroys not only the old order, but any order. Its destructive force becomes manifest in the arrangement of merchandise in the department store. Everything is displayed in the wild, promiscuous confusion that is the new rational principle: textiles and Japanese curiosities, furniture and children's clothing, umbrellas and perfume. The old order of the specialized trades, in which each merchant had a well-defined selection of merchandise, is jumbled. Upset by this apparently relationless side-by-side is also the order of resemblance that ruled the old cosmos of commodities. The honor of the well-ordered trade is given away in this new "bazaar," in which the consumer is assailed violently by the chaos of seductive goods. The mass, artificially banked up, the crowd, skillfully organized, that multiplies itself in its errands, is an image of overflow, of the senseless and direction-less abundance of the department store.[8] The department store be-comes a labyrinthine cabinet of mirrors, in which the client, on her devious detours, goes astray. The department store is the staging of sheer abundance wrought from nothing, reduced to nothing, the stage on which the mass of consumers mirrors itself in the masses of commodities in a vertiginous mimesis. Dancing in this mirror is the spark of desire, fusing distinctions in its tautological whirl.

The hierarchy of the sexes collapses; the opposition male/female is subverted. Shopwomen and shopmen are equal in their fight for the survival of the fittest. Their rivalry, erasing their sexuality, leads at best to some kind of neutral "cameraderie" (143; 165). And be-cause women no longer behave in a womanly fashion—instead of submitting, they compete—men cannot be men. Patriarchy, depen-dent on complementary role models, is thereby corrupted. Zola gives as an exemplary case a family that carries as its patronymic family name the name of man: "les Lhommes." Father, mother, and son work at the Bonheur des Dames. Mr. "Man," in spite or because of his name, does not live up to his male role. Instead of exercising his male-fatherly authority as master of the house and head of the family, he is completely devoted to his wife. Making three times more money than he, she definitely is the one who wears the trousers. Mrs. Man, well equipped in her silk dress, her face an im-perial mask, does everything to deny the male lineage. She wants to be called by her first name rather than by her family name; she re-fuses to bear the name of her husband, the name of man. She also refuses the inheritance of her father: she never uses his theater box. Mme Aurelie is the uncontested head of the family, boss of husband and son, boss of the Lhommes, whom she governs not in their name. All her love goes to cajoling, pliant young women. Mr. Man has no authority over his son, whom he reveres almost as much as he looks up to his wife, "because he comes from her" (81). One-armed, disabled, Mr. Man blows the horn in his spare time. The Lhommes are a family out of place. Their apartment has nothing of the *douceur du foyer,* nothing of the warm inwardness of a space that protects from the outside. It is rather a *"hôtel banal"* (168), a kind of profane passage everybody traverses on the way to amusements. And the award for so much dissolution comes promptly: the amassed fortune, in this case a "matrimoine" rather than a "patrimoine," is consumed by the consuming passion of the son: actresses. Piece by piece, it falls prey to his "terrible teeth" (419).

Just as the hierarchy of the sexes is turned upside down and the underlying opposition of the sexes is subverted, the hierarchy of classes is threatened. It is the class of saleswomen that causes the trouble. Their social indeterminacy turns out to be a moral problem. Because of their low starting salaries, saleswomen of the time were practically reduced to taking paying lovers, and thereby verged on prostitution. But the novel presents this economic problem as a topical problem: "The worst of all was their neutral, badly defined position between the shopwoman and the lady. Thrown into the midst of luxury, often without any previous instruction, they formed a singular, nameless class. Their misfortunes and vices sprung from that" (330; 276). This class of working women who can be defined no longer in patrilinear terms as mother, sister, or wife is nameless, in-famous. Like the silk they sell, beautifully called *ciel de Paris,* their success depends on effect rather than on quality. And beneath their glaring surface their "grâces marchandes" (23) do not fulfill their promise. They are a copy, a counterfeit of the society ladies. Despite themselves, they even copy the hierarchies prevailing in the bourgeois world. In this carnivalized world the problem of mimesis, of copy and imitation, is anything but innocent.

In the end the only question is whether the "real ladies" have been infected by frequenting their copies. The bourgeois opposition of *honnête femme* and *fille* is unsettled. Does not Mme Desforges, the prototype of the *grande bourgeoise,* behave like a shopwoman, or worse, like a prostitute, when she discloses the most intimate secrets of her alcove in public? Egon Friedell has described the fashionable type during the era of Napoleon III as "the grande dame, who plays the cocotte."[9] This play of fashion is literalized in Zola's novel, where it maintains its reversibility; whereas the cocotte plays grande dame, the grande dame turns out to be a cocotte. "Toutes les mêmes!" might be Zola's conclusion. The female world is shaken by a frenzy, in which all oppositions, all distinctions disappear. Last but not least, the opposition of private and public is turned upside down. At home in the department store, women's *intérieur* goes public. The inmost of the inner, the alcove, is staged on a public scene. What until then has been jealously hidden from the world and kept for the husband or lover is displayed before everybody's eyes.

The Capitalist as Divine Seducer; or, The Fall of Patriarchy I

The bachelor Octave Mouret, owner of the Bonheur des Dames, is not only a man of extraordinary genius and inexhaustible willpower. He is more than a brilliant businessman. He has the charm of the conqueror, the grace of a smiling god. In his eccentric excesses, in his willingness to risk everything innumerable times to multiply his returns, Mouret has superhuman qualities. He is not a player, but a creator. As an architect whose artificial city landscapes can compete with the rolling green fertile hills of the Cotentin, he is a poet of the sublime. This reversal of nature can be euphorically celebrated as gaining control and power over the elements; a control that makes dreams come true and fairy tales real. The enchanting impression of such artificial paradises has been described as "a fragment of midsummer night's dream in the midnight sun."[10] But the same artificial reversal of nature can also be seen as breeding flowers of evil luxuriating in an overheated, glaring atmosphere. The reversal of nature in the Bonheur des Dames appears in this all-too-glaring light, which literally casts nature into shadow. Mouret erects a city within the city that strongly resembles a *phalanstère à la Fourier*. On his building sites, he turns night into day. The department store, overheated by the electrical, glaring light, becomes a place of hellish erotics, a Babel consumed by consumer intoxication. It can be redeemed only by the advent of the fairy-tale princess, who transforms the consuming lasciviousness of this huge alcove into reproductive fertility through the consummation of marriage.

Mouret's omnipotence swells boundlessly, and the novel lives on this swelling and its apocalyptic connotations. *Tout Paris* is at his feet. He rules an empire that stretches to the limits of Europe, to the limits of the world. The department store is a miniature of the universe, whose treasures flow together under its roof only to be delivered by railway all over Europe. All these movements need organizational skills equaling those needed for the movement of troops in an empire. No wonder military metaphors crop up: Mouret is the commander in chief of an ever-growing army, and with Napoleonic overtones he conquers one industry after another. But instead of bloody spoils, he brings home as trophies commodities.[11] Mouret is compared to an absolute king; from a benevolent ruler who seems to care only for the well-being of his subjects and who cleverly delegates the execution of unpopular measures to his inferiors, he is transformed into a cruel despot: "multiplying the victims and pushing them into the streets" (355; 301). Finally, his empire drinks not only the money of Paris, but the money of the universe. Four monstruous brazen trumpets launch a publicity campaign and announce the last judgment in the middle of this earsplitting triumph (404).

As a ravishing seducer, Mouret understands the "côté fille" of success; the city of Paris, loving success like all women, gives herself in a kiss to the most audacious (71). Mouret, adventurer from the south, enters on the stage of the city as a ladies' man. He wastes no time and starts his career by bringing sexuality into the open. His debut is, appropriately, a "flagrant délit," a public scandal still ringing in all the shops of the quartier (59). He makes his way by "ceaselessly exploiting women" (59): he exchanges love for money. He gets the shop through marriage; the "sudden and inexplicable conquest" (59) of Mme d'Hédouin transforms him into a man of means. He gets the credit he needs for expansion through his lover, who serves as "lien aimable" (105) between himself and the baron Hartmann, a former lover of hers: "He knew how much the mutual possession of a mistress serves to render men pliable and tender" (106; 65). He is notorious for making love with the shopwomen. Mouret only thinks of "the woman"; he is obsessed with defeating her. He does not want to be consumed by passionate longing; he wants her to ruin herself in a consuming passion before his eyes. This he manages by showing her her own seductive image.

He proves to be immune to the weapons of women, which he uses in turn to defeat them. Even in the hour of tenderness, the hour of twilight, he does not get carried away by their sensual charm but remains coolly in control. Sexual act and selling merge. The one becomes a metaphor for the other, and Zola does not spare us any of the usual symptoms, ranging from trembling lips, turning pale, and whispering, dying voices to the *piccol' morte*. Mouret puts on an act in front of women. He talks with a fluting voice and presents himself as completely entangled by their charms. It is in the role of the seduced that he is the most perfect seducer. But Mouret is so seductive only because he is also a woman: "He seemed to be a woman himself [Il était femme], they felt themselves penetrated and overcome by this delicate sense of their secret that he possessed" (117). Once he is even infected by the collective female intoxication, by their feverish, whipped-up desires to consume without end: "His face got redder, his eyes had a little of that rapture with which the eyes of his customers ultimately vacillated" (277; 226)—but that remains an exception. Mouret's genius consists in not letting himself be tempted. This conqueror of femininity owes his invincibility to his ability to remain immune to the forces with which he plays, untouched by the desires he stimulates. Mouret is victorious as long as he remains an unseduced seducer.

The Bonheur des Dames, this machine for erotic production, sells as its real merchandise seductive femininity that attracts women like moths to a flame. Enraptured, they lean "as if to see themselves" over an imitation waterfall made from fabrics. What they see, Narcissuslike in this "motionless lake," is what makes them fit to be seen: something that makes them complete, total.[12] In their specular gaze they see the material of their flesh transformed into fabrics, into the inorganic that mimics the organic and precludes corruption and death: total femininity toward which all their consuming desires are directed. The department store is a women's house, impregnated with their odor, cast in a dubious light. Femininity, intoxicated with the addiction to consumption, appears to be consumable, venal.[13] Desiring femininity, endlessly reflected, is put on sale. The dummies, animated by the warm breath of seduction, come alive (44). Next to the laughing, bare-breasted women on the logo of the department store, the already surrealist dummy, with her perfect material body animated by desire, who is headlessly offered for sale is the best allegory for this store. The clients stray with guilty looks in this labyrinth and, intoxicated, ravished, succumb to the seduction to which they are addicted. With trembling hands they wallow in mountains of lace, they caress velvet, they are feverishly excited by the burning colors of the silks. They succumb compliantly to vice, a vice that strangely resembles making love with a stranger in public—a truly consuming consumption.

Women become weak; nerves racked, they indulge in an orgy of shameless vice. After one of the big sales, the department store looks as if they had undressed right on the spot, torn off their clothes in an attack of irrepressible desire (171). The department store is no school for honor, but rather the place where the secret vices of women are shamelessly bared in public, as they expose themselves without veil in the glaring, hot artificial light. Ravished, they bathe in the caresses of the "offre public," they touch everything and let themselves, pale with desire, be raped: "la clientèle, dépouillée, violée, s'en allait à moitié défaite, avec la volupté assouvie et la sourde honte d'un désir contenté au fond d'un hôtel louche" (437).[14] The novel talks of a "détraquement de cette névrose des grands bazaars," of a sharp crisis of passions (288). The money of Paris oozes away in this frenzied, shameless spending, in this public orgy of female vice. Blazing, the store trembles with their passionate energy. After the big sale, the store looks as if bulldozed by an invading horde; the ruined conquerors sit on a heap of ruins.

Capitalism as Church; or, The Fall of Patriarchy II

The cult practiced in this cathedral of commerce that is the Bonheur des Dames is set against the background of religion. What is at stake, however, is not the mixing of the profane with the sacred, of the high with the low as expressed in a typical bon mot attributed to Louis Philippe: "Dieu soit loué et mes boutiques aussi." There are few texts that better illustrate what Baudelaire meant when he wrote of the "religious intoxication of the big cities." Seldom have the theological intricacies of the commodity, discussed by Marx, been staged more impressively in their play of mystical veiling and unveiling than in *Au Bonheur des dames*. The religion that Octave Mouret establishes by erecting this cathedral of commerce is a religion of love, a canticle on femininity. The department store, guarded by a whirl of smiling, kissing Cupids, is a temple of female beauty, a "chapel raised to the worship of woman's beauty and grace" (44; 8). The sanctuary is the alcove, half veiled by trembling lace; the owner himself, the beautiful, audacious priest of this new cult.

The new cathedral takes the place of the old church. Like the old one, the new church appears in Zola as a hostile alliance among priest, God, and woman against patriarchy (438). The old as well as the new church is depicted as the threatening locus of troublesome consuming female passion.[15] Like his contemporary Charcot, who—on the other bank of the Seine—made hysterics act out the classical attitudes of the enraptured saints before a huge male audience, Zola stages in his department store the type of the neurotic, hysterical woman, whose very illness seems to be in a dark way her femininity.[16] Like all cathedrals, Mouret's temple has a—appropriately female—relic in his fundament: the blood and the bones of his wife, who fell to her death at the construction site (59). In the middle of the department store, as in the middle of a cathedral, stands the sanctuary, this alcove, that enshrines seductive female flesh for consumption. The covenant founded in communion, wherein the flesh and blood of Christ is consumed together, is opposed to this covenant where everyone eats everybody. The department store is described as a cannibalistic Baal that gets its trembling energy from devouring human flesh. Mouret is a bloodsucker who drinks the blood of women and sells their flesh "like a Jew," by the pound. Salesperson eats salesperson, woman eats woman, Mouret is eaten by "deux ou trois coquines à la fois" (324), the clients consume the fortunes of their husbands or other male relatives or are man-eaters of a different kind. These modern temples have espoused the cult of the female flesh toward which their consuming desire to consume is directed. Femininity and money have become interchangeable.

The turning point of this devouring economy is the "incendie final du blanc, un feu d'artifice, un éblouissement singulier qui fait comme une apothéose de féerie sur les ruines du quartier en cendres,"[17] where the marriage of Denise and Mouret is triumphantly acted out in the end. The underlying logic of this "grande exposition du blanc" is a slow striptease, in which the lingerie in all imaginable materials and variants is spread out in public in order to expose the naked flesh. The secrets of the alcove, publicly exposed in this indiscreet unwrapping, lead to a "dépravation sensuelle" (422). The burning white is at the same time the sparkling, glaring color of voluptousness and the softly gleaming snowy white of virginal, fertile love. The guilty white of female skin, of which one can catch glimpses in the dressing rooms, the seductive white of voluptuous temptation, is metamorphosed by this fire that feeds on the ruins of the quarter into the sacred white of the virginally veiled bride, who wakes up only to be mother, to move to the innocent white of breast-feeding and to end with the white of the children's clothing. The turning point of this metamorphosis is at the same time the highest point of crisis. In this sanctuary, the strongest seduction, the most obvious depravation, lies next to possible redemption. Consumption is replaced by the sanctified, fertilizing consummation of matrimony. The veiled, virginal, all-powerful fairy queen, coming from an epoch before capitalism, redeems capitalism for a short moment from the ceaseless—and ruinous—flow of money and libido. The new covenant between Denise and Mouret that replaces the sexual economy of consuming consumption by a reproductive sexuality miraculously transfigures and purifies this orgy of white.

The fetishistic character of the economy of consuming consumption is so obvious that it might have come straight out of a textbook. The fetish connotes the moment that precedes the unveiling of the missing female phallus. It stands for the last moment when woman can still be imagined as possessing a penis. The establishment of the fetish consists in a displacement of value deinvested from the original object and transferred to an inanimate object. The last memory that precedes the trauma of castration masks it at the same time. The fetishistic object allows the subject to defend this denial: the fetish, identified as a replacement for the maternal penis, makes the very ambiguity of this denial concrete, because it functions at the same time as the memorial recalling castration anxiety as well as the sign of triumph over the castration threat.[18]

Though the logic that determines the choice of the fetishistic object is often hidden, Freud states that next to shoes, velvet, fur, and lingerie are preferred fetishes. In the *Bonheur,* the fetish not only attracts the appreciation of the missing piece; it is literally found in its place. What should we think of the stolen goods the clients in luxurious dressing rooms fix underneath their slips, of the parcels that "dangle along the tights" of these thieves (357)? And what should we think of this "tissu miraculeux de finesse" that the ladies spread in their laps and caress much too long with "guilty hands" (177)? For the reader weaned on Freud it is supremely comic that Zola in the department of the trousseau, which like nothing else calls up the wedding night, arranges his impressive array of fetishes; he thereby fends off the moment when the view of the missing part is inevitable and reenacts the traumatic experience and its triumphant denial. Upside down and as seen from below woman is here shown to us: "la femme retournée et vue par le bas" (422). That sounds like a paraphrase of Freud, who tells us that "the inquisitive boy spies at the woman's genitals from below." And the "pieces of underclothing, which are so often chosen as a fetish," that are spread in an incredible variety all over the *Bonheur,* "crystallize the moment of undressing, the last moment the woman could still be regarded as phallic."[19] The only topic of the *Bonheur* is the reenactment—and thereby the denial—of this traumatic scene in the fetish.

What makes the *Bonheur* interesting, however, is more than just an early illustration of what Freud's psychoanalysis described. In the novel, femininity itself comes to stand simultaneously as the memory of and the masquerade for the traumatic lack in women. Femininity is the absolute, the ultimate fetish. Femininity in Zola is either an organic state that is described in an inorganic way or an inorganic material that gets animated in the description. Woman's body is a body made of fabrics, of velvet, satin, and silk, or a body made of marble or ivory. But the dead materials that constitute it can come alive. Thus, another constitutive character of the fetish is focused: "the transfer of value to an inanimate thing." What femininity masks, according to one of the protagonists of the novel, is of course not the lacking penis, but death. The dark riddle of femininity, so fears Bouthemont, is that virginal beauty is a mask only for death (348). To banish this fear is one of the most important functions of the fetish. The inorganic masks mortality. The animated dummies, like the women turned into dead fabric, have the sex appeal of the inorganic. They incarnate the quintessence of the structure of modern desire: a desire for the inanimate perfection of what is outside of time, of corruption, of decay. The inanimate uncannily apes the animate; suddenly, the animate turns into the inanimate. In *A Ladies' Paradise,* femininity is transformed into a commodity, and that commodity is femininity. In the commodity, femininity is animated without bearing the stigmata of life: decay and death. The flesh as fabric, soft, smooth, gleaming, caressing like silk, denies the corruption of the flesh.[20] What seems to be dead, the inorganic material of the flesh, denies the death beyond whose decay it points. Within the commodity, femininity reanimates what is deadened in the commodity; the desire for what is fetishized in the commodity becomes the animation of what has become the exchange value of the commodity, femininity. Femininity thus is the secondary animation, self-animation, of something whose deathlike appearance has to be overcome as life itself has been overcome. The fetish is the triumph over death in that it overcomes life; it precludes, and bans, the return of the dead in the appearance of what it sucessfully excludes, life.

The New Femininity; or, The Restoration of Mankind

Repeatedly, an angel of revenge is announced to Octave Mouret: what he has gained through women, he will lose through them. One will come to revenge her exploited sex. The advent of this woman who will turn Mouret into a seduced seducer is the event everybody is ardently waiting for—obviously in vain. Denise is no Nana, who would have been Mouret's equal if not superior, who would have defeated him with his very weapons and to whose indifferent beastly femininity he would have happily succumbed. Denise is no Eve, who would have seduced and ruined him, but a saving Mary. She is represented as a pietà figure, with her sleeping brother in her lap. In the middle of a whirl of children she finds herself rejuvenated. Denise, alone of her sex, is not part of the female world, but stands in determined negation to this world. Miraculously, she is exempt from the corruption of femininity.

Denise is a strange generic cross among fairy tale, legend, and saint, life. Despite her being so reasonable, despite her logic and her understanding of commerce, she is not the child of her time but appears in the aura of a bygone epoch. This impression is underscored by the wildly romantic love adventures of her brother, which seem to come straight out of courtly medieval romance. She is orphaned and poor, she is a child, a virgin, a mother. Denise is, in short, soft, reasonable, economical, zealous, generous, patient, kindhearted, humble, and courageous—and constructively on the side of Life. As a modern Saint of Work, she preserves her spotless virtue in the midst of vices, in the hot wind of desires, ceaselessly exposed to the temptations of this world. The law of the convertibility between money and femininity that informs the novel is suspended in her. Contrary to all other women, she does not conduct money and does not function as a communicating vehicle. She remains unstained by money or man, unstained by femininity. Denise interrupts the finally ruinous circuit of money and femininity. She is exempt from the vice of femininity, exempt from consuming consumption.

Zola demonstrates dramatically in Denise's cousin Geneviève, her tragic counterpart, that sterile consumption is the very vice that characterizes femininity. Geneviève is the daughter and the heiress of the house of Baudu, fiancée to the spiritual son of her father. Her heavy black hair is contrasted with Denise's blond. Parallel to the consumption of the house's fortune in a hopeless battle against the Bonheur, her femininity consumes her body, meant to transmit the money to the next patriarchal generation. This anemic white girl, almost already in the grave, who grew like a cellar flower without the light of the sun, is literally consumed by her only feminine adornment left. She will die, consumed by her ever more luxuriantly growing hair, heavy with passion, which eats her up with its "voracious vitality" (380; 324) and thirstily drinks her blood—pure vampirism that, lacking nourishment, feeds on itself. In front of our eyes, a strange metamorphosis takes place: the source of life, blood, is turned into the black stream of tresses. The biological femaleness of Geneviève is monstrously consumed by her passionate femininity. Her virginity is consumed because no consummation has taken place. In the end, she is not a woman anymore, but dies "returned to the first infantile slimness of her young days" (381; 325).

Denise does not partake in this cannibalistic, vampiristic circulation; she is beyond the unleashed contagion of desire. Her cardinal virtue is her willingness to renounce completely personal interests and passions, to sacrifice and immolate herself happily. Denise does not play desiringly with desire; she is ready to renounce it. Zola shrinks from no effort to cleanse her of the suspicion of being nothing but a scheming manipulator of passions, "an artful jade, a woman learned in vice" (347; 293). To her fellow creatures, incapable of understanding this almost extraterrestrial purity, she appears as "a disguised female flesh-eater" (348; 293), who in the war of the sexes strategically spurs desire by delaying its fulfillment. But when Denise in the end gets everything, it is only because she was ready to renounce everything, ready to turn away from the world and live in almost monastic solitude in the countryside. Whereas her sisters, sucked into the ravaging neurosis of the big department stores, are within the contemporary spectrum of female types the newest version of the hysterical woman, Denise is rather a sister of Thérèse de Lisieux, humble pioneer of the "small road." In the figure of Denise, Zola secularizes the Christian virtues: work in the world takes the place of prayer to the beyond; the fertile, chaste, bourgeois marriage takes the place of monastic continence. Because this kind of marriage is based on *caritas* rather than on passion, there is no place left for passion in his dire secularization.

Denise and Mouret's relationship is in a strange way influenced by "superior forces" and has strong religious overtones. Denise's patron saint is the picture of the first wife of Mouret, Mme Hédouin, which hangs like a smiling icon over the desk of the young widower. Toward the end, Denise appears to be the resurrection of his wife, her voice becomes the echo of her voice. This voice says something the whole novel contradicts: "One ought always to believe a woman to be virtuous, sir" (365; 312). Mouret's empire is based upon contrary knowledge and owes its success to the systematic exploitation of this knowledge. And against better knowledge, but perhaps persuaded by the only righteous figure in this modern Sodom and Gomorrah, Mouret loses faith in the omnipotence of the economy he maintains.

Mouret's divine pride and activity reach their limit at Denise's "no," which, repeated like a litany, has the force of prayer. In the face of this "no," he not only feels impotent; his complete triumph over women and therefore over Paris, his empire that spans the earth, his incredible fortune, the turnover of his department store that that very day has reached the legendary and much-awaited figure of one million—all this seems to him empty and vain, nothing but worldly vanity, the hollow erection of his pride, that cannot fulfill his heart any longer. Suddenly, the idols of this world lose their beguiling glare; by turning his back on them and on the libidinal economy that characterizes them he turns to another economy and to true value: Denise transfigured in a halo. And when he sees her in his raging crisis as the revenge of the eternally feminine, against which he had to rebel obstinately so as not to end up defeated under his millions, he feels as if he has blasphemed his idol and, taken by some "sacred terror" (349) this New Woman inspires, he wants to get down on his knees to worship her—a very good inspiration indeed, as he himself recognizes, because what is at stake here is the triumph not of the eternally feminine, but of the eternal mother, into whose hands men "can deliver themselves without fear" (415). All Mouret desires is to be loved by her as she loves her brothers; and that desire strikes him the very moment she handles them like babies whose diapers have to be changed. Denise's love for her husband will have to be a mother's love.

Mouret's decision to marry Denise, against all his principles, is enacted and must be modeled on the schema of a religious conversion. First, Mouret becomes a martyr of love, gains stature through suffering, and is redeemed from his faults by torturing love. Thus prepared, he overcomes his pride; the conqueror throws himself at the feet of this virginal child-mother, whose very weakness is her strength. Something incomprehensible happens to Mouret, a man of will and action, that he suffers passively. The glorious conqueror is defeated by complete weakness. But this defeat is his final, his true triumph. Mouret is redeemed from being a ladies' man to become a family man, a "brave homme" (367), husband and father. He is delivered from his femininity—and from his godliness—through a new womankind.

Postscript

"There is simply no limit, in fine, to the misfortune of being tasteless"—thus notes Henry James as he attempts to articulate his mixed feelings about Zola: "It [being tasteless, that is] does not merely disfigure the surface and the fringe of your performance— it eats back into the very heart and enfeebles the source of life."[21]

James's ambivalence relies on the structural metaphor of the doubled vampire that informs Zola's novels. Moreover, James sees the self-defeating energy that Zola gathers against the grain of his writing. The source of life, eaten from within, is at the same time an overflow of life, too much of a life, life turning against itself: "The singular doom of this genius, was to find, . . . with life, at fifty, still rich in him, strength only to undermine all the 'authority' he had gathered."[22]

In *Au Bonheur des dames,* Denise, the New Woman, is the protagonist of hopeful news of redemption. Zola consolidates what he has propagated through Denise in his later work, where woman has become the "libre compagne de l'homme," a pillar of patriarchy, that is. The happiness of the New Woman is the happiness of living only for a husband and children; motherhood fulfills her and makes her immune to being eaten from within—and thus from having to engulf everything. The transition from the earlier novels' subversive moral message of consuming femininity to the later novels' propagation of the supermother who is no longer a threat to man because she produces life without the threat of vampirized and vampiric femininity is fluid.

When Denise finally agrees to marry Mouret, she throws herself weeping into his arms. He, whose eyes are filled with tears, holds her in his lap. Their flowing tears purify; they cleanse Mouret of the dirt from the flows of money that stream together on the desk on which they are sitting. They purify and eliminate the consuming desire that was streaming through the department store and that also pulsed between them. The tears extinguish the gold in Mouret's velvet eyes that attracted Denise at first sight. Washed away is his pagan godliness that grounded his brutality and immoderateness. The purification is a thorough one, with dire consequences. Denise does not end up with a god. Her tears mark her departure from the god Mouret cannot be. Her Mouret shrinks to human proportions, and in the end this happy ending leaves him with a motherly wife and her with a good provider.

NOTES

This chapter is part of a work in progress, *Fetisch und Phantasma: Der andere Zola* (Frankfurt: Fischer, forthcoming). For help with the English I would like to thank Michèle Lowrie and Margaret Cohen.

1. See, for this topos of research, Naomi Schor, *Breaking the Chain: Women, Theory, and French Realist Fiction* (New York: Columbia University Press, 1985), 29.

2. All page numbers are from Emile Zola, *Au Bonheur des dames* (Paris: Garnier-Flammarion, 1971). The second number in the parentheses refers to the English translation, *A Ladies' Paradise* (Berkeley: University of California Press, 1992). When there is only one number, the reference is to the French original.

3. Letter of Huysmans, March 1883, quoted in Colette Becker, "Préface," in Zola, *Au Bonheur des dames,* 18.

4. Walter Benjamin, *Das Passagenwerk* (Frankfurt: Suhrkamp, 1983).

5. See Kristin Ross, "Shopping," in Zola, *A Ladies' Paradise.*

6. See Avital Ronell, *Crack Wars: Literature, Addiction, Mania* (Lincoln: University of Nebraska Press, 1992), 122ff. For the emblematic role of the trope of consumption, see also Jennifer Wicke, "Vampiric Typewriting: Dracula and Its Media", *English Literary History* 59 (1992): 467–93.

7. The feminine connotations of consumption go back at least to the eighteenth century; women are seen as consumers, consumed by their vain desire for luxury. A specific form of government is favored and indeed brought about by these typically feminine vices—monarchy, which is seen as effeminate. The political critique of monarchy is nourished by a misogynistic discourse that finds its privileged field of articulation in a critique of the addiction to luxury, seen as an anthropological given for the female sex. In the all-male republic, all luxury is banished as the agent of corruption par excellence. See not only Jean-Jacques Rousseau, *Discours qui a remporté le prix à l'Académie de Dijon. En l'année 1750. Sur cette question proposée par la même Académie: Si le rétablissement des Sciences et des Arts a contribué à épurer les moeurs,* in *Oeuvres complètes,* vol. 3, *Bibliothèque de la Pléiade* (Paris: Gallimard, 1962), and his *Lettre à M. d'Alembert sur les spectacles* (Lille/Geneva: Droz, 1948), but also Montesquieu's *De l'esprit des lois,* in *Oeuvres complètes,* vol. 2, *Bibliothèque de le Pléiade* (Paris: Gallimard, 1951), especially book 7, fittingly titled "Conséquences des différents principes des trois gouvernements, par rapport aux lois somptuaires, au luxe et à la condition des femmes."

8. See Michel Serres, *Feux et signaux de brume: Zola* (Paris: Bernard Grasset, 1975), 282–95.

9. Egon Friedell, *Kulturgeschichte der Neuzeit,* vol. 3 (Munich: Beck, 1931), 203 (my translation).

10. Lothar Bucher, here quoted in Benjamin, *Das Passagenwerk,* 1:248 (my translation).

11. The comparison between economic and imperial campaigns was frequently drawn at the time; see examples in Benjamin, *Das Passagenwerk,* 1:252.

12. Rachel Bowlby, " 'Traffic in her desires': Zola's *Au Bonheur des dames,*" in *Just Looking: Consumer Culture in Dreiser, Gissing, and Zola* (New York: Methuen, 1985), 73.

13. In a certain way, Rousseau's *Lettre à d'Alembert* prefigures Zola's department store, a house, where—like in Rousseau's theater—money, femininity, luxury, and the public exhibition of women are brought together in such a way as to connote prostitution.

14. Prudishly, the English translation here offers the following reading: "whilst the customers went away, their purses completely empty, and their heads turned by the wealth of luxury amidst which they had been wandering all day" (378).

15. This is by no means a topos Zola invented. See, for example, Denis Diderot,

"Sur les femmes," in *Qu'est-ce qu'une femme?* ed. Elizabeth Badinter (Paris: Flammarion, 1989), 171–72. Diderot relies on the doctor as the only help against God and the priest when woman is "dominée par l'hystérisme." Diderot also associates women with violent revolutions and describes them as a mass that by contagion gets out of control. For this threatening aspect of the female crowd, see Susanna Barrows, *Distorting Mirrors: Visions of the Crowd in Late 19th Century France* (New Haven, Conn.: Yale University Press, 1981).

16. See Jean-Martin Charcot/Paul Richer, *Die Besessenen in der Kunst,* ed. Manfred Schneider (Göttingen: Steidl, 1988).

17. Letter of Huysmans, March 1883, quoted in Becker, "Préface," 18.

18. See Victor N. Smirnoff, "La Transaction fétichiste," in *Nouvelle Revue de psychanalyse,* vol. 2 (Paris: Gallimard, 1968).

19. Sigmund Freud, "Fetischismus," in *Gesammelte Werke,* vol. 14 (Frankfurt: Fischer, 1964), 311–17. In English, see Sigmund Freud, *The Standard Edition of the Complete Psychological Works of Sigmund Freud,* vol. 21, trans. and ed. James Strachey (London: Hogarth, 1964), 155.

20. See Benjamin, *Das Passagen-Werk,* 1:130 (Konvolut B 9,1 "Mode"; my translation). See also Barbara Vinken, *Mode nach der Mode: Geist und Kleid am Ende des Jahrhunderts* (Frankfurt: Fischer, 1993), 38–41, 152–63.

21. Henry James, "Emile Zola," in *The Future of the Novel* (New York: Random House, 1956), 180.

22. Ibid., 177.

The Morgue and the Musée Grévin: Understanding the Public Taste for Reality in Fin-de-Siècle Paris

Vanessa R. Schwartz

On June 6, 1882, the *Moniteur Universel* reported: "The inauguration of the Musée Grévin, an essentially Parisian event, took place yesterday. At the Musée Grévin resemblance is perfect, striking, extraordinary. You begin to ask yourself whether you are in the presence of the real person." An immediate success upon its opening in 1882, this wax museum attracted nearly a half a million visitors yearly. During the same period, crowds of as many as 40,000 a day gathered at the Paris Morgue to see dead bodies publicly displayed behind a large glass window in the *salle d'exposition*. The Morgue attendant remarked, "The Morgue is considered in Paris like a museum that is much more fascinating than even a wax museum because the people displayed are real flesh and blood."[1] A Parisian newspaper summarized the state of late nineteenth-century Parisian culture by noting, "It is in real life that [one finds] the sensational incidents that excite the crowd."[2]

One hundred years later, a *Wall Street Journal* article proclaimed, "Reality is here to stay," as though it were something new.[3] The article concerns the boom in "reality TV"—the proliferation of shows labeled "docutainment" and "infotainment"—such as *Unsolved Mysteries, Rescue 911, Top Cops, Sightings, Code 3,* and *Cops.* Produced by the networks' entertainment divisions rather than their news divisions, "reality TV" programs reenact events, often featuring the victims and rescue workers (police, firefighters, 911 operators) originally involved. In the cases of *America's Most Wanted* and *Unsolved Mysteries,* viewers are asked to help catch a criminal or solve a mystery. And it seems to work. To date, 259 out of 634 fugitives profiled on *America's Most Wanted* have been apprehended through the aid of viewer phone calls.[4]

Critics have labeled reality TV programs "voyeuristic diversion"[5] and rebuked their "excesses and sleight-of-hand";[6] certain advertisers have "blindly said: 'I don't want any part of reality programming, no matter what the content.' "[7] Responding to the genre's sensationalism, these critics believe that reality TV is yet another new development in the decline of American civilization. They point to the proliferation of such programs as evidence of an increasingly prurient and violent American society.

The popularity of a represented and sensationalized reality, however, is neither an invention of the late twentieth century nor a testimony to what cultural critics, including Jean Baudrillard and Fredric Jameson, have called the "postmodern" and American condition of hyperrealism and simulation.[8] In what follows, I identify a sort of "postmodernism" *avant la lettre* in late nineteenth-century Parisian mass culture in both the popularity of visits to the Paris Morgue and the success of the Musée Grévin, a wax museum, in particular in their re-presentations of a sensationalized reality.

Realism has been well studied in high art and literature in nineteenth-century France, but it also characterized popular cultural forms. Rather than positing a chasm between "high" and "low," in what follows I suggest that "realism" operated across a wide spectrum of cultural forms and practices. A reconsideration of realism in the context of early mass culture in France must account for Parisian spectacle as a historically specific development. In this context, art historian T. J. Clark has argued that Paris became "simply . . . an image, something occasionally and casually consumed."[9] Yet, whereas Paris may have become a show—an object to be looked at—shows in Paris featured real life in the city, represented in as realistic a way as possible.

The flaneur has drawn attention as the quintessential "spectator of modern life." A privileged bourgeois male as a type, he has been described by a long line of critics, from Charles Baudelaire to Walter Benjamin. He has subsequently been used by feminist critics to exemplify the masculine privilege of public life in Paris.[10] According to Janet Wolff, he had no female counterpart: "There is no question of inventing the *flâneuse:* the essential point is that such a character was rendered impossible by the sexual divisions of the nineteenth century."[11] Yet, by casting a much wider net around what constitutes the "texts" of modernity, I will show that the burgeoning Parisian mass culture required women's participation in the emergent spaces of the spectacular city. Women of all classes could be found eagerly "looking" at the "reality" represented at the Morgue and the wax museum.

It is through the imbrication of realism and spectacle that *flânerie* became a cultural activity for all who participated in Parisian life. As such, realism cannot simply be dismissed as one in a litany of representational practices that reproduced male privilege. Rather, by focusing on realism during the moment of the emergence of mass society in France, we can begin to understand how realism in the age of spectacle (which is not yet passed) necessitated the transformation of all subjects into spectators—offering men and women alike the opportunity to participate in social life by looking at the "real thing."

Public Visits to the Morgue

"There are few people having visited Paris who do not know the Morgue," wrote Parisian social commentator Hughes Leroux in 1888.[12] Listed in practically every guidebook to the city, a fixture of Thomas Cook's tours to Paris, a "part of every conscientious provincial's first visit to the capital,"[13] the Morgue had both "regulars" and large crowds of as many as 40,000 on its "big days" when the story of a crime circulated through the popular press and curious visitors lined the sidewalk waiting to file through the *salle d'exposition* to see the victim.

A large and socially diverse audience went to the Morgue. The crowd was composed of "men, women and children," of "workers . . . *petits rentiers* . . . flaneurs . . . women workers . . . and ladies" (Figure 14.1).[14] In fact, the location was so well frequented that vendors lined the sidewalk outside, hawking oranges, cookies, and coconut slices.[15]

The morgue in question was built in 1864 in the center of Paris, behind Notre-Dame on the Quai de l'Archevêché (where the Memorial to the Deportation stands today) and was open to the

Figure 14.1. Destez, *Le Mystère de la rue du Vertbois: exposition du petit cadavre a la Morgue,* from *Le Monde Illustré,* August 15, 1886.

public seven days a week from dawn to dusk. The institution began in the eighteenth century as the *basse-geôle* of the prison, the Châtelet, in a dark and dank room where "visitors could only present themselves one after another; they were forced to press their faces against a narrow opening" in order to identify corpses that had been found in the public domain.[16] Visitors almost exclusively consisted of relatives searching for missing family; the *basse-geôle* was where "parents, lantern in hand, went to recognize [their missing children]."[17]

In 1804, the Morgue, as it was now called, was transferred to its own building at the Place du Marché-Neuf on the Ile-de-la-Cité. Believed at the time to be a great improvement over the *basse-geôle,* the new Morgue revealed both a rationalization of space and an emphasis on the display of the corpses. The building featured a *salle d'exposition,* in which two rows of five corpses, each on its own marble slab, were displayed behind a large glass window that separated the dead from the living. Unlike the *basse-geôle,* at this site large crowds could gather and gaze at the corpses. The Morgue's administrators hoped that by making the display readily accessible they could encourage random passersby to wander in and perhaps identify otherwise unknown corpses.

Napoleon III's and Baron Haussmann's mid-century changes to the Parisian landscape forced the destruction of this Morgue to make way for the Boulevard Sébastopol. Despite the "sanitization" of the city center and its marginalization of bloody spectacles,[18] the new Morgue, with an even larger *salle d'exposition* for the improved display of corpses, was opened behind Notre-Dame in the city's historical center.

The new building's interior heightened the institution's theatrical quality. A green curtain hung at the display window's sides and was used to close it off during a change of scene, when a body was either removed from or put on display. Of the three large doors at the front, the middle one remained shut, and visitors filed through, entering at the left and exiting at the right, prompting the Morgue's registrar to comment that it was nothing more than an *entresort* (a carnival attraction in which one paid and walked through a barrack to gape at the sight within).[19]

The *salle d'exposition* was comparable to other displays that dotted the Parisian landscape in the second half of the nineteenth century. Ernest Cherbuliez, in an article in *La Revue des Deux Mondes,* highlighted this quality by recounting an anecdote in which a man walked down the Boulevard Sébastopol and stopped in front of a store window, asking the window dressers for work. They suggested he ask at the Morgue.[20]

Most often, however, the Morgue was celebrated as public theater. As Emile Zola remarked in *Thérèse Raquin,* it was a "show that was affordable to all. . . . The door is open, enter those who will."[21] A poem in a popular publication called *Les Chansons de la Morgue* described the scene in the *salle d'exposition:* "The crowd, gay and without remorse, comes to the theater to takes its place."[22] Upon the closing of the Morgue to the general public in March 1907, one journalist protested:

The Morgue has been the first this year among theaters to announce its closing. . . . As for the spectators, they have no right to say anything because they didn't pay. There were no subscribers, only regulars, because the show was always free. It was the first free theater for the people. And they tell us it's being canceled. People, the hour of social justice has not yet arrived.[23]

In a time of increasingly private and commercial entertainment, the Morgue was open and free and the display of dead bodies existed for the public to come and see.

As a municipal institution, however, the Morgue's principal goal was to serve as a depository for the anonymous dead whose public display administrators hoped might aid in establishing their identities. Yet the Paris Morgue was like no other municipal institution. Despite the Morgue's location in the shadows of Notre-Dame, its deliberately undramatic facade and its seemingly somber subject matter, the identification of dead bodies was turned into a show, one that made the Morgue "one of the most popular sights in Paris."[24]

Why did this show attract so many visitors? The historical record does not offer many direct answers. Descriptions of the Morgue in the popular press and in administrative literature, however, offer a means through which we may attempt to reconstruct the Morgue's allure. The vast majority of visitors probably did not go to the Morgue thinking they actually might recognize a corpse. They went to look at real dead bodies under the pretense of acting out of civic duty. This was public voyeurism, not for financial gain, but for the social good. Senator Paul Strauss urged passersby to enter and "take a look at the corpses,"[25] and Dr. Gavinzel insisted that the public "enter boldly, and if something strikes you or awakes in you some memories, go to the registrar and make a declaration."[26] These pleas implied that people might care about the anonymous dead, an assumption that had not been built into the structure and practice of the old *basse-geôle.* The state's interest in identifying the bodies and creating civic duty was part of what one police decree concerning the Morgue called "social order."[27]

Many commentators suggested that the Morgue satisfied and reinforced the desire to look that permeated much of Parisian culture in the late nineteenth century. Clovis Pierre, the Morgue's registrar and a sometime poet, wrote that visitors came "to exercise their retinas at the window."[28] No doubt urban life, and Paris in particular, was "characterized by a markedly greater emphasis on the use of the eyes than that of the ears," as early urban sociologist Georg Simmel observed, but why go to the Morgue when there was so much to see in the city most often associated with the "spectacle of modern life"?[29]

The Morgue served as a visual auxiliary to the newspaper, staging the recently dead as sensationally detailed by the printed word. The late nineteenth century in France has been called the "golden age of the press,"[30] and it is critical to understand the central role played by the press in the development of Parisian spectacle. Current events became the daily fare of the popular Parisian dailies, whose overall circulation increased 250 percent between 1880 and 1914.[31] Newspapers replaced opinion with so-called truth as the world "entered the age of information."[32] In the Parisian press, political life took a backseat to theater openings, horse races, and charity events, but it was the *fait divers*—reports of horrible accidents and sensational crimes—that above all else filled the columns and the coffers.

The *fait divers,* a genre defined as such during the last third of the nineteenth century, was technically a newspaper rubric. What distinguished the *fait divers* from its predecessors, especially the *canard,* was its reproduction in extraordinary detail, both written and visual, of stories that might have seemed unbelievable but were actually true, as oppposed to the earlier genre of tall tales. As Gérard de Nerval explained, the *canard* "was sometimes true, always exaggerated and often false."[33] The *fait divers,* by contrast, offered representations of reality sensationalized.

Because of its featured role in so many *fait divers,* the Morgue regularly appeared in the newspaper. As Alphonse Devergie, the medical inspector of the Morgue, explained, "Once the newspapers announce a crime, one sees a great number of the curious arrive at the Morgue."[34] And, of course, when a large crowd gathered at the Morgue, *it* then became the subject of further news reports, which in turn kept the corpse, the unsolved crime, and the Morgue in the public eye, guaranteeing a flow of people to the Quai de l'Archevêché.

Press coverage heightened public awareness and interest. Guillot argued that the newspaper was a source that stimulated public interest for what "in newspaper jargon is called the *plat du jour*."[35] He believed that all the reporting turned the Morgue into a "glass house," and that if the Morgue could be considered a theater of crime, then the newspaper was its program.[36] One of the Morgue registrars argued that newspaper reading prompted the visits of women workers to the Morgue because their spirits had been haunted by the newspapers' serial novels.[37] Other comments suggest that the Morgue was a version of the newspaper's *feuilleton*. *L'Eclair*, for example, described the Morgue as "this living illustration of a serial-novel mystery."[38]

Both the newspaper and the serial novel were complexly perched on the border between reality and representation. The newspaper claimed to tell the truth, to present a nonfictive drama of contemporary life. Articles purported to be nonfiction; their relation to each other was entirely nonnarrative. By the late nineteenth century, however, almost all newspapers offered "fiction" in the form of the serial novel, clearly demarcated from the rest of the newspaper by a bar across the bottom of the page. Yet these popular narratives were often derived from the stories above this line of demarcation, and their literary conventions placed them squarely within a "realist" frame. For an English reporter of the time, it was "the passion developed more and more by a diseased realism in the world of fiction"[39] that produced a public fascination with the Morgue.

Some people believed that the popularity of public visits to the Morgue, like the interest in the newspaper itself, stemmed from the public interest in "reality." "What if rather than your stories, your most frightening paintings, they prefer reality and what a reality," Firmin Maillard, one of the Morgue's earliest historians, suggested.[40] An article in *Le Paris* boasted that the Morgue was worth a visit because what one saw "are not imitations, not trompe l'oeil."[41] The Morgue registrar expressed the same sentiment about the display by commenting that the Morgue was better than a wax museum because the bodies were "real flesh and blood." Yet, while the newspapers may have encouraged many visits, a look at one of the most notorious of the many *causes célèbres* of the Morgue reveals that the show in the window was far more spectacular than the ordinary placement of corpses on slabs facing the public. The case of the "woman cut into pieces" dramatizes how the Morgue administration, in conjunction with the press and the Parisian public, turned "real-life" crime into spectacle.

On November 8, 1876, a report of the police prefect to the minister of the interior indicated that a corpse split into two packages had been found in the Seine just outside of Paris in St. Ouen and had been sent to the Morgue to be put on display.[42] Three days later, a special security force at the Morgue controlled the crowd of 4,000-5,000 people who had already come to see the "woman cut into two pieces," as the case became known.[43] The newspaper Le XIXe Siècle noted that the body was laid on one of the slabs closest to the glass "to be seen better" and that a cloth smock of the material in which the body had been wrapped was thrown over it so that only the head and feet were exposed.[44]

During the next few days, "From the opening of the doors [in the morning] the movements of the public have not stopped," the police noted. They estimated that in the morning, one person went by the window each second, and that in the afternoon between 5,000 and 6,000 people filed through in an hour.[45] By nightfall November 13, 3,000 people still remained in line, so the administration put two candles next to the face and continued the exhibition until 5:10 p.m., when everyone present had filed through the salle d'exposition. Anywhere from 10,000 to 20,000 people visited the Morgue each day during the next two weeks, leading the popular crime newspaper L'Audience to remark, "There is perhaps at this time not as well visited a place in all Paris as this sad museum."[46]

By November 20, the still-large crowd was no longer gazing at the actual corpse in the display window. The Morgue could generally display corpses for only a few days, because, despite the use of a flow of cold water over the bodies, decomposition rapidly set in.[47] No positive identification of the corpse had been made in what had obviously been a case of foul play (as a popular song about the case concluded, "For one cannot commit suicide and then cut oneself up afterward"),[48] but authorities found a way of "holding over" the display. The Morgue administrators removed the corpse from the salle d'exposition and replaced it with a a wax reproduction of the head, sculpted by Jules Talrich, the anatomical sculptor at the Paris Medical School. The head was then placed on a mannequin covered with a white sheet.[49] The police prefect reported that "this reproduction whose resemblance is striking . . . has already attracted a considerable crowd."[50] The Morgue guard reported that the bust "is a perfect resemblance" and the newspaper echoed the police by saying, "The effect is thrilling and the resemblance with the victim of the mysterious crime is striking. . . . Everyone was struck by the truth of the cast."[51] Now Parisians were lining up to see two spectacles in one: the corpse of the victim of a crime and the wax bust, which "seemed so real."

The story continued to grip the public, and by November 24, *Le Voleur* estimated that between 300,000 and 400,000 people had filed through the Morgue without making a positive identification. Even when there were no developments in the story, dailies mentioned the Morgue in their *faits divers* columns, if only to report that there was no news about the case. The cover of *Le Journal Illustré* on November 26 featured the story with the cover caption "Le Crime de Saint-Ouen—LA FEMME COUPEE EN MORCEAUX" (see Figure 14.2). As in an illustrated serial novel, the story narrativized the investigation. Its five images, moving from the discovery of the body to an image of the police photograph of the victim's upper body, to the police showing the photo around the neighborhood where it was found, to the bottom of the page, which depicted the "lines and conversations" outside the Morgue, centered on the scene inside the Morgue. Here, the illustration makes clear the large number of visitors and the crowd's diversity, and shows the victim (or actually the wax head on a mannequin) seated in the center of the window, facing the visitors. The "mise-en-scène" represented in the newspaper illustrates how the body had been pulled out of the context of the other corpses in the display window, creating a further dramatization of what had already been "framed" by its placement in the window.

The Morgue's visitors came neither to identify corpses nor simply to see them laid out on slabs. No doubt, the Morgue was a morbid attraction.[52] More significant, however, is the fact that the Morgue was "part of the cataloged curiosities, of things to see, under the same heading as the Eiffel Tower, Yvette Guilbert, and the catacombs."[53] In other words, this public service was conceived as a Parisian attraction. Newspapers featured stories about the crowds at the Morgue and, like newspapers, the Morgue re-presented a

Figure 14.2. Méaulle, *La Femme coupée en morceaux*, engraving, from *Le Journal Illustré*, November 26, 1876.

spectacularized Parisian life. The *salle d'exposition,* its curtain, the lines outside, wax masks, corpses dressed and seated on chairs, and newspaper illustrations guaranteed that the Morgue's reality was represented and mediated, orchestrated and spectacularized.

Paris's "Journal Plastique"

"Yesterday, all of Paris was at the Musée Grévin," reported *Le Gil Blas* upon the wax museum's opening in 1882.[54] During the museum's first week, *Le Voltaire* remarked, "The crowd presses morning and night."[55] Nearly 400,000 people visited the new attraction at 10 boulevard Montmartre during the next six months.[56] *Le Petit Journal* concluded that "the Musée Grévin's success is assured."[57]

Newspapers alluded, sometimes with a tinge of sarcasm, to the reasons for the museum's popularity. A cartoon of its opening showed two men looking at a corpse on a slab. One remarks to the other, "This is almost as much fun as the real Morgue."[58] This cartoon, like the comment about the Morgue being like a wax museum, only better, suggests that the two institutions were linked in the popular imagination. But what might the two institutions have had in common? Like the Morgue, the Musée Grévin fit into a Parisian landscape in which versions of reality were spectacularized. At the wax museum, people visited a realistic representation of Paris.

The museum's association with "reality" operated in several ways. First, visitors stepped inside a model of the city that they had just left to enter the wax museum. In addition, the museum's founders, Arthur Meyer and Alfred Grévin, were associated with Parisian public life because they were important figures in the Parisian press. The museum's location on the boulevard Montmartre, described as "the center of Paris" by one observer,[59] also contributed to its reputation as Parisian.

Critics celebrated the Musée Grévin for being fundamentally Parisian. One review noted, "Only after the Louvre, which is a universal museum, was there room for a Parisian museum."[60] Another simply proclaimed, "Here are Parisian current events!"[61] The Musée Grévin stood for Parisian life for the reasons above, but more significantly because it represented the Paris that was "representable" and sensational—the city that inhabitants had come to know through the newspaper.

Above all, the museum's effort to be "like a newspaper" made it seem Parisian because, like a newspaper, it claimed to be about its own world. In a long review of the museum's opening, *Le Temps* summarized the museum's attractions:

> To do with wax figures what illustrated newspapers do with their drawings, that is to say, to reproduce the characters and scenes that interest the public, that is the goal of the organizers of the newest Parisian novelty. It will be a type of plastic newspaper, full of celebrities of all varieties, with the usual eclecticism of the press. . . . In a statue the artist creates in broad strokes, but here it is reality itself that must be slavishly reproduced.[62]

The wax museum's content matched the newspaper's, but its plastic means of representation was considered superior because it approximated reality better than the printed word. The preface to the museum's catalog, written by *Le Figaro*'s Albert Wolff, touted the museum's improvement upon newspapers:

> By adding an image to the text, illustrated newspapers have already made a decisive step in modern information. The museum's founder . . . rightfully decided that one could go further and create a sort of plastic newspaper, where the public would find, reproduced with a scrupulous respect for nature, the individuals, who, in a variety of ways, occupy its attention.[63]

The museum resembled a newspaper in its choice of subject matter. One review explained that the Musée Grévin would "recount recent events, gripping happenings, and reproduce for the spectators the dramas and comedies that play daily on the Parisian stage and on the bigger stage of the entire world."[64] Another review noted, "It is definitely a newspaper with all its rubrics: politics, the world, the theater, the arts, literature, the *Gazette des Tribunaux*."[65] At the time of its opening, for example, the first room featured a tableau of the signing of the Treaty of Bardo, through which Tunisia became a French protectorate; the "foyer at the Comédie Française," in which actors and literati mingled; "Le Tout Paris at Grévin's Studio," in which musicians such as Charles Gounod and Massenet were seated in conversation at a piano, while journalists Wolff, Francisque Sarcey, and J. J. Weiss chatted and watched Grévin sketch; the president of the Republic in his library; a meeting of the Chamber of Deputies; a scene from the just-opened opera "Françoise de Rimini"; and Louise Michel, the radical communard known as "the Red Virgin," giving a speech. As in a newspaper, politics and social life mingled, and the random juxtaposition of the wax museum dioramas mimicked the way articles were placed side by side in newspapers.

The museum also promised to represent the latest events. During its opening week, the staff began work on both a figure of Garibaldi, who died the week the museum opened, and a tableau of Arabi-Pacha, the leader of the revolt against the Khedive Tewfick in Egypt, who had just been imprisoned by the English and sent to Ceylon.[66] When the "Crime de Pecq," the murder of a pharmacist by his former mistress and her husband, filled the pages of every newspaper in Paris that week, the museum decided to do a series of tableaux reproducing the story. The catalog boasted that the museum satisfied "the public taste for current events" that newspaper culture, no doubt, had helped create and sustain.[67]

In effect, the museum formed a pantheon of the present. In fact, a letter from a critical English visitor indicated the extent to which the museum was associated with contemporary Paris:

> Your journalists are of no interest to me and I would rather see the great men of the battlefields than the heroes and heroines of the boulevard. . . . Where are historical memories? Where are the characters from your history?[68]

Jules Clarétie, popular journalist, novelist, and eventually director of the Comédie Française, lauded the museum thus: "O glorious transitory wax figures! Celebrities of the day! Pantheon of the moment!"[69] This pantheon of Parisian current events celebrated its breadth:

> All that is of interest to the public has found or will find its place in this museum: the honest humble man crowned with the Monthyon prize by the Académie and the famous criminal whose deed has upset the public conscience . . . authors who write plays and those who review them; men of state who make history and journalists who write it; in one word the Musée Grévin will be a *carte d'échantillon* of the big city in its flights and its falls, in its luxury and in its misery, in its talents that are its glory and in the crimes that are its shame.[70]

The directors insisted that they were responding to public interest in choosing their subjects for the museum. But the public's knowledge of those "celebrities," not to mention their interest in them, had been primarily constructed by newspapers and other sites of "modern" cultural life.

The museum also attracted visitors by offering seeming proximity to celebrities. One review explained, "The likenesses of our great men, of our famous artists or society people pleases us . . . and it is to see them up close that the public crowds to the Musée Grévin."[71] For tourists who arrived in the city to "see it all," the wax museum made their trips easier. As *Le Temps* noted, "The tourist who comes from the provinces or from abroad can visit in an hour all the celebrities that it would take a lot more time and perseverance to see in reality."[72] The museum was like reality, only better, because it both glamorized and simplified its visitors' lives.

The breadth of the display contributed to the seemingly democratic nature of this pantheon at the same time that it bolstered its realism by seeming, like a newspaper, to leave no subject unrepresented. One of the museum's attractions was that it offered access to the "real world" that was actually unavailable to the vast majority of people in Paris. The museum catalog noted, concerning its tableau "Les Coulisses de l'Opéra: Foyer de la Danse," that "everything contributes to give the spectator the illusion of a visit to this curious corner of the grand Parisian stage, a visit that only the very few privileged are allowed."[73] If everyone could not go to the real Opéra, the Opéra would be brought to them.

The museum's ever-changing display, its rejection of the notion of a museum as a definitive collection, and the potentially ephemeral nature of wax sculpture itself matched the newspaper's premium on constant change. Yet the two differed in terms of producing verisimilitude. Wax sculpture's power of illusion was so great that critics claimed to be "fooled." A reporter recounted, "I stopped for a long time in front of 'Grévin's atelier' and could no longer distinguish between real people and the wax statues."[74] Yet the wax figures were not the only element in exacting the illusion of reality; the museum used dioramas and in them compiled details to increase verisimilitude. Accessories, ornaments, the framing effect of the diorama, and even the diorama's narratives created the illusion of reality at the same time that they turned reality into an aesthetic.[75]

Unlike most waxworks that preceded it, the Musée Grévin employed the full-scale diorama. The tableaux offered recognizable, taxonomical, and appropriate settings for the figures, creating "peepholes" into Parisian life.[76] The claims about the veracity of the tableaux might also have been claims about the reality of society. In the dioramas, the wax figures were placed in their "natural" social setting—society *comme il faut*. Although the dioramas were obviously constructions, the tenacity with which the directors of the museum claimed they were just like "the real thing" and the overall attempt to deny artifice suggest an organic and natural order to the socially produced world of the Musée Grévin.

The museum reproduced the details of its settings as closely as possible. For example, the library of Jules Grévy, the president of the Republic, "was copied exactly from [his library] at the Elysée." The tableau from the opera "Françoise de Rimini," from costumes and furniture to backdrops, was copied with the generous permission of the Opéra's director. The success of the tableau "Arrest of Russian Nihilists" lay in its details, according to one review: "Not a detail is missing, the icons, papers, cartons, thick newspapers."[77] The tableau included paper imported from Russia on which real Russian characters were written, and a samovar and tea glasses that came from Moscow. Whereas in the opera scene the museum featured facsimiles or "doubles," in the Russian tableau it displayed "authentic" Russian items.

The museum self-consciously went far in its quest for authenticity in order to keep up with the representational conventions of the day, including dressing the wax figures in the actual clothes belonging to the persons represented. A letter from Grévin to Emile Zola requesting a suit epitomized the contemporary quest for authenticity as a representational style. The former promised, "The Musée Grévin will be Naturalist or will not be,"[78] echoing Zola's own well-known, "The Republic will be Naturalist or will not be," which itself was an echo of president of the Republic Adolphe Thiers's remark that the Republic would be conservative or would not be.

Authenticity did not stop at conventions of representation, however. A few years after its opening, the museum introduced its first historical diorama around its purchase of the tub in which Marat had been murdered (Figure 14.3). The scene, which opened in the fall of 1886, also included a real map of France from 1791, copies

Figure 14.3. "Le Mort de Marat," tableau at the Musée Grévin (Musée Grévin Archives).

of Marat's newspaper *L'Ami du Peuple,* and a knife and a pike dating from the period. In an annual report to stockholders, the museum directors reported that "this scene, whose reconstitution is perfectly loyal to the official reports of the era... was well worth the extraordinary price of 5,000ff paid for the tub. The authenticity of the tub has increased the attraction of the tableau tenfold" and contributed, they argued, to a significant rise in receipts in the two months following the tableau's opening.[79]

The tableaux's narrativity also fostered a sense of reality through the familiarity of the stories they represented. The museum's biggest "hit" in 1882 was its seven-tableaux serial novel, "The Story of a Crime," which the catalog promised was "more moving, more striking, more dramatic in its living reality than any written story."[80] The tableaux portrayed the vicissitudes of a crime, from the murder to the arrest, to the confrontation of the murderer with his victim's corpse at the Morgue, to the trial, to the prisoner in his cell at La Roquette, and finally to his preparation for execution and his being led to the guillotine. Reviewers insisted that the display was a newspaper brought to life. "[It is] . . . a *fait divers* in seven tableaux with an extraordinary reality of execution."[81] Just as part of the "realism" of the Morgue was its embeddedness in newspaper narratives, what was, at least in part, so strikingly real about "The Story of a Crime" was its familiar narrativity. It seemed "real" because it was just like newspaper stories and serial novels that claimed to be about real life in Paris.

The Musée Grévin represented other *fait divers* by directly reproducing newspaper illustrations. For example, in December 1897 the story of the murder of an innocent receipts clerk by Carrara, an Italian mushroomer, filled newspaper columns. The mushroomer, terribly in debt, robbed and murdered the young man, who regularly carried large sums of cash as part of his job. Carrara then boiled the corpse in a mushroom cleaner. The illustrated supplement of *Le Petit Journal* published three-color engravings of the incident on December 26, 1897. When the Musée Grévin decided to do a two-tableaux series featuring the crime the next month, one of the tableaux was an exact copy of the newspaper's engraving (Figures 14.4 and 14.5).

The newspaper was not the only point of mediation for the reality of the wax museum. When, in January 1886, the museum opened

Figure 14.4. *Le Crime du Kremlin-Bicêtre,* engraving, from *Le Petit Journal Supplément Illustré,* December 26, 1897.

a scene from Zola's *Germinal,* which originally appeared in serial form in the newspaper *Le Cri du Peuple* in 1885, it purported to represent the scene from the theatrical adaptation that had been forbidden by the censors. The scene chosen was the flooding of the mine

Figure 14.5. "Le Crime du Kremlin-Bicêtre," tableau at the Musée Grévin (Musée Grévin Archives).

in the end of the novel, in which Etienne kills Chaval and he and Catherine, caught in the mine, make love with the corpse nearby. The museum's tableau (Figure 14.6) represented the moment following the sexual encounter and depicted the lovers clutching each other as they confronted the corpse. The museum catalog boasted of the "scrupulous exactitude" of the representation, and reported:

Figure 14.6. "Germinal," tableau at the Musée Grévin (Musée Grévin Archives).

All of the accessories, hats, lamps, tools, are authentic. The mine is the exact copy of the gallery at Anzin, from where the museum got some of the wood and blocks of schist in order to give the public a complete illusion.[82]

Although the wax museum claimed to represent a scene from a play, it did not make doubles of the play props. Rather, because the play was "naturalist" theater based on a "naturalist" novel that attempted to be as realistic as possible, the museum went to what it believed was Zola's source: the mine at Anzin.[83] Yet, the museum would never have built a tableau of the mine had it not figured as part of Zola's narrative. In this case, the familiarity of both the novel and the play, not to mention the censorship of this particular scene, drew crowds to look at the tableau.

The tableau's evocation of and the crowd's familiarity with Zola's *Germinal* were critical to the "realism" of the spectacle, although reviewers consistently commented solely on the diorama's verisimilitude, as though its mere illusionism constituted its interest. *L'Illustration,* for example, wrote:

Here is a real mine shaft, black and deep with pieces of real coal and its stays that were taken from the depths of the shafts at Anzin. Everything is of the most exact nature. . . . As we already said, all is real . . . the stays, the lamps, the tools, right down to the clothing that is worn by real miners.[84]

What was "real" in this tableau? Its re-creation of the theatrical adaptation, of Zola's novel, or of a mine? What was its claim to reality when juxtaposed with other scenes at the Musée Grévin, such as a tableau of the Chamber of Deputies? Perhaps for the visitors who had seen neither the president of the Republic nor a coal mine, and who were unable actually to assess the quality of a likeness, the diorama was as real as the people and places they had never seen.[85]

Differences between the Musée Grévin and the Morgue abound. For one thing, the former represented celebrities, the latter unidentified people. The dioramas at the wax museum placed people in "natural" social settings; at the Morgue, dead people were wrenched by death from their usual locations. What these two popular nineteenth-century Parisian attractions shared, however, was that they generated and responded to the public taste for reality.

Much of the recent critical interest in simulation and "hyperrealism" describes these as essentially American and recent phenomena. Umberto Eco, for instance, concludes that "the American imagination demands the real thing, and, to attain it, must fabricate the absolute fake."[86] In fact, he goes so far as to say that in Europe, wax museums are "negligible features in the urban landscapes, on side streets."[87] Fredric Jameson dates the simulacrum, a postmodern effect, to a time "with a whole historically original consumers' appetite for a world transformed into sheer images of itself."[88] The contemporary nature of "hyperrealism" is also central to Jean Baudrillard's three-stage model of simulation, in which "a panic-stricken production of the real and the referential" is the last and current phase. These observations suggest a fundamental blindness on the part of postmodern theorists to the historicity of postmodern theory, a historicity that raises questions about the proclaimed postmodern divide.

Yet, these critics are hardly alone in their belief that the mass cultural re-production of reality is American. The response to the opening of EuroDisney is perhaps the best evidence of the association of this kind of entertainment with the contemporary United States. When Disney executives announced plans for the park at the Paris Stock Exchange in 1987, they were pelted with eggs and tomatoes.[89] During the park's opening week, the French satirical newspaper *Le Canard Enchaîné* remarked that "Disney is to culture what the bacon-cheeseburger is to gastronomy."[90] And who can forget Ariane Mnouchkine, the director of the Théâtre du Soleil, whose description of EuroDisney as a "cultural Chernobyl" seemed to epitomize the French reaction.

What no one has said, however, is that in the nineteenth century the French were innovators, not imitators or resisters, of mass cultural activities and technologies that, like the Morgue and the wax museum, re-presented reality. Thus, while critics and participants alike act as though "reality TV" and the Disney parks are new and peculiarly American, I want to suggest that no visitor to the Morgue or the wax museum from late-nineteenth-century Paris would find them entirely unfamiliar.

This historical look at the public taste for reality suggests a cultural continuity between the late nineteenth and late twentieth centuries, one in which reality seems to become an effect of representation. This continuity is attributable as much to "modern" Paris as to "postmodern" America—a continuity that questions the claims of the Continental and epistemic divides between late-nineteenth-century France and late-twentieth-century America.

NOTES

I want to thank Susanna Barrows and Tom Laqueur for their suggestions, and espe-cially Margaret Cohen for her help and for the lively intellectual exchange through-out the writing of this essay.

1. Quoted in *La Presse,* March 22, 1907. Unless otherwise noted, all translations are my own.

2. *Le Voleur,* August 19, 1886.

3. Meg Cox, "Reality TV Shows Continue to Spread Despite Critics and Nervous Advertisers," *Wall Street Journal,* May 11, 1989, B1.

4. Information provided by the public relations department of *America's Most Wanted.*

5. Harry F. Waters, "America's Ugliest Home Videos," *Newsweek,* June 15, 1992, 59–69.

6. Alan Bunce, "TV's 'Cops' Puts Cinema Vérité to True Test," *Christian Science Monitor,* February 6, 1992.

7. Cox, "Reality TV."

8. Jean Baudrillard, *America,* trans. Chris Turner (New York: Verso, 1988); Jean Baudrillard, *Simulations,* trans. Paul Foss et al. (New York: Semiotext[e], 1983), 13; Fredric Jameson, "Postmodernism, or the Cultural Logic of Late Capitalism," *New Left Review* 146 (1984): 53–92. See also Umberto Eco, *Travels in Hyperreality,* trans. William Weaver (New York: Harcourt Brace, 1986); Stephen Fjellman, *Vinyl Leaves: Walt Disney World and America* (Boulder, Colo.: Westview, 1992).

9. T. J. Clark, *The Painting of Modern Life* (Princeton, N.J.: Princeton University Press, 1984), 36.

10. Janet Wolff, *Feminine Sentences: Essays on Women and Culture* (Berkeley: University of California Press, 1990), 35.

11. Ibid., 47.

12. Hughes Leroux, *L'Enfer parisien* (Paris, 1888), 353.

13. *Le Temps,* September 25, 1882.

14. Ernest Cherbuliez, "La Morgue," *La Revue des Deux Mondes,* January 1891, 368; Emile Zola, *Thérèse Raquin* (Paris: Flammarion, 1970), 131; Adolphe Guillot, *Paris qui souffre: Le Basse-Geôle du Grand-Châtelet et les morgues modernes,* 2d ed. (Paris: Chez Rouquette, 1888), 177.

15. Leroux, *L'Enfer parisien,* 353; Guillot, *Paris qui souffre,* 177.

16. Guillot, *Paris qui souffre,* 43.

17. Alphonse Devergie, *Notions générales sur la Morgue de Paris* (Paris: Félix Malteste, 1877), 4.

18. Alain Corbin, *Le Village des cannibales* (Paris: Aubier, 1990); Alain Corbin, "Le Sang de Paris: réflexions sur la généalogie de l'image de la capitale" in *Ecrire Paris,* ed. Daniel Oster and Jean-Marie Goulemot (Paris: Editions Seesam, 1990).

19. Clovis Pierre, *Les Gaietés de la Morgue* (Paris: Gallimard, 1895).

20. Cherbuliez, "La Morgue," 360.

21. Zola, *Thérèse Raquin*, 131.

22. Angelin Ruelle, *Les Chansons de la Morgue* (Paris: Léon Varnier, 1890).

23. Pierre Véron, "La Morgue," *Le Magasin Pittoresque*, March 1907, 171–72.

24. E. A. Reynolds-Ball, *Paris in Its Splendours* (London, 1901), 2:312.

25. Paul Strauss, *Paris ignoré* (Paris: Libraires Imprimeries Révnis, 1892).

26. J. C. Gavinzel, *Etude sur la Morgue au point de vue administratif et médical* (Paris: Baillière et Fils, 1882), 46.

27. Firmin Maillard, *Recherches historiques et critiques sur la Morgue* (Paris: Delahays, 1860), 42–43.

28. Clovis Pierre, *Les Gaietés de la Morgue* (Paris: Flammarion, 1895).

29. Simmel as cited in Walter Benjamin, "Some Motifs in Baudelaire," in *Charles Baudelaire*, trans. Quintin Hoare (London: New Left, 1973), 151.

30. Jacques Wolgensinger, *L'Histoire à la une: la grand aventure de la presse* (Paris: Découvertes Gallimard, 1989).

31. Anne-Marie Thiesse, *Le Roman du quotidien* (Paris: Le Chemin Vert, 1984), 17.

32. Emile Zola, cited in Wolgensinger, *L'Histoire,* 67.

33. Gérard de Nerval, "Le Diable à Paris," in Romi, *Histoire des faits divers* (Paris: Editions du Pont-Royal, 1962), 140.

34. Devergie, *Notions générales,* 11.

35. Guillot, *Paris qui souffre,* 182.

36. Ibid., 199, 258.

37. *La Presse,* March 22, 1907.

38. *L'Eclair,* March 21, 1907.

39. *Morning Advertiser,* January 14, 1893.

40. Maillard, *Recherches historiques,* 94–95.

41. *Le Paris,* August 31, 1892.

42. Archives of the Prefecture of Police (hereafter, APP), BA/87: November 8, 1876. I am indebted to the very interesting article by Alan Mitchell, "The Paris Morgue as a Social Institution in the Nineteenth Century," *Francia* 3 (1976): 581–96. See also the *maîtrise* of Bruno Bertherat, "Le Morgue et la visite à la Morgue au XIX siècle, 1804–1907" (University of Paris I, 1990).

43. APP, BA/81, November 11, 1876.

44. *Le XIXe Siècle,* November 12, 1876.

45. APP BA/87 and BA/81, November 12, 1876; APP BA/81, November 13, 1876.

46. *L'Audience,* November 26, 1876.

47. In 1881 the Morgue administration introduced a system of refrigeration into the *salle d'exposition* that prevented rapid decay and allowed a longer display time.

48. Complainte de "La Femme Coupée en Morceaux," APP, BA/81.

49. *L'Audience,* November 26, 1876.

50. APP BA/87, November 20, 1876.

51. *L'Audience,* November 26, 1876.

52. See Anne Higonnet, Margaret Higonnet, and Patrice Higonnet, "Façades: Walter Benjamin's Paris," *Critical Inquiry* 10 (March 1984): 391–419, in which the Morgue is discussed as part of the nineteenth-century bourgeois obsession with death.

53. *Le Voltaire,* July 22, 1892.

54. *Le Gil Blas,* June 7, 1882.

55. *Le Voltaire,* June 11, 1882.

56. Report of the Board of Directors of the Musée Grévin, March 30, 1883 (Musée Grévin Archives).

57. *Le Petit Journal,* June 6, 1882.

58. Cartoon from the illustrated press, no source or date; probably *Le Charivari,* May 1882 (Musée Grévin Archives).

59. Laffond de Saint-Mir, *Impressions et voyage dans Paris* (Paris, 1893), 166.

60. *L'Evènement,* June 6, 1882.

61. *L'Illustration,* June 10, 1882.

62. *Le Temps,* June 7, 1882.

63. *Catalogue-Almanach du Musée Grévin,* 2d ed. (Paris: Maison Chaix, 1882), 4.

64. *Le Monde Illustré,* no date; probably May 1882 (Musée Grévin Archives).

65. *Le Moniteur Universel,* June 6, 1882.

66. *Le Petit Journal,* June 11, 1882.

67. *Catalogue-Almanach du Musée Grévin.*

68. *La Gazette de France,* June 8, 1882.

69. Jules Clarétie, *La Vie à Paris* (Paris: Victor Harvard, 1883), 275.

70. *Catalogue-Almanach du Musée Grévin.*

71. *L'Indépendance belge,* June 12, 1882.

72. *Le Temps,* June 9, 1882.

73. *Catalogue illustré du Musée Grévin,* 82d ed. (Paris: Maison Chaix, n.d.).

74. *L'Univers Illustré,* June 17, 1882.

75. See Naomi Schor, *Reading in Detail: Aesthetics and the Feminine* (New York: Methuen, 1987), for an important discussion of detailism and verisimilitude.

76. See Donna Haraway, "Teddy Bear Patriarchy: Taxidermy in the Garden of Eden, New York City, 1908–1936," *Social Text* (Winter 1985): 20–63. Haraway argues that the dioramas at the American Museum of Natural History presented "peepholes into the jungle." Whereas the jungle dioramas socialized the natural order, I am suggesting that the Musée Grévin's dioramas naturalized the social order.

77. *L'Indépendance Belge,* June 12, 1882.

78. Letter from Grévin to Zola, July 6, 1881 (Bibliothèque Nationale, manuscripts).

79. *Report of the Board of Directors of the Musée Grévin,* for the General Assembly of stockholders, March 28, 1887 (Musée Grévin Archives).

80. *Catalogue-Almanach du Musée Grévin.*

81. *L'Express,* June 7, 1882.

82. *Catalogue du Musée Grévin,* 39th ed. (Paris: Maison Chaix, c. 1886).

83. The mine in *Germinal* was actually a composite of several mines, including the one at Anzin.

84. *L'Illustration,* January 2, 1886.

85. Unlike today, when celebrity images abound in photographs, films, and video, visitors then probably could not always judge the verisimilitude of a figure, having never seen the person in the first place.

86. Eco, *Travels in Hyperreality,* 8.

87. Ibid., 12.

88. Jameson, "Postmodernism," 66.

89. "Voilà, Disney Invades Europe, Will the French Resist?" *Time,* April 20, 1992, 82–84.

90. *Le Canard Enchaîné,* April 15, 1992.

Bayadères, Stéréorama, and Vahat-Loukoum: Technological Realism in the Age of Empire
Rhonda Garelick

*Under the Eiffel Tower, near a little lake, was hidden the Tonkinese
village with its junk and women chewing betel . . . The entire hill was
nothing but perfumes, incense, vanilla, the aromatic fumes of the
seraglio . . . the cries of the Ouled Nail with their mobile bellies; I
followed this opiate mixture, this perfume of Javanese dancing girls,
sherbets, and vahat-loukoum, as far as the Dahomean village. Among
the mosques and straw huts, tall negroes walked about barefoot, still
savages . . . old and recent enemies who had become our liegemen.*
—Paul Morand, *1900 A.D.,* 1931

The Pageantry of Empire

The Exposition Universelle of 1900 marked the end of the nineteenth century with a grand-scale spectacle of mass consumerism,
imperialism, and tourism, illuminating it all with cascades of jewel-
colored electric lights. The largest exhibition of its kind that Europe
had ever seen, the fair brought millions of tourists to Paris from virtually every country. It appears that a visit to the Exposition was an
experience powerful enough to remain in the imagination for
decades, for frequently people who had gone as children returned
to their memories to write about them, as many as thirty years later.

In 1889 and 1900, the French government strove to use the
World's Fair to market its colonial conquests in Western Africa and
Indochina. In 1889, the French bourgeoisie in particular seemed in-

sufficiently interested, for the government's taste, in the imperialist gains of their country. "All that interests the French about the Empire," lamented Prime Minister Jules Ferry, "is the belly dance."[1] But even appreciation of *la danse du ventre* was a step in the desired direction, for the World's Fair deliberately sought to ally the progress of the Empire with the charms of dancing women of color and countless other such Orientalist luxuries.

Besides Orientalism, the main marketing tools of the fair's imperial promotion were trade and technology. The fair commission attempted to link colonialism in the public imagination with a desirable expansion of French foreign trade as well as with the miraculous advances in science and machinery. "France will emerge . . . yet more splendid," proclaimed the director of the 1900 exhibition, Alfred Picard, "at the vanguard of civilization."[2]

But there was more to the World's Fair than belly dancing and nationalist propaganda. The fair beckoned spectators into alternative worlds in which the thrill of the new or exotic merged with the wonders of a kind of "realism." By *realism* here I mean the exactitude with which the fair technologically re-created other countries and distant lives for the enjoyment of the European public. In this essay, I will attempt to articulate the relationship between the experience of entering the exhibition's technological realism—its mechanical simulations of colonial (and other far-off) landscapes—and the experience of entering *literary* re-creations of unknown worlds.

Naturalism and the Theme Park

My point of literary comparison here will not be the high realism of James or Balzac, but rather the more minutely, and often grotesquely, detailed world of naturalism, and of Zola in particular. Lukács reproaches Zola and the naturalists for lacking a dialectical relation to their world, for creating "gigantic backdrops in front of which tiny, haphazard people move to and fro and live their haphazard lives."[3] "Naturalism," he claims, "results from the direct, mechanical mirroring of the humdrum reality of capitalism." For Lukács, naturalist characters are "puppetlike" and disconnected from their social realities. But, of course, the line separating realism from naturalism has never been easily negotiated. Sandy Petrey, for example, has reconsidered Lukács's criteria for effective realism, and argues suggestively for the inclusion of what Petrey calls "constative referentiality." For Petrey, what so dismays Lukács—the naturalists' tendency to amass obsessively detailed, highly reified descriptions of objects—bespeaks not so much a socially disconnected distortion as a rethinking of referentiality, of the connections between the "outer trappings" of life and the larger ideological worlds of protagonists.

What interests me in the debate over naturalism's place within realism is the emergence of theatrical and mechanical subtexts. Naturalism teases out of realism, and magnifies, all of its disjointedness, emphasizing its "constructed" quality. One might say that naturalism is realism with its seams showing, its inner mechanisms exposed. This constructed quality, this mechanically exposed element in naturalist texts, immerses the reader in a brand of realism that recalls the effect produced by the World's Fair's technological worlds.

Many of the mechanically realist attractions at the Exposition Universelle—all the stereorama and panorama displays, for example—involved rotating backdrops of painted or filmed landscapes against which plaster monuments stood and mannequins posed, simulating postcard venues in the Empire's outer reaches. Sometimes live actors took part in the scene, serving as "extras"—as café waiters or cabaret dancers. Against these elaborate backdrops, curious spectators could play out their own lives for a moment, marveling at the realistic exhibitions, while fully aware of the complicated scientific workings hidden within. The experience of entering the very absorbing world of Zola's Rougon-Macquart series can be seen to comment upon and illuminate the experience of attending the Exposition Universelle; and perhaps there is something to be gained in the comparison.[4]

Because, paradoxically, the quintessential mark of both verisimilitude and mechanicity is so often the presence of a woman, I will be focusing here on representations of gender. A literary heroine, particularly in naturalist texts, can signify biological life as well as an unsettlingly machinelike side of existence. (One need only think of Zola's female characters who are practically baby-producing automatons, the so-called *pondeuses*.) In the same way, the many Oriental women on display at the Exhibition of 1900 served a double function within their worlds, at once revealing and occulting the scientific effort at stake in their presentation.

Because many issues are going to come together in this chapter, it is important that certain distinctions be articulated at the outset. First of all, I will make a primary comparison here that may trouble some: the comparison between theatrical or diversionary spectacles and literature. At the World's Fair, spectators paid their money, boarded the electrically propelled walkways, and let themselves be carried away to other lands: Algeria, Indochina, Ceylon, Peking. In transporting visitors to these re-created landscapes, the fair incorporated them into an "elsewhere," a concept that was increasingly extensive and hard to grasp in the heavily imperial France of 1900.[5] To marvel at the verisimilitude of these attractions was to admire French ingenuity and knowledge, and to do that was to be co-opted into that other French undertaking: the dominion of Indochina and Western and North Africa. Imperialism had become a breathtaking sound and light show.

All of this may appear to have little to do with realism in literature. Certainly, these re-created "dream" worlds cannot be labeled part of "realism" simply because they attempted to re-create an exterior reality. However, there is a deep connection between late-nineteenth-century naturalism and the mass cultural and imperial production that found its apogee at the World's Fair of 1900. The relationship of spectator to attraction needs to be examined in the context of the relationship between the reader of naturalist novels and the texts read. One key issue will be the question of "absorption": the phenomenon that draws participants so deeply into a fiction that they are temporarily "lost" to the outside world. Often absorption comes along with bodily responses provoked by the fictive world: tears in the case of the novel; vertigo, nausea, or breathlessness in the case of physical entertainments. To lose oneself in a fictional world is often the goal of reading a realist novel.

I began thinking about this essay when I spoke with a friend about our mutual tendency to turn to nineteenth-century realist novels when homebound by illness. We both loved, we agreed, to lie in bed and immerse ourselves in the worlds of those fictional characters whose entire lives we could follow through hundreds of pages—indeed, sometimes through several novels. (I refer here to the *roman-fleuve* convention.) Reading these novels, one "travels" alongside the characters, projecting one's own desires onto those of the protagonists, seeing oneself moving through the story. Perhaps these novels are so inviting to us when we are ill because the nineteenth-century novel concentrates so heavily upon the body, and particularly the female body. To lose oneself within these worlds may involve a temporary exchange of one's own body for those of the characters. Or perhaps the reader abed with the flu feels all too keenly her own "constructedness"— her own body's (faulty) mechanics—and may narcissistically identify with the mechanized corporeality of realism, and specifically naturalism.

What, then, is the difference between that phenomenon of identification with a novel and the experience of literally traveling through a strange world that has been re-created by technology? How does the suspension of the awareness of the distinction between text world and life world compare to the suspension of disbelief required to enjoy the verisimilitude of, say, the World's Fair's "Cinéorama," in which a simulated hot-air balloon ride provided aerial views of the earth?

The question of genre must also be taken into account. One might argue that the area of literature most compatible with such fair attractions is not realism, but rather adventure or romance—the domain of Jules Verne, for example. And there is certainly truth in this. During this period of literary history, the paradigm of the fantastical world into which one loses oneself would definitely be found in adventure literature. But it is not the plot of the adventure story that interests me here, but the complex world of character provided by the naturalist novel. What is at stake is the difference between escape and identification. I would argue that the spectators moving through the "foreign" landscapes of the World's Fair had experiences more akin to their reading of naturalist fiction than to their reading of adventure romance. These mechanically transported participants resembled characters let loose in a novel devoid of characters. It was their social and political task, as I will try to show, to lend humanity to these exhibitions, or to lend them the status of the possible. The slightly detached wonderment implied by the literary genres of adventure and romance would simply not suffice here.

Louis Marin has said that spectators of utopian *divertissements* are as much narrators as they are visitors—that they produce the narrative for what they are seeing.[6] In 1900, the World's Fair did indeed ask of its participants that they provide a narrative that would enchain or link the hundreds of different exhibitions, stretching over 350 acres. It is this narrative explanation that I will be examining here.

The Showcase and Narration of Empire

One of the main aspects of the demanded narrative is a sense of proprietary recognition, the implicit understanding that "this is our world, and we recognize this vast expanse as part of our existence." The Exposition Universelle of 1900 was only the second international exhibition to make attractions out of colonized peoples. Of course, there had been earlier exhibitions of imperial power in France and Britain, but it was only in 1889 that the French government got the idea of encasing colonial people in exhibitions, enframing them as consumable attractions on the famous rue du Caire exhibition of Arab and "Oriental" cultures at that year's World's Fair. They had borrowed this notion from Paris's Jardin d'Acclimatation, which, in order to attract more visitors, had begun in 1870 to include wax figures of colonized people inside their glass cases, along with the plants and animals. This idea was born of the period's fascination with biology and anthropology, disciplines that promised to render human mysteries comprehensible, and most important, *visible.* One could turn the living world inside out and see the secret interior. In a sense, the Empire itself contained a secret underside, which was its status as an "elsewhere" so hard to conceive of. But science could help here. The magic of science could magnify a drop of Seine water one thousand times to shock and horrify visitors at the fair's Palais de l'Optique. Spectators gasped as they discovered the thousands of tiny creatures and plants that lived inside the innocuous drop. This same science could reveal the unseeable, far away in the colonies of Senegal, Indochina, and North Africa. Science, and consequently the scientificized World's Fair, could place colonized peoples under the microscope in similar fashion and render them consumable wonders—allied with all the laudable progress of technology.

The Theme Park, the Department Store, and the Consumer

Before going any further, I would like to discuss briefly the implied relation between audience and spectacle both at the World's Fair and in naturalist fiction. In order to examine some of the assumptions underlying this relation in the two domains, I shall turn to a third realm: the French department store. The *grand magasin* shares several qualities both with Zola's naturalist style and with the consumerism of the World's Fair.[7] This three-way resemblance makes the nineteenth-century department store a particularly illustrative point of comparison.

In the cases of the novel and the *grand magasin,* the implied audience (reader and customer) was female. Zola's naturalism partook quite openly of the period's explosive consumerism. His novels entice the reader into the spectacle behind the *vitrine,* constructing highly visual stories that invite the scrutinizing regard of the consumer/reader.[8] It is this peculiarly spectacular allure of Zola's work that allies it most strongly with the department store. Like the merchandise in the windows of Au Bonheur des Dames that so fascinated Denise Baudu, Zola's novelistic world is seductively absorbing and designed to lose the reader in a contemplative reverie. In *Les Rougon-Macquart,* it is not complex psychological portraits that provoke the reader's daydreaming, but rather the scientifically transcribed social detail, the heaping up of fascinating, mechanical minutiae, all arrayed for our observation. Whether shopping at Au Printemps or reading Zola, the consumer's pleasure comes from observing; "looking is itself the commodity," as Rachel Bowlby has remarked.[9]

Women constituted the majority of the stores' clientele, just as they made up the majority of the novel-reading public; and the great success of the French department stores stemmed, in large part, from their deliberate incorporation into the female customers' domestic realm. By providing reading rooms, tea salons, and other inviting amenities, the department store strove to make the bourgeois woman feel at home. And in so doing, the *grand magasin* transformed a merely utilitarian exchange into a day-long leisure activity, spread out over a diverse—but recognizably domestic—space.

The World's Fairs also promoted strolling and browsing among their hundreds of attractions; they were, in a sense, outdoor ver-

Figure 15.1. Oriental dancers at the World's Fair of 1900 (Bibliothèque Nationale, Paris).

sions of the Parisian department stores. Like naturalism and the department store, the World's Fair—particularly in 1900—relied upon a heavily visual appeal. The various attractions resembled the department store's many *rayons* and, like them, were spread widely apart to create as many purchasing opportunities as possible. But just as bourgeois shoppers were encouraged to recognize their own homes in the domesticized space of the *grand magasin,* so were fairgoers expected to look upon the re-created foreign worlds as representations of their own (newly extended) country.

If the typical department store shopper was a middle-class woman, the typical World's Fair visitor in 1900 was a middle-class family. In both cases, however, consumerism was tied—with equal success—to an erotic female spectacle. The stores used seductive images of women to sell their merchandise just as the Exposition Universelle relied upon seductive dancing girls to promote imperialism (Figure 15.1). And whereas the intended appeal to male and female shoppers alike was sexual, for the female visitor there was the additional element of narcissistic identification.

But there was a third component implicit in the fair's marketing of colonial sexuality, and this aspect reveals again a proximity to the department store. By 1900, the department store had become a respectable place where bourgeois women could stroll alone—unaccompanied, that is, by men. In similar fashion, the World's Fair "domesticized" and tempered the strongly erotic valence of colonial sexuality.

Popular entertainment in Paris at the turn of the century often found its themes in the forbidden attractions of women of color. Music-hall reviews habitually featured scantily clad "native" dancers. The World's Fair of 1900 relied heavily upon such attractions, but at the same time endeavored to make them acceptable to female visitors as well, in part by toning down the salaciousness, but mostly just by bringing the reviews out into the open air during the afternoon. The fair thus provided a place where women could enjoy themselves while keeping an eye on their husbands. By creating a daytime, family entertainment from what had been a late-night attraction for men only, the World's Fair managed to connect the naughty with the nice. The allure of the colonized world could now be appreciated by the whole family in broad daylight; this furthered the government's goal of promoting bourgeois acceptance and awareness of France's imperialist expansion.

Identification and the Naturalist Microscope

Recently, one of my students turned in a paper that posed some knotty problems for me. The paper—a discussion of depictions of motherhood in Zola—focused on the character of Adélaide Fouque or Tante Dide in *La Fortune des Rougon*. Tante Dide is the genetically tainted matriarch of the Rougons, who suffers spasms and nervous crises of unspecified origin. In his trademark style, Zola devotes some exaggeratedly horrific details to descriptions of Tante Dide's contortions and bestial cries.

In researching her paper, the student read through several of Zola's personal notebooks, in which he mused about how best to portray Tante Dide. In one notebook entry, Zola remarked to himself that Tante Dide's fits should resemble epileptic seizures. My student found this particular detail helpful and commented upon it at length in her essay.

The problem was that in Zola's private remark to himself, this student saw a "key" to Tante Dide—a new truth that could liberate this character from the misogynist constraints of the frequent label "hysteric." In her paper, the student made a case for Tante Dide's being an epileptic whose disease was not respected, and therefore a faultless victim deserving only sympathy, and not horror. She saw Adélaide's "epileptic" condition as a mitigating factor, an element that could forestall Zola's theory of Dide's guilt in founding the defective family. In reexamining this character's medical condition from a decidedly modern point of view, the paper's author sought to highlight Zola's prejudices against women, his unconscious disdain for female characters, and his inability to be "scientific" when it came to women's medical disorders.

I believed that my student had gone too far in looking for a behind-the-scenes truth about Tante Dide. I thought it unhelpful to say that Tante Dide was "really" an epileptic whom Zola should have depicted differently. I needed to explain just how far I thought one could go in using an author's private notes to illuminate his fictional text. But when I attempted this explanation, I found that new and troubling issues arose.

Zola's naturalist *roman-fleuve,* the Rougon-Macquart series, lures the reader into a familial world, a world in which characters appear and reappear in different novels, their fictional boundaries differentiable from the covers of the individual volumes. Indeed, the characters seem to "travel" on their own from novel to novel, meeting up with new intrigues and life crises, while still remaining themselves. Similarly, readers of the series "travel" in time with these characters, whose effect on them is intensified by the familiarity established by the characters' continual reappearance, and by the series's generational cycle. Zola's world has a profound aura of scientificity, and in the Rougon-Macquart novels the author passes the social fabric under the microscope—in much the same fashion that the Exposition Universelle's Palais de l'Optique magnified the drop of Seine water. We, as readers, scrutinize Zola's magnified specimens of humanity as they struggle for life in a Darwinian, sometimes degenerative, universe painted in meticulous detail. The repulsion felt by visitors to the Palais de l'Optique stemmed from seeing at close range minutiae that are usually hidden from sight. This brand of fascinated horror, evoked with the help of a scientifically probing gaze, is reminiscent of our horror (and interest) upon witnessing the intimate details and sordid adventures of Zola's protagonists.

My student had been so affected by Zola's naturalism that she sought to extend it beyond the confines of the text. She probed for hidden truths in places that were, I felt, inappropriate. That part was relatively easy to explain. But there was more to figure out. The inherent question seemed to be how to negotiate the boundaries between a fictional text and its real-world context, how to understand at what point the scientific gaze no longer reveals a deeper truth. The Tante Dide of *La Fortune des Rougon* or *Le Docteur Pascal* is not the Tante Dide of Zola's notebooks, because in the first case she inhabits her fictional universe, and what Zola creates there must remain inviolable; and in the second case, she is merely a reference that Zola makes to himself, with no narrative voice granting her status. My student had been so absorbed by the novel that she dissolved these boundaries, extending a bit too far her identification with the Naturalist's behind-the-scenes gaze. She tried to grant Tante Dide an existence detached from Zola's point of view. I see this phenomenon as similar to the loss of self that is connected both to reading naturalist and realist novels and to participating in "technological realism" or those attractions in which an alternative reality is created for the specific purpose of absorbing people into it.

It is not incidental that my student was seeking a bodily or medical excuse for Tante Dide. Her emphasis on this character's diagnosis demonstrates the seductiveness of naturalism's medicalized gaze. This student's search for a biological truth about a fictional character offers a paradigm for the phenomenon of absorption. The particularly medical quality of this absorption, of this transgressing of representation's boundaries, appears as well in the display and reception of the "technological realism" of the World's Fair of 1900.

Why the Exposition Universelle?

I choose to focus on the Exposition Universelle for several reasons. The first is that this World's Fair represented the vastest and most ambitious promotion of imperialism in European history, a shameless vaunting of France's tremendous expansion into Africa and Asia. Indeed, France was the first country in the world to display imperial gains at exhibitions.

The second reason for my interest in this Exposition Universelle is that, although much of music-hall entertainment in France at this time already included technological trompe l'oeil effects and early cinematographic marvels, the Fair of 1900 featured more of these entertainments than had ever before been together in one place.

Finally, I write here of the Exposition Universelle because of its complex showcasing of gender. It is commonplace to speak of the feminization of colonized countries. We are all familiar with the metaphorical practice whereby the colony emerges in the metropolis's imagination as a supine and languid female creature awaiting the culturally fertilizing power of the invading First World. And the 1900 World's Fair certainly promoted this typical connection between colonies and women. The most famous of all the attractions in Paris that summer were the Algerian *danse du ventre* and the Javanese *danse de la gorge.* Indeed, all the expected connections between what was "racy" and "racial" were played out by the French government's emphasis on the highly acclaimed Algerian female dance troupe the Ouled-Nail. In addition to performing nightly, members of this troupe entertained fairgoers by simply walking around the grounds scantily dressed, as their contract dictated.

But there is more to explore in the representation of femaleness at the World's Fair of 1900. It was not simply the French colonies that were implicitly feminized at this fair; instead, all of French culture itself took on a feminine cast here, and deliberately so. Typically, the French do not balk at seeing their cultural ideals in female form; on the contrary, they have a tradition of employing such feminine allegories as *la liberté, la Révolution,* and *la Semeuse* as expressions of patriotism. The World's Fair participated in the usual nationalist celebration of idealized femaleness and placed itself under the sign of the woman. The first and most dramatic manifestation of this was the enormous statue of a woman—known as *La Parisienne*—that loomed over the main entrance at the Porte Binet. The sculpted outfit worn by this giant "consumer goddess," as she has been called, was designed by the famous pret-a-porter couturier, M. Pacquin.

Europe's international exhibitions were also among the very first places that explicitly exhibited women's art; at the 1900 exhibition, the Arts de la Femme pavilion ranked among the most popular attractions. This pavilion featured primarily handiwork, miniature paintings, and small sculptures. And, of course, there was the extremely feminine nature of the aesthetic movement that reached its apogee at the Fair of 1900: art nouveau.[10]

All this is not to say, however, that the World's Fair of 1900 was in any way a feminist endeavor. On the contrary, the burgeoning French feminist movement of the late nineteenth century may have been partly responsible for the fair's aesthetic insistence upon an idealized, maternal, and domestic version of femininity.[11] And furthermore, the overall femaleness of the fair contributed structurally to its scientifically imperial gaze, for the strolling spectator wound up something of a medical researcher peering into a hard-to-reach, feminized other space—be it an art nouveau interior or a colonial hut. It is for this reason that one can detect a faintly obstetrical quality in the implied position of the fairgoer, and this stance is not all that distant from that of the reader confronted with one of Zola's graphically described childbirth scenes.[12]

Of course, cultural studies has often pointed to mass culture's "feminine" nature, and I have already discussed the fair's resemblance to that most feminized of institutions, the French department store. In fact, it is often precisely the issue of the consumer's "absorption" into mass culture—his or her self-abandonment to it—that suggests its passive or feminine quality. "The lure of mass culture . . . has traditionally been described as the threat of losing oneself in dreams . . . of merely consuming rather than producing," writes Andreas Huyssens.[13] Tania Modleski discusses the extent to which "mass culture is condemned as feminised culture," specifically because of its tendency to lure its participants inside of it.[14] My argument here does not contradict this reading, but it adds a new wrinkle. If mass culture is feminine, and beckons spectators or audience members to lose themselves inside of it, that does not mean that the spectator is completely feminized or rendered totally passive. It may mean that this same spectator is being given two roles at once: one of identification and its result, passive absorption or self-abandonment, but also another, of exploring curiosity and an almost medicalized empowerment. I am particularly interested in the tension between these two roles.

"A Thousand Marvelous Journeys without Moving a Single Step": Attractions at the Fair

In order to talk specifically about the effects of technological realism, I must outline some of the major attractions of the World's Fair of 1900. From among the staggeringly diverse and complicated attractions Paris offered that summer, I will limit myself to those most relevant to questions of imperialism and gender.

Perhaps the most significant shared aspect of the attractions at this fair was the theme of travel. Of thirty-three major attractions, twenty-one involved dynamic illusions of voyage of some kind. Among the most stunning were the Cinéorama aerial tour exhibition, the *"stéréorama mouvant"* that "visited" Algiers, the Trans-Siberian Railway exhibition, and the *"globe céleste."*

The Cinéorama took visitors on a hot-air balloon ride above the world. From their realistic but earthbound balloon, the spectators toured Africa, South America, and Asia. Harnessing the new technology of the cinematograph, the Cinéorama featured ten screens that rotated films of these regions. Occasionally, diorama and plaster reproductions of key monuments were positioned in front of the screens.

The *stéréorama mouvant* restricted its travel to a purely French colonial site. In this attraction—one of several *maréoramas* at the fair—spectators boarded a boat that would lurch and sway as it made its way from the re-created city of Bone toward its destination, Oran. As a "sea breeze" wafted by, the boat mechanically agitated the passengers while the ride exposed them to a series of rotating panoramas depicting an approaching, ever larger and more detailed Algerian coastline (Figure 15.2). When they arrived, the passengers disembarked to find themselves in an Algerian café, complete with musical entertainment and the all-important *bayadères* performing the *danse du ventre.* So lifelike was this ride

Figure 15.2 A maréorama ride at the fair, which simulated an ocean crossing (Bibliothèque Nationale, Paris).

that some passengers regularly needed to be escorted off, overcome with seasickness. I will return later to the significance of such a physiological reaction to a theme park attraction.

The strength of the celebrated Franco-Russian Alliance prompted the French government to dedicate considerable space at the fair to the exhibition of Russian culture. Part of this exhibition involved a re-creation of the world-famous Trans-Siberian Railway. Here, passengers would board a life-size replica of a luxurious wagon-lit furnished with crystal tables, onyx tea services, and fur lap rugs. "We crossed great rivers. . . huge forests. . . and vast deserts," wrote Paul Morand. "We left the carriage to find ourselves magically transported to the other end of the earth at the foot of one of the gates of Peking."[15] This effect was produced by moving the railroad car eighty meters, from the Russian to the Chinese exhibition, while painted canvases depicting Siberia were unrolled outside the window.

Another fair attraction combined the theme of world travel with the timely motif of astronomy. At *le globe céleste,* spectators sat back in easy chairs and voyaged through space via a series of rolling panorama canvases depicting the known wonders of the universe. Nearby, the world's largest telescope offered views of the moon in closer detail than anyone had ever seen.

Regardless of the ostensible "destinations" of these simulated voyages, the technological emphasis of the World's Fair allied itself inextricably with the might of empire. The power of science and France's advances in human knowledge were used overtly and implicitly to justify the domination of Third World peoples. From marveling at French technology's ability to bring the moon's surface within view it is not a big leap to marveling approvingly at the Empire's power to conquer and package Algeria or Indochina for the public's viewing enjoyment. Even those exhibitions that referred more to inter-European affairs—such as the pro-Russian Trans-Siberian Railway—participated in this great imperialist justification; for, as Fredric Jameson points out, early imperialism expressed itself more as relationships and rivalry between nation-states than as a tension between metropolis and colony.[16]

Even beyond the formally cordoned off "voyages," the entire exhibition contained an element of simulated travel, because 350 acres of Paris had been transformed into a miniature world. Paul Morand, who wrote extensively of his boyhood experience of the World's Fair thirty-one years later, was particularly struck by his "travels" there: "I passed my days [on] a quiet Paris hillside [that was] suddenly bearing upon its back all Africa, Asia. . . . Like Huysmans' Des Esseintes I went a thousand marvelous journeys without moving a step."[17] Here, Morand refers specifically to the Parc du Trocadéro, whose vast expanse had been transformed into what the *Guide Figaro* called the "grand rendez-vous colonial," a landscape of huts, temples, markets, and theaters, all showcasing the wonders of the colonies, both French and foreign.

But in addition to the official exhibitions, such as the stereorama ride to Oran and the diorama called "Splendeurs sahariennes," there was also the fairwide realistic Oriental backdrop, created by the exhibition committee. Before the exhibition, committee director Alfred Picard had imported hundreds of indigenous workers and craftsmen to create various attractions, including much of the Parc du Trocadéro. Then, once summer came and the fair opened, Picard employed these people as "extras" to add exotic ambiance to

Figure 15.3 Congolese village at the fair (Bibliothèque Nationale, Paris).

the exhibition. Indigenous people were encouraged to walk around the exhibition grounds in their national costumes, performing their "normal" daily duties in full view of European spectators. "Native villages" were formed from all the French empire holdings, and people lived on the fair grounds for up to six months. To increase the realism, the government provided them with food and the raw materials with which to build their own "authentic" dwellings. Sometimes whole families were imported; each "native village" contained anywhere between fifty and two hundred persons (Figures 15.3 and 15.4).[18] The presence of these "native extras" blurred the boundaries between entertainment and backdrop, and between spectacle and spectator, because the strolling natives were at once spectators *and* exhibitions. The authentic extras staffed restaurants and cafés and, in this way, "outside" activities such as having lunch or coffee became bound up with the grand imperial spectacle. As Paul Greenhalgh remarks, the purpose of these native villages was "to allow the public to see at a glance *their* empire."[19]

But they accomplished more than that. The presence of these extra-muros human exhibitions dismantled the distinctions between fairgoer and fair, between backdrop and panorama, drawing

Figure 15.4 Under the Eiffel Tower, a re-created North African street (Bibliothèque Nationale, Paris).

the strolling visitors into the very spectacles that they had paid to see, absorbing them into the imperial fiction. Even the *Guide Figaro* acknowledges this breakdown of boundaries in its description of the Algerian "native village":

> Let us cross the threshold of Babel-oued, here we are in the rue de la Kasbah. The steep path snakes around . . . behind the barred doors and windows pass the shadows of mysterious veiled women. . . . The street is dotted with bazaars where artisans work under the eyes of the public. We pass huts where belly dancing, sword dancing, . . . restaurants proudly displaying Arab cuisine, laughter, shouts and songs . . . all form a multicolored tableau, most animated and alive.[20]

Here, the guidebook first invites the European spectator to consider the novelistic or theatrical appeal of the setting, "Let us cross the threshold." The women, supposedly glimpsed in their daily life, add verisimilitude or homeyness to the scene. As "racialized" female bodies, they inject the necessary sexual secret. It is no accident that the tourist's guidebook presents these Algerian women not only veiled, but behind barred windows and doors, and mere shadows at that, "*des ombres.*" The women dematerialize under the imperial gaze, inside the framing narrative of the World's Fair. They become simulacra of themselves, glimpsed *through* and *between* obstructions or barriers. Enframed and partially obscured by prisonlike bars, the *algériennes* become peep show attractions, even when presented as being at home. Despite the "realistic" settings, the fair's technologizing gaze transforms them into filmic ghosts of themselves, less real women than cinematic shadows, and resembling nothing so much as the stereoscope show, in which, for two centimes, customers could briefly ogle erotic pictures of women. Just as the distinction between audience and spectacle was dismantled, so was the distinction between the technologized body and the "natural" body blurred.

Writing of the explosion in late-nineteenth-century France of commercially produced photographs depicting North African women, Malek Alloula has commented, "History knows of no other society in which women have been photographed on such a large scale to be delivered to public view."[21] In a sense, these Algerian women of the fair became photographs for spectators, so that even when we are not referring to actual panorama or cineorama displays, we must understand the living persons of this exhibition as potential photographs or films before the fact. "These *algériennes,*" writes Alloula, "are themselves but simulacra (that is, phantoms),"[22] and the same could be said of the Algerian women at the World's Fair.

The *Figaro* guidebook provides further evidence of dismantled distinctions between stage and audience, and between technology and human life, in its description of the rue du Kasbah. The Kasbah is a "multicolored tableau, animated and alive [*animé et vivant*]." Here the writer protests too much by insisting upon the "lifelike" and "animated" quality of the exhibition. This description also makes indirect reference to that very famous French entertainment, the *tableau vivant,* in which a group of persons is arranged into a perfectly immobile composition that embodies some static concept or aphorism. Like the English *still life, tableau vivant* is an oxymoron, an expression that deadens the very life it lays claim to. *La Femme au foyer*— present in this exhibition to lend the realistic touch—becomes an inanimate, mechanical detail, a phantom reminding the visitor of the artifice of the scene, even while signifying its verisimilitude. She is enframed as living corroboration of Flaubert's distasteful remark that "the Oriental woman is no more than a machine."[23]

Constructing Reality

In exploring the contradictory role of the Oriental woman at the World's Fair, it might be profitable to return to the paradigm of the shift from realism to naturalism. Lukács complained of naturalism's backdrop/puppet quality. Bad realist art allowed its seams to show and was disjointedly "mechanical." For Lukács, effective, pure realism allowed its characters to interact with those backdrops, to shed their marionette strings. And yet, realism needs to show its seams. "As representation, the novel's realism is a system," writes Stephen Heath, "that includes the reader as the subject position of its coherence. . . . the common reality must needs be constructed."[24] This construction turns often on the representation of women, their bodies and their lives. When the issue is the rendering visible of what is normally invisible, the female body emerges as a gauge of effectiveness. As the body that hides, but also generates, the female body is the one into which the realist/naturalist gaze peers most intently. It is the female world of the interior that appears in insistent, even obsessive detail in Zola—the washhouse, the cabaret dressing room, the dining room. But, of course, the massive heaping up of naturalist details achieves a paradoxical end: the real is conjured only to be exaggerated to the point of mechanized monstrosity—as seen, for example, in the meticulous description of the heroine's decaying corpse at the close of *Nana*. Femaleness is at once the most natural and the most *made* or constructed of concepts—hence the profusion of female automatons in late-nineteenth-century fiction.

It is for this reason that the gaze of the naturalist novelist, and, by extension, the gaze of the reader of such novels, resembles the obstetrical gaze, the technologized gaze into the hidden, *female* part of society. Zola's insistence upon the horrors of motherhood illustrates well this merging of the obstetrical and the naturalist gaze. "[The] model for such [compulsory] visibility is the mother."[25]

The desire to lay open the hidden (feminized) passageways of a society appears not only in naturalism, of course, but in the very landscape of late nineteenth-century Paris itself. Baron Haussmann's accomplishment was to tear up the narrow, winding secret passageways of Paris and replace them with great vistas and boulevards. The remodeled Paris of the Second Empire flaunted its increasing (imperial) power through its urban *visibility*. The hidden inside had been probed by technology and opened up for the public's enjoyment. And this was the paradigm for the technologically realist attractions at the Exposition Universelle. Paris, a panoramic city that had produced a panoramic literature, created with the World's Fair a wonderland of panoramic vistas—especially vistas of the Empire's unseeable, other lands.[26]

Fredric Jameson has explored the imperialist agenda in modernism's fascination with seeing the unseeable, with space, and the materialization of space. He writes of the difficulty in conceiving of that vast "elsewhere" of empire:

> Colonialism means that a significant, structural segment of the economic system as a whole is now located elsewhere, beyond the metropolis, outside of daily life and existential experience of the home

country. . . . one's simplest first thought faced with the problem of global space that escapes is to make a map.[27]

According to Jameson, the effort of conceiving of the Empire's vast expanse leads to a "new kind of value: even if infinity and imperialism are bad, its *perception,* as a bodily and poetic process is good, an achievement."[28] I would argue that this perception of infinity, of a world beyond, is at stake in all the "magical voyage" attractions at the World's Fair. But then what happens to the spectator of such entertainments? And what is the relationship between this experience and the experience of the reader of a naturalist novel?

Here, I will return to something I mentioned earlier: the physical sensations experienced by many fairgoers. The exposition represented the first time that such large groups of people were electronically manipulated en masse. Even before entering some of the mechanically re-created worlds, fairgoers often grew sick simply from mounting the machine-propelled walkways. Unaccustomed to such devices, many grew dizzy or nauseated on the walkways; others simply fell down when the ground started to move beneath their feet. Once on the *stéréorama mouvant* or the Cinéorama hot-air balloon, visitors suffered vertigo and motion sickness. These physical discomforts were more than incidental side efects; an important relation exists between the obstetrical gaze implicit in the imperial project of the fair and the spectators' various maladies.

The gaze of the metropolis upon the colonies presupposes a certain masculinized, unified, penetrative force. The Parc du Trocadéro opens up and examines the normally hidden daily life of colonial interiors. And yet, once again a blurring of boundaries occurs. Not only does the realism of the "native villages" shade off into cinematic simulacra, but participants themselves begin to lose their bodily seamlessness. In experiencing vertigo or nausea, spectators necessarily become aware of themselves as conglomerations of bodily parts and mechanisms that are subject to failure. As I have suggested, the countless details added to these re-created worlds for verisimilitude often contribute more of a mechanical than a lifelike effect. The same may be said for the sensations provoked by technological realism. Faced with a constructed "reality"—a voyage to Algeria, a glimpse of the Kasbah—the fair spectator becomes something of a bodily "construction." The surprising result, then, of the absorption into an alternative world is that this absorption takes place as it decomposes the spectator. With the visitor now a potentially fallible organ system, his or her obstetrical gaze no longer presupposes indivisibility or seamless subjectivity. The staged intruder into the inner workings of the colonies becomes an amassed heap of mechanisms, individuated organs that assert themselves, decomposing the subject-fairgoer into a potential series of working parts whose wholeness—whose realism, if you will—is gone.

What are the ramifications of this phenomenon? And how does it comment upon the realist project in general, and on gender within that project? To begin with, it further strengthens the argument of identification. My student's desire to search for a "real" Tante Dide beyond Zola's text contained an element of the medical; such enthusiasm for finding an explanatory or excusing diagnosis for Adélaide Fouque's malady bespeaks the desire to uncover the hidden, medical truth about a female character. In seeking this truth in Zola's notebook, this student blurred the borders of fiction and reality, but she also began dismantling the borders between herself as "visitor" in the naturalist world of the Rougon-Macquart series and the internal world of the novel's characters. In seeking a "behind-the-scenes" truth about a two-dimensional literary character, this reader—drawn in by the plethora of amassed natural, bodily details—merged her world with the text world, as if Tante Dide's medical, corporeal self were as diagnosable and as open to a medically informed gaze as this student's own body.

In this case, the effect is less one of bodily fragmentation than one of interpenetration of the textual body and the reader's own body. At the World's Fair, participants' bodies merged with the mechanical systems that were transporting, agitating, and entertaining them. Confronting naturalist texts, the reader is similarly drawn into a world of blurred distinctions. The scientifically realist gaze of naturalism breaks down the social order depicted into great and fallible mechanical and bodily systems.[29] Readers of such texts are susceptible to a desire to extend the already present bodily identification with the text to its fictional bodies, with the result that they are encouraged, as my student was, to appropriate the naturalist text's peering gaze and use it themselves, even in inappropriate situations. Just as the mechanicity of the fair's attractions seems contagious, so, too, is Zola's scientific, probing gaze.

"The ticking which enhances reality"[30]

Electronically propelled through mechanical simulacra of other countries and dream landscapes, the World's Fair visitors enacted physically the process that is only implicit in the reading of naturalism's mechanized texts. Traveling through *Les Rougon-Macquart,* the reader stops and starts at the various novelistic attractions, drawn in, touched by the contagion of what Angus Wilson calls the text's "whirring," and then moved onward by the curiosity to explore and marvel at the next set of "lifelike" details. The contagion of Zola's scientifism lends the reader what amounts ultimately to a filmic gaze. Like a camera, we move through the novels, peering through the lens in search of secret truths.[31] The scientific gaze of the World's Fair is similarly contagious, only in this case the private, domestic act of reading explodes into collective movement. The fair harnessed this filmic contagion in an effort to persuade Europeans of the charms inherent in rendering the colonized world visible and domestic, a diversion for a Sunday afternoon.

NOTES

1. Quoted in Sylviana Leprun, *Le Théâtre de colonies: scénographie, acteurs et discours imaginaires dans les Expositions 1855–1937* (Paris: Editions L'Harmattan, 1986), 135.

2. Quoted in Paul Greenhalgh, *Ephemeral Vistas: The Exposition Universelle, Great Exhibitions and World's Fairs 1851–1939* (Manchester: Manchester University Press, 1988), 118.

3. Georg Lukács, *Studies in European Realism,* trans. Edith Bone (New York: Grossett & Dunlap, 1964), 92.

4. In *Expositions: Littérature et architecture au XIXème siècle* (Paris: José Corti, 1989), Philippe Hamon discusses the relationship between nineteenth-century realist texts, including Zola's, and the culture of the exposition. Hamon focuses on the compulsion for visibility and display during this period of arcades, department stores, and World's Fairs. He sees Zola's insistence upon the *detail* as a conscious display of the author's (textual) *product,* a display analogous to the exposition's displays of products of a more material nature. Hamon compares Zola's work directly to the Exposition Universelle, seeing it as "a world of characters on display or on exhibit [*exposition*], but having lost all density or fleshly 'volume' " (166) (my translation). Hamon does not, however, address the underlying gender issues implicit in his comparisons.

5. Within the last fifteen years of the nineteenth century, France had increased its territories from 1 million to 9.5 million square kilometers. See Raoul Girardet, *L'Idée coloniale en France de 1871 à 1962* (Paris: La Table Ronde, 1972), 80.

6. "Sa promenade est le récit mille fois renouvelé de l'harmonisation leurrante de contraires" See Louis Marin, *Utopiques: jeux d'espaces* (Paris: Editions Minuit, 1973), 299.

7. Noting the similar structures of naturalist-realist text and the department store, Philippe Hamon speaks of the "texte-magasin." Hamon, *Expositions,* 112.

8. Zola was particularly aware of his role as a packager of literary merchandise, and his early years in journalism had left him with a talent for self-promotion and the sensational. His celebrated motto, "Nulla dies sine linea [No day without a line]," encapsulates his investment in a highly regulated, quantitative, almost factorylike literary production.

9. Rachel Bowlby, *Just Looking: Consumer Culture in Dreiser, Gissing, and Zola* (New York: Methuen, 1985), 6.

10. Art nouveau celebrated the female form in its most biological and maternal incarnations, showcasing decorative themes based on reproductions of smooth-curved women; undulating, feminine lines; and a new smaller, "feminine" scale. The movement raised the small *objet*—the jeweled brooch, the table lamp, the figurine—to the status of serious artwork.

11. See Deborah Silverman, *Art Nouveau in Fin-de-Siècle France: Politics, Psychology, and Style* (Berkeley: University of California Press, 1989), for a description of the relationship between feminism and the World's Fair of 1900.

12. I would like to acknowledge here the work of Mark Seltzer, whose recent book *Bodies and Machines* (New York: Routledge, 1992) constructs a compelling argument for the medical or obstetrical model of naturalist texts.

13. Andreas Huyssens, *After the Great Divide: Modernism, Mass Culture, Postmodernism* (Bloomington: Indiana University Press, 1986), 55.

14. Tania Modleski, "Femininity as Mas(s)querade: A Feminist Approach to Mass Culture," in *High Theory/Low Culture: Analysing Popular Television and Film,* ed. Colin MacCabe (Manchester: Manchester University Press, 1986), 38.

15. Paul Morand, *1900 A.D.,* trans. Rollilly Fedden (New York: William Farquhar Payson, 1931), 103.

16. Fredric Jameson, "Modernism and Imperialism," in *Nationalism, Colonialism, and Literature* (Minneapolis: University of Minnesota Press, 1990), 43–66.

17. Morand, *1900 A.D.,* 88.

18. Greenhalgh, *Ephemeral Vistas,* 79.

19. Ibid., 89.

20. *Guide Bleu de France à l'Exposition de 1900* (Paris: Le Figaro, 1990), 88 (my translation).

21. Malek Alloula, *The Colonial Harem,* trans. Myrna Godzich and Wlad Godzich (Minneapolis: University of Minnesota Press, 1986), 5.

22. Ibid., 64.

23. From a letter to Louise Colet, in *Flaubert in Egypt: A Sensibility on Tour,* ed. and trans. Francis Steegmuller (London: Bodley Head, 1972), 220.

24. Stephen Heath, "Realism, Modernism, and 'Language Consciousness,' " in *Realism in European Literature,* ed. Nicholas Boyle and Martin Swales (Cambridge: Cambridge University Press, 1986), 110.

25. Seltzer, *Bodies and Machines,* 95.

26. Walter Benjamin writes, "Contemporary to the panoramas is a panoramic literature." "Paris, Capital of the Nineteenth Century," in *Reflections,* trans. Edmund Jephcott (New York: Harcourt Brace Jovanovich, 1978), 150.

27. Jameson, "Modernism and Imperialism," 52.

28. Ibid., 58.

29. In *Nana,* for example, the obsolescent economy of Paris's aristocracy breaks down when the monkey wrench that is Nana's body is thrown into the works.

30. "In *Germinal* and the later great novels [the whirring of the mechanism] has been reduced to a ticking which enhances the reality of the atmosphere." Angus Wilson, *Emile Zola* (New York: William Morrow, 1952), 57.

31. It should not surprise us that Zola himself was interested in photogrpahy, and took many excellent photographs of the Exposition of 1900.

A Question of Reference:
Male Sexuality in Phallic Theory
Charles Bernheimer

Psychic Reality and Sexual Difference

Reality is a problematic idea in psychoanalysis. In phrases such as *reality testing, reality adaptation,* and *reality principle,* the term *reality* refers to the external world of objective phenomena. As one of the two principles that govern mental functioning according to Freud, the reality principle serves the ego by assessing the conditions imposed by the material world and proposing adaptive strategies to obtain the satisfaction of desired goals. Reality testing involves the ego's capacity to discriminate between subjective representations and actual perceptions and its ability to rectify mental pictures by comparison with factual data. The function of "reality" in these processes appears to be normative and conforming, as if their purpose were to cure the subject of whatever is unrealistic in his or her personal world.

But, of course, unrealism is a primary characteristic of the neurotic psyche as Freud analyzed it, and he was careful to point out that "one must never allow oneself to be misled into applying the standards of reality to repressed psychical structures, and on that account, perhaps, into undervaluing the importance of phantasies in the formation of symptoms on the ground that they are not actualities."[1] This comment could refer to the famous instance in which Freud believed that he himself had been led to undervalue badly the importance of fantasies, that is, his early conviction that hysteria originates in actual acts of seduction and abuse perpetrated on young children by older family members. No moment in the history of psychoanalysis exemplifies more vividly its prejudice in favor of psychical reality over material reality than Freud's abandonment of the seduction theory, or rather of its universal applicability (he never denied that abuse occurred in some cases). "The firm ground of reality was gone,"[2] Freud wrote about his determination that his patients' seduction scenarios were most often wishful fantasies, a turn away from traumatic experiential history that has come under one-sided attack by Jeffrey Masson in *The Assault on Truth*.[3] "As far as the neurosis was concerned," Freud commented on another occasion, "psychical reality was of more importance than material reality."[4]

In becoming psychical, reality loses the bond to the external world forged through the mimetic insistence of the ego and becomes subject to the pleasure principle, to unconscious desire, and to fantasy. Thus is formed the sphere of symbolic activity proper to psychoanalytic investigation. It operates through such processes as displacement, condensation, repression, repudiation, sublimation, and introjection. The premise of these complex functions is, in Freud's words, that "*psychical* reality is a particular form of existence not to be confused with *material reality*."[5] Although he does not say that psychical reality has no relation to the material world of bodies and objects in history, his own theorizing reinforces a split that, as we shall see, was deepened yet further by Lacan.

It is in defining sexual difference that Freud offers his most striking illustration of the priority he ascribes to psychical over material reality. Offering little clinical evidence to support this claim, Freud maintains that both boys and girls start out believing that all human beings have penises. When the little boy sees that girls/women actually do not possess this organ, he does not allow this confrontation with anatomical reality to discredit his unisexual theory. He does not observe an absence and on that basis recognize difference. Rather, he performs what Freud terms a "theoretical advance":[6] he comes up with the idea that women have been castrated. The progress Freud speaks of here involves a denial of physical reality and a valorization of fantasy. Although in the Little Hans case Freud acknowledges that the boy's failure to "report what he really saw" could be seen as a sign of the "premature decay of a child's intellect,"[7] Freud endorses Hans's allegiance to psychic reality by repeatedly referring in his own texts to castration as a fact. Factuality thus becomes for Freud himself a function of unconscious fantasy. Like Little Hans, he welcomes castration as a "theoretical advance" enabling him to preserve his regressive fantasy of sexual sameness while accounting for difference in its terms as loss.

Freud's fetishistic valorization of psychic reality as the medium for understanding sexual difference extends to his analysis of girl children. According to Freud's scenario, no sooner does a normal little girl see a penis than she immediately "acknowledges the fact of her castration"[8] and wants to compensate for it by acquiring a male organ. Denying the girl any knowledge of her vagina or any allegiance to the anatomical reality of her own body—and never asking why she does not wonder how, when, and by whom her penis was cut off—Freud attributes to her an instantaneous adoption of phallocentric theory. Were a girl to refuse to believe in her castration, this would not signify, for Freud, a healthy insistence on her anatomical difference. Rather, it would represent, he says, "a conviction that she *does* possess a penis," which might compel the girl "to behave as though she were a man."[9] And this, of course, is to be avoided at all cost. The girl's castration complex "encourages femininity"[10] in that it endorses her revulsion from her body as a necessary means for the discovery of the "truth" of her sexuality. To ensure her psychic health, she must learn to interpret her genitals as a mutilated organ explicable only by phallocentric theory.[11]

If Freud's account thus denaturalizes female sexuality, which becomes equated with the purely psychic reality of castration, one might assume that it would be more realistic in its description of male sexual identity, the patriarchal norm. After all, the male does actually possess the organ that, according to psychoanalytic theory, is signified in the unconscious as the emblem of truth. But it is precisely against this essentializing claim that Lacan argues that no semantic link exists between the real penis and the symbolic phallus. He defines the phallus as "the signifier intended to designate as a whole the effects of the signified."[12] Lacan thus takes to its logical conclusion the derealizing thrust of Freudian psychic reality, removing the phallus as rigorously from the male body as the theory of castration had removed the vagina from the female body. Lacan's followers, many of them women, have continued to stress the completely unnatural, disembodied, unrealistic quality of the phallus. "The importance of the phallus," explains Jacqueline Rose, "is that its status in the development of human sexuality is something which nature *cannot* account for."[13]

Of late, however, some feminists have been taking a more critical tack, arguing that Lacan's phallus is too closely tied to the penis to be able to soar freely as a transcendental signifier. Jane Gallop, Mary Ann Doane, and Diana Fuss all argue that the word *phallus* cannot help but conjure up an image of an actual penis,[14] thus contaminating with male essence the construction of the phallus as a neutral signifier "set up regardless of the anatomical difference between the sexes."[15] But these feminist critics have little to say about the penile image that confronts them once the phallus has been unveiled. The implication seems to be that the penis in itself is uninteresting; bears little looking at; is obvious in its unambiguous meaning; is in itself somehow outside theory; represents, perhaps, a limit of the theoretical. For instance, in her wittily demystifying article "Phallus/Penis: Same Difference," Jane Gallop asserts the value of extricating the penis as an object of female heterosexual desire from its pernicious, but historically inevitable, association with the hegemonic phallus. Although she brilliantly exposes the way Lacan's denial of the phallus's penile reference is a political move that perpetuates patriarchal inequalities, theory remains for her in the domain of the signifier, where the penis appears only as a tempting outsider.

The argument I want to make here is that the penis as phallic signified has a more complex theoretical function than has generally been recognized. Feminist critics have argued that Lacan reinscribes patriarchal domination by camouflaging the phallus's anatomical reference. Their point is that reference to the penis has a naturalizing and essentializing function and that penile realism is therefore necessarily reductive. Although I join the feminist attack on the hegemonic pretensions of the phallic signifier, I do not agree that penile reference is necessarily essentializing. I will argue that it can have the opposite effect. My perspective on the male sexual body as a potential site of subversion has something in common, paradoxically, with Luce Irigaray's claims for the antiessentialist power of female sexuality. The paradox, of course, is that Irigaray constructs her reading of the polymorphous plurality of the female body against a view of the phallocentric sameness of that sex which is one. But she also notes that male anatomy is not an adequate signified for this monolithic signifier: "The passage from erection to detumescence does pose some problems," she wryly observes.[16] Although her remark is intended to undermine the inflated grandiosity of the phallus, I want to consider the problems raised by the passage she evokes in a more positive light— positive, that is, for a materialist, feminist-informed, straight male reading of male sexuality that works to resist phallocentric cultural symbolizations.

A useful, if perhaps unsettling, starting point for this argument is the image that appears in the mind's eye when the word *penis* is heard. Will not this image differ significantly from person to person, depending on such factors as gender, race, class, and experience? The most salient differences are likely to concern the penis's size and state: Is it large or small, erect or flaccid, circumcised or not? One may wonder about its color: Is the skin white, black, yellow, or some in-between shade? Does your picture include the testicles? What kind of context have you constructed for your penile image: How much of the rest of the body do you see, if any? What background have you imagined for the penis's display? Is there any suggestion of sperm? With what affective qualities have you invested your penis: Does it desire you? Do you desire it? What do you fantasize doing with it? How does it feel? Smell? Is it associated with pain, pleasure, disgust, delight? Is its preference heterosexual or homosexual or both? To what degree have you imagined one particular penis; to what degree is your picture a generic version? Perhaps your penis is not made of flesh at all, but is a plastic or rubber facsimile . . .

Many other such questions are, of course, relevant, and the formulations would no doubt be quite different were they being made by someone of a different gender, sexual orientation, race, and so forth. My point in provoking this train of thought in my reader is to suggest that the risk involved in giving the phallus a penile referent is not the self-destruction of theory on the bedrock of essentialism but the liability of theory to account for such "external" contexts as race, class, social convention, and individual history. Consideration of these particular and material contexts insistently challenges the exclusively psychic reality of theoretical speculation. This insistence has been effectively championed in recent years by female feminists, who have stressed the importance of speaking from an acknowledged subject position and in relation to a personal bodily history. But that position and that history do not constitute having a penis or looking at it as someone who has one (assuming that we exclude the prosthetic option that I evoked above). Granting the value of the gesture of unveiling the Lacanian phallus, it remains for men to speak their response to what they see revealed there and to analyze its political function in the elaboration of theory. This is the task I have set myself in this essay.

Penile Caprice and Phallic Lack

The most evident effect of penile reference on the transcendental phallus is the onslaught of temporality and the consequent variability of the penis between its rigid and limp states. Lacan's phallus has no such variation, a point that Derrida rightly interprets as proving that the Lacanian phallus is a metaphysical delusion, an ideal signifier not itself subject to semantic mutilation.[17] Derrida's critique, however, does not help us get any closer to the bodily origin of the penis's changeability. Indeed, his theoretical fantasy constructs the phallus as an even more lost and surreal nonorgan than Lacan's: it is always-already castrated; it is forever suspended and vulnerable to further division; it has no place to which to return. (Lacan, in contrast, appears to suggest in his Poe essay that the phallus always returns to its place, that is, to woman, whose lack-in-being it signifies.) Although both Lacan and Derrida conceive of the phallus as a signifier of differential effects, neither thinks of these effects as being internal to the male subject's somatic awareness. In discussing the phallus, neither man risks conjuring up an image of a temporarily erect penis. In discussing the loss of the phallus, neither risks evoking an image of the detumescent male organ. For them, phallic loss or lack is always an absence, not a change, and it occurs symbolically in the place of woman, not realistically in the genitals of men.

The word *phallus* has a certain referential instability even in common usage. A phallus, the dictionaries agree, is "a representation of the penis and testes as an embodiment of generative power" (this particular wording comes from the *American Heritage Dictionary*). The outlines of this mimesis are imprecise, because the state of the penis is not described. "Can a phallus be flaccid?" Jane Gallop queried in the margin of an earlier version of this essay. The question is pertinent, because the many symbolic meanings of *phallus* and *phallic* in contemporary culture all evoke images of the erect organ, this being the form in which male sexuality most effectively asserts power, dominance, potency, and so forth. This usage has etymological justification in that the Indo-European root of the word *phallus, bhel-,* signifies (again according to the *American Heritage Dictionary*) "to blow, to swell; with derivative reference to various round objects and to the notion of tumescent masculinity." The phallus thus would be more precisely defined as a symbolic representation of the erect penis.

What, then, is the relation of this image signifying patriarchal hegemony to any particular erect penis that presumably could be seen as the symbol's referential vehicle? More concretely, what would it mean if my lover were to qualify my penis as phallic? Should I consider this a compliment? The epithet could imply a certain distanciation on my lover's part, a viewing of my organ as inert, insensible, unresponsive to variations in context and circumstance. A phallic penis is impersonal and unchanging, always erect, impervious to differences in desire—whether the other's or one's own. To bring the phallus into the scene of erotic exchange is to freeze that scene outside of time and to require the body to become an inexhaustible performative machine. For a penis to be phallic, the blood would have to be drained from it and replaced by an enduring artificial substance. It would have to become a dildo.

And yet—might I not after all feel a certain pride in my lover's perceiving my penis as phallic? Might I not after all see in the connection to symbolic meaning a compliment to the impressive power of my sexuality? I don't simply have a penis: my penis is greater than itself; it embodies an erotic force worshiped in ancient rituals; it is the representative of a cultural function that regulates laws of inheritance and exchange; it grants me access to the privileges of patriarchy; in Lacan's terms, it connects me to the very principle of signifying production.

But my initial hesitations return: If the mimetic bond between particular penis and hegemonic phallus assumes the former's erection, do I then lose my privileged cultural status when my organ becomes flaccid? If the phallus alone signifies, does the penis then have any significant role to play if it is not erect? If I embrace the immutability of the signifier as desire's mark, do I not thereby abandon the whole narrative dimension of desire, with its dialogic give-and-take, advance and retreat?

Lacan's theory encourages precisely this abandon. Desire in Lacan is a function of signifying structure; it is not instinctual; it is not driven by energetic drives and impulses. Lacan argues that desire works in the unconscious through the same signifying operations that structure everyday linguistic expression. The main difference he would see is that everyday speech relies on meanings produced through the assumed convergence of signifier and signified, whereas the unconscious forgoes this assumption and operates through the independent mobility of the signifying chain. For Lacan, the phallus, originating principle of this mobility, refers to no body. But he is wrong: the link between signifier and signified in the sign cannot be severed and produces an effect of reference that inscribes bodily experience into the psychic reality of the unconscious. The phallus's pretense to universality and transcendence thus is challenged in the unconscious by the penis's claim to historical specificity.

Most subversive of the phallus's unchanging identity is the penis's capricious variability. The penis justifies phallic apellation only at certain moments, which may actually be difficult to determine. Sexologists speak of the "quality" of an erection. Some are supposedly better than others, more impressively phallic. But who is to say when a particular penis has achieved its full erectile potential? Duration of an erection is equally uncertain. Some last longer than I may wish, others not as long as I might have hoped. My only certainty is that whatever phallic symbolism I may attribute to my penis is sure to prove illusory. The condition of phallic plenitude is subsequent deflation.

The more phallic reference is invested with symbolic meaning, the more it comes to represent, in Lacan's terms, the "all" for either a male or female subject, the more the shrinkage back to penile banality will seem like a castrating loss of patriarchal power and masculine identity. This form of castration anxiety runs rampant through psychoanalytic theory. Think of Freud's "reconstruction" of the erection the fourteen-year-old Dora (must have) felt when Herr K. embraced her. Outraged by Dora's failure to respond with grateful excitement, Freud labels her disgust a hysterical symptom. Positing the growth of a fine erection on a man he calls "still quite young and of prepossessing appearance,"[18] Freud rushes anxiously to defend the irreproachable attraction and irresistible power that he attributes to this sterling phallic appearance.

Lacan's strategy to defend the phallus against potential deflation is more sophisticated than Freud's: he links it so closely to castration that conceptually it incorporates its own loss. The phallus depends for its founding illusion on the reflection of its absence in the place of the Other. Man has it only insofar as woman lacks it, or, put otherwise, he *has* it insofar as she *is* it. Both gender positions come up short before the Law of the Symbolic, making of Lacanian theory, as Judith Butler observes, a kind of slave morality.[19] Crucial to the subjection required of this morality is that there be no imaginable outside to the Law's prescriptive domain. The phallus cannot be undone by reference to the real, because that reference can occur only within an orbit of theoretical jurisdiction that produces the real as an effect of signification. The machinery of Symbolic production absorbs the subject's exegetical attention, much as the Law in Kafka's novel demands Joseph K.'s totally concentrated devotion. In both cases, the discursive manipulation of lack is so powerful that the hermeneutical slave never asserts the authority of his or her physical embodiment to attack its castrating empire.

How can we extricate ourselves from this slavery without abandoning what is valuable in the Lacanian critique of the unified patriarchal subject? We need, I think, to recognize that Lacan's view of the subject as appropriated by language rather than expressed in it does not tell the whole story. The story that it tells, as Mikkel Borch-Jacobsen has brilliantly shown, derives from a specific historico-philosophical context of Hegelian thinking, which constructs the subject as a self-negating fiction and reduces the real, through the alienating operation of language, to nothing.[20] This is a powerful mode of thought, with enlightening connections to some of the most radical moments in Freudian theory. But its privileging of negativity as the medium of the subject's constitutive lack excludes any connection to the body and its social and cultural history. A claim such as Freud's that the ego is "first and foremost a bodily ego" and that it is "ultimately derived from bodily sensations, chiefly from those springing from the surface of the body"[21] is dismissed by Lacanians as leading to the naive holistic illusions of ego psychology.

Sensations on the body's surface do not, however, necessarily synthesize an image of totality—quite the contrary. We have noted the precarious ontology and discontinuous temporality of the penis. This contrasts with Lacan's association of the phallus with "all" and of its essentially feminine absence with "not all." Such designations, which suggest that there is only one kind of genital, derive from the kind of thinking Freud identified with the phallic phase of development *preceding* sexual maturity. This construction of the phallus's symbolic power depends, as Nietzsche says about the construction of concepts that later appear as truths, on "overlooking the individual and the real."[22] In actuality, "all" and "not all" are differential categories internal to the penis and subject to further qualification: there is no way to judge when a penis has become all it can be anymore than there is a way to determine the extent of its potential detumescence. As an object of mimetic reference, the penis is not single, whole, self-identical, unchanging. Insofar as the phallus refers to the erect penis, it refers to something whose temporality is erratic, whose appearance is sporadic, and whose duration is uncertain. The phallic referent, in short, is not phallocentric.

Now, a Lacanian might argue that the phallus theorized by Lacan is similarly decentered. For instance, Jacqueline Rose explains that, for Lacan, "the status of the phallus is a fraud. . . . The phallus can only take up its place by indicating the precariousness of any identity assumed by the subject on the basis of its token."[23] The crucial difference is this: Lacan views the inherently fraudulent phallus as constitutive of the subject's fundamental division and lack-in-being, whereas I would argue that whatever might be called fraudulent about the erect penis reveals not the subject's constitutive negativity but the collapse of the metaphysical, idealizing basis of that founding premise.

One of the means by which Lacan perpetuates this idealizing fraud is his refusal to acknowledge any contextual limitation to the phallus's signifying domain. The phallus may circulate, as it does, famously, in Lacan's reading of "The Purloined Letter," but its meaning is never determined by the context in which it finds itself. On the contrary, the context becomes readable in terms of who is provisionally in possession of the phallus. The positioning of the phallus creates the psychic choreography of the scene. But, once again, this argument ignores the phallus's reference to the erect penis, whose status depends on the provocation of an exciting context. The particular context can, of course, vary enormously, given that what excites one man may well leave the next indifferent and that what excites a man on one occasion may turn the same man off on the next. The animating context, moreover, can vary from the almost purely fantasmatic, as in the case of an erotic (wet) dream, to the purely physical, as in the case of frictional stimulation. But, whatever the stimulus, a penis always requires an inspiring conjuncture for its erection.

Metonymy, Repression, and the Feminine

Lacan's refusal to contextualize the phallus is part of his strategy to detach the unconscious from history. This strategy further requires that, in theorizing the way the unconscious is structured like a language, he distort the meaning of the trope that operates by privileging the semantic value of context, metonymy. Given its importance in denying the inscription of bodily experience into the Lacanian unconscious, this distortion warrants a short analysis.

Metonymy operates rhetorically by deleting one or more items from a commonly understood context of reference. Classic examples would be "fifty sails" for "fifty ships," taking the part for the whole; in French, *boire un verre,* to drink a glass, where the container replaces the contents; and, in the sphere of conventional symbolism, "the crown" used to designate royal power, taking the symbolic attribute for the concept. In all these cases, the trope functions by evoking a shared context of sensual and perceptual experience, whether of spatial contiguities in the world or of traditional attributions in cultural symbolism. It is precisely because of metonymy's dependence on a knowledge of the material and conventional contexts for relations such as those of cause and effect, container and contained, sign and thing signified that Roman Jakobson associates this trope with literary realism.

Although Lacan, in a few passing remarks, endorses Jakobson's link between metonymy and "the so-called realist style,"[24] his definition of metonymy actually subverts the function of contextual reference that is crucial to the rhetorical understanding of metonymic figuration. This subversion is analogous to the divorce from reference that Lacan attempts to effect in his un-gendering of the phallus. In his view, metonymy operates through the combinatory potential of contiguous signifiers in linear discourse, thereby excluding any connection to a signified. This relation of signifiers, he claims, is analogous to the mechanism of displacement in dreams and is the vehicle of desire—as we read or speak, the displacement of one word by the next points to a meaning that is always postponed and thereby generates an insatiable desire for semantic closure. The analogy is neat, but it makes nonsense of Freud's conception of displacement, which functions not to express desire but to defend against it and which does not privilege any particular type of associative connection, such as contiguity. For instance, in the *Introductory Lectures,* Freud observes:

> The allusions employed for displacement in dreams are connected with the element they replace by the most external and remote relations and are therefore unintelligible; and when they are undone, their interpretation gives the impression of being a bad joke or of an arbitrary and forced explanation dragged in by the hair of its head.[25]

This description of an arbitrary, disjunctive process has nothing to do with either the rhetorical trope of metonymy or the literary genre of realism, which aims to create an intelligible world where semantic relations are based on shared knowledge and common experience. Without acknowledging his difference from Freud, Lacan forges his own notion of displacement and then uses it to fulfill his desire to detach signification from reference: he displaces metonymy from any constraining context and then equates its function with that of displacement itself.

Some notion of reference nevertheless remains latent in Lacan's writing about metonymy, and I think Jane Gallop is precisely right to read this latency as connoting the feminine.[26] It is not metonymy as desire that is feminine—on the contrary, that Lacanian interpretation, passed over by Gallop, might be thought of as Lacan's masculine version of the trope—but metonymy as context-bound.

"This form [metonymy]," says Lacan, "which gives its field to truth in its oppression, may it not manifest some servitude inherent in its presentation?"[27] This rhetorical question suggests that, for Lacan, the insistence of the signified in metonymy expresses the figure's servitude to the "truth" of female oppression.

Relating this to Lacan's theory of the phallic signifier, it would appear that his refusal to contextualize the phallus reflects a desire to keep it free of any taint of subjection to the feminine. His language becomes quite violent as he describes the way the semiotic bar splits the signified away from the signifier. To illustrate this split, he evokes the demon of Shame in ancient mystery cults, which rises up just at the moment when the phallus is unveiled and "strikes the signified, branding it as the bastard offspring of its signifying concatenation."[28] The allusion to illegitimacy fits in with Lacan's other suggestions about slavery and oppression: in some sense, it is shameful for theory to make any biological reference, biology in whatever gender being coded as feminine. Thus, when Lacan insists that the phallus "can only play its role as veiled," this assertion brands with shame the anatomical signified, whose image he has just evoked in the previous sentence: "One might also say that by virtue of its turgidity, it [the phallus] is the image of the vital flow as it is transmitted in generation."[29] Here Lacan takes the risk of conjuring up an image of the real erect penis, swollen with blood and sperm, but then he immediately veils its gross crudity, consigning this vital signified to "the latency with which everything signifiable is struck as soon as it is raised [*aufgehoben*] to the function of signifier."[30]

Associating this latency with the feminine, Gallop credits Lacan with having theorized "a metonymic, maternal, feminine phallus."[31] But this is, I think, to give credit where none is due. The latent phallus exists for Lacan precisely insofar as it is struck with shame and branded as illegitimate. Thus marked, it cannot be *aufgehoben* into the universal sphere of the signifier, where any referential bond to the penis is strategically veiled. Barred from transcendence, it must remain behind in the shameful world of the signified. But here no referential context exists for a metonymic, feminine phallus. The attribution to woman of an unveiled phallus—that is, of an erect penis—can produce only a monster, not a symbolically phallic woman, but a biological woman who is also a man. Lacan uses his notion of latency to hide what I take to be his vision of a monstrous physical world that is latently feminine in much the same way as the phallic signifier is latently masculine.

Indeed, it would probably not be an exaggeration to say, as Malcolm Bowie suggests in his excellent critical introduction to Lacan, that the Lacanian signified can be understood as the repressed.[32] Lacan did not develop this interpretation, Bowie supposes, because it would have introduced "vagueness and pathos"[33] into the cohesive autonomy of the systematic structures he privileges, such as metonymy. I would go a step further and say that Lacan's distortion of the rhetorical meaning of metonymy, which detaches its function from any reference to a signified, serves to repress his associations of the signified with feminine vagueness, pathos, disorder, and monstrosity. Thus, Lacan designates the phallus to signify desire's structure, whereas he relegates the penis to the debased realm of female biological needs and domestic contexts. Significantly, when he does admit that certain fixed meanings may after all be necessary for a subject to maintain sanity, the image Lacan uses to describe these convergences of signifier and signified derives from the domestic interior, *points de capiton*, upholstery buttons. His implication is that a "strong" subject, that is, one who accepts his—I use the pronoun advisedly—conditioning by the impersonal structures of language, will need few anchoring buttons yet not become psychotic. This daring proximity to psychosis characterizes the phallic subject, which is penisless, empty, "without subject-matter,"[34] dead to the world.

Metaphor, Desire, and Fatherhood

Thinking the Lacanian subject through metaphor rather than metonymy does nothing to breathe life into it. Lacan defines metaphor as the process of substituting one signifier for another and identifies the law of that process with the Name-of-the-Father. He voids that name of physical reference in precisely the same way that he detaches the phallus from its penile embodiment. Indeed, it is only Lacan's pretense that the phallus is genderless that obscures its identification with the paternal metaphor. The father is granted metaphorical status in Lacanian theory through the denial of his bodily life, just as the phallus is granted universal signification through the denial of its reference to the anatomical penis. That the conceptual identity of the terms *phallus* and *Name-of-the-Father* has gone unobserved, even by a critic as sensitive to Lacan's phallocentrism as Malcolm Bowie, attests to the power of the psychoanalyst's structural logic to obfuscate his political agenda.

Once the phallus is connected to its penile referent, it becomes evident that the phallus attains its privileged status as signifier only through the authority of paternal law. That law is metaphoric for Lacan because its operative principle, like that of the phallus, is substitution: fatherhood is a condition that passes from man to man, with no individual father ever being able to stop the movement of the signifying chain. The father is generated as metaphor on the basis of his death in the flesh. His place is then revealed to exist in name only, as the agency of the law that, by restricting desire's primary goals, sets in motion the process of substitutive (dis)satisfactions.

Lacan metaphorizes the father for the same reason that he veils the phallus: he derives prestige as a theoretician largely from his identification of/with an authority that cannot be confronted. Its power, like that of Kafka's Castle, is a function of the Symbolic order, where, says Lacan, "nothing exists except on an assumed foundation of absence. Nothing exists except insofar as it does not exist."[35]

This comprehensive claim sweeps everything into the dustbin of negation. Whereas Freud speaks of the death *instinct,* which links death to the living organism as a source of bodily stimuli, Lacan inscribes death into language as the principle of the signifier's mobility. This mobility, though it appears to have the forward thrust of desire, is so much an effect of synchronic structure that it effaces the historical dimension of lived experience.

As to the category of the Real in Lacanian theory, it is anything but realistic. Indeed, it refers to what is outside the symbolizing process, to what cannot be integrated into psychic reality, whether this be a material object or a mental trauma. Whereas in Freud the exigencies of reality require certain adaptive strategies on the part of the psyche, in Lacan the Real is precisely what cannot be the object of any adaptive conciliation—an obdurate, alien force that resists any signifying appropriation. Interesting as this interpretation may be for the understanding of psychosis (in which hallucinations attack the subject with the traumatizing force of the Real), it reinforces the radical split in Lacanian theory between symbolic processes and the material world. My argument, in contrast, is that the concept of the Symbolic can and should accommodate a less defensive attitude toward the Real—especially as the latter is manifested in the bodily experience of sexuality. This experience, far from being outside signification, is referentially inscribed in the tropological structure of the unconscious.

Focusing on male sexuality, I have argued that its dependence on a stimulating context for sexual arousal can be read as a metonymic imperative. A process that could be considered metaphoric takes over when a man's desire to maintain an erection gives way to an urge to intensify pleasure to the point of orgasm. In the drive toward climax, a similarity of aim is projected onto all aspects of physical and psychic experience. Another way of putting this would be to use the term *condensation,* not as Lacan does, to refer to the substitution of signifiers, but more in Freud's spirit, to describe the way energies dispersed among different associative chains become concentrated on one idea that stands at their point of intersection. As my desire for orgasm intensifies, erotic energies previously diffused over the surface of my body become concentrated in my erect penis. My awareness of the variety of stimulations available from the context diminishes. My fantasies become less mobile, more focused on a single scenario. Formulating this process abstractly, I could say that my desire tends to equalize differences in order to arrive at an intense sensation of sameness.

What is metaphoric about this process can be explained by a playful appropriation of Jakobson's famous definition of the poetic function, the superimposition of similarity upon contiguity. Poetic effects are created, Jakobson claims, by the projection of similarities in the purely sensuous, material qualities of words from the vertical axis of metaphorical identifications and equivalences onto the horizontal axis of metonymic combination and sequence. In this process, semantic differences are reduced and reference becomes ambiguous. A sense of pervasive similarity overtakes an awareness of contiguous distinctions. In Jakobson's phrase, "Anything sequent is a simile,"[36] which is his translation into technical language of Goethe's "Alles Vergängliche ist nur ein Gleichnis

[Anything transient is but a likeness]." The movement here is the contrary of that by which Lacan imagines the phallus exercising its "function of equivalence in the emergence of all objects of desire."[37] Whereas Lacan's phallus absorbs all meanings into itself, dissolving their differences by the machinery of structure, Jakobson's model projects equivalences among signifiers onto a sequence of contiguous signifieds. The signifieds are not thereby repressed, as in Lacan, but are made "symbolic, multiple, polysemantic."[38] In Freudian terms, this compression of meaning is an effect of condensation. In terms of male sexual experience, it is a result of the signifiers of desire becoming focused on the penis as an active agent of orgasmic fulfillment.

Now, seminal discharge may, under certain propitious conditions, determine fatherhood. But the name of the father is the secret of the mother. Far from being a symbol of phallic privilege, as Lacan would have it, the paternal name is a potential source of male anxiety. At issue is not the substitutability of signifiers, but the substitutability of penises. The fear that fatherhood could be nothing more than metaphorical, an arbitrary identification, an empty speech act, is ubiquitous in the male imagination. Thus understood and affectively weighted, metaphor is indeed a function of secrecy and absence. But the familial scenario also demonstrates that the ground of metaphor is not negation and that the slippage of signifiers is not unending: the laws of female biology and genetic inheritance can ultimately reveal the truth of paternity. Similarly, the laws of male physiology prove that the penis's metaphorical performance has its ground in bodily presence. The penis loses its erection after orgasm, but detumescence is not castration. There is no absolute loss, no permanent lack. The return to flaccidity forms the familiar, realistic basis for the organ's expression in both its metonymic and its metaphoric modes.

My discussion in this essay of the behavior of the male sexual organ may appear to be essentializing and reductive because of its anatomical specificity. But my point, to reiterate, is that the body, whether male or female, is as undecidable and shifting as any semiotic construction. I am championing penile reference not to give theory an anchor in physiology but to show how the body's uncertainties challenge the truth value assigned by Lacan and others to transcendent structures and systems. The penile signified reveals the phallic signifier to be the theoretical projection of a dream of perpetual erection and symbolic potency. The phallus is maleness elevated to the level of universality at the expense of the body's castration. That body is both male and female, for the phallus's erection in theory at once denies men their genital experience and identifies women constitutionally with deficiency and mutilation. Granted, men may feel compensated for their loss by the promotion of their organ to the status of arch signifier, and women may feel compensated for their supposed lack by its earning them the position of Truth. But neither mode of compensation is worth the body's strangulation by the signifying chain and the consequent elimination of such material factors as history, race, and power from the theorization of subjectivities.

NOTES

A number of friends gave me helpful feedback on the first version of this article. I want especially to thank Jane Gallop, who, at a memorable lunch at the Hanover Inn, convinced me of a fundamental problem in my conceptual formulation. I also owe a debt of gratitude to Susan Suleiman, Jeff Kline, Humphrey Morris, and Betty Louise Bell, all of whom helped me at various stages to clarify my ideas. A somewhat different version of this essay appeared as "Penile Reference in Phallic Theory," *differences* 4 (Spring 1992): 116–32.

1 . Sigmund Freud, "Formulations on the Two Principles of Mental Functioning" (1911), in *The Standard Edition of the Complete Psychological Works of Sigmund Freud,* trans. and ed. James Strachey (London: Hogarth, 1953–74), 12:225. Hereafter, references to the *Standard Edition* are abbreviated SE.

2. Freud, "On the History of the Pschoanalytic Movement" (1914), in SE 14:17.

3. Jeffrey M. Masson, *The Assault on Truth: Freud's Suppression of the Seduction Theory* (New York: HarperCollins, 1992).

4. Freud, "An Autobiographical Study" (1925), in SE 20:34.

5. Freud, *The Interpretation of Dreams* (1900), in SE 5:620.

6. Freud, *Leonardo da Vinci and a Memory of His Childhood* (1910), in SE 11:95.

7. Freud, *Analysis of a Phobia in a Five-Year-Old Boy* (1909), in SE 10:11.

8. Freud, "Female Sexuality," in SE 21:229.

9. Freud, "Some Psychical Consequences of the Anatomical Distinction between the Sexes," in SE 19:253.

10. Ibid., 256.

11. For a more detailed critique of Freud's account of the genesis of sexual difference in fantasy, see Charles Bernheimer, " 'Castration' as Fetish," *Paragraph* 14 (1991): 1–9.

12. Jacques Lacan, "The Meaning of the Phallus," in *Feminine Sexuality: Jacques Lacan and the Ecole Freudienne,* ed. and trans. Juliet Mitchell and Jacqueline Rose (New York: W.W. Norton, 1985), 80. Translation modified.

13. Jacqueline Rose, "Introduction," in *Feminine Sexuality: Jacques Lacan and the*

Ecole Freudienne, ed. Juliet Mitchell and Jacqueline Rose (New York: W.W. Norton, 1985), 40.

14. See Jane Gallop, "Phallus/Penis: Same Difference," in *Thinking through the Body* (New York: Columbia University Press, 1988); Mary Ann Doane, "Women's Stake: Filming the Female Body," *October* 17 (1981): 23–36; Diana Fuss, *Essentially Speaking: Feminism, Nature, and Difference* (New York: Routledge, 1989).

15. Lacan, "The Meaning of the Phallus," 76.

16. Luce Irigaray, *This Sex Which Is Not One,* trans. Catherine Porter with Carolyn Burke (Ithaca, N.Y.: Cornell University Press, 1985), 26.

17. See Jacques Derrida, "The Purveyor of Truth," *Yale French Studies* 52 (1975): 31–113.

18. Freud, *Fragment of an Analysis of a Case of Hysteria* ("Dora") (1905), in SE 7:29.

19. See Judith Butler, *Gender Trouble: Feminism and the Subversion of Identity* (New York: Routledge, 1990), 57.

20. See Mikkel Borch-Jakobsen, *Lacan: The Absolute Master* (Stanford: Stanford University Press, 1991).

21. Freud, *The Ego and the Id* (1923), in SE 19:26.

22. Friedrich Nietzsche, "On Truth and Lie in an Extra-Moral Sense," in *Friedrich Nietzsche on Rhetoric and Language,* ed. Sander Gilman, Carole Blair, and David Parent (New York: Oxford University Press, 1989), 249.

23. Rose, "Introduction," 40.

24. Jacques Lacan, *Le Séminaire de Jacques Lacan, livre III: Les Psychoses* (Paris: Seuil, 1981), 266 (my translation).

25. Freud, *Introductory Lectures on Psycho-Analysis* (1917), in SE 15:174.

26. See Jane Gallop, *Reading Lacan* (Ithaca, N.Y.: Cornell University Press, 1985), 125–32.

27. Lacan, *Ecrits: A Selection* (New York: W.W. Norton, 1977), 158.

28. Lacan, "The Meaning of the Phallus," 82.

29. Ibid.

30. Ibid.

31. Gallop, *Reading Lacan,* 131.

32. See Malcolm Bowie, *Lacan* (Cambridge: Harvard University Press, 1991).

33. Ibid., 73.

34. Ibid., 76.

35. Quoted in ibid., 92–93.

36. Roman Jakobson, "Linguistics and Poetics," in *Selected Writings,* vol. 3 (The Hague: Mouton, 1981), 42.

37. Lacan, "The Meaning of the Phallus," 91.

38. Jakobson, "Linguistics and Poetics," 42.

Courbet's *L'Origine du monde*: The Origin without an Original

Linda Nochlin

Nothing could be more Freudian than the scenario I am about to rehearse in this narrative, for it concerns the endlessly repetitive quest for a lost original, an original that is itself, in both the literal and figurative senses of the word, an origin. I am referring to Courbet's painting, *The Origin of the World,* a work that is known to us only as a series of repeated descriptions or reproductions— an *Origin,* then, without an original.[1] But I shall also be discussing notions of origination and originality as they inform the discipline of art history itself: the founding notion that through the logic of research—that is, the repetitive act of searching over and over again—one can finally penetrate to the ultimate meaning of a work of art. In the case of Courbet's *Origin,* this ultimate-meaning-to-be-penetrated might be considered the "reality" of woman herself, the truth of the ultimate Other. The subject represented in *The Origin* is the female sex organ—the cunt— forbidden site of specularity and ultimate object of male desire; repressed or displaced in the classical scene of castration anxiety, it has also been constructed as the very source of artistic creation itself.

Hot on the Trail

The first part of my scenario has to do with a failure: the failure to locate the original of Courbet's *Origin of the World* for a forthcoming exhibition of the artist's work. I had gone about my art-historical business in the usual way: tracing the work back to its origin in the Courbet literature, and then, working forward, attempting to discover its present location—to no avail. Not only was the original *Origin* impossible to find, but the clues to its location seemed to be perversely, almost deliberately, misleading, fraught with errors in fact. Nor did the errors seem to be entirely fortuitous. Rumors that *The Origin,* now veiled behind a canvas by André Masson, was actually in the collection of Sylvie Bataille Lacan—former wife of both Georges Bataille and Jacques Lacan—seemed almost too good to be true, even when they were confirmed by a French expert who claimed to have seen *The Origin* in Mme Lacan's apartment. This hot lead, sending my colleague and myself to a sure address in the sixth arrondissement, left us standing frustrated in the lobby.

On a subsequent trip, another French expert, the head of the Societé des Amis de Gustave Courbet, assured us that the work was not in France at all, but in the United States, in a collection on the West Coast the name of which he had forgotten—perhaps the Norton Simon Collection, perhaps not. My heart leaped when I discovered a photograph of the work accompanying Neil Hertz's provocative article, "Medusa's Head: Male Hysteria under Political Pressure,"[2] credited to the Boston Museum of Fine Arts—certainly the most unlikely possible location, one would imagine, for a work that might be thought of as prototypically "banned in Boston"! A call to the curator of the Boston Museum confirmed my doubts. After helpfully going through all the files of the museum, including those of the visiting exhibitions, he assured me that there was no record of *The Origin* in Boston.

A call to Neil Hertz revealed that the attribution to the Boston Museum had been a printer's error—an error more recently repeated by Denis Hollier in *his* provocative article, "How to Not Take Pleasure in Talking about Sex"[3]—perhaps Boston is the literary critic's preferred mislocation of *The Origin?* Hertz told me that he had really meant to credit the *Budapest*—not the *Boston*—Museum of Fine Arts. Yet the hope that *The Origin* might be in Budapest was dashed by further research. Peter Webb, in his discussion of Courbet's work in his 1975 publication, *The Erotic Arts,* states that this painting, which had been reproduced in hand-tinted full color in Gerald Zwang's *Le Sexe de la femme*[4]—a limited edition, luxe, pseudoscientific, soft-porn production—with the provenance "Museum of Fine Arts, Budapest, formerly collection of Professor Hatvany," was not in fact in the Budapest Museum anymore than it had been in the Boston one. Says Webb, "In a communication to the author dated 4 February, 1972, the Director of the Museum of Fine Arts at Budapest (Dr. Klara Garas) wrote, 'Courbet's painting has never been in our museum; it was in a private collection in Budapest and disappeared during the war.'" Webb continues, "During a visit to Budapest in October 1972, the author learned that the painting had been stolen by the Germans during the war and had then been appropriated by the Russians. Professor Hatvany had bought it back and later taken it to Switzerland. Wayland Young, in *Eros Denied,*[5] reports a rumor that the painting was sold in America in 1958." At this point, Webb simply throws up his hands in despair: "This painting has rarely been seen or even heard of, and judgement of its quality is difficult from the blurred photograph that remains." He concludes rather lamely, "This painting was last heard of in Budapest in 1945"[6]—which leaves us more or less where we began, although, to be sure, Robert Fernier, in his catalogue raisonné of Courbet's work, asserts, without further substantiation, that *The Origin* returned to Paris after the war, where it was sold to an unspecified "amateur" in 1955.[7]

More secure, in terms of the art-historical quest for the original *Origin,* is the reference to the Hatvany Collection. In his 1948 publication *Courbet et son temps,* Charles Léger, one of the major Courbet scholars of the earlier twentieth century, states that the work was bought in about 1910 by the Baron Francis Hatvany of Budapest.[8] Baron Hatvany had seen the painting at the Bernheim-Jeune Gallery in a double-locked frame, hidden by a panel representing, Léger asserts, not a "church in the snow" as Edmond de Goncourt had described in his diary in 1889, but rather a "castle in the snow." Even the supplementary details relating to *The Origin,* it must be reemphasized, tend to be fraught with error. One might almost say that no statement can be made about it—including my own—that does not contain some deviation from empirical factuality, much less from "truth" in a larger sense. Léger continues, "M. de Hatvany, with whom I was formerly in correspondence, for he owned *The Wrestlers* of Courbet [a work now in the Budapest

Museum], naturally spoke to me about this *Origin of the World,* acquired at Bernheim-Jeune, with the frame, while the little panel hiding the canvas, the *Castle in the Snow,* became the property of Baron Herzog, of Budapest."[9]

Goncourt and Gambetta

Working ever backward in our search for the original *Origin,* we come upon a sighting in June 1889, recorded in the pages of Edmond de Goncourt's journal. Goncourt writes that a picture dealer had shown him a painting of a woman's *bas-ventre* that made him want to make "honorable amends to Courbet." That belly, declared Goncourt, "was as beautiful as the flesh of a Correggio."[10] Also dating from the 1880s—May 27, 1881, to be precise—is Ludovic Halévy's account of Gambetta's spirited recollection of the work, which the latter had encountered, many years earlier, in the company of Courbet, at the home of its owner, the notorious art collector and Turkish ambassador to St. Petersburg, Kahlil Bey.[11] Here is Gambetta's rather scrappy reminiscence, as recorded by Halévy in his memoirs: "*L'Origine du monde.* A nude woman, without feet and without a head. After dinner, there we were, looking . . . admiring. . . . We finally ran out of enthusiastic comments. . . . This lasted for ten minutes. Courbet never had enough of it."[12] Still earlier, we have the notorious "hysterical" description of the work by Maxime du Camp in his four-volume denunciation of the Paris Commune, *Les Convulsions de Paris,* written ten years after the fact:

> To please a Moslem who paid for his whims in gold, and who, for a time, enjoyed a certain notoriety in Paris because of his prodigalities, Courbet . . . painted a portrait of a woman that is difficult to describe. In the dressing room of this foreign personage one sees a small picture hidden under a green veil. When one draws aside the veil one remains stupefied to perceive a woman, life-size, seen from the front, moved and convulsed, remarkably executed, reproduced *con amore,* as the Italians say, providing the last word in realism. But, by some inconceivable forgetfulness, the artist, who copied his model from nature, had neglected to represent the feet, the legs, the thighs, the stomach, the hips, the chest, the hands, the arms, the shoulders, the neck, and the head.[13]

The search, then, ends fruitlessly, in the dressing room of an Oriental bon vivant, or rather in a textual allusion to Khalil Bey, who commissioned the work from Courbet in 1866. Ultimately we find the origin of *The Origin* in the desire of its possessor, the exotic collector of erotica, Khalil Bey, but it is still an origin without an original: we have come no further in our search for the lost painting itself. In this almost parodic—because failed—rehearsal of a familiar art-historical scenario, which has turned into a kind of allegory of the scholar's enterprise itself, I wish to emphasize the repetitiveness at stake here, within the context of a discussion focused on originality and repetition. Each new find simply repeats, as though original, a new set of false clues. Each so-called discovery simply mimes the "truth" it supplants without bringing the quest any nearer to completion. One might go further and say that art-historical practice is itself premised on the notion of originality as repetition, an endless rehearsal of the facts that never gets us any closer to the supposed "truth" of the object in question.

Yet the presumed origin of *The Origin* in masculine desire leads to still another scenario of orgination, that of the origin of art itself. In an article titled "The Origins of Art," Desmond Collins and John Onians attempt to "trace back" historically the origin of art to the engraving of crude but recognizable vulvas on the walls of caves in Southern France during the Aurignacian period, about 33,000 to 28,000 B.C.[14] According to this scenario, masculine desire literally led lusting but frustrated Aurignacian males to represent in stone the desired, absent, object—the female sex organ—and thereby to create the very first artwork. In the light of this assumption, all other artworks ought to be considered simulacra of this originating male act, and representation must itself be considered a mere simulacrum of that desired original. What a perfect example such art-historical scholarship offers of the assumption that "everything has to begin somewhere."[15] What a perfect disregard of the "always already" is demonstrated by such an enterprise!

Courbet's *Studio*

It is equally clear that Courbet shared in this myth of the originating force of the artist's desire. To construct still another scenario implicated in the quest for *The Origin* without an original, one must turn to *The Artist's Studio,* a work in which Courbet clearly and literally turns his back on the social and political contextualization that had marked his earlier achievements—*The Stonebreakers* or *The Burial at Ornans.* The central portion of *The Artist's Studio* constitutes Courbet's most complex and profound meditation on art as an originating act and the position of the artist in relation to that act of origination.

In *The Artist's Studio,* Courbet positions himself at the very heart of what must be read as the oedipal triangle, classic site of origins, a configuration constituted by the female model (the mother), the little boy spectator (the son), and the dominating figure of the painter (the father). In a single, powerfully determined image, Courbet has locked into place patriarchal authority and pictorial originality as the inseparable foundations of Western art—great or ambitious art, needless to say.[16] Turning away from the nude model and her forbidden sexuality, the patriarch-painter is absorbed in his act of progeneration, the supremely originating thrust of brush to canvas. And what he is represented as creating in the painting-within-a-painting is not an image of the nude model, who functions unthreateningly as a kind of motherly muse behind his back, but rather a landscape. The reading of landscape as a manifestation of the psychoanalytic process of displacement in Courbet's oeuvre becomes even clearer if we consider a work like *The Source of the Loue*—itself the representation of an origin, or source—whose morphological relationship to *The Origin of the World* has often been asserted in the Courbet literature. Nor is it any accident, to continue this Freudian scenario, that, at the crucial heart of a crucial painting, Courbet-as-patriarch is represented as inscribing sheer matter—the actual pigment on the palette—as the origin of his creation. Not only is the pigment emphasized by its denseness, thickness, and brightness; not only is it unequivocally centralized; but also, by calling attention to the shape of the canvas-within-the-canvas, as well as the shape of the *actual* support of the painting, the rectangular palette that supports the pigment focuses our attention on the manipulation of matter, the application of paint to canvas, as the originating act of the artist. It is this that makes his work authoritatively original. Here, the strict Freudian, or the reductivist one, might say that the patriarch/originator becomes identical to the child who plays with his feces.

This leads us to the final scenario: that of the quest for originality in Courbet's *Origin*. In the absence of the painted materiality of the original, that incontrovertible evidence of the father-generator's presence constituted by Courbet's unique mode of applying his *matière* to the canvas; in the absence, in short, of all identifying signs of the artist's imperious originality in the available images of his work, there is really no satisfactory way of differentiating Courbet's painting from a thousand ordinary beaver shots available at your local newsstand. In its blurry reproduced repetitions, most of which seem to have been printed on bread, *The Origin* is literally indistinguishable from standard, mass-produced pornography—indeed, it is identical with it.

The Signs of Origin

Critics have, understandably, attempted to read the signs of originality back into these inadequate reproductions of Courbet's *Origin of the World*: it is a practice in which almost all of us who work with reproductions must inevitably engage. Here is Neil Hertz, in an otherwise exemplary article, having a try at establishing the authoritative originality of *The Origin*:

> The darkness of the paint combines with the pull of the erotic fascination to draw the eye to that central patch, but this centripetal movement is impeded, if not entirely checked, by the substantiality of the figure's thighs and torso, by details like the almost-covered breast . . . and by what I take to be (judging from black and white reproductions) Courbet's characteristic care in representing the surfaces of his model's body—the care, at once painterly and mimetic, that can be observed in his rendering of the rocks surrounding the cave of the Loue. *The Origin of the World* . . . explores a powerfully invested set of differences—the difference between painting and flesh, between a male artist and his female model, between sexual desire and the will to representation.[17]

Surely, the last two sets of differences fail to distinguish Courbet's *Origin* from any other representation of the female nude, in whole or in part; and in the absence of the original, the first set of differences is unsubstantiated by the visual evidence. This passage simply indicates the degree to which eyes have been strained and discourse put under pressure in the vain attempt to find traces of the patriarchal caca, the spore of genius, in an unprepossessing black-and-white, infinitely repeatable, reproduction.

But it is this infinite repeatability, ironically enough, that characterizes the very *subject* of Courbet's *Origin*: a metonymy that, in Lacanian terms, poses the question of lack and desire. Desire itself, according to Lacan, is a metonymy, for metonymy expresses itself "as eternally stretching forth towards desire for something else."[18] Courbet's *Origin of the World,* then, finally reenacts the infinite repetitiveness of desire, the impossible quest for the lost original. Or, to return to our original Freudian scenario, one might say that in the case of Courbet's *Origin of the World,* as in that of the founding myth of Oedipus, the search for lost origins leads ultimately to blindness.

Postscript

The Origin of the World came to light shortly after the publication of an earlier version of this chapter in 1986. It appeared in the exhibition "Courbet Reconsidered," and is reproduced as no. 66 in the catalog of that exhibition. For a fuller consideration of *The Origin* and its relation to Masson's painting, see the catalog of the exhibition organized by Jean-Jacques Fernier: Ornans, Musée Natale Gustave Courbet; "Les Yeux les plus secrets" Gustave Courbet "La Naissance du monde" 1866; André Masson, 56 Dessins Erotiques de 1921 à 1970: Le Romain de Mathilde, Correspondance avec Courbet 1873, exhibition catalog 1991.

NOTES

1. For a reproduction of this work, see Sarah France and Linda Nochlin, *Courbet Reconsidered* (exhibition catalog 66) (New York: Brooklyn Museum, 1988), 178.

2. Neil Hertz, "Medusa's Head: Male Hysteria under Political Pressure," *Representations* 4 (Fall 1983): 27–54; with responses by Catherine Gallagher and Joel Fineman and a reply by Hertz, 55–72.

3. Denis Hollier, "How to Not Take Pleasure in Talking about Sex," *Enclitic* 8 (Spring/Fall 1984): 84–93.

4. Gerald Zwang, *Le Sexe de la femme* (Paris: La jeune Parque, 1967).

5. Wayland Young, *Eros Denied* (London: Corgi, 1968), 96.

6. Peter Webb, *The Erotic Arts* (London: Secker & Warburg, 1975), 166, 451–52 n. 67.

7. Robert Fernier, *La Vie et l'oeuvre de Gustave Courbet* (Lausanne: Bibliothèque des arts, 1977–78), 2:6 n. 530.

8. Charles Léger, *Courbet et son temps* (Paris: Editions universelles, 1948). Léger does not reproduce the work; I have not been able to find any reproductions of the *Origin* dating before the 1960s.

9. Ibid., 116. Unless otherwise noted, all translations are my own.

10. Edmond de Goncourt and Jules de Goncourt, *Journal: mémoires de la vie littéraire* (Paris: Fasquelle, Flammarion, 1956), 3:996.

11. For information about Kahlil Bey, see Francis Haskell, "A Turk and His Pictures in Nineteenth-Century Paris," *Oxford Art Journal* 5, no. 1 (1982): 40–47.

12. Ludovic Halévy, *Trois dîners avec Gambetta,* ed. Daniel Halévy (Paris: Grasset, 1929), 86–87.

13. Maxime du Camp, *Les Convulsions de Paris,* 7th ed. (Paris: Hachette, 1889), 2:189–90.

14. Desmond Collins and John Onians, "The Origins of Art," *Art History* 1 (March 1978): 1–25.

15. Rosalind Krauss, "Originality as Repetition: Introduction," *October* 37 (Summer 1986): 36.

16. This is of course neither the first nor the last time a major artist will resort to such a gesture; both Michelangelo in his *Creation* and David in *The Oath of the Horatii* offer memorable analogues.

17. Hertz, "Medusa's Head," 69.

18. Jacques Lacan, "The Insistence of the Letter in the Unconscious," in F. DeGeorge and R. DeGeorge, *The Structuralists: From Marx to Lévi-Strauss* (Garden City, N.Y.: Doubleday, 1972), 313; see also Holly Wallace Boucher, "Metonymy in Typology and Allegory, with a Consideration of Dante's *Comedy,*" in *Allegory, Myth, and Symbol,* ed. N. M. Bloomfield (Cambridge: Harvard University Press, 1981), 141.

Select Critical Bibliography

Alliston, April. *Virtue's Faults; or, Women's Correspondences in Eighteenth-Century Fiction*. Stanford, Calif.: Stanford University Press, forthcoming.

Alloula, Malek. *The Colonial Harem*, trans. Myrna Godzich and Wlad Godzich. Minneapolis: University of Minnesota Press, 1986.

Armstrong, Judith. *The Novel of Adultery*. London: Macmillan, 1976.

Armstrong, Nancy. *Desire and Domestic Fiction: A Political History of the Novel*. New York: Oxford University Press, 1987.

Baguley, David. *Naturalist Fiction: The Entropic Vision*. Cambridge: Cambridge University Press, 1990.

Barrows, Susanna. *Distorting Mirrors: Visions of the Crowd in Late 19th Century France*. New Haven, Conn.: Yale University Press, 1981.

Barthes, Roland. *S/Z*, trans. Richard Miller. New York: Farrar, Straus & Giroux, 1974.

Baudrillard, Jean. *Simulations*, trans. Paul Foss et al. New York: Semiotext(e), 1983.

Benjamin, Walter. *Charles Baudelaire*, trans. Harry Zohn. New York: Verso, 1989.
————. *Das Passagenwerk*, 2 vols. Frankfurt: Suhrkamp, 1983.
————. "Paris, Capital of the Nineteenth Century." In *Reflections*, trans. Edmund Jephcott. New York: Harcourt Brace Jovanovich, 1978.

Berger, John. *About Looking*. New York: Pantheon, 1980.

Bernheimer, Charles. *Figures of Ill-Repute: Representing Prostitution in Nineteenth-Century France*. Cambridge: Harvard University Press, 1989.

Bersani, Leo. *A Future for Astyanax*. Boston: Little, Brown, 1976.

Bhabha, Homi. "Of Mimicry and Man: The Ambivalence of Colonial Discourse." In *October: The First Decade, 1976–1986*, ed. Annette Michelson, Rosalind Krauss, Douglas Crimp, Joan Copjec. Cambridge: MIT Press, 1987.

Bowlby, Rachel. *Just Looking: Consumer Culture in Dreiser, Gissing, and Zola*. New York: Methuen, 1985.

Boyle, Nicholas, and Martin Swales. *Realism in European Literature*. Cambridge: Cambridge University Press, 1986.

Brooks, Peter. *Reading for the Plot*. New York: Knopf, 1984.

349

Butler, Judith. *Gender Trouble: Feminism and the Subversion of Identity*. New York: Routledge, 1990.

Certeau, Michel de. *L'Invention du quotidien, I: Arts de faire*. Paris: Gallimard, 1980.

Chambers, Ross. *Story and Situation: Narrative Seduction and the Power of Fiction*. Minneapolis: University of Minnesota Press, 1984.

Clark, T. J. *The Painting of Modern Life*. Princeton, N.J.: Princeton University Press, 1984.

Darnton, Robert. *The Great Cat Massacre and Other Episodes in French Cultural History*. New York: Vintage, 1985.

Doane, Mary Ann. "Women's Stake: Filming the Female Body." *October* 17 (1981): 23–36.

Freud, Sigmund. *The Standard Edition of the Complete Psychological Works of Sigmund Freud*, 24 vols., trans. and ed. James Strachey. London: Hogarth, 1953–74.

Furet, François. *L'Atelier de l'histoire*. Paris: Flammarion, 1982.

Fuss, Diana. *Essentially Speaking: Feminism, Nature, and Difference*. New York: Routledge, 1989.

Gaillard, Françoise. "Histoire de peur." *Littérature* 64 (December 1986).

Gallop, Jane. *Thinking through the Body*. New York: Columbia University Press, 1988.

Garb, Tamar. "The Forbidden Gaze." *Art in America* 79, no. 5.

Gellner, Ernest. *Spectacles and Predicaments: Essays in Social Theory*. Cambridge: Cambridge University Press, 1991.

Gilman, Sander. *Sexuality: An Illustrated History*. New York: John Wiley, 1991.

Ginzburg, Carlo. *Myths, Emblems, Clues*, trans. John Tedeschi and Anne C. Tedeschi. London: Hutchinson Radius, 1990.

Girard, René. *Mensonge romantique et vérité romanesque*. Paris: Livre de poche, 1961.

Gombrich, Ernst H. *The Sense of Order: A Study in the Psychology of Decorative Art*. New York: Columbia University Press, 1979.

Grossberg, Lawrence, Cary Nelson, and Paula A. Treichler, eds. *Cultural Studies*. New York: Routledge, 1992.

Hampton, Timothy. *Writing from History: The Rhetoric of Exemplarity in Renaissance Literature*. Ithaca, N.Y.: Cornell University Press, 1990.

Hertz, Neil. *The End of the Line*. New York: Columbia University Press, 1985.

Higonnet, Anne. "Secluded Vision." In *The Expanding Discourse*, ed. Norma Broude and Mary D. Garrard. New York: HarperCollins, 1992.

Hunt, Lynn, ed. *The New Cultural History*. Berkeley: University of California Press, 1989.

Hunter, J. Paul. *Before Novels: The Cultural Contexts of Eighteenth-Century English Fiction*. New York: W. W. Norton, 1990.

Hollier, Denis. "How to Not Take Pleasure in Talking about Sex." *Enclitic 8* (Spring/Fall 1984).

Irigaray, Luce. *This Sex Which Is Not One*, trans. Catherine Porter with Carolyn Burke. Ithaca, N.Y.: Cornell University Press, 1985.

Jameson, Fredric. "Magical Narratives: Romance as Genre." *New Literary History* 1 (Autumn 1975).

———. *Signatures of the Visible*. New York: Routledge, 1990.

Johnson, Barbara. *The Critical Difference: Essays in the Contemporary Rhetoric of Reading*. Baltimore: Johns Hopkins University Press, 1985.

Kaplan, Amy. *The Social Construction of American Realism*. Chicago: University of Chicago Press, 1988.

Keller, Evelyn Fox. *Reflections on Gender and Science*. New Haven, Conn.: Yale University Press, 1992.

Kelly, Dorothy. *Fictional Genders: Role and Representation in Nineteenth-Century French Narrative*. Lincoln: University of Nebraska Press, 1989.

————. *Telling Glances: Voyeurism in the French Novel*. New Brunswick, N.J.: Rutgers University Press, 1992.

Knight, Chris. *Blood Relations*. New Haven, Conn.: Yale University Press, 1991.

Lacan, Jacques. *Ecrits: A Selection,* trans. Alan Sheridan. New York: W. W. Norton, 1977.

————. *Feminine Sexuality: Jacques Lacan and the Ecole Freudienne,* ed. and trans. Juliet Mitchell and Jacqueline Rose. New York: W. W. Norton, 1985.

————. *The Four Fundamental Concepts of Psychoanalysis,* trans. Alan Sheridan, ed. Jacques-Alain Miller. New York: W. W. Norton, 1978.

Laqueur, Thomas. *Making Sex*. Cambridge: Harvard University Press, 1990.

Levin, Harry. *The Gates of Horn*. New York: Oxford University Press, 1963.

Lowe, Lisa. *Critical Terrains: French and British Orientalisms*. Ithaca, N.Y.: Cornell University Press, 1991.

Lukács, Georg. *Studies in European Realism,* trans. Edith Bone. New York: Grossett & Dunlap, 1964.

Marin, Louis. *Utopiques: jeux d'espaces*. Paris: Editions Minuit, 1973.

Matlock, Jann. *Scenes of Seduction: Prostitution, Hysteria, and Reading Difference in Nineteenth-Century France*. New York: Columbia University Press, 1993.

McKeon, Michael. *The Origins of the English Novel, 1600–1750*. Baltimore: Johns Hopkins University Press, 1987.

McTighe, Sheila. "Perfect Deformity, Ideal Beauty, and the *Imaginaire* of Work." *Oxford Art Journal* 16, no. 1.

Modleski, Tania. "Feminity as Mas(s)querade: A Feminist Approach to Mass Culture." In *High Theory/Low Culture: Analysing Popular Television and Film,* ed. Colin MacCabe. Manchester: Manchester University Press, 1986.

Moretti, Franco. *Signs Taken for Wonders: Essays in the Sociology of Literary Forms*. London: Verso, 1988.

————. *The Way of the World: The* Bildungsroman *in European Culture*. London: Verso, 1987.

Miller, D. A. *The Novel and the Police*. Berkeley: University of California Press, 1988.

Miller, Nancy. *Subject to Change: Reading Feminist Writing*. New York: Columbia University Press, 1988.

Nesbit, Molly. *Atget's Seven Albums*. New Haven, Conn.: Yale University Press, 1992.

O'Brien, Mary. *The Politics of Reproduction*. London: Routledge & Kegan Paul, 1981.

Petrey, Sandy. *Realism and Revolution: Balzac, Stendhal, Zola, and the Performance of History*. Ithaca, N.Y.: Cornell University Press, 1988.

Porter, Dennis. *Haunted Journeys: Desire and Transgression in European Travel Writing*. Princeton, N.J.: Princeton University Press, 1991.

Prendergast, Christopher. *The Order of Mimesis: Balzac, Stendhal, Nerval, Flaubert*. Cambridge: Cambridge University Press, 1986.

Rouillé, André. *Le Corps et son image*. Paris: Contrejour, 1986.

————. "Les Images photographiques du monde du travail sous le Second Empire." *Actes de la Recherche en Sciences Sociales* 54 (September 1984).

Said, Edward. *Orientalism*. New York: Random House, 1978.

Schor, Naomi. *George Sand and Idealism*. New York: Columbia University Press, 1993.

————. *Reading in Detail: Aesthetics and the Feminine*. New York: Columbia University Press, 1985.

Sedgwick, Eve Kosofsky. *Between Men: English Literature and Male Homosocial Desire*. New York: Columbia University Press, 1985.

Segal, Naomi. *The Adulteress's Child: Authorship and Desire in the Nineteenth-Century Novel*. Cambridge: Polity, 1992.

Seltzer, Mark. *Bodies and Machines*. New York: Routledge, 1992.

Showalter, English. *The Evolution of the French Novel, 1641–1782*. Princeton, N.J.: Princeton University Press, 1972.

Silverman, Debora. *Art Nouveau in Fin-de-Siècle France: Politics, Psychology, and Style*. Berkeley: University of California Press, 1989.

Solomon-Godeau, Abigail. "The Legs of the Countess." *October* (Winter 1986).

Steinberg, Leo. "The Algerian Women and Picasso at Large." In *Other Criteria: Confrontations with Twentieth-Century Art*. New York: Oxford University Press, 1979.

Watt, Ian. *The Rise of the Novel: Studies in Defoe, Richardson, and Fielding*. Berkeley: University of California Press, 1957.

Wechsler, Judith. *A Human Comedy: Physiognomy and Caricature in Nineteenth-Century Paris*. Chicago: University of Chicago Press, 1982.

Weinberg, Bernard. *French Realism: The Critical Reaction 1830–1870*. New York: Modern Language Association, 1937.

Welsh, Alexander. *Strong Representations: Narrative and Circumstantial Evidence in England*. Baltimore: Johns Hopkins University Press, 1992.

Wolff, Janet. *Feminine Sentences: Essays on Women and Culture*. Berkeley: University of California Press, 1990.

Wright, Elizabeth, ed. *Feminism and Psychoanalysis: A Critical Dictionary*. Oxford: Basil Blackwell, 1992.

Žižek, Slavoj. *Looking Awry: An Introduction to Jacques Lacan through Popular Culture*. Cambridge: MIT Press, 1991.

Contributors

April Alliston teaches in the Department of Comparative Literature at Princeton University. She is the author of *Virtue's Faults; or, Women's Correspondences in Eighteenth-Century Fiction* (forthcoming) and a number of articles on French and English women's writings in the Enlightenment and romantic periods. The essay published in this volume is part of a book in progress, *Fictions of History: Gender and the Genres of Historical Narrative, 1650–1815*.

Emily Apter is professor of French and comparative literature at the University of California, Los Angeles. She is the author of *Feminizing the Fetish: Psychoanalysis and Narrative Obsession in Turn-of-the-Century France* (1991) and coeditor, with William Pietz, of *Fetishism as Cultural Discourse* (1993). She is currently at work on a book titled *Colonial Subjects/Postcolonial Seductions*.

Charles Bernheimer is cochair of the program in comparative literature and literary theory at the University of Pennsylvania. He is the author of *Figures of Ill Repute: Representing Prostitution in Nineteenth-Century France* (1989) and is currently writing a theoretical study of the idea of decadence in fin de siècle European literature and painting.

Margaret Cohen is assistant professor of comparative literature at New York University. Her publications include *Profane Illumination: Walter Benjamin and the Paris of Surrealist Revolution* (1993) and essays on modernity, aesthetics, and gender. Her essay in this volume comes from *Why Were There No French Women Realists?* (forthcoming).

Rhonda Garelick is assistant professor of French at the University of Colorado at Boulder. She has published articles about gender and performance in early modernism and is currently finishing a book-length study of the relationship between women's performances in early European mass culture and turn-of-the-century literature.

Judith L. Goldstein is professor of anthropology on the William R. Kenan Jr. chair at Vassar College. She is currently completing *Passions and Possessions,* a book about consumer culture and its impact on the categories of everyday life in nineteenth-century France and the contemporary United States. She has written articles about religious, ethnic, and gender identity based on her fieldwork in Iran and Israel, and about gender, aesthetics, and popular culture in the United States.

Anne Higonnet teaches in the Art Department of Wellesley College. She is the author of two books on the impressionist Berthe Morisot (1990 and 1992) and a dozen articles or book chapters on aspects of modern visual culture. She is currently writing a history of private art museums and organizing a symposium on Victorian and contemporary images of children.

Roger Huss teaches at Queen Mary and Westfield College, University of London. His publications include work on verbal aspect, gender, and constructions of the natural in Flaubert, Joyce, and Michelet. He has recently written on femininity and masculine homosexuality in *La Dame aux camélias* and is now working on representations of dirt and literacy in Zola.

Dorothy Kelly is associate professor of French and director of women's studies at Boston University. She is the author of two books on gender and French literature: *Telling Glances: Voyeurism in the French Novel* (1992) and *Fictional Genders: Role and Representation in Nineteenth-Century French Narrative* (1989). She is now working on a book about constructions of women in the nineteenth-century French novel.

Diana Knight is senior lecturer in French at the University of Nottingham. She has published *Flaubert's Characters: The Language of Illusion* (1985) as well as essays on nineteenth-century fiction, feminist theory, and Roland Barthes, and is currently completing a book on Barthes as a utopian writer. She is a member of the editorial boards of *Paragraph* and *Nottingham French Studies*.

Jann Matlock is associate professor of Romance languages and literatures at Harvard University. She is the author of *Scenes of Seduction: Prostitution, Hysteria, and Reading Difference in Nineteenth-Century France* (1993) and coeditor, with Marjorie Garber and Rebecca L. Walkowitz, of *Media Spectacles* (1993). Her current project, from which her chapter in this volume is drawn, is a book titled *Desires to Censor: Spectacles of the Body, Moral Vision, and Aesthetics in Nineteenth-Century France*.

Linda Nochlin is Lila Acheson Wallace Professor of modern art at the Institute of Fine Arts of New York University. She is the author of *Realism* (1971) and *Women, Art, and Power and Other Essays* (1988). She is currently working on a study of French nineteenth-century bathing and bathers titled *Bathtime*.

Patrick O'Donovan is professor of French at University College, Cork. He has written on Stendhal, Flaubert, Beckett, and Barthes, and is completing a book on language, literature, and the public sphere in nineteenth-century France. He is coeditor, with Wendy Ayres-Bennett, of *Syntax and the Literary: New Approaches to the Interface between Literature and Linguistics* (forthcoming).

Christopher Prendergast is reader in modern French literature at Cambridge University and a fellow of Kings College. He was formerly distinguished professor of French and comparative literature in the Graduate School of the City University of New York. His publications include *Balzac: Fiction and Melodrama* (1978), *The Order of Mimesis* (1986), and *Paris and the Nineteenth Century* (1992). He is coeditor of the *World Reader* (1994) and editor of a University of Minnesota Press volume on the work of Raymond Williams. He is currently writing a book on Napoleon and history painting.

Vanessa R. Schwartz is assistant professor of history at the American University in Washington, D.C. A French cultural historian, she is coeditor, with Leo Charney, of *Cinema and the Invention of Modern Life* (forthcoming). She is completing a book-length study on the taste for reality in early mass culture in late-nineteenth-century Paris.

Naomi Segal is professor of French studies at the University of Reading. She is the author of numerous articles as well as five books, most recently *Narcissus and Echo: Women in the French Récit* (1988) and *The Adulteress's Child: Authorship and Desire in the Nineteenth-Century Novel* (1992). She is currently working on two books: *Lesbian and Gay Studies: Coming out of Feminism?* and *Pederasty and Pedagogy: The Case of André Gide.*

Barbara Vinken is assistant professor of French at the University of Hannover. She is the author of *Unentrinnbare Neugierde: Richardson's* Clarissa *und Laclos'* Liaisons dangereuses (1991) and *Mode nach der Mode* (1993), and editor of *Dekonstruktiver Feminismus: Literaturwissensschaft in Amerika* (1992). Her forthcoming books are *Der Ursprung der Ästhetik aus theologischem Vorbehalt: Ästhetische Kontroversen von Port-Royal bis Rousseau und Sade* and *Fetisch und Phantasma: Zola.*

Index

Compiled by Douglas J. Easton

Note: Citations followed by the letter f designate figures.